COLLECTED CLASSICS OF SOARING

researched and edited

by

TRISH DURBIN

at the request of the Board of Directors of the
ARIZONA SOARING ASSOCIATION

with illustrations and cover design by
Rohn Brown

Published by
Arizona Soaring Association
P.O. Box. 11214
Phoenix, AZ. 85061

October 1988
ISBN 0-9620668-0-X

Publisher's Note.

The manuscript of this book was prepared using WordPerfect software. Camera ready copy was printed on a LaserJet series II laser printer in 10 point Century Schoolbook font.

Printed by
Braun-Brumfield Inc.,
P.O. Box 1203, Ann Arbor, Michigan 48106

ACKNOWLEDGMENTS

I would like to thank Rohn Brown for the great illustrations included in this book, completed at very short notice. If you are familiar with the folk depicted, you'll know what excellent likenesses Rohn has achieved.

Special thanks to Charles Franklin, son of R.E. Franklin and nephew of Wally Franklin, both for taking the time to tape the Uncle Wally stories and for his permission to include them in this volume. Thanks also go to Anna Hutchinson for her contributions and to Paul Dickerson for taping his stories. I would also like to acknowledge past Air Currents editors and contributors whose efforts created such a valuable archive of superb material.

Thanks are also due to Mrs Dorothy Lincoln-Smith, Wally Raisanen, Roc Cutri, Jeff Turner, Steve Fahrner and John C. Lincoln II for their accolades and constructive suggestions. Yet more thanks go to John Joss and to Gren Seibels.

Finally, extra special thanks to Andy Durbin, (GY), who worked tirelessly as my resident computer consultant, and solved all the mysterious problems of type faces, fonts and layouts to produce the final camera ready document. Golf Yankee's love of flying introduced me to this great sport and he taught me all I know about soaring and crewing. (I taught him a few things too!)

Trish Durbin.

CONTENTS

CHAPTER 1 - THE UNCLE WALLY STORIES

The Uncle Wally Stories have been transcribed and edited from a tape specially made for Collected Classics of Soaring by Charles Franklin, Wallace B. Franklin's nephew, who still lives in Ann Arbor, Michigan. We are grateful to Mr Franklin for permitting us to include this superb material which has never before been published.

My Dad, R.E. Franklin, was born in 1895 in New York. When he graduated from high school he took a Degree in Chemical Engineering. He got his first taste of aviation when he joined the Army in 1916 and was assigned to the Air Corps in aerial photography research. After the war he came to the University of Michigan and took degrees in Mechanical Engineering and what was then called Automotive Engineering and stayed on at the University to teach.

Uncle Wally was born in 1909 so he was 14 years younger. He came to Ann Arbor to live with my father and mother. About 1923 or 1924 he went to school just across the street from West Engineering where all the engineering courses were taken. So Uncle Wally spent most of his time in the University environment, in and around things having to do with the School of Engineering. Glider development was a major preoccupation. There was another fellow who was about the same age as my Uncle, his name was Walt Graves. He was a student at the University, extremely brilliant and always involved with gliders.

The Golden Years did not extend over a very long period. They started probably in 1928 and were pretty much all over by 1935. My Uncle's involvement was from the beginning until sometime in 1933 or 1934. What spurred the whole thing on probably was the attitude that everybody had toward aviation due to the flight by Lindbergh across the Atlantic in 1927. Uncle Wally couldn't help but get interested in the gliding club that was started at the University of Michigan and I think this was probably in late 1927. A bunch of students got together and then West Engineering decided to build a primary glider from some German plans. Wally talked my Dad into building a glider alongside it so two of these gliders were built.

Ann Arbor is not known for its hills but they took the ships to the largest hill they could find and tried to get the darn things to fly off the hill by shock cord launch. For one reason or another they never could get them to fly. So they took both ships back to West Engineering and my Dad, my Uncle, Walt Graves and the rest of the students got redesigning the wing and a few other things. Increased the size, changed the airfoil and what have you. By then it was winter time and presumably 1928. There is a large lake close to where we live. Being winter it was frozen so they decided they'd tow these things behind automobiles on the frozen lake. At the time the primary glider just had a wire braced skid.

They had a lot of success teaching people to fly by towing up and down Barton Pond with a 200 foot rope. The instructor was in the back of the convertible tow car and giving instruction to the student in the glider. This training system was quite successful. This continued with the usual amount of crack ups and rebuilding of gliders until in late summer of 1928 they decided to do a little different design. By this time Uncle and my Dad were quite involved in the University gliding club and they designed a new sort of ship. They used a steel tubing fuselage. It was still open, not fabric covered, and they spent the following winter with that ship which looked an awful lot like a primary except it was strut braced, and continued their program on the ice. This was the way both my Dad and my Uncle and in fact I myself learned to fly.

One day, while they were building the new ship, Wally and Walt Graves were welding up the fuselage in West Engineering and Walt started to cut away part of the bottom of the ship.

"What the heck are you doing?" said Wally.

"Look at this," answered Walt. "If you guys are gonna shove this damn thing all over the airport out there in the spring time, you're crazy. We're gonna put a wheel on this."

"Oh if you want a wheel in the thing, put it in." And he did and he completed it and somehow he managed to get the wheel so that it was just behind the C.G. and it was the first wheel ever put in an American glider.

So this ship was considerably different than the previous ones. It had, as I recall, a six foot root chord and about a 45 foot wing span. It was strut braced and it had one of the Monk section airfoils in it. Its wing tapered straight down from 6 feet to something like 3 feet at the tip. So it was a lot of wing area. And the designation number given by the CAA was 9491. This was the ship which was used for the first aerotows and the blimp tow and a lot of the early flying. The whole ship was trailerable. Where this innovation came from I really don't know. All of these gliders had to be lugged around so the idea of a trailer already existed.

UNCLE WALLY AND THE FIRST AMERICAN AEROTOW

Since both my Uncle and my Dad had lived in New York not that long ago, they decided to go back to some of the airshows out there in the summer of 1929. When they reached Albany, New York, they got to talking with a guy by the name of Slim Emmerson, who was a pilot for a very young Allegheny Airlines, or Mohawk Airlines, I can't remember which. Slim had an old Hisso powered Standard. He got talking with Wally and Walt and asked, "You guys ever tow in a glider behind an airplane?"

2

Remember at this time Wally was maybe 19 or 20 years old, something like that, and a little bit of a gung ho type guy. So he said,

"You fly the airplane, we'll sure give it a try!"

Walt got to thinking and said, "Are you sure you want to go up that high?" At that time the fuselage of 9491 was not covered. So they went down to the store and bought some cotton bed sheets and a couple of gallons of nitrate dope and they proceeded to cover the fuselage and this took most of the day. By the time everything got together the sun was just about ready to set and Slim Emmerson said,

"Say, one thing I forgot to tell you about, this old engine, the bearings are getting a bit worn and when it gets warm I lose oil pressure. When that happens I have to shut the thing down and land. So when I wiggle my wings you better cut loose 'cos I got to go down and land."

So Wally said that was no problem, he'd do that, and they were trying to figure out how much of this rope they should use and decided on 500 feet. So they tied it on the tail skid at one end and put a ring in the other and hooked up the glider. The sun was just setting as they took off, probably with some overcast, so night came a little bit quick. Wally took off remembering Slim Emmerson's instruction to watch his wings but he couldn't see the wings! All he could see was the blue exhaust coming from each side of the fuselage out of the exhaust stacks.

There was no airspeed indicator as far as I know. I'm sure there wasn't any altimeter and he couldn't have read it if there had been because it was so dark. But Wally just hung on and he'd never been this high before. Actually he couldn't see the ground too well. He could see the outline of the airport. So after he released and flew around a little while, by the time he came in it was pretty black. One of the landing systems they used at that time was a spotlight down at the end of the runway. They had a guy that had a round silhouette and as soon as he saw the ship coming in, he would cast a shadow on the ship by holding the round disk in front of the spotlight. That was the method for a night landing, at least at Albany Airport at that time.

However, with no engine noise, this guy couldn't find Wally and the glider. So Wally was flying into this bright light and it completely blinded him. Somehow or other it all turned out even and he hit the runway going like the devil.

"Even when I got out of the spotlight," said Wally, "it was a couple of seconds before I could finally see the hangar. I ran the glider over on the apron and came to a screaming halt right in front of the doors. It took people a little while to find where I was." Wally confessed later on, "I was scared to death!"

UNCLE WALLY AND THE FIRST "C" FLIGHT

Later on they went down to Williamsport, Pennsylvania. Apparently there are some rather substantial ridges that run parallel and very close to the airport at Williamsport. And Wally found somebody else down there to tow him up in the air. This was getting to be a habit with him. There was quite a wind blowing and he stayed up on the ridge for a considerable length of time. He came down and put it all in his log book and later tried to claim the flight as a record. At that time Orville Wright was the record keeper and he was the one that said, "You should have launched off the mountain with a bungy cord." Orville probably would not have recognized an autotow. He certainly wasn't about to acknowledge an airplane tow and declared the attempt invalid.

UNCLE WALLY AND THE LONG TOW

Tows had always been short up to that time but now they were going to tow from Ann Arbor down to Akron behind a J5 Waco. This is a flight of considerable distance and remember the ship had a lot of wing area and was quite light. If it weighed more than 325 pounds I'd be surprised. Of course nobody was buying any parachutes. Wally had never had one on in his life. So they took off and incidentally the pilot of the J5 Waco was only doing this out of kindness. He was going off someplace else and they didn't have any way back once they got down there but they took off anyway.

Toledo was about 35 to 50 miles southeast of Ann Arbor and right on route towards Akron, Ohio. Wally said the air used to be so turbulent over Toledo, and this particular time he could not control the glider. It was rolling behind the tow plane on tow. Those old ships had an awful lot of parasite drag which undoubtedly did not help. Wally wouldn't have had control at those speeds which were probably something in the order of 85 mph. You never knew for sure because you didn't have an airspeed indicator and he always told me, "I hated to fly over Toledo."

UNCLE WALLY AND THE BLIMP TOW

Anyway, other than Toledo the flight apparently was uneventful and they arrived at Akron, Ohio. Akron was where the Goodyear company was building blimps. After World War 1 there were some really knowledgeable German dirigible pilots, notably Wolfgang Klemperer.

Apparently it was some festive occasion that was going on in Akron at this time, and the guy who was flying the Goodyear blimp, Vigilant, was a German who, as Wally said, didn't really look like he had it all together. He was absent minded and a lot of the things he did were the protocol from years and years before. He'd get a bunch of dignitaries loaded on to the blimp and all the crew would be hanging on the handrails. Then the Captain would open the window and holler out, "Up ship!" at which point the crew would throw the blimp up in the air. As soon as it was up fifteen or twenty feet the German Captain would turn the engines on, and off they'd go on their little tour of Akron.

So Wally discussed it with Wolfgang, and when the Captain came back they persuaded him to hook the blimp up to the glider for a tow. Unfortunately he was having a little bit of trouble with the German language. He knew none at all, and Wolfgang was busy elsewhere and wasn't a very good interpreter. So Wally said, or tried to say, "I'm going to be towing behind you. Can you take this thing off like an airplane? Just run on the ground and take off and when you get up to a good speed, 20 or 30 miles an hour, just go ahead and take it off and fly like an airplane." The German thought he could do this OK.

There were two engines side by side, and they didn't want to get the tow cable hooked up in the propeller so the only thing they could find to tie the trope on the blimp was one of the tether lines at the rear. So they just did a square

4

knot, hooked it up to the glider and stretched the thing out relatively straight. Wally got in the ship and all the dignitaries that were going along for the ride got into the blimp. The Captain opened the window, leaned out and yelled, "Up ship!" and the crew threw the ship up in the air, as usual. And it kept going up and up and up. Eventually all the slack came out of the rope and the nose of the glider started to come up and eventually Wally was just hanging a few feet off the ground. He was going up behind the blimp like a hooked fish. All of sudden the German pilot realized what had happened and he pushed the blimp throttles and they sort of staggered off with enough speed for Wally to fly the glider behind it.

So they took the tour over Akron, though not too high, but more was in store. Apparently when this Captain got out over the town, he just pulled back the throttles to give all the people enjoying the ride a nice view of Akron. And that's what he did with Wally on behind him. So with no more airspeed, Wally was left flying in ever decreasing circles around the blimp with the tow line hanging just below the idling propellers, shaking his fist at the Captain and shouting at him to get going again. Eventually the Captain did see him and gave the call to the crew of the Goodyear blimp Vigilant. As soon as he could make the airport, Wally cut loose, brought the ship in safely and swore to himself he'd never tow behind a blimp again.

Meanwhile, the absent minded blimp Captain brought the blimp in over the edge of the runway and somehow managed to get the dangling tow line wrapped over a couple of phases of the main power bus that was providing power to the city of Akron, taking out literally all of it. So it was quite a memorable event - the first and, as far as Uncle Wally was concerned, the last blimp tow.

UNCLE WALLY AND THE BIG SHIP

Remember the pilot of the J5 Waco had some place else to go, so they were stuck down there in Akron, and so they put up in the YMCA. There were three of them, R.E. Franklin, Wally Franklin and Walt Graves. These guys spent every waking moment during that period of time breathing and eating gliding. While they were stuck in the YMCA they got some butcher paper from the local fish market, and on their own they started the design for what was known as The Big Ship. As I recall the wing span was 50 or 54 feet, and this ended up being the Texaco Eaglet. 9491 had the taper wing which was about 6 feet at the root and tapered down to 3 feet at the tip. They had come up with a method where they were going to make a straight section that would go from the root out to about where the ailerons started, and then they would taper the wing down using the rib jigs with which they'd built 9491, and they would use one of the rib stations some place mid way to make the constant chord for this new ship.

So all their innovations are all laid out on a piece of butcher paper down in Akron, Ohio, in the YMCA. The ability of those guys to work day in and day out to get things done was quite amazing. The Texaco Eaglet, or as it was known then, The Big Ship, only took three weeks from design until completion and there were not that many people working on it, 3 or 4 at the outside.

UNCLE WALLY TOWS TO THE CLEVELAND RACES

The reason for hurrying was that there was going to be a Pilots Glider Derby at the Cleveland Air Show in the late summer or fall of 1929. They were starting to get some sort of name in gliding and they had the idea that they were going to take The Big Ship to the Cleveland Air Races. That was the reason for the hurry. They managed to get the ship done but Wally literally was staggering around - none of them had had very much sleep for three weeks. They didn't manage to get it painted, however, and didn't even have the silver on it. It was covered but had nothing but clear dope. An unusual thing about the ship was that it had round struts. The struts of modern ships are streamlined or tear drop shaped, but these were just round tubing, primarily because they couldn't get the material they wanted. It also lacked jury struts. Four struts, two for each wing. Jury struts are struts that run some place around mid span of the strut up to the wing to stabilize the struts. They didn't have time to put the fairing on either.

In addition to The Big Ship, they decided they were going to take 9491 which now boasted a highly innovative Eagle Beak canopy. The forward visibility of this was poor but remember in those days they only had windshields. For the most part, nobody had flown under a canopy. The innovation of the canopy was done, I believe, by my Uncle, Walt Graves and my father, but the celluloid type material could not be bent satisfactorily. Everything had to be a simple shape but with plywood they could do some pretty fancy stuff. The Eagle Beak had terrible forward vision and two portholes in either side. The idea was you'd stick your head up against the porthole and get one eye looking forward. They modified 9491 with this so called Eagle Beak canopy. No plexiglas, it was all plywood and veneer. In any case, between doing the modifications on 9491 and completely building the Big Ship, Wally was totally exhausted and so was everybody else.

So came the day of the races and they decided to airtow 9491. There were some last minute things Walt Graves was going to do to the Big Ship while Wally towed 9491 from Ann Arbor to Cleveland, Ohio. The route took them right along Lake Erie, again over dreaded Toledo. Uncle Wally packed two apples for the journey but unfortunately in his haste and excitement forgot to go to the bathroom before he took off.

Once airborne, Wally quickly discovered a strange thing happened with this new canopy. "When I put my head just in the right spot, my head was whipped round like the ball in a whistle. That was terribly disorienting and I was having a good deal of difficulty keeping from being sick." As it turned out, that was the least of his worries. He had more pressing needs.

"Eventually I just had to go," reported Wally, "so I let it go in the bottom of the fuselage. Then I got to thinking, Gee, we're gonna have all these famous pilots flying these gliders, I can't land with urine sloshing around in the bottom of the ship. What am I going to do?" All this time his head was bouncing around in the cockpit like the ball in a whistle. Finally he came up with a brilliant idea. He would use his pocket knife to cut a small hole in the fabric at the bottom of the ship and just let it drain out. Unfortunately, that's not what happened.

Instead of urine flowing out through the hole, as Wally intended, air blew in and blasted urine all round the cockpit and out through the portholes. Even the apples received a liberal coating but by this time Wally was thirsty so he wiped them off as best he could and ate one.

Once he finally landed at Cleveland Uncle Wally had to go back to Detroit to help finish The Big Ship, still only coated with clear dope. He took the overnight ferry boat and enjoyed the first decent night's sleep he'd had in three weeks. Plus the bonus of a nice shower next morning.

That day they got The Big Ship out to the airport and did a couple of auto tows to make sure everything was fine and took off on tow to take the Big Ship to Cleveland. This was the first time they'd ever flown the thing.

So they took off and this time he didn't have trouble over Toledo and this was a very different ship. It was bigger and it was apparently a nicer handling ship, the best performing glider ever made, before or since! The only thing that really bothered Wally on tow was that the round tubes on either side that were supporting the wing, the struts, were wobbling back and forth a lot. He was really concerned they were going to collapse. However, they didn't and he made it.

He released over Cleveland airport at a fairly good altitude, 2000 feet or so, just as the Top Hats, Lindbergh's touring air show, were putting on their act. At this juncture Wally suddenly saw a Top Hat pilot come right up on the port wing and it suddenly occurred to him that his ship, being clear and of no color, could not be seen. In his haste to get the heck out of there he went the wrong way - down wind! Pretty soon he thought, "Gee, the airport looks a long way off." As he tried to fly back he figured, "I'm not gonna make it!" Later he said, "Chuck, I was coming back at speed, and that dumb ship didn't sink at all." It came over the threshold of the airport, over the fence, and he saw all the rest of the gliders up ahead of him. He put the thing down, rolled up and parked right in the line with the rest of them. Like a big hero, he said, "I was just lucky to get there." That was the finest glide ratio he'd ever known. He always remembered that final glide into the airport. The performance of the Texaco Eaglet was something else.

Finally able to turn his mind to other things, Uncle Wally realized 9491 was nowhere to be seen. Eventually he saw the ship with a large group of people around it. So he went over and discovered the Glider Derby had already begun. Amelia Earhardt had selected 9491 as the ship she was going to fly, put it into a spiral, spiralled it right into the ground and dinged up the wings. Frank Hawks was there too, one of the pilots who was going to fly the gliders. Amelia Earhardt was saying to Frank,

"I put it into a turn and it wouldn't come out. It just kept right on turning."

"Well, you darn fool," said Frank, "any ship will do that. You have to take it out of the turn."

Then Wally walked up, saw the damage to the ship and asked what happened. Of course he felt quite attached to 9491. This was the ship in which he had done most of his flying. He realized it shouldn't take too long to fix the damage but he decided he'd go ahead and put an act on anyway. He was moaning over his bruised ship to Amelia Earhardt and finally she said,

"Oh, Wally, I'll do anything to make it right."

"Well, I'll have to fix this and I'll have to fix that."

"Will a check for $400 fix the damage?"
Wally sat there for a while and finally said,

"That probably would just about do it."

To me later he said, "Heck, the whole ship didn't cost more than $200 or $300!" This was right after the Depression and the Big Crash and things were a lot cheaper then. Anyway, that $400 ended up being the money they'd needed for the prototype PS2 glider so in a way Amelia Earhardt was the one who financed the development of what finally became the PS2, the production ship of which they built so many.

UNCLE WALLY AND THE TEXACO EAGLET

Right after the Cleveland air races in the early fall of 1929 there was a short two day meet at Detroit. Wally had two ships there, The Big Ship and 9491. A local pilot, Milo Oliphant, and his mother, actually lived on Barton Pond and had quite a bit of money. I think he owned a Waco at the time and it was decided they would do a double tow. As far as I know this was the first time anybody had done a double tow in America and Milo Oliphant was the pilot and 9491 and The Big Ship took part.

Apparently Captain Frank Hawks was right there watching. For him it had a lot of romance to it and this was when he actually came up with the idea to do a transcontinental flight from the West coast carrying the mail to New York City. Having seen both The Big Ship and 9491, Frank's feeling was that 9491 was a stronger ship and that was the one he wanted to buy to fly from San Diego to New York. They talked about a deal and Frank was all set to buy 9491.

Until he could collect his purchase and sign the final documents, flying continued in 9491 during the winter of 1929 on the ice on Barton Pond in Ann Arbor. Some of the more senior members of the University Glider Club were flying the ship off the ice. Several students had progressed to the point were they were doing some pretty good auto tows.

Anyway Frank Hawks came to Ann Arbor to collect his ship. It was to have a paint job and Frank was going to pay the money so the work could be done. One of the pilots that day knew Frank Hawks was there and happened to be in the air in 9491 and decided to show Captain Hawks how well he could fly. He put the ship into a vertical bank and promptly spiralled the dumb thing right into the ice and just busted it all to pieces. There wasn't enough left to pick your teeth with. The amazing thing was that the guy came out of it without a scratch, but 9491 was no more. So at this point they had to sell Frank The Big Ship and that's how The Big Ship turned out to be the Texaco Eaglet. Wally took it in and did the special paint job that's on the ship now in the Smithsonian Institute.

That flight from San Diego to New York is probably pretty well known. There were some incidents that happened that I'm sure nobody knows about and I think very few people realized what a physically taxing thing that flight was for Frank Hawks. He did have telephone contact. They had taped a telephone line to the tow rope, it was actually a wire. This wire and the towline was rolled up back into the fuselage of the tow plane and Wally was on the flight, I think in the front seat. Pilot Jenkins was in the rear seat of the biplane and he would roll this up after Frank released so they didn't have to drag it all over the place and the phone line wouldn't get damaged by pulling it along on the runways and such.

If you have ever towed on long flights in the early ships, especially those that didn't have good trim controls on them, you'll know you had to put a lot of forward pressure on the stick and that was the case with the Texaco Eaglet. Being towed at those speeds demanded great physical effort for a long period of time and it taxed the stamina of Frank something terrible. By the time they reached Albany he was pretty well worn out and Wally said that when they took off for the final flight from Albany to New York City, they had a horrible horrible headwind. They were flying down the Hudson River valley and there was a railroad track, a road, and, at that time, there was also barge traffic on the Hudson River. They were flying into this horrible horrible headwind and the flight was just dragging on and on and on. Frank was getting more exasperated and he finally said,

"Look, a train has passed us by, the traffic down there is passing us by, and if that damn barge passes us by I'm going to land this thing and we're going to carry the mail on our backs to New York City." So he was getting pretty short of patience but finally they made it in. He did land in Central Park and the mail was delivered.

The thing nobody knows was that Frank had to go to the hospital for three days to recover from the whole episode. His hands were so raw they were bleeding by the time he got to New York City. And so he spent three days in the hospital to get himself back in shape so he could face the people.

THE FRANKLIN PS2

During this time the prototype PS2 was developed. The first one had a Monk section wing. Wally spent virtually every weekend fixing that thing after the students had bust it up. Finally they had to do something so they changed the airfoil to what my Dad described as a modified Clark Y and that ended up being the airfoil that went on the prototype glider.

I think there were 54 built, amazingly in a relatively short period of time and with relatively few people working on it, mostly Wally. They started building jigs and fixtures and started to produce the Franklin PS2 glider. As they went into production Mrs. Oliphant, Milo's mother, got into the act and did some financing of the glider factory which was moved out of West Engineering over to Ypsilanti.

It was a pretty good ship and they were winning some of the contests with it, especially those at Harris Hill. But Wally and my Dad were not satisfied with the standard Franklin so they decided to add a four foot wing panel to each side. The original wing was 36 feet for the PS2, rectangular with elliptical wing tips. Adding four feet to each panel meant 44 feet of constant chord wing. They didn't have time to change the strut points. It was easy enough to modify the wing but by not changing the strut point it ended up in the middle of the wing which set up a primary oscillation point. Wally was going to fly this ship at, I think, the 1931 Nationals at Harris Hill. They worked on this ship and the only way to get it to the Contest was by airplane tow.

UNCLE WALLY BAILS OUT

Mrs. Oliphant said, "You're doing an awful lot of test flying. You really should be wearing a parachute."

"Gee, I can't afford one," said Wally.

"Well," said his concerned benefactor, "if I buy it for you will you wear it?"

"Sure," grinned Wally. "It will make me feel pretty great to put on a parachute all the time."

They bought an Irvin chute that was made in Buffalo, New York, and, as fate would have it, the chute was delivered by truck the morning before they were to leave to fly this long wing Franklin to Harris Hill.

So Wally adjusted the harnesses on the parachute and did the usual checks, a couple of auto tows with the glider back and forth along the field. It was pretty windy and Walt Graves said, "Are you guys going to be OK? The wind is picking up pretty good."

"If it doesn't settle down pretty soon we may have to wait until tomorrow to go," agreed Wally. Just about the time they'd planned to take off it got real calm and everybody said, "Isn't this great?" So they took off but in fact it was the lull before the storm. Wally took off with this new ship and they started heading round Lake Erie and had to go over Toledo again. He climbed out and not very far from the airport they hit a really bad gust and the wings folded up! Wally was spinning behind the towplane and his first thought was, "I can't leave all this garbage on behind the towplane." So he cut loose and pushed up on the canopy to get rid of that. That flew away OK but he didn't have any sense of up, down or anything else. All he knew was that he was spinning pretty violently. He undid the seat belt and said later, "I didn't have to jump or anything. I just flew out of the ship. I pulled the ripcord and I don't know if it was a dry year or something but I landed in a lily pond. Waist deep. The ship all came down not too far around me." The tow pilot went back and landed and told what had happened. He'd seen the 'chute so they figured Wally must be OK.

So they brought the trailer and put the wreckage on it and took it all back to the factory and locked the door. Just as they were leaving, the local newspaper called up and said,

"We understand there's been a crash. Was it a glider?"

"Gee," said Wally, all innocence. "I don't know what you're thinking about. It's news to me." He wasn't going to admit a problem at all because they were in the process of trying to sell gliding and the Franklin glider so they weren't looking for adverse press.

It was then decided they were going to have to drive to Harris Hill. They couldn't fly in it that year but at least they were going to drive and on the way they stopped in Buffalo and took the chute to the parachute company to be repacked. As soon as the old guy that ran the place saw the chute he recognized it as the one he'd shipped out the day before.

"You kids can't keep your hands off that equipment, can you?" he said sternly. "You pulled the rip cord and the thing went all over the place, didn't it?"

"No, no, no," said the misjudged Wally. "I put the thing on, I didn't have it on for more than five minutes and the airplane fell apart on me and I had to use the chute."

"My Gosh, is that right?" If it hadn't been for Mrs Oliphant he would have been gone a long time ago.

There's an interesting sidelight to that story. During the early 1950's Wally was working in the Styling Department of Kaiser Frazer, the automobile manufacturer based at Willow Haven Airport. He could spin a pretty good yarn and his co-workers probably didn't believe half his stories. One day he was talking to Joe Kluska, a colleague he didn't really know, who was about his own age. He was telling about the time he had had to bail out of a glider and Joe said,

"Yes, I saw that! I was sitting on the mountain in back of the barn trying to stay out of the weather and I saw this airplane go over." He went on to describe exactly what happened and said, "I actually saw that." So they were the best of friends after that. I don't know if he was the person who told the newspaper about it but he had to have been one of the few people who saw that accident happen. And here the two of them were working together a good number of years later and they got to be good friends.

UNCLE WALLY SURVIVES DOPING GLIDERS

Another guy that was always around the glider plant used to be an ex-prize fighter. His name was Rudy Fedus. Rudy was a pretty bright guy and he decided he would get out of the fighting business because there was no future in it. He went to college and was working in his spare time in the glider factory. He was the guy who came up with the idea of using ordinary clothes pins to hold the fabric over the trailing edge and in place when you're putting fresh fabric on the wings. He did a lot of innovating that way.

Rudy was the dope man, covering and doping the ships. There was a room in which they did this but the ventilation wasn't very good in there. They did have enough sense to use a face mask to keep from breathing the particulates from the overspray and so forth when they were painting the ship. Now airplane dope has a lot of alcohol in it and if you breathe it for a long period of time you can get a pretty good jug on. So when you went to the dope room you'd get a little drunk and time would just stand still, you lose all track of time.

Anyway, one night Rudy and Wally were working on one of the ships, painting it, a rush job, and it was getting on towards 8 or 9 o'clock at night. Remember, this plant was right next to the road. It was during the Depression and there were a lot of hobos and tramps around, hitching rides back and forth on the trains and living in the area. Anyway, Wally and Rudy were working in the dope room and they were half shot themselves when all of a sudden the door opened and one of these unsavory looking characters walked in. There was a bench adjacent to the door and he sat down on the bench and Wally and Rudy looked at each other and shrugged their shoulders. The guy wasn't doing anything, just sitting there. Soon he got up and walked out but about fifteen minutes later he came back and in trooped a half dozen more of these guys behind him. They all lined up on the bench and simply sat watching the progress on the ship.

Wally figured Rudy was an ex-prize fighter so he felt reasonably safe. He wasn't sure he and Rudy could take on all six if necessary but here were these guys all just sitting there. They didn't say anything. So Wally and Rudy went on with their work and sort of kept their distance. They had been spraying, there was dope all over the place so everyone was feeling pretty good. Soon the first guy nudged the others with his elbow and they all got up and staggered through the door. The last one out looked back and said, "Hey, thanks for the free drunk, buddy!"

UNCLE WALLY, BARNSTORMER

By this time, Wally was starting to burn out. He wasn't getting paid much money; he was selling gliders for about $600 and sometimes it was hard to collect even that so wages were low and he was working far too hard. He had been going with my aunt and they decided to get married. He quit the glider business, they got married and lived out west for a number of years. He managed to get a Franklin glider and he used to fly airshows out there. He got into the circuit and used to go all over the country. South Dakota, North Dakota, Nebraska and so forth. That was how he made spare money.

He said the people who ran the shows were not very ethical. If you didn't fill your contract by doing so many flights regardless of the weather they didn't pay you anything.

One day he was planning an airshow flight when two guys from the CAA came by and said, "You're not going to be able to airplane tow this ship unless you get a waiver to say its OK." Apparently it was a new rule that had come in since Wally had left and they were starting to write rules for how the gliding thing was to be controlled. So Wally wrote my Dad and they wired out a waiver that it would be OK to fly a glider behind the airplane and do airplane tows for the show.

One of his favorite things was loops and what he called vertical turns. But the PS2 was an open cockpit ship and one time he got off tow and started into his first loop but didn't feel he was getting too much speed. "But my head was hanging out," he told me later, "so I pulled back on the stick and about the time I got vertical I was dead in the air. Slipping backwards. I had to do something so I decided to turn it into a vertical turn. I slammed the rudder over real hard and heard metal bending back there." The ship flipped over and came down and he didn't try any more loops. He did a bunch of what ended up being wing overs instead. When he finally landed he discovered the rudder was badly bent, jammed against the elevator. So he got in there with his knee and straightened out the wrinkles just as the two CAA men came up and Wally thought, "Oh oh, this is it, I'm really gonna get it now."

And one of the CAA men said, "Those are the damndest wing overs I've ever seen in my life. How d'you do that?" Wally just grinned and said,

"Oh, that's one of my specialties."

Uncle Wally had a lot of stories about a bunch of local pilots who flew in pilot races. One guy had a fairly good airplane and was flying in the pilot races but he lost it. Wally said when he went in he was going like the devil. There just were pieces all over the place. Wally knew the people who held these shows were not particularly ethical so he was real mad when they got on the PA system and said, "That's OK, folks. Pilot So-and-So will be OK. They're gonna take him to the hospital and make sure there's nothing seriously wrong with him, then he'll come back."

Wally thought to himself, "Those sons of guns, they can't even tell the people the guy is no longer with us and just got killed." Then about two hours later the pilot came back! He had a sling on his right arm and a patch on his head and got up and told the audience all about the accident.

Wally told of another airshow where one of the pilots had a power plane and would get up and spin it right to the ground. It had a pretty big engine in it and what he'd do was spin the thing down and just about a turn before the ground he'd jam the engine wide open and it'd catch up and pull right out of the spin and it could stop practically on the ground. Wally had seen this done a number of times and he always liked to watch because it was probably the most daring thing he'd ever seen done in the air. This particular time it was coming down and he heard the pilot push the throttle wide open and that big engine just coughed and half a second later he just hit the ground and there wasn't anything left.

From this Wally decided the airshow circuit had a certain number of drawbacks and if he was going to live to a ripe old age he probably ought to get out of it. His suspicions were confirmed while practicing for one of these airshows. He had a guy who was helping him and a length of rope but instead of going to an airport they were out in the plains of South Dakota. Using the road as a runway they would tow the glider up, fly around and land back on the road again. However, off to the side of the road were the local telephone lines. The poles were some way apart with just one line hanging down with quite a bit of sag. They were party lines in those days. Wally had it all picked out where he was going to land when all of a sudden some guy in his truck came right where he was going to land the glider. The only thing he could do was turn off the "runway" and land adjacent to the road. Unfortunately, he completely forgot about the telephone lines but he was quickly reminded of them. The wire hit Wally right between his eyes and the bridge of his nose. He said, "It hurt like the devil. It pushed me back against the back of the glider, the whole thing just sort of stopped as the wire stretched and the glider just finally dropped ten feet to the ground." He said everything had been fine except the strut ended up hitting one of the posts and was bent pretty bad. Other than that, and a broken nose, he came out of the thing in good shape.

So just a broken nose wasn't too much damage to his person, considering all the risks he had taken. Uncle Wally in fact lived to a ripe old age and died in Mexico in November, 1984.

CHAPTER 2 - THE UNPUBLISHED JOE LINCOLN

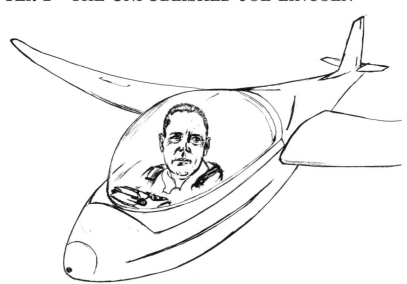

The following stories are the original, uncut versions as they first appeared in Air Currents, the newsletter of the Arizona Soaring Association. Most of them are, as the title suggests, unpublished. However, in places, some parts may be familiar to you. This is because Joe cut and polished extensively, and used some of the material in his books. It is my sincere belief that the repetition is well worth while, in order to show how the pieces originally appeared. But first, a little history...

THE JOSEPH C. LINCOLN STORY by Don Barnard, January 1957.

Born in Cleveland, Ohio, June 15, 1922, and moved to Arizona in December 1931. Attended Judson's Boys School from 1931 to 1939. Graduated to North Phoenix High School from 1939 to 1940. Attended Pomona College from 1940 to 1942. At that time with war coming on, entered the Army Air Corps and was in service up to 1945. Upon release he entered the University of Arizona for the years 1946-47, then returned to Scottsdale where he taught grammar school from 1948 to 1950. Took his M.A. Degree in 1951 at A.S.C. Started his own business in 1952, Flemish Glazenier, stained and leaded glass shop, located in Scottsdale at 47 W. 5th Avenue, which he operates at the present time.

Mr Lincoln's interest in flying led to his getting his private license in 1947 and purchasing a Piper Tri-Pacer in 1954. He received his commercial license and has built up around 850 hours of power time. His interest in gliding started in 1956 when he and Don Barnard soared for over an hour above 5,000 feet. Thus the bug bit and the die was cast which led to his buying the Baby Albatross. He earned his private glider licence on June 10, 1956.

Since then he has made quite a name for himself in the soaring world by attending the 1956 Nationals and winning the Class C Championship, also the Tail-End Tony Trophy. He at present holds the Arizona Soaring Association altitude record with a flight up to 13,100 feet, or 11,600 feet gained. He has earned both the "C" and "Silver C" awards and his soaring time totals up to over 100 flights and close to 80 hours. His popularity led to his being elected President of ASA for the year 1956-57.

Mr Lincoln's generosity and foresight for the advancement of ASA led to his buying the Stiglmeier Pratt-Read, for the sole purpose of giving the members of ASA a chance to create a club and have a very fine 2-place ship to fly.

Without a doubt, Joe's enthusiasm will carry him to the top of the soaring world and it can be predicted his name will be linked with future soaring records and championships.

JOE LINCOLN   Author Unknown - probably Jean Doty, December 1968.

Joseph Colville Lincoln began his soaring career on February 19, 1956 when he had his first ride with Don Barnard in an LK-10A. During the following May, he acquired his C pin with a flight which lasted two hours and carried him up to 13,100 feet above terrain at Falcon Field. Joe's first National contest followed later that month when he towed his Baby Bowlus over to Grand Prairie, Texas, and competed in the 23rd National Soaring Contest. He came in 40th out of 44 competing pilots. During this contest he got acquainted with a number of the great figures in American soaring, and he got all three legs of his Silver C.

In January, 1957, he ordered a Schweizer 1-23D which was to be named Cirro-Q. In early July, 1957, he competed in the 24th National Contest at Elmira, coming in 18th out of 33 pilots. On the way back home from this contest, he flew Golden Distance from Grand Prairie, Texas, to Guthrie, Oklahoma - 218 miles. On Labor Day that year, he flew Cirro-Q up to Golden C altitude out of Rittenhouse Field. During the course of this flight, he passed over the terrain where a Pratt Read which he owned had been cracked up early in the year. In 1958 he flew the 25th National Contest at Bishop, Ca., finishing in 11th place and narrowly missed the magic top ten.

In 1959 he flew Diamond Distance on the 4 July from Prescott to West Mesa in Albuquerque. On the 24 July he got Diamond Altitude North of Prescott, soaring up to 26,000 feet in Cirro-Q and on August 8 that year, he completed his Diamond C with a goal flight from Odessa to Esperanza, Texas, 204 miles.

In 1960, Joe won the Barringer Trophy for a flight of 455.5 miles from Prescott to Variadero, New Mexico. Later that summer he flew the National Contest at Odessa, where, starting in 11th place on the first day, he resolutely worked his way down to 25th place by the end of the contest. In 1961 he was elected to the Helms Hall of Fame.

1965 saw the arrival of Cibola, a new Schweizer 2-32. On his first cross country he flew 288 miles in an attempt to beat the 19 year old two place National Distance Record. The landing at the end of this flight was up on the Mesa Chivato, which is north east of Grants, New Mexico. This landing required an all-night, twelve hour walk out before he and his passenger, son John, finally arrived at San Mateo an hour after dawn.

1966 was the first year Joe made record attempts with George Locke from London as crew. The best flight that year was a heart breaking 294 miles - 17 miles short of tying the 20 year old National Two Place Distance Record. This flight ended on an Indian Reservation east of Mount Taylor, and there was heavy landing damage when his right wing struck an unobserved post, throwing Cibola off the road.

1967 brought new record attempts with George Locke, back from England to crew once again. This year brought two successes: on the 30th April he flew from Prescott to Tucumcari, New Mexico, with Bruce in the passenger seat. He was credited with an official distance of 500.64 miles and exceeded the ten month old record of Minghelli by 91 miles. Two and a half weeks later, he flew from Prescott to Tonalea and back with Chris Crowl as a passenger. This beat Harland Ross's 9 year old two place National Goal and Return record by 54 miles, but the record was not accepted because of photographic mistakes.

In 1968 his flying was limited in the spring and he got married in June. In September of this first year he flew in the 3rd Annual ASA Contest, coming in second. A noteworthy flight was made on the second day of the contest. The task was a triangular race from Prescott to Seligman to east Flagstaff and back to Prescott - 300 Km. The existing two place world speed record is 57.5 mph. He made the course with Bruce as a passenger at a speed of 68 mph for an unofficial world record. He had no barograph, no sealed camera to photograph turnpoints, no declaration to photograph and his passenger, Bruce, was approximately 40 pounds under legal weight.

Plans are to seek new records in the spring of 1969 out of Kingman, with other attempts at 100 Km triangular speed record flying from Wickenburg.

Joe Lincoln has recorded large parts of his career in soaring. He began by writing up a detailed account of his flying in the 23rd Nationals which was published in the first issue of Arizona's Air Currents. His first work in Soaring magazine was called "Beginner's Luck" and appeared in June, 1957. Other works to appear in Soaring were "Flight to Variadero", "The Retrieve", and "The Walkout". In 1959 he conceived and began his book, Soaring For Diamonds, which was finally published in October 1964. In 1967 a second edition came out and in 1968 a third printing was needed. He had the lead article in the July 1967 issue of Arizona Highways. The story was titled "Soaring in Arizona".

In addition to record flying planned for 1969, he hopes to finish a soaring anthology which has been worked at intermittently ever since January 1962. In 1968 Joe was commissioned by the Encyclopedia Britannica to write their new article on gliding and soaring. This piece was turned in three days before his wedding.

(Editor's Note: After the above piece was written in 1969, Joe covered the Nationals at Marfa, Texas, for Soaring magazine that same year, and the Internationals there in 1970. His piece on gliding and soaring for the Encyclopaedia Britannica appeared in the 1970 edition and a similar piece for the Encyclopedia Americana appeared in 1971. His major work, "On Quiet Wings", was published in 1972. In 1975 Joe was posthumously awarded the Warren E. Eaton Memorial Trophy, awarded each year to the person who has made an outstanding contribution to the art, sport or science of soaring flight in the U.S. It is considered the Society's highest award.)

FIRST TIME ON HARRIS HILL by Joe Lincoln, December 1957.

May, 1956. My first time on Harris Hill. Temperature 28°F. Wind N 28 knots. Ceiling 28 feet. Good Elmira soaring conditions (!) I was new and eager, wanting to help and learn. They were getting a sailplane out of the hangar and I was assisting. All names were new: 1-26, 1-23, 1-24, 2-22; I could recognize LK and Cinema, but the numbers meant little more than the symbols of a different equation. A white haired old timer kept looking at me suspiciously. Then I did it.

"What kind is that?" I asked, pointing to a sailplane that was known only by its numbers. He gave me the most searingly contemptuous look I have ever received, as if he did not know anyone could be quite that stupid. Not even to look at the front end!

"It's a glider!" he snapped.

CACTUS CLIPPER by Joe Lincoln, March 1957.

Some observations about the Pratt Read accident. Sunday, March 3rd was a day of beautiful cumulus. I had intended to take my kids out to Cave Creek for the afternoon, but it looked like too good an opportunity to miss. After checking with Sally Schmid I found out that Charlie had no crew, and he lacked only his distance leg of the Silver C. I raced out to Falcon to offer services as crewman and at 3:20 he was off the ground with the barograph running.

This flight was a failure, but had several lessons which should be learned by others. The day is coming soon when cross country flights by ASA members will not be so unusual an occurrence. For those who have never crewed before, you should know that it is the thrill of a lifetime. This was my first experience, and it is almost as much fun as distance soaring. It should be explained at this point that this piece is in no way intended to be critical; if gliding accidents can be instructive there is something to be gained. Otherwise each pilot has to learn only by his own mistakes.

About fifteen minutes after takeoff, Chuck Schmid turned east on course, with what appeared to be good altitude. His goal: Superior Airport, 38 miles away, Silver C distance. We left immediately in the Ford with the Pratt Read trailer and maintained a speed of over 60 miles an hour almost all the way to Apache Junction before catching up the first time. After five minutes there we left again on the way to Florence Junction. His speed was excellent - there was a small break in cloud development east of Apache Junction, but he made contact with the good clouds. I thought the next stop might be Superior, and we would have a new Silver C pilot in our ranks. It seemed he was just a little short of straight gliding distance away, since there was a strong west wind.

Half way to Florence Junction we passed him after he had stopped to circle in lift. This time it was a longer stop. After 15 minutes we drove two miles into the "Don's Trek" road toward Superstition Mountain. Altitude was still good but Chuck seemed to be having trouble. I thought momentarily of flagging traffic on this almost unused road to give him a chance to get down if necessary. The good clouds were moving eastward rapidly and he was holding a position above a small but sharp ridge which was evidently producing intermittent lift. Lower and lower came the sailplane, below the crest of the mountain, then a little above it, then down again. Up and down but always getting a little lower as each thermal gave out. We turned around, got on the main highway, and promptly lost him. At a turn off for the King Ranch there was a boy waiting. We turned in, picked him up and got the news. He had apparently gone down behind the ridge somewhere. Where? The country was rough and had a heavy growth of saguaros, cholla, palo verde, and greasewood. We headed in.

Once past the ridge the country rapidly got worse. With every hundred yards we traveled I got less worried about the sailplane and more worried about Chuck. A fork in the road. Which way? We tried right. In half a mile we came to a house where we caught up with Kenny Bawden and Willie Rogers. The owner of the house had seen him go down. He offered to lead us to the spot. We all took off. After a very anxious ten minutes we got to the place. Chuck walked out to us looking very embarrassed.

"Are you OK?"

"No sweat." So far so good.

"How is the aircraft? The man said you just banged a wing tip."

"It's bad enough."

We left the car - one crewman, four kids, two dogs, Willie, Kenny and Chuck. A hundred yards away we came to the Pratt-Read, headed into the wind with stones over a cushion on the good low wing. Its right arm was broken at the inboard end of the aileron, and hanging down forlornly in the wind. Marcel Godinat was undoing the control cables. It took an hour and a half to de-rig and load it up on the trailer for the trip back. No Silver C today.

LESSONS:

1. I violated the first cardinal rule of all aviation safety. DON'T HURRY. The aircraft was well preflighted, barograph set and running, pilot strapped in, everything seemed fine. BUT, not enough time had gone into the planning of the flight. Crewmen: Never Hurry. Pilots: Never let yourselves be hurried. Ray Jackson of Michigan almost killed himself in Texas by taking off without checking his ailerons. Good luck saved him. Again - NEVER HURRY UP.

2. Don't be carried away by a sky of good looking cumulus. How much vertical development do they have? (Sunday the cumulus were quite flat). Get careful right now if you can't even get to cloud base.

3. Always leave yourself an "out" to get down. And don't feel you have to apologize for being careful. Two quotes: "Any danger is too much danger for me, I'll leave that kind of flying to younger men." Paul MacCready, age 30. "Take a chance over northern Arizona? No, I don't fly that way, I always have a place to come down." Richard H. Johnson. (Both to the writer).

4. Decide early on a "base altitude" below which you will make full use of any lift, regardless of how weak.

5. If trouble looms DON'T WAIT too long to make a run for a good landing area even if cloud development and terrain seem better for lift where you are. This saved the LK on my first forced landing in the Salt River bed last May. I had worked two areas of weak lift which were promising but were not maintaining altitude. Result of leaving was five hours of back breaking work, but only a few paint scratches on the sailplane.

The landing: he came in low, had to make a last minute decision not to use the road because it was fenced and lined with palo verde trees which had not shown up from the air, around a low bluff, around a house, over the wires, down into a clear area the size of an overgrown dish towel - all in a gusty cross wind. Fifty feet to either side, ten feet too high or low, and the sailplane would have been kindling, and Chuck might have been badly hurt. The only possible explanation for this landing was composure, high self confidence, and extraordinary skill. A little more luck and he would have done nothing more than scratch the paint. Ill fortune emerged in the form of a slender ironwood tree which broke the wing. Anyone subject to getting rattled after an agonizing letdown would have been in great danger.

6. If, in the last emergency you find yourself down with no escape, over bad terrain, keep your head, plan carefully and with unflinching resolution, then execute the plan. You might save yourself and the sailplane both. Chuck Schmid did.

THE GOLDEN C by Joe Lincoln, September 1957.

After getting my Golden Distance in Texas, finishing the pin with an altitude flight had almost become an obsession. The first time Cirro-Q was off the ground in Arizona was at Rittenhouse for a 15 minute glide in stable air. This was followed by a weekend in Prescott with Chuck Schmid, Sally, and Bob Sparling, theoretically for an automobile launch. The weather there at 10:00 am must have been fabulous, but we got to town at 11:30, and by noon the cumulonimbus clouds joined hands and covered the sky until 6:00 pm. Next week further auto-tows with Jerry Robertson as crew chief, assisted by Bob Sparling, Joe Vest, and one other Prescott enthusiast. Three tows netted altitudes of 150 feet, 350 feet, and 600 feet, after which a zoom put me at 700. I gained another 100 up to 800, but it was under a thin cirrus overcast and I could not get away. Total flying time for the two weekends was 21 minutes. I had spent 4 hours in the sun at Rittenhouse untangling a thousand feet piece of cable for this flight, and many man hours as well as five hundred miles of trailing went into the two weeks effort.

Sunday, September 1st was different. An early morning wash job preceded the jaunt out to Rittenhouse, but there were delays and I was not airborne behind Don's tow plane until 3.30. How good the towplane looked after threading an auto tow cable through gates and over cattle guards! The flight carried to 9000 A.T. over Superstition Mountain. At dinner with the Barnards and Kenny Bawden that night, Kenny said he heard over the radio that the Labor Day weather looked even better. We were at the field early, and the Cinema and Baby were both aloft when I took my tow a little before 12:30 with two barographs running behind my head.

Release was at 1700 feet followed by two dives to 1500 feet to notch my barograms. Sgt. Beam had found me a wonderful thermal to start the flight, and I went up to 5500 feet above Rittenhouse at 500 fpm. There it weakened and I headed for the happy hunting ground of Superstition Mountain. Getting over to the road half way between Apache Junction and Florence Junction, (known locally as the Schmid ridge country!) produced very little lift but plenty of 600 to 900 fpm down. I was getting a little nervous as the top of the mountain went over my head when a new 900 fpm down was followed by a powerful thermal. This time we went up almost to 9000 feet at which time I stopped to blow up my pneumatic cushion which had conveniently gone flat. That erratic flying you might have seen was not caused by a swarm of bees in the cockpit, it was me trying to jam the cushion

19

back underneath the hind end while keeping the Cirro-Q more or less upright. It took 1200 feet to do it, but there was lift all over the place.

Slowly we went up again in strong patchy lift intermingled with strong sink - still far below cloud base. I finally attained base over the mountain at above 10,000 feet or 12,000 ASL. There was a series of moth-eaten clouds over the mountain, two or three good ones to the west over Apache Junction, and some bigger ones in the distance toward Superior. I took the direction of Apache and soon got into one with the electric turn and bank on. Lift in this one weakened at 11,300 AT just a few feet under Golden altitude, so I came out and spotted a bigger one two miles west with finer vertical development. The sink in between lowered me to cloud base as I reached it and then went in. The next seventeen minutes were about as pleasant a time as I have ever spent. I had no difficulty flying on instruments in soup thick enough that I could not see the wingtips, and wet enough that my yarn yaw indicator lay down on the canopy like a wash rag. Lift varied from 100 fpm sink to 1000 fpm climb, and I tried to stay in the best part as well as possible with the shallow turns allowed on the turn and bank. At high point the altimeter read 13,700 feet above terrain and I was heading for 15,000 but never got it. The cloud had passed its development stage and became very patchy in lift with holes developing in the mass.

The cushion was flat again and the backside felt like it was ready to fall off. I tried one or two other clouds and then gave it up. I had used the oxygen mask for three quarters of an hour but still felt very tired. The return to Rittenhouse was made at 100 to 120 mph (different from the Baby Albatross!) and then I did three consecutive loops, one registering 5 G's, almost passed out, did a six turn spin and came in to land.

Golden C complete! And a new ASA altitude record to burn. 15,250 feet ASL. For those who might think it is good luck, you should consider that this was on the 10th try for this altitude. My other high flight which was to Golden altitude was made before the ASA barograph had arrived, in April of 1956, and all the other ones carried from 3000 feet to 9000 feet in the Baby, Pratt-Read, and the Cirro-Q. Just stay with it and you win. The next news should be Silver C's for Chuck Schmid and Bob Hawkes.

FLYING THE 24TH NATIONALS AT ELMIRA by Joe Lincoln, September 1957.

A few days before Jerry Robertson and I left for the East, Derek Van Dyke was in my shop and gave the stern command to come back from the Nationals with my shield or on it. No such luck. The first contest day I lost my shield, the second day I lost my shirt. And before the competition was over I had to hold on to my pants to keep them damn yankees from stealing my drawers. Nothing that is said here should be construed as an attempt to rationalize 18th place into a creditable performance. It was not. My flying was like a sleepy baseball team that cannot get started; then in the fifth and seventh inning they rap out a sharp triple with nobody out, and proceed to leave the man on third base.

It should be mentioned here that the new aircraft is magnificent. I understand why so many Schweizer owners are fanatical Schweizer salesmen. It is more fun to fly the 1-23D than any other type I have ever been in, with or without power. I have never had any special skill at spot landings and was much impressed with

Paul MacCready's statement that he had put the Breguet-901 down in 200 feet of field. The third day I flew the 1-23D I was able to better this consistently, and stopped it once beyond and within 180 feet of a point on a level field. This gives one a necessary confidence in short field ability which is invaluable in competition flying. The instrumentation is excellent; put together largely on the advice of Wally Wiberg of Texas. I had never flown a Kollsman Direction Indicator. For those who contemplate serious cloud flying it is worth many times the cost. Oxygen equipment (which was never necessary in this contest), consists of a Zepp Aero rig which is good up to 40,000 feet or 43,000 feet in emergency. Radios in both car and aircraft are by Skycrafter and results in their limited use were excellent. I was inexperienced with them and found the soaring so difficult in Elmira that most of the flying was done without their benefit. This improved flying somewhat and made crewing more difficult - but Jerry Robertson did a consistently excellent and steadily improving job as his experience increased.

My practice was limited because there was a great deal of final installation and checking to be done. I flew on four days before the contest and got a taste of accurate landings, ridge soaring, cross country soaring and thermal work. The only cloud I tried produced humorous and highly unsuccessful results. Lack of practice in the 1-23D should not be blamed for my final standing. Three times the practice, I am convinced, would have changed it little. It is an uncontrovertible fact that I was unprepared by experience for Elmira-style soaring. In general, conditions were moderate to weak. My analysis of the final standing of all pilots would put a mark of 35% to luck; 50% to pilot; 15% to aircraft. Very different from Texas where no medium penetration ship did too well in the single place category.

First Day: A 150 mile out-and-return flight to Norwich, New York and back. Direction ENE; wind NNW at 20 to 25 knots. Best flight of the day: Paul Schweizer, about 110 miles.

Having anticipated this take-off for eleven months, I was so excited that I had some difficulty eating a short lunch. We towed aloft around noon and after getting to 5000 feet I set off on course, crabbing heavily into the crosswind. I had John Serafin's cruise control chart that he had made for the 1-23D but after 15 minutes decided that the main problem was to stay aloft and finish the course, not to win a race. My speed between thermals thus became Max L/D or 48 mph. Four thermals and 12 miles away from Harris Hill I found myself over the town of Erin, 35 minutes out, and struggling to get upwind to a good looking ridge. The thermal which would have taken me there did not materialize and I sank like a stone, landing in a short field. In the last struggle there was no time to send a radio message to Jerry. He went the wrong way and we were several hours getting together, so there was no chance for another try. I was very depressed; then when we returned to the Hill we found out that Graham Thomson in the RJ-5 had made only 7 miles and Ray Parker in Tiny Mite 6½. He had rushed back for another try but found things so weak he did not leave the ridge at Harris Hill.

Day 2: Conditions were much weaker today and the Contest Committee set the task of a race to Tri-City Airport, 42 miles away, straight down wind, a few miles SW of Binghampton, NY. Bill Hoverman made the best flight of the day.

A weak thermal took me to 4000 feet over the Hill and I left on course only to get in such heavy sink that I thought I was going to have to land on the east side of Elmira. A ridge there kicked up a good thermal which took me to 5000 feet and I left again sinking rapidly all the way until I was down on another one 18 miles out. This time I was right down to the trees and Jerry could not receive my transmissions. The ridge was perhaps a quarter of a mile long and I sawed up and down it for 35 minutes applauding myself at the foresight I had shown in picking out the ridge before it was too late, and thinking about how I would tell everyone what a jam I had been in, but flew on to reach the goal. Three or four phony thermals came by which gave up to 300 feet of extra altitude and all quit dead and became heavy sink. The big one which was going to get me out was almost in sight when the wind quit and I landed at the foot. Thirty miles in two days! Stan Smith was on a ridge over an hour and a half that day but he made the goal.

Day 3, July 4th. Weaker still, a solid overcast in the sky. The task for the day was a 100 kilometer triangle race to an airport 17 miles SE, then to Ithaca and back. The public address system went blaring on and on to the large gallery that it was an exciting day because they would be able to see the sailplanes come back in at the end of the day. The gallery did not have to wait. A score of sailplanes were towed aloft and came drifting back like leaves on a windless autumn day. Some of the more adventurous pilots took their 2000 feet tow and glided down to O'Brien's Restaurant, fifteen miles away, and collected their free steak dinner. I took one tow and found not a ripple so I landed. An hour later the sun came out and Maxey took his second tow. He seemed to be doing well. That night I found out he made seven miles and landed in the Elmira City dump. What a place for the National Champion!

The sky promptly clouded up again and I took my second tow, this time finding very weak and smooth lift. At 4000 feet I left the area and headed on course at 45 mph, about half way between max L/D and what I thought was minimum sink, to make the most of the slight tail wind. Schreder had been 300 feet above me over Chemung Valley and I could not catch him. In ten minutes a little puff took me up 400 feet and then later a thermal took me clear up another 4000 feet again. I passed a 1-26 several times. It was time to navigate. All hills and dales in Elmira look just the same; so do the rivers, roads and railroads. This is in clear air. On a dim day with a smog-like haze beneath a solid overcast, finding anything is quite a trick. I thought I found the turnpoint and then saw Schreder struggling below me at ridge top height. After spotting what I thought was the turnpoint I went around it and headed north on the second leg with about 2500 feet in hand. As things turned out I did not see the marker but passed over the field below O'Brien's and so close to the turnpoint that many people who observed me thought I had gone over it. I passed over the field as marked on the air chart, but found out the chart was in error - the field was a mile away on the other side of the river! How improbable can things get?

The second leg took me over a long hill and then into a valley on the lee side of which I tried to find ridge lift. No lift or sink, but the sailplane was only going down at 120 fpm and sometimes there were areas of only 100 feet sink a minute followed by 200 feet. It was a flat glide. I passed over the ridge I knew so well from yesterday, said hello to the field, and flew north, getting closer and closer to ridge top height. Finally, I was down to the top and then below. We kept going. When I was down to 100 feet I dropped the nose to get a screaming 55 mph, pulled up over telephone wires, a railroad track and trees, then made an easy landing in a young cornfield.

The rules required two flights over 50 Km. to make it a contest day. I prayed to be beaten by at least two people after calculating my distance at 29½ miles.

Helen Thomson came by and we honked the horn. She stopped. Graham had made 36 miles. Anyone else? As it turned out, no. He and I were the only ones to get past the turnpoint. If I had been able to squeeze out an extra 500 feet in the last thermal it would have made the necessary two miles to give him 1000 points and me about 950. I could afford to be philosophical. For the first time in my life I had made second best flight of the day in a National contest. What I missed in points was more than made up in morale.

Day 3: The task: a 78 mile speed dash to Sidney, New York, ENE, with a 25 knot tail wind. Best flight of the day: Graham Thomson in the RJ-5, 62 minutes for an average speed of 75 mph. My time was 98 minutes.

On this day the conditions far outstripped the forecast, and were perhaps the best of the entire contest. Nobody who stayed high had any trouble making the goal, and several people got down to ridge height but made it aloft again. I released in good lift and departed from the hill with 3500 feet in hand, only to get the usual inverted Elmira thermal which put me down on the ridge east of Horseheads about 7 miles out. After only one minute I started to get visions of sitting here until sundown when the wind would quit, but things were different today. Perhaps five beats were made on the ridge when a powerful thermal took me up to 6000 and I never got below 4500 until the letdown at goal. The flight was made with great conservatism; never forgetting that even spirals were carrying me toward my destination at good speed. Half way out there was a ten mile cloud street which I cruised at 85 mph, and I tried some cloud flying but was still so erratic that I thought cloud base altitude would give me a better speed. This was the street which the RJ-5 used much better. Graham saw me, but I missed him. His flying that day was brilliant.

Navigation was difficult in the extreme, and I started my final glide very late when there was no possibility of landing in the wrong place. I had never finished a contest task in my life and wanted to break that habit today. The wish came true. Final glide was made at 110 mph with spoilers on part of the way and I landed at the goal where it seemed every sailplane in the US had congregated. The time - about average.

This was the day that impressed Barney Wiggin who had been the meteorologist for the American soaring team at St. Yan during the 1956 Internationals. He said that under almost identical conditions there, only one third of the pilots had completed their goal instead of three quarters as at Elmira. The United States is getting depth for future International soaring teams.

Day 4: The first open day. Best flight: Schreder in the new Airmate HP-7, 305 miles to a goal at Logan airport in Boston. Longest flight: Compton in an old LK, 320 miles to Plymouth. These flights were only the second and third in Elmira history over 300 miles - the longest being by Dick Johnson in the RJ-5 of 360 to Norfolk, Virginia. I made 158 miles to Coxsackie, New York, 21 miles south of Albany, and within two miles of the Hudson River. It was the most interesting and skillful soaring flight I have ever made. I came within 20 seconds of having zero points for the day and scored about 500. Three days later in a much easier flight I scored 959 points.

My take off was about three quarters of the way down the list and a weak thermal took me up to 3500 feet above the hill - not quite enough altitude to risk leaving, and in the heavy wind I did not want to hang on to the thermal too long to get back. I decided to leave presently and fly upwind to something better. It was not there; I sank at 500 fpm no matter where I looked and had to duck back onto the hill which was now vacant except for Ray Jackson and John Bierens in the Alibi. 20 minutes aloft followed by 20 minutes on the ground, then came my second tow. The wind had shifted enough to fly ridge lift on the hill which I started to do and I worked 3 thermals up to 3000 feet only to have them quit and put me back down. Time was getting short because a cirrus overcast had come in from the west and the ground was already shaded. Then the wind abated and my altitude thinned out. I was down to 400 feet above the hill, less than pattern altitude. What to do? Try it another 20 seconds and risk a downwind landing or one at the county airport, or quit and burn the rest of the day. This was a National contest. I hung on.

The thermal came after 10 or 15 seconds and I started going up, expecting it to quit like the others, but we kept on and on until I had over 5000. Forty five minutes on the ridge but we are off now, and might hope to get into the sunlight there on the horizon. The first half hour was good but had nothing that justified flying over max L/D. Once in a while I put the speed up to 55 mph but rarely, and I stopped to circle in every scrap of lift. The wind was carrying over the ground at these times and shaded ground is not famous for producing explosive Texas thermals. The altitude range went up from 4000 to 6000 feet and slowly we flew toward Binghampton, 55 miles out, where I saw Ray Jackson for the first time since leaving the hill. He was 500 feet below me in the same thermal and he left before I did, going like a cannonball. Too fast Ray - slow down. Ten minutes later I caught up with him, 800 feet below me in the same thermal. His white 1-23 with copper numbers was beginning to shine because we had worked out of the shaded area at last. He took off ahead of me again flying very fast and landed soon after. I went on in conditions which improved a little over sunny ground but still unable to get up into cloud although I could always get up to the base. Past Sidney I ate a candy bar and had a swig of water.

We were approaching the Catskill Mountains, homeland of Rip Van Winkle. It was my first mountain crossing in a sailplane, but eastern mountains are not like Arizona ones. The country is populous and there were many fields which would have been suitable for landing in a pinch. I know. Three times during the crossing I was below ridge top height, within 800 feet of the ground, when I struck lift. Another minute without lift at any of these points would have let me down. You get used to seeing ridges above you! After the second lift I was over a mountain valley several miles wide and could see that if I made it past the ridges on the other side, the land fell away, giving effective altitude without further climbing. The sun was getting lower in the west; I had a late start and had been aloft over 4 hours already. At the far side there was a ridge which ran like the vertical arm of a T up to a mountaintop. This ridge faced the wind. From the peak there were two ridges parallel with the wind - the cap of T - falling off both upwind and down wind. The downwind ridge had a notch in it which I hoped to sneak through. I started across the valley toward the distant ridge which might give lift. The level ground was not over 2000 feet below me.

The crossing was made in stable air at 48 mph and tension mounted as the ridge came slowly closer and I sank toward the floor. At last I made it. There was no lift! Then in a few seconds it came, first zero sink, then slow lift which kept me a few feet above the ridge crest as it ran at a gentle angle up to the summit. We were approaching the point at which to make the plunge for the notch in the downwind ridge. With 200 feet above the crest I went over. 600 fpm sink and nothing but forest below. Instantly I did a 180 and got back in lift, running toward the summit. A second try. No violent sink this time. You have it. And also the indescribable thrill of solving a tricky problem in cross country flight.

Over the top we ran parallel to the downwind ridge for half a mile just even with its crest as it fell away from the summit, and turned left through the notch, flying out over a much broader valley below. I had expected great sink here but none came. After a few minutes instead arrived the last thermal of the day and I squeezed every foot I could get, then headed for the far side as the land fell away again into the final Hudson River valley. The passage seemed very long and when I was down to 400 feet I had cased a good many fields which I thought of using, but just ahead was a tantalizing ridge with another notch in it through which the road passed into the big lower valley. I went on.

We hit this final ridge about 250 feet above the immediate terrain. The notch was on my left. I turned right to try to gain a little more altitude from the ridge. None was there. Not quite zero sink. A quick 180 headed us for the notch, and when we brought it up we turned right and slipped through. The land fell away sharply; we crossed a large freeway and were again 600 feet above terrain in stable air. The last glide brought us over a group of large brick buildings, across the street from which was a big field of newly mown wheat. At 300 feet speed was increased, I turned base leg and final, then went in. 4 hours and 58 minutes after takeoff I was down again after a memorable flight.

A man came over from the group of brick buildings which turned out to be a juvenile penal institution. (What if I had landed inside the fence?) He was wonderfully helpful in calling contest headquarters. After the call I went back to Cirro-Q where a crowd was gathering. There were men and women of all ages, and I explained the operation of the aircraft, how you used the parachute, how you were towed aloft, what the instruments were for. Came the inevitable question about the relief tube from a 7 year old boy. What do you say with all these ladies present? Desperately racking my brain for a quick answer, I was saved by a mature 9 year old boy. "It's a fire extinguisher, stupid!"

Fifth Day: On this day Stan Smith won the 24th National Soaring Contest with a flight to the task goal of Rochester, 85 miles to the north. Del Miller made it a contest day by making 42 miles. Bikle got 22 miles in the longer of his two tries and nobody else got up to 20.

Early in the day the sun was out and it might have been possible to stay airborne if you had been aloft when the solid cover moved in. Stan got his tow at exactly the right time to contact a strange and ominous looking wave which appeared as a writhing black line moving across the sky with the overcast. Paul Bikle was aloft only three minutes later and he missed it. This wave carried the champion over half way to his goal after which he flew thermals in rain which reduced his visibility to the vanishing point.

I considered an early start but Jerry had obtained a take off time at 2:00 pm which theoretically should be at the height of the day and thus ideal for a fairly short speed dash. I kept it, and lost a chance to make a good score. After the wave had passed there was a series of violent rain squalls, but never an opening in the sky. Several people tried tows and got no father than the county airport. Late in the afternoon I went up and to my amazement found heavy lift on tow 1000 feet above Harris Hill. Thinking I might not find it again if I took the full 2000 feet allowed, I released and played about in lift and sink for over fifteen minutes without gaining over 50 feet. I headed back for the Hill to take the full 2000 for my glide out, then changed my mind, did a 180 and headed on course in strange air that kept my sinking rate down to about 100 fpm. There was an airport on Montour Falls, just below the southern extremity of a lake, 15 miles out. I headed for it at slightly less than max L/D reasoning that the tail wind might flatten my glide a trace. We flew on in glassy air, getting down to hilltop height, then well below; the lake was getting very close and south of the waterline was a great field of cat tails at least 6 feet deep, but no airport where the chart promised one. The country all about was virtually unlandable - forest, vineyards, areas of tightly packed houses. 400 feet left and still no airport. Had it been abandoned or closed since this chart was published? Things like that happen. Then at 350 feet it materialized right where it was supposed to be, marvelously disguised by the color of the sod strip on the dark afternoon. A base leg and final brought us down, and within 20 minutes the RJ-5 came down with Thomson on the same field.

Fifteen miles, and oddly there were only 4 or 5 longer flights on that day. If Del Miller had made 10 miles less it would not have been a contest day. If I had made two miles more on July 4 it would have been a contest day. If... but then, that is why you go to contests.

Sixth Day: A 200 kilometer triangle course to the airport just SW of Binghampton, then to Ithaca, and back to Harris Hill. Weather forecast: good, although it looked completely impossible with a dull solid overcast during the pilots' meeting. Best flight of the day: a tie of 73 miles which both Fritz Compton and Paul Bikle made. I made 70 for second best flight and 959 points, and also had the pleasure of beating Graham in the RJ-5 and Maxey in the Prue 215-A, on a day when it was more than blind luck.

It was a comparatively simple flight. The wind was WNW at 18 knots which gave a strong direct tail wind to the first turn point. I made this in 50 minutes of easy flying, using some cloud lift, then got blown far downwind of the turn point before getting high again in another cloud. My instrument flying was very nervous but improving rapidly. Forty minutes after passing the turn point I had worked my way back upwind to a station 3 miles north of the turn. This was averaging 4 miles an hour so far on the second leg! A good brisk walk. Then a fine cloud street appeared and I flew under it straight back toward Elmira and gained fifteen miles advantage on the deadly wind. For the rest of the day I was able to crab into the wind only 25° or 30° instead of 60°, and my speed greatly increased.

Three hours out I stopped to circle in a thermal which was near a cloud and had the unusual experience of seeing the clear air turn into cloud on all sides and above and below me as I spiralled. I had entered the thermal just as it reached condensation level and flew out of cloud when the lift weakened.

Near the second turn point I saw a mountain which seemed to have a soarable ridge on the far side. The cumulus up wind had disappeared and this ridge promised to keep me aloft until things improved as they seemed to be doing on the horizon. I headed straight upwind and back toward the course to avoid the off course penalty in case I got let down. My last 4000 feet was spent in this maneuver going down at 500 fpm, and I landed on the side of a hill inclined at about 25°. Just below the touchdown point the hill pitched down at 45° and made climbing down a little tricky. Only 250 feet away the sailplane was out of sight and I had trouble getting my landing card signed by a farm lady who was too shrewd to believe the fantastic story that I had landed a glider up there. She took me for a city slicker out to slap a mortgage on her property.

Last Day: The second open day, and one with a forecast for good distance soaring. After yesterday's performance my standing had come up and I had one of the first choices for time off. I decided to go early. If anyone should ever compete against me on open distance days, the right technique is to find out what I plan to do and then do the opposite. It cannot fail to bring success.

Rushing madly to get everything ready, I was airborne at 11:00 with a sealed barograph ticking behind my head, no food, a goal in Virginia 230 miles away, and a solid strato-cumulus overcast above. 1200 feet over Harris Hill three sailplanes were circling in weak lift, but I went on up to 2000 feet for the release. Almost immediately I got weak lift and made the insane decision to hold on to it in the bristling north wind. The lift held up exactly long enough to put me out of range of Harris Hill, then quit dead. In steady sink I went down as we flew over west Elmira and never made a turn until I was on the ridge at South Mountain, just seven miles from the Hill, and still in sight of Jerry Robertson who was watching through field glasses. The ridge soaring was easy. Occasionally, a weak thermal would come along and take me up to 200 or 300 feet. Other sailplanes joined me. The RJ-5 went over a scant 1000 feet above and I was worried when he headed for the forest country to the south.

Back and forth in endless beats. If any of you ever get in a position like this look out for the feeling of safety. This illusion of absolute security was new to me, but it kept growing stronger even though my wingtip was often only a span and a half from the trees. Jerry saw at least one man escape from the ridge. I must have flown it wrong. Thermals with strong lift would become violent sink when I had gained 300 or 400 feet. The overcast had begun to break up. My optimism increased for a getaway and a long flight. Then the wind abated and four sailplanes landed at the foot of the ridge within five minutes. I had the doubtful honor of being first down. Seven miles and 29 points for the day. Paul Bikle made it to Cape May, New Jersey, about 240 miles out, and landed on the beach for his second consecutive 1000 point day.

My time on the ridge was 1 hour and 35 minutes, and I felt so completely disgusted and defeated that I did not make another try. This was an unforgivable mistake. For me it was over. 18th place in my second National Contest.

TUCSON FLIGHT by Joe Lincoln, April 1958.

Saturday, 22 March, I had thought of flying. The day had a powerful west wind, strong convection, and good cumulus which dumped light rain periodically. It was on such a day that I had been let down on my first cross country out of Elmira 127 miles out on the way to a 202 mile goal. I decided against it, worked on the Pratt Read, checked weather for Sunday which looked better. Convection was still to be good, wind WNW to NNW at 20 knots. Perfect for a goal flight to Douglas. Preparations were well under way by Saturday night.

Sunday, I was up at 6:20 with a date to meet Bertha and Marcel (Godinat) by 9:00 am. Chet Howard was going to be at the field at 10:15. I had not counted on having the Cosim variometer needing minor repair. The rubber tubing needed to be cut and re-set. Jerry Robertson also went along and set a new record for washing down Cirro-Q. We met Marcel and Bertha at 10:00, and dashed out to Turf Paradise. Final preparations, rigging, sealing the Peravia, and loading up took another hour and a half. I had too much gear along - food, coffee, an extra jacket, charts, kneeboard, pen, cruise control curves, and finally my new Swiss knife which Marcel thought I might need. I put it in the pocket of my jacket, under a parachute strap. This had roughly the effect of a burr under the saddle of an unbroken horse. I found a new location.

Takeoff was at 11:50 and lift began at something over 500 fpm to cloudbase at 7000 feet. I waved goodbye to Don Barnard in the TG-3 and headed SE on course, giving the crew a call on the Skycrafter radio. Conditions were tremendous and I ran 80 mph between the first thermals. It seemed to take longer than I had expected to get over Camelback Mountain, but I got there after deciding that my altitude range for the day's work would be somewhere between 8000 and 5000 feet. Over the mountain I saw a newspaper which had been carried aloft almost to my altitude.

South of Scottsdale I looked for the first time at cloud shadows to see them racing toward Douglas. The ground wind at Turf Paradise had been in the wrong direction, by the hefty margin of 170°, but I knew this was only a surface condition. At first glance, I was satisfied with the wind aloft, then looked again, blinked, rubbed my eyes, and looked hard again. The wind was almost directly out of the south at what appeared to be 20 knots. The weather office had hit all other conditions on the nose, but missed this wind vector by 135°. Half way between Scottsdale and Mesa the clouds ahead on course all but disappeared, and by the time I reached Chandler my speed had been cut in half by weaker lift.

Jerry suggested an out and return to Tucson, which still seemed possible, but I was flying for a Diamond, and did not want to abandon the goal. They caught up with me just beyond Chandler and began the leisurely drive to Tucson, with frequent stops for me to catch up. Most of the rest of the day they had me in sight, and once or twice I saw the Ford and trailer.

Two hours and 15 minutes out I was near Coolidge airport, not quite in gliding range, and in trouble for the first time. Down to 1000 feet above terrain. I worked out of that and went slowly on, pressing toward Desert Peak, across from Picacho. My course had been altered to stay over better landing country. This side of Desert Peak I was down again to 1400 feet and looking over the fields with more than academic interest. Then I got a good one and worked up well over the top of the mountain. I flew by it and caught another good lift on the south side. Up again at 6500 I set course for Redrock, half way between Picacho and Marana Airbase. Here there was a big hole and I went on and on with no lift. Finally the altimeter read 2400 feet, only 500 feet above the terrain. I told the crew to keep me in sight; the flight was just about flown. Then a weak lift! Five minutes of desperate soaring gained me 300, then it quit, and I went over to the field I was going to use. New lift appeared momentarily. Generally in this position I get 100 up for the first half circle and 250 down for the second half. To my surprise this time the second half gave me 300 up. The flight was saved. In 20 minutes I had safe altitude again. The headwind had somewhat abated and my loss of distance was not close to the altitude gain I had made.

I foresaw that by using a technique Dick Johnson calls austerity gliding there was a faint possibility of making Tucson, still 40 miles away, even though it was 4:30 pm. You fly at max L/D and use every shred of lift to the maximum. I knew if I got low again after 5:00 the flight was over. This worked better than hoped for and at altitude the lift was good, up to 300 fpm. Slowly I went on, then came the last thermal of the day, 15 miles out of Gilpin airport, which is 6 miles north of Tucson. This took me up to a point where Gilpin was in the bag, and there was a possibility of making the downtown airport. I headed on course at 50 mph. Altitude was slowly converted into distance. The sun got lower. At 5500 feet or 3300 feet A.T. the impossible happened. I got another thermal! It took me clear back to 8000. Now Tucson Municipal was easy and I instructed the crew to go there and wait for me.

All over Tucson there was lift, and I soared up under the first cloud I had been with since leaving the Motorola Plant on East McDowell Road. Altitude went up to the highest point of the day, 8840 feet ASL. I reached Tucson Municipal over a mile above terrain, 6 hours after takeoff. My knees were a little wobbly, feet were freezing, and I was afraid I had gangrene in the rear end from lack of circulation.

Two new ASA records had been set. Distance: 123 miles; and duration. It seemed a crime to land and throw away all this altitude so I radioed Jerry and Marcel to see if they were in a hurry to leave. They politely said no, even though Jerry was very short of sleep, having returned from a California track meet the night before, and Marcel had to work the next day. I decided to make the new ASA duration record 7 hours if I could. Over Tucson there must have been the condition known as the evening thermal. Lift was over tremendous areas, and I went back up almost to the high point of the day. Then it gradually lessened, but one time I got nervous and timed my sink. It took eleven minutes to lose 300 feet. I had radioed the Tucson tower and they knew I was in the area. The sun was almost down, then it set and I was still close to a mile high. A decision was made to end the flight before darkness fell, and when cleared for landing behind a Piper the strip lights were already on. Touchdown was at 6 hours and 55 minutes after takeoff. The first minutes I was out of the sailplane I had great difficulty walking. It had been a memorable flight.

Three observations might be made for the benefit of ASA members who have not yet flown much cross country.

1. For distance flying, wind conditions are paramount. This flight easily carried 220 miles through the airmass, with a goal 209 miles away. It could have been successful with similar convection and no wind. With the predicted wind it might have carried over 300 miles, although it would have to have been cut off because of the international border at Mexico.

2. When in trouble, alter course to assure yourself of good landing terrain underneath you. This was done, and a forced landing would never have caused embarrassment anywhere on this flight. Also for long flights, take great care of your comfort. My parachute has a buckle in the back which grew very painful after 4 hours. At Elmira Jerry had always stuffed a T-shirt between the 'chute and my back before a flight. This was forgotten on Sunday.

3. Late in the day reduce speed and stay as high as possible. This flight was lengthened by 2½ hours and 50 miles using this technique. My final altitude over Tucson Municipal could have added on at least another 20 miles. (30 to 1 glide less wind drift). Finally, a criticism of your flight by an old hand like Marcel Godinat, or Don Barnard, can give you some pointers which you might have overlooked. If you keep your ears open you can always learn something new about soaring.

COLORADO WAVE SAFARI by Joe Lincoln, April 1968.

December 27, 1967, dawned clear, cold and hung over. After two years of thinking about it, I was finally going to go up to Dave Johnson's and Mark Wild's Black Forest Gliderport, outside of Colorado Springs, for some real live wave flying. The morning got off to a bad start as a result of recurring vertigo which was my souvenir from a tremendous Christmas party the night before. I could not summon quite enough co-ordination to get the bag packed on time and missed my scheduled flight.

I left Phoenix in late afternoon and flew over the vast snowfields of northern Arizona, covered with their heavy blanket after the December storms. It was nearly dark when we landed at Colorado Springs and night had fallen when Dave Johnson picked me up. Wave flights had carried up to 20,000 feet that day and at 10:00 pm that night he pointed out a fabulous lenticular cloud straight over his house in Colorado Springs. It looked like the flying was going to be extremely good.

I spent the night at Dave Johnson's place in company with his dog, his young tow pilot, and his beautiful new Libelle which was parked in the living room. Early next morning we got up and drove out to the Black Forest Gliderport which I saw for the first time. The morning was quiet; the wave was not waving. I met Mark Wild, Mrs Wild, and some of the people in the operations shack, then after a while I went over to the lounge where a sizeable group of pilots sat around in various amounts of flight gear, waiting for the wave to begin. Wally Scott was there with his son; Hod Taylor was there, and we met for the first time. On the last day of November he had flown his bright yellow Standard Austria up over 42,000 feet in a flight which was good for his Three Lennie Pin. Ruth Oelrichs was there. On that same day in November she set a National Feminine Altitude and Altitude Gained Record.

That morning there was no activity. We had lunch and watched the weather. That afternoon there was no wave activity. A promising front had gotten stuck in a snowbank somewhere on the far side of the Rockies. We went back to Dave Johnson's house and had supper. That night we listened to the weather report on the radio. There was no activity.

December 29 dawned cold, clear and beautiful. Meteorologically there was no activity. We went out to the field and Dave Johnson gave me my wave orientation flight which is required before you can go solo in the wave. A trace of wind picked up and after we had released from tow, we found one very good patch where the condition was such that our rate of sink was reduced to 40 fpm. After working this for a few minutes, we turned ENE and flew back to the Black Forest Gliderport, passing over Colorado Springs, over the snow fields, toward the black pine trees and the strip which grew closer until it was time to make the pattern and land. I was very heavily dressed but still got cold even during this brief flight.

That afternoon Gleb Derujinsky, the famous fashion photographer and soaring pilot, came in. Ed Mack Miller, the writer for Flying Magazine, flew in to say hello. There was lunch and a long afternoon filled with soaring talk. We watched the weather. There was no activity.

That evening Mark and Ruth Wild threw a wonderful party at their new house and after dinner showed still photographs and movies of wave flying in Colorado - pictures of days with great flying weather, days of activity.

December 30 dawned cold, clear and beautiful. There was promise of very fine wave soaring. The valley at Colorado Springs was covered with heavy fog, and we just emerged from this as we came up toward the Black Forest. Half a dozen sailplanes were already aloft. I got my place on the takeoff list and spent 40 minutes dressing for a flight after seeing a number of pilots, heavily dressed in their Eskimo clothing, bundled into their sailplanes and taking off for the wave. The day looked very good. After I was dressed, I went over to the operations office. It was still before mid-morning and the wave had not yet picked up its expected strength, although one man was nearing 20,000 feet which is more than a mile above the summit of Pikes Peak. I began to watch the clock and anticipate when I would be able to take off.

Then came the first ominous report of a wall of snow blowing in toward the Black Forest from the northeast. The reports of this storm kept growing more and more frequent. Interest in this phenomenon, which we could not see on the ground, gradually became concern and started tipping in the direction of anxiety. The first sailplane reported that he was coming home in order to beat the storm to the field. Three more quickly followed. Within a few minutes, all of the sailplanes were headed for the field. From where we watched on the ground, it looked like they were throwing away a wonderful day; then 5 minutes later a snowstorm with northeast wind rustled the tree tops. Two of the sailplanes had beaten it in and a number came in during the early wind flurries. Everyone sprang into action, helping the pilots get their aircraft off the strip and into the hangars before heavy wind came. It was astonishing how soon one ran out of breath while working hard in extremely heavy flight clothing at the altitude of 7,000 feet.

Presently all aircraft were secured and most of them were safely in the hangar. The storm settled in for an all day blow. Wally Scott spent 3 hours trying to get his twin engine airplane started for a flight back home and everyone's ingenuity was called into play before he succeeded. They taxi-ed down to the far end of the strip, disappearing in the snow before they were one third of the way down. We watched the airplane as it re-emerged out of the snow haze, thundering over our heads 100 feet high. We waved farewell, and one by one other people were leaving the field and leaving Colorado Springs. Toward nightfall, I gathered up my things and drove back into town with Dave Johnson. We all had supper together, then one of the other pilots took me to the airport for my flight home.

My first wave camp was over. Everyone talks about the standing mountain wave. I had experienced my first sitting wave.

JOE LINCOLN, WORLD RECORD HOLDER

In the June, 1970 issue of AIR CURRENTS, Editor Nancy Hume wrote, "On May 23, 1970, Joe soared 404.6 miles to earn the World Multi-Place Out and Return Record. He released at Sante Fe, New Mexico, soaring 202 miles north to a predesignated turn point at Salida, Colorado and back to Santa Fe. Total flight time was 7½ hours, giving an average speed of 54 mph. Joe's passenger in his 2-32, Cibola, was Chris Crowl. Upon acceptance, this record will replace that set by Klaus Keim of West Germany on December 28, 1967, for a distance of 385.66 miles. We're all mighty proud of you, Joe!"

A WORLD RECORD WITH JOE by Chris Crowl, June 1970.

There are two major types of competitive soaring. One is contest, the other record flying. Although contests are recognized as more strenuous to the nervous system, they test only half of a pilot's skill.

Record flying, as does contest flying, relies on speed, in-flight weather observations, course changes, pilot ability and, as Ross Briegleb said in the June 1970 Soaring, "If he has an average IQ or better, that kinda helps too." But record flying involves more than this. It involves hundreds of hours of planning and preparation. All items must be completed before the day of the flight. Imagine trying to accomplish a flight preparation hours before a flight begins: wash and wax sailplane, thoroughly inspect and repair trailer (in case of 500 mile retrieve) put fairings on sailplane, chart course and alternate, check weather, make flight declarations, seal and install cameras and barographs, make tow arrangements...

Record flying also involves inhuman patience. Thermal strengths of 500 fpm are nice, but are not record weather. Thermal strengths must be near 1,000 fpm without the accompaniment of 1,000 fpm sink. Weather conditions must be nearly ideal on the entire flight path. One poor area can destroy your record.

During our record trip, Joe, Don and I waited 21 days for a record day to appear. When it did appear we had to take appropriate measures. From weather information gathered the day before our flight, a task decision would have to be made. No person would tell us the day's task. All information pointed to a goal and return flight from Santa Fe, New Mexico (our base of operations) to Salida, Colorado and return, a respectable flight but not a pace setting flight, as we had hoped. We all were in agreement that this would be the final flight. That Friday night was the most sleepless night I have had since Joe and I made the national goal and return attempt two years before. (Disqualified due to photographic error.) Joe had a dream of a goal and return flight he and I had in a 1-26. I am not sure why it was in a 1-26. Guess he likes to stick with Schweizer equipment. The weather man had been correct about the lack of cirrus (first item checked in the morning), and we hoped he was correct about the rest of his information. After making other necessary arrangements, we were ready to start the flight.

Saturday, May 23rd, looked like an excellent day. There was no sign of cirrus to the north. This had called an abrupt halt to past flights. By 9:30 Cibola was near the runway ready to fly. This is when Joe and I started our cooling off period. With the high altitude undergarments, a person can get warmer than on a summer day in Phoenix. During this rest period cu's started developing over the mountain.

We started our tow at 10:30. Through past experience we had found that lift started over the mountains one hour before it started over the valley. For this reason we had picked a dirt strip close to the mountains as a starting point.

At 11:15 we released and made our start at 9500 feet. Heading straight for the mountain range we slowly sank to 8500 feet. This must appear high to the reader, but not to the writer. The ground level was about 500 feet below us. At 8500 feet we hit our first thermal and climbed back to 11,700 feet. Not wasting any time, we continued up-range, slowly sinking down to the scenic view. I was just getting interested in the pine needle patterns on the trees when Joe hit another thermal. We slowly climbed back to economy cruise in the area of 14,000 feet. This is the economy cruise because you're not yet using oxygen and still not on the ground.

As we passed Truchas Peak, I remembered our first practice day. We were to fly to Taos and back. When we got to Truchas Peak the task was clearly evident, get back. We unintentionally started our final glide from Truchas Peak toward Santa Fe. The range runs north and south with ridges running east and west. We managed to clear one ridge but we were too low to clear the next ridge when we hit the saving thermal.

One hour flight time, 16,400 feet and only 30 miles. At this rate we will be back at two in the morning. Another solution would be to speed up. On the north side of Taos over Lama we were up to 17,200 feet when the whole sky started going up. I couldn't help feeling sorry for the guys where all the air was going down, because they probably couldn't get their tow plane in the air!

As we passed Lama we encountered our first cloud street. We quickly flew to the north averaging 75 mph the second hour. We cloud hopped from the Colorado border to Blanca Peak. Here we visualized possible tragedy. That cirrus was back. We moved north as fast as possible.

Three hours, 180 miles and 75 mph during the third hour, 35 miles to the turn and we started encountering cirrus. This was the time for careful flying. We slowly edged our way toward our turnpoint. Seven miles short of the goal we took time to get all the altitude we could. We left the thermal and headed for the turn like a bat-out-of-!!!! The pictures were taken and we were homeward bound. Still in trouble from cirrus we worked our way back along the mountain range running to the southeast of Salida, Colorado.

After breaking loose from under the cirrus, we were surprised to see how promising the sky looked. We worked our way to Blanca Peak. To the south the sky started to disintegrate. Over Blanca Airport came the turning point of the flight. A 60° turn to the southeast was accomplished, putting us 2000 feet above ground and climbing. From where I sat, the battle was over.

We headed under clouds toward Taos. Over Taos, with what we thought was a dying day, we climbed to cloud base. We cruised towards our goal, decreasing our glide angle and increasing our hopes.

We contacted Don Barnard, who had chased us as far as Alamosa, and he said we would beat him by a good half hour (he was already traveling over red line). We told him we would try to stay aloft until he got there. Seven and a half hours into the flight, seven miles short of the goal, we caught another thermal and slowly started climbing.

Don got back to the ranch strip about 8 hours into the flight and looked up the owner, Jack Gallette. We had made prior arrangements with Jack, a Civil Air Patrol man, and he was most willing to have us use his strip. Jack also brought the beer and champagne. Then the idea, why not call the newspaper?

Meanwhile, Joe had talked to John Wheatly, a 3 diamond pilot, on his way back from a retrieve. John said he would act as a landing witness. After 8 hours and 30 minutes of flight time we cruised over Santa Fe Airport and back towards the ranch for a landing. Then Don called and said, "Can you stay up for thirty more minutes?" The newspaper people would take that long. Sure! Just find a thermal and stay in it until the sun sets. What could be easier!

As I finished thinking of every profound word I could think of, we hit a thermal. Finally our crew chief on the ground gave us the okay to land. In the pattern, which was made in the 120 mph range, I watched the sun set on a day that was to go down in my mind as the most instructional of my life. But, for the moment, I was recovering from the fact that we had actually made it!

ANOTHER RECORD FLIGHT by Joe Lincoln, June 1970.

Takeoff in my Schweizer 2-32 was approximately 11:40 am on the 30th May behind a Cessna 180 towplane. Chris Crowl was flying passenger in the back seat and the declaration had been properly photographed. I released some 10 or 15 minutes later just east of the soaked bottom land of the Rio Grande River, which runs through Alamosa, Colorado, over the beginning of dry valley terrain, a few miles east of the town. There had been evidence of a good thermal before release, but it vanished. We sank from nearly 2,000 feet to an altitude of only 400 feet above terrain before usable lift was found. This was at a point roughly 6 miles west of Blanca Airport. From there we worked up to 13,000 feet in a somewhat disappointing thermal and flew out along the course toward the first turnpoint of the 100 kilometer triangle. The first turn is some buildings on the eastern border of Great Dunes National Monument, 24 miles north and a trace east of the airport serving Blanca, on which our start gate was set up.

Roughly eight miles SSW of the turn, we turned south and worked back toward Blanca and the start gate. In due course, we made a pass through the starting gate and flew northward toward the first turn at high speed, but at very low altitude along the lower slopes of Blanca Peak. This time we went clear to the first turn as we had done twice the day before - once at a speed of nearly 85 mph for the first leg. There appeared to be no workable lift on the second leg between the first turn and the hamlet of Mosca, so we gained altitude and flew back toward Blanca above the ridge between Blanca Peak and the turn.

Weather over the course consisted of fairly strong cumulus clouds with bases around 17,500 feet, no cirrus overcast, few dust devils and wind running from southwest at the surface at approximately 15 knots to WSW at cloudbase at approximately 30 knots. Lift at the lower levels was discouraging, frequently being in the neighborhood of 300 fpm. Up toward cloudbase, lift in a good thermal ran from 800 to 1,000 fpm. Above the ridge, running north from Blanca Peak, we were able to get some ridge soaring effect.

When we returned to Blanca Field, there was a great hole in the sky to the southwest and it was necessary to wait over half an hour before we made our next start.

Two hours and 14 minutes after takeoff, we made our next high speed run through the starting gate and turned north toward Blanca Peak, which lay 9 miles northeast. Altitude lost in our dive through the gate was promptly regained as we started cruising northward at slightly over 11,000 feet, 3,300 feet above the surface of Blanca Field. Lift in the next 7 miles was very disappointing, and there was one area of heavy sink. I was just about to abort the flight when we found a solid and respectable thermal on the southwest flank of Bianca Peak. Lift began at about 600 fpm and worked up to 800 or 900 feet, while we soared from about 11,000 feet up to summit altitude, 14,317 feet. From here we passed over the summit and worked ridge lift while we cruised with quite good actual speed toward the first turn. North of Blanca Peak a cloud was worked which put us up over 15,000 feet and over the ridge. While we were nearing the first turn, we worked solid 1,000 fpm lift up to

17,500 feet. During this fast climb the wind carried us a little east of the ridge. From here we flew WNW to the buildings of the first turn and photographed them.

WSW of the turn there were two clouds lined up in a street ahead toward Mosca. With impressive brilliance, I flew under this cloud street and was rewarded with solid 900 fpm sink until we flew out from under the clouds.

The sink ended approximately where the lift should have ended, and we were down to roughly 14,000 feet, perhaps a quarter of our way on the second leg, bucking a 30 knot headwind. For the next few miles sink was moderate, and we got a good thermal as we approached big San Luis Lake, which lies 8 miles east of the second turn, just north of Route 150 which goes toward Mosca. In this thermal we regained our lost altitude while we discouragingly blew back toward our first turn. From 17,000 feet I was determined to make the second turn without further circling to escape the damage of the headwind. We slowed down in lift and speeded up in sink and presently rounded Mosca where we made our photographs from a point outside the town.

Glide angles for the last 40 miles of the course had been worked out at 20/1, 30/1, 35/1 and 40/1. My passenger, Chris Crowl, was on duty giving me glide angles. The initial leg measured 24 miles, the second leg was 22 miles, and the final leg was 24 miles, for a total distance of 70 miles. As we left the second turn, we were 500 feet beneath a 20/1 glide angle for the last leg.

We set course for Blanca Field marked by the large Smith Reservoir which is beyond. Using the technique of slowing down for lift and speeding up in sink, we were able to make good time without further circling while we flew our cross wind leg home. Half way back we got above a 20/1 glide angle and started increasing speed from 70 mph indicated until we gradually worked up to 100 mph indicated. Twelve miles out we contacted Don Barnard on the radio to be ready for our pass through the gate and were able to continue gradually increasing speed until we were indicating over 120 mph for our last few miles.

We passed through the finish gate 50 feet high, 56 minutes after the start, pulled up and did a 270° left turn for our landing on the main runway. Shortly after landing, we photographed our declaration with the amended time, and Don removed the barographs, one of which had not worked. Immediately after landing, Chris Crowl estimated our speed at 75 mph, roughly 6 miles per hour faster than the existing World Multiplace Speed Record for the 100 kilometer triangle.

EPILOGUE: This was our last flying day in Colorado. Later that afternoon, I soared back to Alamosa and we de-rigged. On May 31, Don left the field at Alamosa and started trailering Cibola home, while I flew back in the Cessna carrying John Spealman, who had helped man the starting gate, and my young passenger, Chris Crowl. Two nights later, the four of us worked from 8:00 pm until midnight on a massive assault on the paperwork necessary to substantiate world records. On Wednesday, the first of June, all the paperwork was shipped off to Bertha Ryan, along with calibrations, four photographs, four maps of the flight and four copies of all the required record forms: one for the FAI in Paris, one for the NAA in Washington, one for the SSA and one which comes back to the pilot.

Five days later the telephone rang just as we were finishing supper. It was Bertha Ryan. The record came unglued because of an unconsidered technicality: there was no possible way to establish that we had photographed the first turn on our actual speed run rather than on our aborted first flight, which had passed through the starting gate and carried north as far as the initial turn.

RECORD TRY IN RENO by Joe Lincoln, May 1972.

Early in 1971, major steps were taken in preparation for a very long wave flight out of Reno. These preparations included the commissioning of a new 20 meter wing from Schweizer Aircraft, the acquisition and assembly of an extreme cold weather kit, and the construction of a heavy insulated box for the back seat of my 2-32 which would contain a new long-range radio, a transponder, a place for 3 barographs and space for a very high capacity nickel cadmium storage battery.

Don Barnard also worked out and constructed a block-and-tackle device and other rigging machinery for a very heavy wing.

The last week of April and the first week of May, 1971, were devoted to flying in Reno, the first 3 days of which went into finishing details and learning how to use the rigging machinery. As things worked out, we got to Reno a bit too late for wave flying and too early for any impressive thermal flying. The air was full of holes, and I never really left gliding range from Stead Air Force Base where we kept the ship in the Lear hangar.

Later on in the year, good fortune came in the form of a Multiplace World Record around a 100 kilometer triangle out of Alamosa, Colorado at 72.93 mph.

1972 saw full preparations under way. First of all, Don Barnard completely re-worked and replaced the deck of the 2-32 trailer along with the other main-tenance chores. The decision was made to fly the wave with my standard 2-32 wing rather than the long one. There was a number of reasons for this.

1. The fact that the long wing would have to be flown dry due to extreme low temperatures, 70°F below zero.

2. I thought the standard wing might be a little safer in severe rotor turbulence.

3. In case of landing damage to the standard wing, it would not put us out of commission for the race part of the season with the long wing.

4. The standard wing is equipped with navigation lights for night flying in the case of a long term flight.

The fuselage of Cibola, standard wings, and long wings, were all given a thorough physical examination at Mercury Aviation. All radio and related equipment was given a thorough inspection and up-dating at Rainco. I spent 9 hours training, re-activating my instrument licence - all this training being done in the air rather than in a Link trainer. I spent March 9 taking high altitude physiological training at Williams Air Force Base, followed by a trip in the decompression chamber with some of the personnel at the Base. This trip took us up to 43,000 feet and I was able to check the effectiveness of a diet my doctor had recommended for very high altitude flying.

On March 10, Don Barnard and I left for Reno in the Cessna. We met Dr. John Armitage there. I was able to get my first real wave flight that afternoon in the Cessna with instruction from Dr. Armitage who is a wave pilot. We went to 18,000 feet in the wave at Reno and checked out various areas of it, both under the roll cloud and above the lenticulars.

The following day we started flying from Reno, south 20 miles to a point just east of Mount Rose, then eastward to Virginia City, then eastward across the parallel ranges of Nevada to Ely where we landed and had lunch. After lunch we took off again and flew over the nearly total desolation of central Utah, then got in range of the Umcompahgre Plateau of Colorado, thence eastward across the great

Colorado massif, and as dusk was turning into night, we landed at Alamosa, 20 or 30 minutes after nightfall.

The following day we flew and checked over some courses for a goal and return which would have its beginning at Santa Fe; then we went on to Boulder. I spent the night with the Armitages and came home the next day, on March 13.

I left for the flying in Reno with my boy, John, on March 24 and met Don that evening. Much of the first week in Reno was spent in local thermal flying, and we finally transferred the sailplane to Minden where the Pasco Wave Camp was in progress. My first sailplane wave flight came on April 1st. This was a most satisfying flight which carried up to 27,700 feet and gave a good opportunity to check out my cold weather kit. Cockpit temperature got down to 20°F below zero. Interestingly, at altitude, I was flying above solid undercast horizon to horizon with the exception of a few windows in the wave in the immediate lee of the Sierra. I had one further thermal flight in Reno transferring from Minden to Stead Air Force Base. The following week and a half was devoted to study.

Future plans call for seeking multiplace records out of Prescott in the categories of straight distance, goal, and 300 and 500 kilometer triangles. Distance flying will hopefully carry us from Prescott into the Texas Panhandle.

ON QUIET WINGS

In the Air Currents dated March 1972, Newsletter Editor Nancy Hume said, "On Quiet Wings is now for sale. It's a beautiful book, beautifully written. A tribute to Joe is the fact that Senator Barry Goldwater will review the book for publication in the newspaper. Joe's press conference was successful and his book enthusiastically accepted."

WRITING ON QUIET WINGS by Joe Lincoln, March 1972.

The original idea for the book "On Quiet Wings" took seed at June and Wally Wiberg's Flying W Ranch South of Grand Prairie, Texas, back in the late 1950's when I was visiting them for several days, waiting for the passage of a mid-winter Texas ice storm. I spent my time reading through their collection of old Soaring magazines, and for the first time ran across the story of Dick Johnson's 500 mile flight, E.J. Reeve's piece, "A Summer's Tale", and Wally Wiberg's story, "I Musta Done It Wrong." The storm did not abate for a number of days and before I left I had thought of the idea of making a small book composed of six or eight pieces by other writers and two or three of my own.

Initial work was started in early January, 1962. The reason for beginning in early 1962 was to make a book which would celebrate Soaring magazine's silver anniversary year. Soaring magazine had completed 25 years of publishing with the December 1961 issue.

I allotted three months of work time for the job with a six week cushion of time. This plan completely jumped the track within the initial six weeks of work on the book, and by the time I was 3 months into the task, I already knew I was working on something that had become five times as long and five times as important as what I originally had in mind. By the time I had been working on it 5 months, I had read, selected, and transcribed nearly 700 pages of typewritten material (in triple space).

This work was followed by an interval of 5 years during which nothing further was done on the book. The job was picked up again briefly for six or seven weeks in the spring of 1967, then it was dropped again, this time for two and a half years. Work began a third time on October 1, 1969. When the reading was complete, it covered Soaring magazine over a span of a third century rather than a quarter. With the exception of a five month break during the spring of 1970, work was carried on until it was completed and finally came out on St. Patrick's Day, 1972.

In sum, the book has taken something over two years of solid work, of which seven months were devoted to the acquisition of graphic materials. In its final edited form, the manuscript of "On Quiet Wings", not counting the captions and graphic identification, makes a double spaced, typewritten manuscript of 690 pages.

To my knowledge there has been no previous attempt to make a definitive work on the literature of soaring flight. "On Quiet Wings" begins with the legend of "Daedalus and Icarus" and finishes with the legend of Jonathan Livingston Seagull. It contains stories by writers as diverse as Leonardo da Vinci and Wally Wiberg. It is divided up in classifications which include Mythology and History, Sunday Soaring, Scientific Background, The Glider Goes To War, Duration, Cross-Country, Record Flying, Contest Soaring, The Crash, and The Wave.

AN AUTHOR IN OUR MIDST by Dan Halacy, March 1972.

On Saturday, March 18, 1970, glider guiders, wives, and widows, plus many friends of soaring converged on the home of Al and Nancy Hume to pay homage to author Joseph Colville Lincoln on the publication of his new book, "On Quiet Wings." Against a swinging backdrop of socializing, gourmet food, and a gamut of attire spanning the spectrum and then some, the beaming pilot-author explained to non-writing types just how he put together what must be the definitive anthology of soaring. The task cost Joe a decade of loving labor and Northland Press has spared no expense to do justice to the challenge. The result is a handsome, oversize volume sure to find its way into many soaring homes where it will be enjoyed by the hour.

For much of the evening the author was kept busy brandishing a red pen boldly across the fly leaves of purchased copies -- friendly and pertinent lines that will be treasured in years to come as words of greeting from the guy who wrote this great book.

ASA is eternally grateful to host and hostess Al and Nancy, and tremendously proud of author Joe Lincoln. It has been well said of lovers and fliers that when they are not involved in the actual process they spend all their time talking about it. Thanks be that Joe not only talks about soaring but puts it down on paper so beautifully. So that the rest of us can share soaring adventures from Icarus and Daedalus to the contest greats of today.

Joe was delighted and responded with a thank you letter.

"I would like to thank Nancy and Al Hume once again, this time in public, for their hospitality and for making possible the book party held at their home on

March 18, and I would also like to thank all those who came, and especially those who bought "On Quiet Wings".

The task, which the book represents, has been a long one, and I believe it breaks new ground in the field of aviation anthologies.

Credit for the final appearance of the book goes a great deal to Northland Press in Flagstaff, Robert Jacobson who designed the book, and to the Roswell Bindery here in Phoenix. I feel the work of these people has been outstanding.

During my early years in soaring, I used to hear much about the superiority of European effort in the field. Roughly 85% of "On Quiet Wings" is American work.

Sincerely...
Joe Lincoln.

HE LIVED TO FLY, an Obituary by Fritz Marquardt from The Arizona Republic dated May 21, 1975. Reprinted with permission of The Arizona Republic. Permission does not imply endorsement by the newspaper.

Joe Lincoln was a big man with the heartiest laugh you ever heard. He enjoyed life, particularly when he was flying a sailplane at 5,000 feet above the ground. With only the natural air currents to support him, he went hundreds of miles at a time in his engineless aircraft.

He held many soaring records at various times, and he probably published more about the art of soaring than any other American.

His "On Quiet Wings" is an anthology that goes back to the Bible and Leonardo da Vinci to show man's ability to conquer the skies in powerless flight.

"Few things in soaring are ever certain," he wrote in his autobiographical book, "Soaring For Diamonds". "The most promising clouds will sometimes betray you and give you no lift." But the thermals, the upthrusts of warm air, came that day, and before he landed at Prescott he had broken his second national record, one that had stood for nine years.

Recently the doctors told Joe he had an inoperable tumor. As soon as he was out of the hospital he went soaring, with a copilot to be sure. Last week he told two Phoenix friends that he expected to spend as much of his remaining time in the air as possible.

There was no self-pity, no "Why me?" in his attitude. But as long as he was here, he was going to fly.

Death ended that plan Monday evening. He died quietly, and one can only hope the thermals are with him today.

CHAPTER 3 - SOARING WITH THE RICH AND/OR FAMOUS

MIDAIR! from THE BRIDGE ACROSS FOREVER by Richard Bach, Dell Publishing Co. Inc., Copyright 1984. Chapter 35 - Included by kind permission of the author.

For a while, Richard Bach and Leslie Parrish "lived in a trailer parked in ten thousand square miles of Arizona sagebrush and mountains, on the fringe of an airport for gliders. Estrella Sailport." While there, Richard took part in the 1978 Region 9 Contest in an ASW 19, CZ. The night before the Contest started, Richard dreamed he was involved in a midair collision.

Our launch-time for the race next day put me twenty-third sailplane in line for takeoff, second from last. Full water-ballast in the wings, survival-kit aboard, canopy marked and turn-point cameras checked. Leslie handed me maps and radio codes, kissed me good luck, eased the canopy down. I locked it from the inside. I lay back in the contoured pilot's seat, checked the flight controls, nodded OK, blew her one last kiss, rocked the rudder-pedals side to side; let's go, towplane, let's go.

Every launch is different, but every one is the same aircraft-carrier catapult-launch in slow motion. A great thrashing and roaring from the towplane out ahead on its towline, we creep forward for a few feet, then faster, faster. Speed gives power to the ailerons, to the rudder, to the elevators, and now we lift a foot off the ground and wait while the towplane finishes its takeoff and begins to climb.

Leslie has been mischievous this morning, generously cooling me with ice-water at moments I least expected. She was happy and so was I. What a spectacular mistake it would have been, to have insisted on leaving her!

Five minutes later, a climb on the end of the line, a dive to loosen the tension, and I pulled the handle for an easy release.

There was one good thermal near the airport, thick with sailplanes. I shivered in the heat of the cockpit. A cyclone of sailplanes, it was. But I was almost last one out and couldn't spend all day looking for lift. I was ginger on the stick, careful. Look around, I thought, watch out!

Tight turn. Fast turn. I caught the core of the lift, an express elevator on the way to the top... five hundred feet per minute, seven hundred. Look around.

My neck was sore from twisting fast left, fast right, looking, counting. A Schweizer slid in below me, turning hard. She's right. I do create problems. We've had our bad times, but hasn't everybody? The good times are glorious, they just... LOOKOUT!

The Cirrus above tightened its turn too steeply, sank toward me thirty feet, its wing a giant's blade slashing toward my head. I jammed the stick forward, fell away, in the same instant dodging the glider below.

"You gonna fly like that," I choked, "you gonna get plenty room from me!"

I swung back into the cyclone, looked up the center of the half-mile cylinder of climbing aircraft. Not many pilots, I thought, ever see anything like this.

The moment I looked, an odd moment, way above. It was a sailplane, *spinning*! down through the center of the other planes! I saw, and could not believe... what a *stupid, dangerous* thing, to SPIN! In the midst of so many other airplanes!

I squinted against the sun. The glider was not spinning for sport, it was spinning because it had lost a wing.

Look! Not one plane spinning - two! Two sailplanes tumbling out of control, falling straight down toward my cockpit.

I snatched the stick to the left, floored the left rudder and shot away, out from under.

High behind my right wing whipped and tumbled the two broken aircraft. In their trails floated a cloud of broken pieces, lazy autumn leaves swirling down.

The radio, that had been quiet static for minutes, shouted, "MIDAIR! *There's been a mid-air!*"

"BAIL OUT! BAIL OUT!"

What possible good can it do, I thought, to tell them on the radio to bail out? When your airplane is reduced to pieces, doesn't the idea of a parachute come right quickly to mind?

One of the glider-parts in the midst of the cloud was a man's body, tumbling. It fell for a long time, then nylon streamed out behind it, into the wind. He was alive; he had pulled the ripcord. Good work, fella!

The chute opened and drifted without a sound toward the rocks.

"There's two parachutes!" said the radio. "Contest Ground, there's two parachutes! Going down three miles north. Can you get a jeep out there?"

I couldn't see the other chute. The one I watched collapsed as the pilot hit the ground.

Still fluttered the parts of the demolished gliders, one section with half a wing attached, pinwheeling slow-motion round and round and round.

Never had I seen a midair collision. At a distance, it was gentle and silent. It could have been a new sport invented by a bored pilot, except for the shreds of airplane sparkling down. No pilot would invent a sport that shredded airplanes for fun.

The radio crackled on. "Anyone have the pilots in sight?"

"Affirmative. Got 'em both in sight."

"How are they? Can you tell if they're OK?"

"Yeah. They're both OK, seem to be. Both on the ground, waving."

"Thank God!"

"OK, chaps, let's look alive up here. We got a lot of airplanes in a little space..."

Four of the pilots in this race, I thought, are women. How would it feel to be a woman, flying up here, and be called a "chap"?

All at once I froze in the heat. I saw this yesterday! What are the odds against it... the only mid-air I've ever seen, coming the day after I lay on the floor of the trailer and watched it in advance!

No, I hadn't watched, it had been *me*, hit by the wing! It might have been me, down there in the desert, and not so lucky as the two climbing in the jeep with exciting stories to tell.

Had Leslie left me last night, had I been tired and sad today instead of rested and cool before the race, it could have been me.

I turned on course, in a sky oddly deserted. Once they get started, contest sailplanes don't stay much in clumps if the leaders can help it.

Nose down, my quiet racer hushed top-speed toward a mountain ridge. Rocks close below, we burst into a new thermal, spiralled steeply up in the lift.

The vision, I thought, had it saved me?

I'm being protected now, for a reason.

Having made the decision to love, had I chosen life instead of death?

GEORGE MOFFAT, SOARING TEACHER by John Joss, 1987.

Both gentlemen are famous although neither claims to be rich! John Joss is an aviation writer and an active pilot. In 1976 he was the first civilian journalist to fly, photograph and write about the U-2 spy plane. He is an Honorary Blue Angel, has flown the Navy's Top Gun air combat training course and owns a Discus.

Champions in every sport occupy pinnacles. There is little room for more than a few men and women in those lofty places. The air is rarified. It is hard to breathe up there, let alone speak.

The ordinary mortal, student alongside champion, feels a sense of unease, of not belonging. It is as if one does not really comprehend what is going on. In fact, the student does not truly understand. The master has already forgotten more than the student will ever learn. Both know it. Neither speaks of it.

For many years George Moffat has occupied, with varying degrees of ease and unease, the pinnacles of world soaring competition. Twice World Open Class Champion (Texas, 1970; Australia, 1974) on the U.S. Team in Poland (1968) and Yugoslavia (1972), National Champion and contestant on countless occasions, he has Done It All. Today, although owner of a highly competitive Ventus, he enters only those soaring contests fitting his busy schedule that includes, in the summer, sailing his ocean-racing yacht.

Now, in 1986, George Moffat has entered a new phase of his soaring life. He is passing on skills acquired over more than 30 years of world record and championship achievement. The Japanese have a special word for it, describing a person who has attained mastery of a subject and can thus be honored with the name "sensei", or teacher.

Browning said that less is more. Moffat proves the point. His is the minimalist skill of the truly great. He does as little as possible, with the least motion. He makes no sudden or ill-considered moves. He executes precisely, effortlessly. The hopeful neophyte (the writer is such) comes hat in hand, hoping for the best, dreading his display of incompetence in front of the master.

Patient Teacher: Some who have encountered George in the past, usually at contest sites, have noted his seeming aloofness, his withdrawal, his sense of being (in their eyes) above it all, unwilling to engage in simple human interaction. This judgement is unjust. Moffat is an intense, highly intelligent man whose thoughts occupy his mind fully, especially at contests. Shy by nature, diffident about his extraordinary skills, he feels uncomfortable pushing himself or his ideas on others. A modest, kind man. But let it not be doubted that the fire of a warrior burns in his belly.

Moffat as honored "sensei" does not disappoint. He leads his student forward from the initial goal of a successful flight with a sense of purpose. He establishes an overview of the task (badge leg, contest day), to consider what must be done, how to do it most efficiently. He evaluates, compares options, considers contingencies. He studies everything, misses nothing.

Soaring achievement of any kind, he insists, is based on efficient flying, by which he means understanding the weather, glider and task, taking the correct strategic and tactical view of the situation, planning the day, minimizing the losses and maximizing the gains ("winning by not losing" - G. Moffat), honing the technique and eliminating the mistakes. Sounds simple? It isn't. But it is Very George. He said it all a decade ago in his book Winning On The Wind.

He asks about the student's problems and needs. He is engagingly candid and open, totally devoid of that intimidating aloofness of which he has been accused in the past. He discusses, suggests, recommends, cites examples. He never patronizes or preaches, and he has that innate teacher's skill (he teaches English to support his soaring and sailing habits) of never making the student feel foolish or incompetent, despite continual proof that one is committing grievous soaring howlers. Aloft in the cockpit (in our case a Grob 103 Acrobat) he never raises his voice, comments without chiding or judging, shows by example. Elegant.

Travels With George: Marion Barritt, among the most dedicated, thoughtful and generous spirits in a sport full of unique and decent men and women, decided in 1986 that Soar Minden (the operation she and Linda Draper co-own) needed to attract soaring pilots from around the world. So they arranged to support or sponsor a schedule of events that included cross-country, aerobatic and motorglider camps, the Hitachi "Masters of Soaring", the George Moffat Week and the Eric Mozer Cross Country Seminar. To visit Minden, Moffat had to rush from the Standard Class Nationals at Cordele to the Sierra Nevada. After that, he had to fly back East, then return a week later to compete in the Hitachi.

Six lucky pilots, responding to word of mouth in the soaring grapevine about the Moffat opportunity, signed up for a full day with the master. The horde of would-be students who answered the advertisement in Soaring magazine were disappointed (next year?). The day included the Grob, a tow (no maximum altitude specified), water/O_2/Granola Bars, and a sumptuous dinner. Despite the inevitable weather problems ("It isn't usually like this..." "You should have been here last week..." "I can't believe the weather man!"), it was a memorable experience. Now the precedent is set, more will surely follow.

"My" day was weather dominated and the weather was rotten, unsuited to cross-country work. There would be, said the weather guesser at Reno (NOT U.S.

Team Meteorologist Doug Armstrong), strong surface winds and even stronger winds aloft, leading to wave. Lift? Thermals? The met man predicted that there would be none, and would not even cite a trigger temperature no matter how many ways the questions were posed (Soaring Index? "K" Value? Convection?) This from a National Weather Service Office, supposedly informed, serving what is among the world's busiest soaring communities. The day's high was over 85°.

A "Paper" Task: We sat down, therefore, and designed a "paper" contest task, a 200 mile quadrilateral with four turn points (Air Sailing, Yerington, Bridgeport and back for those with San Franciscan sectionals). It could as easily have been a badge leg, since the same principles of efficient flying would apply and only thermal-marking contestants would be lacking on the badge flight.

George's eye view encompassed everything the pilot needs for a successful flight. Psychology and optimism/pessimism of the weather man? Listen to him on the practice days and see how to factor his attitude. Task-day weather versus winning average speed? We "estimated" a 700 fpm blue-thermal day (500 fpm true average), to 14,000. Operating band? A "floor" (know your proposed landing spots!) of 3,000 AGL, or 8,000± feet MSL in the Sierra to a "ceiling" (lift declining below useful level) of about 13,000 feet MSL - a 5,000 foot band. Getting low? Go slow. High? Speed up!

"Weather" timing? Trigger at noon, peaking at around 3:00 pm and decline around 6. We backed our 500 fpm average into a MacCready, giving 75 mph average speed for a Standard or 15 meter ship. Task time? Not less than two hours nor more than three. Probably two and a half. Start time, then? Optimally, around 2 to 2:20 pm. Tactically, let others go ahead to mark thermals on course. Vow to circle as little as possible. Sniff out the good thermals, discard the bad. Dolphin? Only for height, not speed - the up and down causes drag and slows you. Simple. Very George.

If launch would start around 12:30 pm, with typically 60 ships off in an hour, one might want to go to the end of the line, to reduce excess bug-collecting time before the start. But one would not do this on the first or second day, during which the contest staff would be getting organized. Circling 45 minutes before the start would allow evaluation of actual versus predicted lift rates.

After the start, course selection would use markers and terrain. Minimal (5°) deviations to thermal-producing sites would involve little distance penalty, but over 10° would, and thus should be used only as an emergency/great opportunity diversion. Given the choice, allow a 10 mile-in/10-out altitude to and from the valley turnpoint sinkholes versus the lift-producing sites, and note thermal sources (terrain, other gliders) before committing to the photo run. Watch the weather cycle to avoid being clamped at turns. Proceed on a course to the next turnpoint that would be marked by earlier starters. And observe, observe, observe the universe with close attention. Clouds forming or dissipating, terrain effects, everything. Straightforward. Very George.

Final glide? Don't complete the full climb at maximum distance (about 50 miles from 14,000 feet MSL), but leave that thermal early, below needed glide slope, then check gaining/losing trends en route. Sierra terrain over those 50 miles would be almost sure to produce the "needed" difference in altitude. Faster. Much.

Cockpit aids? George eschews overly complex calculating/navigating varios, preferring to rely on minimum useful information that does not distract. He has prepared a computer-generated set of speeds to fly versus gross weight (empty, half water, max. gross), in 30/20/10 MPH head and tail winds, and a list of MacCready speeds versus the "last thermal". He uses this as a handy paper reference chart he attaches to his panel. Make your own from the Johnson data on the most popular sailplanes, he urges.

Our Actual Flight: ("Follow me through"). Launching into a wind-torn sky, we climbed laboriously in one of those "non-existent" and hard-to-center thermals until we contacted the wave at 8,500 feet and climbed to 16,000 feet (two Diamonds were earned that afternoon, with climbs to 30,000 feet). Moffat wants to see precise speed control, minimum thrashing and flailing with stick and rudder (my specialty) to reduce flow-separating perturbations. He performs very smooth speed control, usually with the trimmer, to reduce flow separation. A minimalist.

Moffat stresses the need to practice when the lift is poor, as it was for us. Anyone, he argues, can go fast and complete badges when the weather co-operates. Citing the poor weather in the Eastern U.S. where soaring character is truly formed and conditions most closely emulate Europe, versus the West where it booms, he points out that no U.S. pilot based West of the Mississippi has ever won a world championship...

Most of us, George shows, turn too early into lift. Give it more time, be patient, to characterize the thermal as to strength and location. But managing to get shot down after 4 hours, and to show that all his guidance was in vain, I delivered one of my all-time-worst patterns (obdurate and deaf power traffic practicing down/cross wind landings on a conflicting runway), needed full spoiler to get down from excess height, flared early and touched down twice, while George explained drily (he hides his fear well) what he would "prefer".

The bottom line: We spend years and countless amounts of our resources learning to soar. A day with George is worth a season of tows and flying experience. He gives and gives and gives. It is up to the student to assimilate the lessons, then practice until perfection (hah!) is achieved. What's more, that signature in your log book will be treasured for ever. George Moffat: soaring pilot, champion, friend. And teacher.

CHAPTER 4 - WISE OLD MEN

THE FOSSIL APPROACH by Bob Sparling, April 1962.

Is some of the old fun of soaring missing? Or have some of us lived too long and remembered too much? It seems that the old days, when Franklins outnumbered all the other ships at the Nationals, (who even knows now what a Franklin looked like?) held a lot more of the things which can make soaring (we called it gliding then) so downright enjoyable. Those were the days of the four-minute flights, the ten-cent winch and auto-tows, and the days when all took their turns in the activities both in the air and on the ground. Performance was low and the flying was easy. Anyone watching the Franklins, the Midwests, the Cadets, or the numerous one-of-a-kind utilities kite to the top of the wire and release, to make lazy circles at 600 feet before floating in to a smooth and easy landing, could not help being enthused and excited. He just knew that he could fly one of those things if he were only allowed the chance. The "high performance" ships were the Wolfs, the Minimoas, the Sperbers, the Bowlus Babies, and the dreamer's home-brews, but they were all alike in their light wing-loadings that gave them the slow and beautiful grace in flight that lifted the heart and stirred the age-old yearning to join the birds on high.

Things are different now. Are they too much different? The war effort absorbed the utilities. The plentiful and cheap, relatively high performance ships that became available at war's end cut the heart from any ambition to rebuild the utility fleet. Airplane tow became almost a necessity. And the affluence of the utility-trained pilots, increasing as they grew older in their work, enabled them to demand ever better performance in their new ships, with the inevitable increase in price that such performance must demand. For the new pilot it has become a matter of starting at the top and working upward.

Now where does this leave the interested onlooker; the man who makes up the group from which we must draw the new blood necessary to keep our sport alive and healthy? Should he happen to arrive at the airport at just the right time he may witness a take-off or a landing. But is this the slow and easy flying taking place where he can see the flights from beginning to end; the kind of activity that puts him right in the middle of things?

Not by a long shot. He sees a noisy airplane laboriously tugging a sailplane slowly higher, and quickly removing it from his vicinity. When it is finally free it is far away and high above. Gone is the thrill of seeing the silent ship climb steeply on the almost invisible wire, or watching it release and wheel in whispering circles, and land almost without having crossed the boundaries of the field. Gone too is the feeling that he could easily master the slow and graceful flight. He realizes that this is a precise and complicated operation that must surely require much training. And he can easily see that considerable sums of money have been expended for equipment of this quality, and must be continually expended in its operation. Is he seized by an irresistible urge to be a part of this exhilarating activity? Unless he is just the right individual, in the right financial circumstances, he assuredly is not. So he goes off to pursue his interests in golf or rock collecting or other earth-bound activities that seem better suited to his abilities and means.

Lost! Another pilot who might have contributed much to the sport, and certainly would have added to it by just being a part of it. Lost too is the continuing activity on the ground that keeps those unable to afford the price of high performance active and interested. Without them the high performance ships cannot get off the ground, and without the pool of maturing pilots that they comprise, the sport can hardly prosper.

Does this mean that we should abandon the wonderful improvements we have achieved in equipment and performance? Does it mean that we should return completely to soaring as it was 35 years ago? Of course it doesn't; who would be so foolish. But should we not make some effort to revive the parts of it that were good then, and remain good today? The use of utilities for training, with the lower costs involved, will surely bring out more people. The use of auto and winch tows, again with the bonus of lower costs, will once more create the atmosphere at the site that is attractive both to the participants and the prospects. All this need in no way interfere with those interested solely in high performance. It only requires that they lend a hand in getting it started. By providing for a sure and steady growth, it can only insure continued improvement in equipment and accomplishment. Isn't it worth thinking about?"

1969 OPTIMUM UTILIZATION OF ATMOSPHERIC TURBULENCE - REVISITED
by Jim George, May 1975.

In doing research for a manual I am writing, I keep running into the problem of the lack of information on certain soaring subjects, techniques and "secrets", especially when it comes to competition soaring. It is difficult to get information from the leaders in this field, so when I do run across some valuable thoughts, I like to share them with you.

During October of 1969, I was fortunate to be able to attend the first symposium on soaring held in the Western United States. This two day affair was sponsored by the Southwestern California Soaring Association and was held in Bakersfield, Ca. The gathering was aptly named: Optimum Utilization of Atmospheric Turbulence.

During a morning session at the Bakersfield Inn, a panel discussion was held, one where questions were submitted from the audience and answered by some of the greatest names in U.S. soaring. This distinguished group of soaring pilots included one World Champion and two times U.S. Champion, three other former U.S. Champions, and two top western competition and instrument specialists. This fine panel was moderated by the holder of the world altitude record in a sailplane and perhaps the most competition-wise U.S. pilot - Paul Bikle. The panelists were Paul MacCready, Jr., Dick Johnson, Dick Schreder, Ross Briegleb, Bob Semans and Bud Mears.

I taped portions of this panel discussion and what follows is my edited and condensed version. The material must be read and understood in light of newer equipment and techniques, but there are some basic thoughts and information from which each of us can benefit.

BIKLE: What ways are used by the panel members to work thermals?

JOHNSON: I use a 270° turn method. When I do find lift, I slow down to where I feel I want to make my turn of approximately 50-55 miles per hour, I watch the rate of climb meter, of course, if one wing comes up I initially turn in that direction. If there is no sign like that, I go straight ahead, and count one, two, three or four: After I reach a good rate of climb, I go all the way around once. This gives me a pattern. Now I may be going up strong on one side and weak on the other. If there is a strong area as I go around the 360°, that is where I should move over to. So I go to a heading of 270° from that heading where I achieve my best rate of climb. Next, I straighten out for one or two seconds, and then continue my turn. Thus, I move over 100 feet. I keep repeating this cycle while I am going around in a thermal.

BRIEGLEB: I use about the same 270° method that Dick has described. You must remember that every variometer has a small lag to it. When you are showing the best lift, you are actually out of it, so you must allow for this lag. I feel the optimum thermaling bank is about 35°. I very seldom go much over 45°, as it starts hurting you a little bit in your sink rate. Thermals are not as large as most people think, this is a common error.

MacCREADY: One wonders what a bird does to locate a thermal in the first place and find the center of it. I am sure a bird uses a great deal of intuition. The sense of feel, the sound of your sailplane, the acceleration on it, all of these help you. Also, when sleuthing out thermals, a total energy variometer is a very important part of your ship's instrumentation.

SEMANS: I very much agree with Paul, I think the fastest response instrument you have is the seat of your pants. What you have to do is calibrate this all of the time by looking at the instruments, making sure that you haven't been fooled. Your mind must continuously build a mental picture of your thermal, and do what ever has to be done to maneuver into the strongest part of the thermal.

SCHREDER: When you enter a thermal, the seat of your pants is probably the best indicator of telling you where the strongest point is in your initial penetrations. I make one full turn and keep track of the cardinal points of the compass in relation to my best lift. If my best lift is on the west side of my circle, I shift my circle in that direction. A good sailplane pilot makes corrections on every turn, and is never satisfied until he gets the same rate of climb all the way around. That is the ultimate goal.

MEARS: When you are cruising at 100 mph, in one second you are half way through the thermal, compared to the circle you ultimately will make. Most people don't realize this. While I am cruising at 100 mph and there is indication of lift, I do a strong pull up into a steep angle (3 to 4G). I watch my total energy variometer for a moment. If it is a short gust, I pitch over and keep on course. If I still get a continual rate of climb, I'll carry on up at a steep angle and into a pitch over at zero G into level flight. In level flight position, I am at my right airspeed for turning. I roll into a 180° turn, constant airspeed, count off a few seconds, make a 180° turn onto the original track. I have worked out this maneuver from practice many times and it is planned to bring me back through the area of original lift at circling airspeed. I keep my head out of the cockpit as much as possible. I set my audio threshold at O and shift my circles to move away from the down, or silent audio. Also, I use the audio exclusively, it is faster than the indicator on the variometer.

BIKLE: What roles do these various aspects of soaring play: sailplane, pilot, instruments, weather and soaring techniques?

SCHREDER: I practice flying as much as possible, it would be better if we flew more and worried less about our ships. Dick Johnson and I work on our ships continually to make them as smooth as possible. There are people who buy the latest sailplanes. I personally don't feel there is enough difference in the better ships, with the possible exception of the AS-W 12. Most of us think the AS-W 12 is a dangerous ship to land. Especially where you are flying in rough country. I am sure this affected Wally Scott's flying, because he had to stop and land at airports, rather than just keep barging on.

JOHNSON: In contest flying, there is the all out flying used at such places as Marfa and El Mirage. Where optimum speed is used all the way to the ground, if necessary. This is because conditions are uniformly good throughout the day. The philosophy of all out flying will change when contests are held at such places as Adrian and Elmira. There will generally be a more conservative type of flying.

BRIEGLEB: To win in contest flying, you take the sailplane, instruments, weather and soaring pilot and his personality. This same pilot would excel in whatever sport he entered. It is his desire to win or his basic need for recognition. I feel this is the motivating factor. The majority of the sailplanes at Marfa this year (1969) were in the same ballpark. A seventeen year old boy flying a doggy SH-1 put it into 17th place. No doubt he had a desire to win.

MacCREADY: In contest flying, there is a group of top pilots who fly all out. They are taking risks. Thus, an excellent conservative pilot will not end up winning, because there are so many willing to take the risks.

SEMANS: For contest flying, I think a distinction of what kind of flying practice you do is important. I feel you should extend yourself, fly away from your home field, find a new area, new air masses, and different terrain. My attitude for contest flying is that you do not make even one single major error in the contest.

MEARS: For contest flying, you must mentally reach a point of winning. I am one of the few that feel you can practice effectively within 20 miles of the field. I practice some of the mechanical things. In working thermals, I quickly locate the core, center it and then leave it. I concentrate and continually force myself to work mentally by looking for dust devils, cloud wisps, and shear lines. I find you can't relax for one minute, if you do, you are not up to the proper competitive edge.

BIKLE: A few of us had a difficult year at McCook in 1964. I believe Moffat, Dick Schreder and I were down close to the start line on the first day. We watched everybody else flying overhead. We figured it would be a tough day, and they wouldn't get far. We watched later in the day as they came trailing back. I believe Dick Schreder said, "There is something about this sport, it teaches a guy humility."

BIKLE: What does all this talk of competition flying mean for the people that are not doing competition flying?

SCHREDER: There is a connection between competition and badge flying. The Diamond distance badge flyer will find the principles and techniques are the same. So that you can travel 300 miles before the lift dies and you run out of daylight, you must be able to identify good thermals and center them and not waste time in weak lift.

BIKLE: How much altimeter error is introduced if the altimeter is not connected to the static source, but is open to the cockpit?

MEARS: Frequently, cockpit static is pretty good. The problem you have if you open your dive brakes and the dive brakes (spoilers) are vented through the wing into the cockpit, your instruments may have a big glitch. Basically, the instruments you put on the cockpit static are the same instruments you don't have to count on. Never put your airspeed on cockpit static. The errors on the altimeter won't be large, even with glitches.

BIKLE: Is there a relationship between the size of the Bernard Cell, and the distance between thermals?

MacCREADY: There is, and exactly what the relation is, in the case of a thermal, I do not know. Cell laboratory work tends to show cell size, the distance between the up currents is approximately 3 times the height of the unstable layer. In the atmosphere, I expect the relationship to hold as a general rule. I would say three or four times the height would be the distance between thermals.

BIKLE: Is there any rough average of cycle time you would have for the average cumulus, not cumulonimbus?

MacCREADY: In observing the typical cumulus cloud in Arizona, we have watched an identifiable cell, one that would have an up current strong enough for a sailplane. The duration of this cell will last around 10-15 minutes. During this time, it will go up around 15,000 feet. Then, it will reach stable air and this will cause dampening effect. It erodes at the edges as it is starting to cool. Then, it starts to decay and decays rapidly.

BIKLE: Shear lines, what causes them? How do you recognize them? How do you fly them?

MEARS: The Elsinore shear line is caused by the smoggy warm air from the Los Angeles basin. This converges with the clear air from the passes down at Elsinore. You fly the shear line as if you are slope soaring. Polaroid glasses help you see the different density gradients.

BRIEGLEB: The Mojave Desert shear line is caused by the different air masses, one of the masses is of a different temperature and possibly moisture content. Some of the strongest thermals I have ever had gave me 2,000 fpm lift a number of turns. Usually, though it is around 800 fpm. When flying shear lines at low altitude, treat them like a line of thermals and work them like thermals. Not until you get high can you fly them like a ridge. A couple of good ways of telling where shear lines are located: watch the dust on the ground blowing and determine where it meets dust being blown from another direction. Also, watch dust devils, they lean toward a shear line.

BIKLE: How often do you calibrate your instruments?

MEARS: I don't calibrate them very often. Maybe every year or so unless I have some feeling I have damaged them. I have a current calibration on most of my instruments.

BIKLE: You can make variometers with one-quarter second time constant, but on the average, I think people feel they cannot integrate the twitching of the needle. I prefer a faster variometer than most people, because I mentally integrate the audio frequency changes. It is a matter of preference. I don't think there is an optimum. It is what the individual likes.

MacCREADY: The total energy variometer is the result of a theory which is derived from the standpoint of vertical up currents. When you are in the real turbulent atmosphere, there are a lot of horizontal components to the wind. When you are flying at very high speeds, you will find the total energy variometer can give very erroneous readings because of these horizontal gusts. I feel whatever damping of the instrument's time constant you put in will depend strongly on your trying to damp out some of these horizontal influences. It is kind of hard to damp horizontal effects out without damping out some of the information you want from the vertical. The instrument itself can't tell the difference between horizontal and vertical. It reads the horizontal much more sensitively than the vertical when you are flying at high airspeeds.

BIKLE: Would you agree, Bud?

MEARS: No question about it. It is one of the unresolved problems. I think by putting a restriction in the pitot line you can by trial and error "time" the pulses racing down the pitot line and the static lines, so that they get to either side of your total energy compensated variometer at the same time. That is about as good as you can do. It is surprising that a large amount of restriction is required in order to pneumatically tune the system, it tends to alleviate the deflections due to horizontal gusts. When you do put up through a shear gradient, this will influence your readings. If there are horizontal gusts, they will give you erroneous readings that you will just have to live with.

BIKLE: How far behind a sailplane will there be a wingtip vortex?

SCHREDER: In the case of flying together with someone, such as formation flying, when you get behind and want to catch up with them, I feel I can get some help from the vortex. I feel that this effect extends possibly up to a half mile behind them.

BIKLE: What is your technique or philosophy for working zero sink or weak lift when down to 2,000 feet or below while on a contest task? What might move you to leave such lift?

JOHNSON: I would seldom leave at 2,000 feet or below, unless I could see somebody else at a reasonable range climbing better, then I would move over to them. I wouldn't leave a thermal at 2,000 feet unless I had some good concrete thing to go on.

SOME ANCIENT HISTORY by John Serafin, May 1970.

Cross country soaring really began after the discovery of thermal type lift during the latter 1920's in Germany. Many amazing distance records were set after that, using strictly "seat of the pants" flying techniques. This included the World Distance Record of 652 Km set in 1937 by the Russian pilot Victor Rastorguyev, who said he flew in good lift of better than 1200 fpm most of the time, but that at times it got bad and dropped to 800 fpm! The 749 Km World Distance Record was set by Mme. Olga Klepikova in 1939, also in Russia, and not bettered until the early 1950's by Dick Johnson, made in even stronger meteorological conditions.

During 1937 the academic soaring group at the Lwow Polytechnical Institute in Poland began the investigation of sailplane performance as related to thermal energy and cross country speed. Outstanding among this group was a gentleman by the name of Witold Kasprzyk who published the results of his work in this field early in 1938 and scientific cross country soaring took off. Immediately the distances flown by Polish pilots in all types of sailplanes were substantially increased. This included the 578 Km. goal flight of Tadeusz Gora, which earned him the first Lilienthal Medal issued. Mr Gora also has World Diamond Badge Number 2.

As originally used, the results of this formula relating to a given sailplane were carried on a convenient cardboard chart in the sailplane. Of course, nowadays this formula is applied to slide rules, variometer speed rings, integrated airspeed variometers and, lately, onboard miniature computers with pictorial display.

I first met Mr Kasprzyk at the 1948 World Gliding Championships in Samaden, Switzerland. He was serving as adviser to the Swiss pilot, Max Schachenmann, who took second place in this competition.

In 1950, the World Championships were held in Orebro, Sweden, and for the first time we had a pilot entered in the event - the famous Paul MacCready. Mr Kasprzyk had moved to Sweden in the meantime, so I quickly arranged for his services as advisor to our team. It was very enlightening to listen to Paul and Mr Kasprzyk discuss the flying strategy to be used for the task of the day after the morning pilots' meeting.

On the last day of this competition, my faith in scientific soaring was badly shaken when Billy Nilsson of Sweden, an adamant "seat of the pants" technique pilot, nosed our MacCready out of first place by a mere 20 points!

Right after the championships I was invited to fly at the Swedish high performance soaring school at Alleberg. While seated in the cockpit of an Olympia-Miese ready to take off on my first cross country flight for my Silver C, Billy Nilsson, the World Champion, came along and gave me some sage advice on how to fly to my goal at Hjo, 55 Km due west, but scoffed at the Kasprzyk chart pinned to the instrument panel. According to the chart and the conditions that day, Hjo was 45 minutes away. Billy said it would take me 1 hour and 20 minutes. I was over Hjo 44 minutes after release from tow, and that, baby, saved the faith!

Mr Kasprzyk is now (1970) a technical translator for a large aerospace firm on the west coast. He has mastered 12 languages and has designed and built two very interesting flying wing configuration sailplanes using his patented control and stability systems.

SOME MORE ANCIENT HISTORY from William Prescott, former SSA State Governor for Colorado.

My interest in airplanes probably began when I was about age 7 (in 1924) when my Dad took me for a ride in an old OX5 powered bi-plane on floats flown by a barnstormer who was hopping rides in the various inland lakes of Michigan. The bug had bitten and I made do with models until I was old enough to get into the real thing. We kids used to ride our bikes out to several active airports. Elmhurst Airport was probably the busiest in those days - it became a housing development several decades ago! There we watched the Hartley Glider Club training students in a very nice Northrop Primary glider. They were towing it up and down the runway with a Model A Ford with a rumbleseat in which the club instructor sat facing the glider madly gesticulating at the students to keep the wings level. (We later learned he had never flown a glider and was not about to fly this one).

This looked like fun to us and the cost was right: $5 to become a member. I don't think any of us had had our first tow down the runway when word came to us that Mr Hartley, in a desire to demonstrate his flying prowess to his girlfriend, had wrecked the glider. So sadly we proceeded to the Elmhurst Airport to look at the remains stuck in a corner of the hangar. Harry Krueger's father was a carpenter by profession and Harry had been brought up with tools and was exceptionally skilled. He looked at the remains with a critical eye and then pronounced he thought he could repair it. Most of the damage was to the fuselage with only minor damage to the wings.

At that time there were four of us who formed the Club, Harry, Dave Miller, a chap by the name of Ray, and myself. The four of us went to Mr Hartley's place of employment (he was a dishwasher in a Chicago restaurant) and told him that we would like to buy the remains. "How much money do you boys have?" he asked. The four of us went through our pockets and came up with $10.47 and Mr Hartley said, "Sold!" Harry acquired the necessary aircraft grade spruce and mahogany plywood and we rebuilt the fuselage, and had the glider ready to fly in a few weeks.

One of the guys had access to a truck so we loaded the parts, and took them out to St. Charles Airport where it was carefully reassembled. A great fellow by the name of Jack Jahnecki was the Airport Manager. He was a great help and let us hangar the glider at a very nominal cost, about $1 a month.

We hadn't been too impressed with the results obtained by the Hartley Glider Club people, so at the Glen Ellyn Public Library we obtained a book called, "Peale's Book On Gliders" which explained how to teach yourself to fly a primary. We found a piece of log at the airport, and as recommended by the book, we balanced the glider on the log and "flew it in the wind" which blew frequently and strongly in Illinois. After the four of us had completely mastered balancing the glider on the log on both axis, we started Peale's Phase 2 which was to tow the glider down the beautiful grass runways at a speed sufficient to level the wings using about 100 feet of rope. About this time, Ray's parents enticed him to drop out of the Club by buying him something much safer - a motorcycle!

We each made just a few tows when (I don't know whether Harry or Dave did this on purpose or if it was just coincidental) on a supposedly slow tow down the runway just to keep the wings level, I suddenly found myself 50 feet in the air. It looked like a thousand. I remembered something from Peale's book - that if you wanted to come down, you pushed the stick forward. I remember seeing a lot of green rushing at me and I instinctively pulled back on the stick. I had remembered to pull the release and I greased her in for a perfect landing. I sat there in the primary with my knees literally knocking together. Harry and Dave rushed over and said, "That was great! Boy! Do you have guts!" I was so damned scared that Harry and Dave had long since graduated to making high tows before I'd take it more than a couple of feet of the ground.

On one occasion as we towed as high as possible without running out of runway, it was decided it was now time to practice our first turns. "Bill, it's your turn!" I towed as high as the rope would allow (maybe 800 feet) and started kicking rudder and pushing the stick over, managing a maximum uncoordinated 90° turn which took me beyond the airport boundary and into a field of ripening corn. I remember cutting quite a swath through the corn and sustaining numerous bruises as I got whacked by the ears of corn.

At this point Jack Jahnecki, the Airport Manager, who had been watching this whole affair and who was undoubtedly concerned about the reputation of his airport, came out and said, "Boys, I tell you what I'm going to do. I'm going to give each one of you 45 minutes dual in the Curtiss Wright, Jr." And so with Jack's patient help we learned to make reasonably well coordinated turns. From then on we flew aggressively and safely with only one minor mishap when Harry stalled on an approach and cracked a wing spar, which we repaired.

We made hundreds and hundreds of flights using our folks' cars and in time pulled the bumper off the Prescott family Buick. Even this did not satisfy us so we decided to continue night operations. The tow car launched the glider down the runway, and when the pilot saw the driver flash his headlights on and off, we knew the car had reached the fence at the end of the runway. The glider would release and the car would race to the other end of the runway, turn around and throw his headlights down the runway so the glider could land. We never even had so much as a close call with our night flying.

We discovered that we could carry passengers if the passenger would sit on the 45° strut behind the pilot, place his feet on the flying wire fittings and grasp the vertical strut directly behind the pilot. We took many of our friends for rides in this manner. Needless to say, the little primary would drop like a rock with two people on board.

One day two brothers from Chicago who had originally built the primary with plans imported from Germany dropped by to watch our operation. The older brother asked, "How does it fly?" We were, of course, astonished, and said, "You built it! Why would you ask?" He answered, "Yeah, we built it alright but we didn't like the looks of the airfoil on the plans so we designed our own. By the time we finished the glider, we knew better so we never flew it and we sold it to Mr Hartley."

Dave Miller was the most aggressive pilot, and one time on his initial climb he pulled up so steeply that the release let go and Dave snapped over on his back before he could correct. With great presence of mind, he pulled back on the stick, completed a loop and made a normal landing.

We eventually sold the glider for $75 to another group who promptly smashed it to kindling wood, seriously injuring the pilot. We then purchased a Waco Primary Glider which was in real mint condition. (By this time I was a senior in high school - 1935). The Waco had a steel tube fuselage, was much lighter and had more wing area and had probably twice the glide angle of the Northrop. In fact, we decided that with a lightweight pod it would probably make an excellent secondary, so Harry, with his great skills, designed and built out of light spruce and plywood a very good looking fabric-covered pod complete with windshield. This machine flew beautifully and we made some considerably extended flights in it.

One of the hotshot power instructors at the airport asked to fly it, spinning it in, doing major damage both to the glider and his own nose. About this time I left for college but the large and active Detroit Glider Club, together with the Purdue Glider Club from Indiana, and others, would come to Sleeping Bear Dunes over the 4th July holidays for a very large and fabulous glider camp. The prevailing winds would blow across Lake Michigan and into the face of 800 foot sand dunes creating beautiful slope soaring conditions for miles up and down the beach. Launch was by means of a winch along the packed sand near the water's edge. Gliders were towed aloft and would soar for hours on end. The country was pine forested and all the pilots camped out in the area and had a perfectly marvelous time. I was thus able to keep my hand in soaring during those periods and earned my C Badge along those dunes in an old Franklin primary.

Then, about 1939, Stan Corcoran and some other notable glider pilots who had flown in the area, found some local merchants from the town of Frankfort near Crystal Lake who had become sufficiently enthusiastic about gliding to finance the building of sailplanes designed by Stan Corcoran. This company was called the Frankfort Sailplane Company. Stan had been a model airplane builder of note in Los Angeles and had owned his own hobby shop there. He designed a Cinema I single seat sailplane and a Cinema 2 two-place. Needless to say, when I wasn't working I spent every spare moment at the Frankfort Sailplane Company. Stan and I became good friends, and when they decided to try for a new National Endurance Record, he asked me to fly with him in the Cinema 2.

SAILPLANE ACCIDENTS: A CRASH COURSE by Judy Lincoln, October 1979. *Although this chapter is entitled WISE OLD MEN, this piece was actually written by a Wise Young Lady!*

I've always said that if I ever (God forbid) totalled an airplane, I hope it's a Schweizer. Obviously, I don't own a Schweizer, so you wise guys are thinking, Oh, she wants to total someone else's plane. Very funny. What I mean to say is that an SGS-anything can crumple itself into a very mangled mess before the pilot's compartment is involved. And "it" doesn't crumple itself, mind you - the plane is in effect the crumplee, the pilot the crumple-or. This brings up my basic philosophy of aviation safety: "You take care of the airplane, it'll take care of you."

Somewhere along the line, that bargain has been compromised. We've had 5 sailplanes totalled in Arizona this year - a Cirrus, two 1-26's and two 2-33's. In the case of the Schweizers, it's my opinion that at least one of them would not have been a survivable crash in any other make of sailplane.

Review the incidents:

1. A partially ballasted Cirrus develops directional problems on the take off roll. Release is delayed, as the pilot attempts to get back on the runway and raise the dragging wing. Finally, just before striking both a tied-down 1-26 and its tie-down chain, the Cirrus releases.

Cirrus totalled, 1-26 totalled, no injuries.

Moral: Don't Give Up The Ship - Give Up The Tow!

2. An eager out-of-state pilot attempting Silver Distance tries to "save" the flight by thermaling below 500 feet in a rented 1-26. A spin entry, probably from an accelerated steep banked turning stall, is followed by an ineffectual recovery. The man had flown Silver Distance to the point of impact, and still wants to claim his FAI Badge.

1-26 totalled, injuries required emergency room treatment.

The Question: What Price Silver Badge?

3. A student pilot has a rope break at 200 feet. According to a CFI witness, there was room enough to land straight ahead safely, if the pilot had assessed the emergency promptly. Instead, the pilot recalled one phrase of his rope-break instruction: "Keep the speed up". He elected to regain the 70 mph tow speed, then initiate a 180° turn from about 100 feet. In the turn, the low wing caught a tree, the glider cartwheeled, and came to a stop inverted with less than 1" to spare between the pilot's head and the shattered canopy-strewn ground.

2-33 totalled, pilot shaken, no injuries.

The Moral: I-know-you-believe-what-you-think-I-meant,

But-I'm-not-sure-you-understand-that-what-you-heard

is-not-what-I-said.

4. On a winch tow, the agreed-upon signal for the winch driver to accelerate for take off was "Wings Level". To re-position the glider, which was connected to the tow cable, the instructor got out of the plane. The line person and instructor leveled the wings to make pushing easier, whereupon the winch driver started up as per the agreement. The empty glider did a reasonable facsimile of a winch tow at first, then dipped a wing, and dived to impact.

2-33 totalled, injuries to both line person & instructor.

The Question: When is a signal not a signal?

The common denominator in these accidents seems to be that each pilot chose a course of action that made disaster unavoidable. At one point or another, almost every dangerous situation demands that the pilot decide NOW what to do and how to do it. As these summaries show, that decision must be based on the pilot quickly and accurately assessing the situation, and considering his knowledge of the plane, the conditions, and his abilities. Also, "Emergency Plan A" had jolly well better have a "Contingency Plan B" to back it up, just in case...

No, I don't claim to be pure as the driven snow with regard to sailplane accidents. My own moment of utter stupidity involved running a perfectly good 1-26 wing tip into a perfectly good tree at 25 mph, some five years ago. Neither the tip nor the tree was perfectly good when I was through with this maneuver. I learned more than I cared to know about clicoes, rivets, and sheet metal repairing the plane. I didn't take very good care of the thing, running it into a tree that way. (And I never flew that particular 1-26 after the incident, for fear it might retaliate). So this treatise does not come to you from some plateau of Holier Than Thou. But I'll stand by my philosophy - take care of your airplane!

ON PULLING THE ROPE FROM BOTH ENDS by John Baird, October 1987.

John Baird has done a considerable amount of towing from both ends of the rope. With 625 tows in sailplanes and 550 tows in power, and over 2500 hours in each, he is a man who knows of what he speaks. He is also the man who dragged a trailing tow rope through power lines and blacked out the entire town of Calistoga.

Pulling the rope from both ends has to do with launching the sailplane. This phase of glider flying generally gets no respect, too bad. The process of getting the sailplane and its pilot free is a very important part of soaring flight. It has a bearing on the success and safety of the entire activity. This article is offered to compensate for all of the inattention given to rope pulling in the past.

In my own soaring experience, the launch part of the flight gets very little thought at all, unless it was frustrating, exciting, or had a profound effect on the day. The launch capers get separated from the flights. This is true of the launches made behind a tow plane, the auto tows and the winch tows. Since I have dealt with both ends of ropes a lot, one would think that should at least generate profound respect for another reason: gliding is done for fun, adventure, recreation, and learning. Towing gliders is a business that we hope is always successful. We hope that there is not very much adventure and a lot of fun for honorable tow pilot. What is the process like? Who does what to whom? and When do they do it?

A bunch or flock of gliders all turn up on the line and they all want to be launched at once, that's when. This is called the flocking instinct by commercial operators and glider club line managers that have a training flight schedule to maintain. This is called monkey business by the flocking glider pilots who are driven quietly mad by the wait while their buddies are launched into the wide blue yonder ahead of them. This causes them to do crazy things later when they actually get connected to the tow plane and are in the process of becoming free. Sometimes they do crazy things that are related to their towing experience even after they are actually free.

The waiting madness is enhanced by scenarios like this. On the take-off line a training ship is next to go and the tow plane is on downwind. The instructor and student are near the ship and the student gets in. You are next after a 15 meter bird and you think this will be quick. There are 6 glass birds, some demonstration flights and your buddies behind you. Some of your buddies have already launched. The second towplane departed with glider about three minutes ago.

Now watch this. The tow plane on downwind flies a huge pattern, lands long and taxis slowly back, waits while the lineman walks over and hooks the rope, then taxis slowly up to the mark. Why are they moving as in slow motion? The reason is that there is lots of time. The instructor who is talking to the student hasn't entered the glider yet. He is getting in now, the canopy is closing, that is good. The canopy is opening again, the second tow plane lands. Two tow planes are now idle. They are bringing over the weights because the student is too light. She should be a tow pilot. (Regular tow pilots are usually big, heavy people). She gets out, the weights get in and she gets back in again. Gadzooks. Both tow planes have cut engines.

The reason that the tow pilot flew the huge pattern is that he would rather wait in the air than on the ground and he knows the routine. He now has lost interest in the rear view mirror and is looking at the clouds and would rather be

57

soaring so he doesn't see that the people in the training glider are now ready to fly. The line person has to walk up to the plane and shout to get the thing going again. The starting is balky since the carb is too hot/cold/lean/rich and/or the pilot forgot to turn the mag/fuel/mixture control (he doesn't feel needed, got it?) The slack gets removed and after a lot of arm waving, they are off!

Now the glass bird is to go, snappy like, we hope, then it is my turn. I am really ready. The second tow plane fires up, lineman picks up the rope and connects the glass bird in front. The pilot is in the cockpit and the canopy is closing. Good show. The canopy is opening again, the pilot gets out and is adjusting straps and calls for someone to bring him his water. OH SHIT!!!!! If this feels like an exaggeration, look again sometime at the real thing.

This kind of operation does not aid the business. If the tow plane is used about 1000 hours per year it has to bill at least $1.00 a minute of operating time to just make expenses if the pilot is a volunteer and $1.35 per minute if the pilot is paid. Except for marketing aspects, losses incurred through hours not flown and operating hours not billable, are easy to make up. Just raise the price of the tows. What cannot be made up is the following. Sloppy or inefficient use of the towplane diminishes the joy of soaring and has a negative impact on soaring safety.

The most visible part of soaring is the launch and landings. If these are haphazard the marketing of soaring is not positive. Negative marketing responses include the position which might be taken by the prospective student/club member who might be a power pilot thinking of making the great transition to real flying. He gets to wait 20 minutes past the scheduled time for his flight. While he waits he observes what appears to be haphazard, careless, hesitating and wasteful handling and preparation of the equipment. If he puts this together with a semi-conservative's view of the advisability and reliability of operating airplanes without engines, let alone learning to fly them, he might do something else.

In the case studies of tow rope pulling selected for analysis, notice the impact on the joy and safety of soaring from the reactions to really slow towing operations or towing operations which just seem to be slow. Real slowness occurs at big contests where there are too few towplanes, or where the towing gets delayed by a passing storm, launching borate bombers, etc.

CASE 1: Most of the interesting and exciting towplane cases have to do with the towplane's engine. Wonder why? On the other hand, the propulsion system for the glider is the entire towplane, pilot and rope. I participated in this one from the back end of the rope.

The density altitude of the field was probably over 9,000 feet, there was almost no wind, the towplane was non-standard and very welcome since not many turned out to tow the regional contest. The towing was going very slowly because of the conditions and the inadequate number of tow planes. Glider pilots were not getting off early either since the thermals were originating in the hills 1500 feet above the airport elevation.

It was well after my selected time when I started to roll slowly down the runway to an imperceptible rotation onto the climb vector. We made no turns, just motored straight ahead with a limp rope indicating only minor energy addition to the glider. Not to worry, this tow plane has launched about 4 gliders already today and more yesterday, right? We are headed toward the base of the hills. He knows where there is a line of lift and that is good since the grass in the small creek-crossed fields still looks strong and tall. We get to the base of the hills and now there is no climb rate at all and the rope is slack. The tow plane starts a shallow turn and the prop reflects the sun. IT IS HARDLY TURNING.

I release and make a max L/D glide back to the airport going straight in with no spoilers and end up at the launch point. How long did I hang on while deciding to do something? Probably about 30 or 40 seconds while being coerced lower and lower and further out from the only reasonable landing area in the territory. The contest line manager is chewing on me for an unnecessary release and screwing up the already late towing, and I am demanding the next tow because of a towplane failure. The towplane has motored back, flying a full pattern and is taxi-ing to the tiedown area. I was given the next tow and all during the task was bugged by the thought that I had over-reacted, looked more inexperienced than I really was and resolved never to be so quick again.

The lesson learned by those observing was that it is essential to make the best of the available equipment and skills for towing, particularly when the line is slow, even if the climb rates are unsafe. See, nothing got bent, the line chief was angry and it was hard to see that the tow plane really had a problem from his actions after my release.

At the next days' pilots meeting the tow pilot thanked me for releasing. Why didn't he release me? I did not ask and by this time in my career I know the answer. He forgot about me and was in the process of saving his pride and perhaps his towplane as well. His plane was on the line for towing. I was happy about not being a wimp and everyone was happy that the towplane was available. I did not find out what was wrong with the engine or pilot. No one else did either. The contest line chief allowed that I had done the right thing. Are there any lessons in this caper? Probably.

CASE 2: Trying the other end of the rope...... Flying the tow plane is a high work-load recreation. Honorable tow pilot is busy, never bored when flying billable time, and removed somewhat from the glider pilot and his problems.

The rope which connects the glider and tow plane is long and softens the input to the towplane to the extent that the glider can make (nearly) wild excursions without affecting the controllability of the tow plane at all. The way that the tow plane is operated, its flight patterns, and the waiting period for a tow can have an important bearing on the hazards presented to the glider pilot.

The way the launch line is operated can have a profound effect on the wait period, the tow plane pilot's work load and the overall safety of the operation. The tow pilot's work load for a normal tow includes the following:

1. Taxi by the launch point, note the glider/number/type or something to bill it with.

2. Pick up any signaled towing instructions from line personnel.

3. Watch to make sure that the tow rope gets hooked or otherwise controlled by the lineman, taxi to the mark with appropriate off-set to account for the glider being past the usual launch point, etc. Stop, set idle r/m, enter the glider identity and estimated launch time on the tow sheet.

4. Check fuel, change tanks if appropriate, think about refueling if near the quarter mark, check trim for take-off and try to see the take-up-slack signal in the mirrors, and wait. And wait.....

5. Finally take up slack, note time and that 3 minutes have been lost from the estimated to the actual take-off time, and stop with the slack-free rope. Let the idle

power keep the slack out while the take-off signal hand shake ritual goes on. More work.

6. Get the go signal, advance the power not too fast and not too slow. Remember them? Make sure that the field is clear, know what is going on with cars, other gliders, other tow planes, other runways, the winch. Think again of the glider that is being towed, how to initiate the climb, at what speed, and the like.

7. Keep the towplane going straight and get some idea of how the glider is doing. This is important later. Try to notice if the acceleration is right and that the glider is tracking OK.

8. Let the tail come up with a little help from the stick and remember what the wind was and is from the rudder trim that had to be carried, with consideration of where the glider was, etc. Make a non-skid lift-off by banking the towplane to fair it with the relative wind before leaving the ground. This saves tires, gives the glider pilot some warning and is neat aviator-wise.

9. Lead the airspeed gain into the climb angle/airspeed so that the glider will not have to follow an abrupt transition from the inflight acceleration to the climb vector. (High priced term). This is a defense maneuver. If the glider pilot is inexperienced and the towplane leaps skyward, he will try to follow it with great precision to be "cool", and incidentally, to avoid flying in the towplane's wake near the ground. If he overdoes it on the pull up, he might lose sight of the tow plane. The tow plane might end up flying very low.

10. When the climb vector is established, different for each glider and its load, check the engine gauges, think of where the release is and where to prang it if the engine quits. If the glider gets way too high it will get there slowly, there will be lots of warning if the indications of impending disaster are thought about and acted upon. If the glider flew the roll off with the spoilers out, and you remembered what it was and how it was loaded, you will have some idea of what the fence and bushes are going to look like up close and so you will not release the glider, unless, of course, you are not getting by with it. This is the only time you release the glider. This action requires that you can remember where the release is and can find it quickly by the braille system.

11. Now you have to see where everything is, make the first turn, proceed into altitudes where gliders might be turning, entering landing patterns and the like so it helps if you have been keeping track of towplanes, gliders' thermal heights, flight times, and incidentally what the glider is doing behind you. If it is a training flight the glider might be doing the wake box exercise, so add to all of the above the task of keeping the towplane going somewhere specific. If it is a tow where the only objective is to get away from the ground, the task is to fly in continuous lift so the glider pilot can get off in the best thermal and the lowest possible altitude. If the glider pilot steers you, you are not relieved of your captain's duties. In this mode you must still fly the airplane and not hit things.

12. When the glider gets off, you do the departure maneuver, with non-fry engine management and plan the fast let down, ending up in the right place for approach at the right airspeed, do not fly through anything on tow in the pattern, do not cut any gliders out of same, do not hang the rope on the fence, do not make a bad landing (with all that practice you should be good at it), do not overwork the brakes. Raise the flaps, check the fuel, reset the trim, taxi past the line, get the signals, look at the glider that is to go next and you are back at #1.

There are reasons to do these things and more that have not been noted, like preflighting the towplane. This should be done carefully. A tailwheel steering linkage failure could kill the towplane in an emergency landing in a cross wind. The tow pilot is busy. It will take more time to read and think about the above than to do it.

CASE 3: At another contest site where the density altitude went over 9,000 feet, in the practice days ahead of the contest the sailplanes were many and the towplanes few. Towing was going very slowly and the soaring weather was poor. The thermals were small, choppy, giving very slow climb rates through about 1500 feet above the surface.

Being ready to fly in this fabulous place to get familiar with the local departures and approaches, I took an early tow, found out how long the take-off roll was and how bad the day was. Not wanting to land and wait again in the take-off line it was necessary to stay up at all costs. Iron clad logic. But it was very hard to stay up near the field. Now I am in the pattern, gear down and hit a bump. With great skill and cunning and some disregard for the pattern, I squeaked away from about 500 feet above ground and worked my way across the valley to low clouds in the foot hills. These promised to get higher during the day to enable a glide return to the airport. Right! It is a bad scene to require a retrieve from a 3 mile outlanding at the beginning of a contest, macho-wise.

After the 500 foot "save" while I was crossing the valley, I noticed a sailplane on tow much lower than I was. He wasn't doing very well. He was looking for a place to land and advising his crew of that fact by wireless while still on tow. Think about that for a second; he was going to select a field for an outlanding while on tow! He landed in a good field near roads and was retrieved uneventfully. The tow plane, using the term loosely, was marginal, full of fuel and had two heavy persons on board, one of which was called pilot.

The glider pilot in this near disaster had only the perspective derived from watching the tow plane from behind, roll the entire length of the runway, getting airborne only after the runway started over the crown of the gentle hill that it climbs during the first 75% of its length. The glider pilot did not have any specifications on the tow plane; he just accepted it as being suitable since it was there. It is not known how or if the tow plane ever climbed back up to the airport altitude to make a landing after the glider release.

Is this funny? Why didn't the glider pilot release? He did not release because he wanted to fly, and he had no perspective on what this tow plane could do at the density altitude of the field on the uphill runway. By the time he knew he was in trouble, he was looking up close at a barbed wire fence with sage brush behind and he did not like the smell of freshly cut sage brush or the sound of snapping barbed wire.

Who qualified the tow plane and pilot? What would have been the assigned faults if the glider pilot had been hurt in the off field landing? What would have been the assigned faults if the tow plane and crew were destroyed by fire after a crash? Is there a way to measure the performance of a candidate tow plane prior to risking the system to the results of marginal performance?

The pre-practice day towing is still going slowly, the pilot that outlanded while still on tow is now with his crew and I am scratching in the foot hills in unreliable thermals near the cloud base which is too low to glide back to the field. There are good fields available for landing however, so the flight feels good.

The radio chatter begins to define a situation that is not good. There is a ritual at soaring contests when not good things happen. It uses the radio. All pilots who have flown contests have participated. This one began with a glider pilot flying near the airport reporting that another glider has landed at some approximately defined location. Contest ground radio requests information on roads and the like to enable retrieve and there is much conversation to ensure that we are all talking about the same roads, fences, fields, compasses and distances to the landing site. Someone flies over the site to get a bearing from the field and in the process gets a good look at the glider on the ground and sees and reports that there has been some glider damage. He advises that the retrieve crew might need a 4 wheel vehicle and some help.

The radio gets quiet when the location has been really established, yet no one knows who has landed. It would be considerate, to keep your own crew from hooking up and finding a 4 wheel vehicle and an extra crew man, to let them know that the landed glider is not you. I never think of this until someone says, "4 Lima, OK", and the entire group that is still up gives similar reports, with long delays between transmissions, trying not to step on each other. The ground crews do not acknowledge. The radio gets quiet again.

While still scratching near the hills, I am reviewing the information between concerns about the unreliable thermals and the non-raising cloud base. The observing glider pilot did not say that he saw the landed pilot near the damaged glider, and the pilot that landed was never on the radio requesting a relay. No one asks if the grounded pilot has been seen. The clock is standing still.

Still reviewing the data: grassy gentle slope, no rocks, no trees, why the damage? No contact with downed glider, battery connection came loose in landing, being low I missed the transmission. Still do not know who it is. The airborne observer should have reported seeing the pilot, shouldn't be any damage in the open field, the thermals are rotten, bending the glider on a pre-practice day does not help your score, he must have stretched a return glide from an aggressive departure attempt, better man than I am, hope the cloud base goes up, better find the highest point in this scud with the best down wind, short course back to the field, it is raining in the mountains.

The first car to the glider which landed out reports that the damage to the glider is serious; there has been a fatality. The glider had been seen very low, banked steeply, then disappeared.

Was the slow towing operation a factor in this accident? We weren't in that seat so do not really know. It was a factor in my decision to work the small rough thermal at 500 feet in my flight earlier. I was returning to the field to land, saw 6 or 7 gliders waiting for tows, ran into the bump at a low pattern entry altitude and worked it to avoid the wait, the cost, the risk and anguish of another possibly marginal tow, and missing the soaring day which was just about to start.

Are there lessons in this case? Of course. The impossible challenge is to give each person the scale that allows measurement of the risk being taken and the other scale that establishes the ability to manage that risk successfully. It helps to be continuously analytic while gaining experience; just before a situation gets unsanitary, do some planned alternative that is within the limits of experience. Notice the word "planned". The existence of the conscious planned alternative that is "familiar" stretches the scale that measures "unsanitary". So there is learning. Safety is a planning activity.

CASE 4: Back to ropes, the front end for Case 4. It is probably human nature to wonder about your own performance when the exciting and probably inevitable chance comes for some application of cool skill. How will you do for a real rope break, landing in a strange field, landing the glider in the boonies with no field. If gliders are flown then these neat opportunities will befall us.

So, I have had the real towplane failure from the back end of the rope and did OK, surviving the period of indecision and getting back to the starting line from a really low tow. Although I have flown a lot of tows from the front end of the rope, there have not been many opportunities to practice real engine failures. There have been engine failures in B-17's and gooney birds, but these have all been from high altitudes with lots of time. They do not count. I have known tow pilots who were very experienced, and did not do well from the engine failure just after take off. It is easy to say, "I would not do that", and keep on wondering how the situation would be handled if real and in your own hands.

I got the chance to find out. Even though all of the check list (informal) items were completed with the associated assurances nested in my subconscious, the experience was illuminating.

The 2-33 being towed was occupied by two big men, there was not much wind and the day was warm, not hot. There was about one third tank full in each wing, the mag was on both and the tank selector on a tank selection, not off, and the trim was in take off position. When the trim is overlooked there is something to do during the early part of the flight after lift off when the amazing stick pressures are discovered. When the trim is set, there is nothing to do except all of those things necessary to really fly the towplane. The glider tracked perfectly, it was an instructor check out flight, and all was great until about 250 feet of altitude was gained.

We were at the point where all the earlier looks at the ground ahead on prior towing flights said all the soft places to prang are now behind us. The climb vector was established. The places ahead are scattered with drainage tracks with heavy plants and fat very heavy indeed cacti. All is OK and very normal with the engine pulling strongly as it had done on about 12 earlier tows. The engine made one loud "POP" and quit.

Surprise! It seems that I debated with myself regarding whether or not the engine was working, including the possibility that it was not really working even though it always worked before, that the ignition and fuel were great, couldn't be water in the fuel since it was not raining and two thirds of each tank had fired the engine successfully, if the fuel was really shut off and not on a tank we could not have gotten this far, so the engine probably was working now, but if it wasn't it would sound like it wasn't running now and if that was true then we would not be climbing any longer and probably the airplane would be going slow and I had better DO SOMETHING!! QUICK!!

The airspeed indicator at this point showed less than 50 mph, it had been indicating about 65 mph and it was clear that this tow plane was now a glider going too slow. So nose down a lot since it is hard to gain speed from a mushing attitude and start a turn to the left, from the subconscious and no other input. I totally forgot about the glider but felt a tug as we got going in separate directions and he released. Rolled out of the left turn, nose back up with about 60 mph on the ASI over a soft spot with a little right turn we are lined up and too high and fast for the TREES by the first DITCH. So I reached for the flap handle, initiated a slip for a few seconds, couldn't really use or find the flap down latch, so wings level and into the light, high creosote bushes. Every time I tried the brakes the tail came up; the bushes should be slowing the plane faster. After the longest roll ever we came to rest about 10 feet from the nearest iron wood tree.

It was crystal clear to me at this point with my lightning quick mind that the engine on this tow plane really did quit. The throttle setting was as it was when that happened and the mag switch still on. The only thing that was expected on the roll out was that the plane would nose over and that it is always necessary to get out fast releasing the belts first. The possibility of fire was never a concern. What was a concern during the glider-like flight portion of this caper was that the towplane was about to get wrecked and what would the club do for tows, the waiting period would be extreme for tows now, etc. These thoughts would give way to advice to myself such as "You better do what is right to survive this."

The club members came in force, moved the towplane through the bushes and through the fence back to the cleared airport area. There was little damage to the airframe or its rags and when an attempt was made to start it, it fired up and checked out normally. There were gliders waiting for tow so it was put back on the line and finished the afternoon towing operation without incident.

Are there lessons in this? Yes, indeed. It would be great if they could really be pulled from the happening since they would disclose the nature of the real attitudes that control what we do and how that interfaces with safety. This is never easy because it is not possible to have all the data or to know what, of all of the data, each participant has. For example, I do not know why the tow plane failed at all yet.

My best guess is that the needle valve that is actuated by the float in the carburetor got stuck in its seat at a worn place because it happened to need to limit fuel flow just at the time that the cooling of the carb after some ground time allowed the seat to close on the worn spot. The sticking fuel shut-off is not uncommon on old carbs and it is a solid shut-off. While the throttle and mags were just left as they were during the roll, lift off, and initial climb, the engine did not fire during the bumpy roll through the desert. The needle valve and seat would have to come to thermal equilibrium to cause a release without the hammer bump on the carb itself. The carb was high time.

Was it wrong to fly the towplane in same condition after this incident? Of course not. Everything that we operate is in a condition where it might fail, and if it checks out OK using the tests that are usually used to make the determination of usability, then it is OK. Right? Almost right.

This position is reinforced by the attitudes that cause people to say, "He did something wrong", "It will never happen to me", and "If he can get by with it so can I". I have said and thought those things. I have had friends that said and thought those things and the ones that are still with us are the ones who approach their energy management tasks on the basis that energy management is best done where we have control of all of the energy in the system. That means that it is necessary to know, think about, and act upon a lot of information ranging from the problems of flying too fast or too slow, exceeding our own capability/experience envelope, preventive maintenance, and where the tow release lever is.

There is a real tow pilot who is still active who once refused to fly a tow plane because it smelled strongly of fuel. There once were two pilots who flew a plane that smelled strongly of fuel. Witnesses said the rags were almost burned off before the airplane hit the ground.

CASE 5: General aviation airport, density altitude over 9,000 feet, 180 hp Super Cub tow plane, light and variable winds, dry, about 11:00 am sun time, first tow for everyone, and the tow pilot steered to optimize ground clearance. We made a shallow right turn and then a shallow left turn over some low hills at the end of the runway. At about 1000 feet AGL we went through a 6 knot thermal and stayed on to assure minimum interference with the airport's traffic. In the middle of a downwind leg position at about 2000 feet AGL another 6 knot thermal big and smooth. Released with 6 knots all around and working two tight spots topped out at 14,000 feet ASL. Oh joy!

CHAPTER 5 - THE PILOTS SPEAK FOR THEMSELVES

I REMEMBER WHEN by Don Barnard, May 1958.

It was a spring day around the year 1930, in Portland, Oregon. This was the day I was going to fly the ship I had put so many hundreds of hours of work on. I had no sleep the previous night thinking of a million things regarding the ship and what I had to do once I had the thing off the ground, as I had no dual instruction of any kind. But there was no fear, I had read all about how to fly in every book that was available in the public library, and anyway, my plans were not to take it up too high...

About 5:00 a.m. I was up and dawn showed the start of a beautiful day, which in Portland in spring is almost a miracle in itself. After some breakfast a gang of friends arrived who were going to help me. We hooked up the trailer and started out. Having spent everything on getting the ship finished, I couldn't afford much of a trailer so what was hauling the ship was a conglomeration of 2 x 4's nailed together on an axle base, wheels but no tires.

We arrived at the hill 5 miles from home about 2 hours later, and started to set up the ship. For those of you who have never seen a primary glider or helped set one up, you haven't lived! There are so many wires... landing, flying, drag... that not to watch where you are stepping is a good way to get hung. There's nothing like getting lifted off the ground and bumped on your backside from a drag wire under the chin! A record-breaking job of assembling a primary will require three hours... that is if everyone knows exactly what they are supposed to do. If they don't, then you end up with one flying wire hooked to the control stick and elevator wires to the drag cables and everything all fouled up, which takes another hour or two to straighten out. Well, this morning everything seemed to go together pretty good so in a matter of three or more hours we were ready for the first flight.

Now a little briefing on the site might be in order. The hill, Mount Scott, the part I was using, had a nice gentle slope cleared off, was about half a mile long and about the same wide... just a nice gradual slope into the prevailing southwest winds and plenty of open field at the bottom of the slope. My method of launch was to be shock cord, and for those of you who have never seen it or ridden through one, it is comparable to being shot out of a cannon. First you are sitting on the ground gritting your teeth and next thing you know you are 50 to 100 feet in the air trying to get your eyeballs back in the sockets from the back of your head.

This method of launching is to have 100 feet of 7/8ths rubberized rope (called shock cord), in the middle is attached a ring which goes on the open hook of the glider, and at each end an additional 8 to 10 feet of rope for the crew to hold on to. The line is stretched out in front in a V-shape so if the ring comes off the hook it will not fly into someone's rear. (I can tell you a good story about a time when that sort of thing did happen and I think the guy is still in the air, but that's another story).

Once you are all secured in the glider, belt tightened up, prayers said, and all apples swallowed from the throat, then you give the commands. This is very important as you can really foul things up if they are not given correctly. There are five big fellows on each end of the rope and there is a short length of rope tied to the end of the skid with one or two heavy fellows hanging on to it and laying down so as not to get their heads taken off as the tail whizzes by. When everything is set you give the first command "WALK", this starts the crew walking forward stretching out the shock cord. After a few yards you give the command "RUN" and away they go running down the slope, the shock cord getting longer and longer and the diameter getting smaller and smaller. As the grunting from the crew holding back on the tail rope gets louder and louder, you wait until you think you've heard a gut pop, then it is time to holler "GO", and that means for the tail crew to let go. With a swish and snap, up you go into the blue... or something. The height from this launching depends on the amount of stretching that has gone into the shock cord, so a good crew is made up of all the beef you can get into helping you stretch the line.

There will be a million firsts in my life yet, and a million firsts are already past, but I know nothing will ever equal that first launch, fifty feet up with the wind whistling through the wires, my eyes all watered up (no goggles), and just a bucket seat and a rudder bar for the feet to rest on, between me and the ground. It seemed I must be at least 1000 feet up. What a thrill! The ship automatically went into a glide and as I floated down the slope I could hear the fellows hollering after me, and I felt like a new soul on the wing, free from all earthly attachments. Everything appeared to have a new look and the fields at the bottom of the hill seemed to be miles away. Through all this new exuberant feeling, my thoughts said... you've got to fly this ship. So I tried moving the controls. Sure enough, the ship responded and the nose dipped. Sitting out in front of the glider, as one does in a primary, there is nothing from which to judge the attitude of the plane and it is very hard to figure out just when or what control to use, but the Lord was with me and a nice glide to the bottom of the hill was made. The one bad fault on the landing, unless you hold the ship up by the stick, is that a pancake landing in a primary with NO shocks of any kind can sure be rough on the spine.

After I recovered my wind from the landing shock, I was never so surprised in my life to think, "Here I am safe and sound after being airborne all by myself. Well, say now, there's nothing to this flying business, haven't I just proved how easy it is!" The heavens tremble when out of the mouths of ignoramuses such statements come... I could hardly wait til the crew came running to get it up the hill for another go at it.

If you think hauling a glider with no wheel up a hill by hand isn't a big job, then you still have a lot to learn; and if you want to lose all your friends in a hurry just try the above method. About three retrieves up the hill will do it. When next you see them and mention their helping launch the glider you will be amazed how much of the population is suffering from back ailments.

As I remember that day, I made 8 or 10 flights to the bottom of the hill, each ending with a grinding of the vertebrae, as the landings were yet more vertical than horizontal, but both the ship and my spine managed to take it and stay together. The setting sun finally stopped any more flying for that weekend. A very tired but exuberant student of the art of birding worked with flashlight getting the ship back on its trailer to get homeward bound, never to forget this first day of a new-born freedom.

BAROGRAPH BLUES by Derek van Dyke, May 1957.

"Daddy, what's a barograph?" asked my eldest son the other evening. There are some questions which answer themselves but this was definitely not one of those. The scientific and mechanical answer might have been proper but it wouldn't have been completely accurate. For, you see, around our house a barograph is special. It has more personality than a box filled with a few working parts was ever to meant to have. A barograph controls the actions of grown men. It has the capacity to make them laugh and cry. It exists to torment the forgetful and tease the proud. No longer can I define a barograph as a mechanical instrument meant solely to measure flights of sailplanes. No longer can I draw a simple diagram for my wide-eyed and respectful siblings and say, "Son, that's the way one of those gadgets looks." On no! I can't say this anymore. Now I have to tell the tale. I have to sit with my head bowed, my eyes closed, and my hands clasped between my knees to conceal their shaking. I now know how the inhabitants of Mudville felt when the third strike streaked across the plate knee-high to the great Casey's knickers.

Listen! The tale unfolds. As Bobbie Burns was wont to say, "The best laid plans of mice and men oft gang agley." Plans have a way of being more human than their mortal progenitors. Ours were no exception.

Don (Barnard) was going to go 218 miles to Needles on a diamond goal flight. This was no premise on our part. It was a fact. We were not planning for failure and at no time during the following hours did it occur to me that Don would miss. This is known in the trade as Good Planning as opposed to the kind which admits to any degree of doubt. The weather was perfect, the ship was in beautiful shape, and the start moved rapidly to a successful launch from an air tow at 10:15 am over Rittenhouse field. I was back on the ground and driving out the gate with the trailer six minutes later.

The plan for the flight called for an average of 25 mph ground speed along a course northwesterly past Falcon Field, to the north of Scottsdale, over Cactus airport, across Deer Valley to intercept highway 60-70-89 between Beardsley and Morristown. Then past Wickenburg, over Salome to Hope, and then on to the Colorado River at Parker, and up the west side of the river over California 93 to Needles. We figured landing time for about 6:30 or 7:00 pm. In the event that Don should land earlier, he was to contact the nearest law officer by phone and have me flagged down and brought to where ever he was. It looked like a good program. All it required was a desire to fly to Needles, and we had that.

Within 20 minutes and 5 miles I had lost sight of the white bird and figuratively went on instruments. Plotting intersection points against Don's estimated flight path and ground speed, I stopped 5 or 6 times on my way across the valley but no amount of straining the eyes showed the whereabouts of the glider. So I just kept going. However, it did become apparent that it was quite possible that Don's ground speed was probably closer to 30 mph than 25 so I revised my plans and began to pelt down the highway at a great rate for I was certain I was behind rather than ahead of the plane.

As I entered Wickenburg, I pulled into the gas station beside the bridge to top off the gas tank for the run across to the Colorado. Have you ever had someone tap you on the shoulder and say your name when you knew darn well there's nobody within 60 miles who knows you? Well, friend, it gives you a turn. There I stood in the shade while the meter ran pennies into the tank with horrifying haste, and this gentle touch tapped my clavicle.

"Mr Van Dyke?" I'm afraid I'm suffering from more tension than I care to admit for I jumped.

"Yes?"

"I'm with the Wickenburg Police Department and Mr Barnard just called in from the Flying E Ranch and asked us to send you along to him."

Don was down. Well, at least I knew where he was and I hadn't been too far off on my estimate. Let's go find out why. All these thoughts moved through my mind as I drove the three miles to the ranch. There sat the LK on the edge of the strip. And there stood Don! Now I know how Casey looked when the umpire's voice rolled across the ball park's acres. He looked just like Don Barnard at 1:30 in the afternoon of April 30, 1957 at the Flying E Guest Ranch strip. Shock, covered with disgust, mixed with frustration, coated with disbelief. What a dictionary of defeated dejection was mirrored in that handsome bald face.

I knew it was bad and braced myself for the worst but nothing could have prepared me for the chilling statement which greeted me.

"What do you think I did?" said Don in a voice loaded with self loathing. "What do you think I did? I forgot the barograph."

And so, son, that's why I say a barograph is more than an instrument. It's a way of life. It's a necessity to record-making sailplane pilots just as food and oxygen are. Never forget, son. Never forget your barograph."

NOW & THEN by Pete Petry, June 1972.

Editor Nancy Hume asked me to write something about the Tucson meet. "If it's clean, I'll print it," she added. The challenge of writing to such an editorial standard flattered me into submitting the following.

I had been looking forward to the Parker meet of the 1972 ASA series as my first contest in 33 years, the previous one being the 2nd Annual American Open Soaring Meet and 4th Midwest Soaring Contest in Frankfort, Michigan, in August 1939. Old clippings state I took third place with a spot landing of 5 inches and on "points" in a Franklin, all of which indicates the caliber of competition I engaged in as a youth. I particularly remember unsuccessfully trying to outlast R.E. Franklin on Sleeping Bear Dune on a violently rough day of that meet. I have framed that particular barogram.

This spring I was working on my gliding instructor rating, when Fran suggested that if I was going to get an additional licence, she thought the 747 might pay better than the glider instructor's, so I switched interests temporarily and missed the Parker meet while following her orders.

However, I bid my flights to be free for the May 27-30 meet, and enjoyed every minute of it. Flying against such competition as Baird, Fellner, Hume, Obershaw, the Robertson brothers, Sczesny, and others, made it impossible not to compare soaring contests today with the Nationals at Elmira which Ruth and I attended in the late thirties (but only participating to the extent of flying the weather instruments to 12,000 feet in a Cub every morning before Barney Wiggins' weather briefing).

My principal impression was of how little things have changed. The ships are faster and even more beautiful, all launching is by aeroplane, radio equipment is in general use, and varios are far superior, but all else was reminiscent of earlier days. I thought the direction and management at Tucson was excellent, and, of course, the level of pilot co-operation with the officials never changes. For example, we were warned in pilots' meeting against over-use of the radios, and later, while inspecting under-wing contest numbers in a gaggle, I noticed a Cirrus with its wheel down. I called this to the attention of the pilot, and although he observed the earlier caution against indiscriminate radio use, I did notice that the wheel disappeared promptly.

Fortunately, I had a wheel brake problem on the 1-34 the first day, and hoped that my fiddling with it at frequent intervals on the ground might somehow be connected in the minds of the other pilots with my failure to stay up on either tow. It was a no-contest day anyway, as it turned out.

The second day I did better, darting from one landable area to another, then climbing to the top of any available thermal, continuing to circle until it had degenerated to 200 fpm down, on the philosophy that a place that could produce as fine a thermal as this had been, was more likely to send up another one than some distant, unknown, and perhaps inhospitable place on down the course. Fran has been trying to tell me that Baird, Hume, Obershaw, et al, don't do it this way. However, I made it my way to Tumacacori Mission and landed by the road while my crew chief, Paul Eskew, was being surrounded by a herd of stampeding horses and hung up on a barbed wire fence while keeping "Old Glory" (my portable radio) from touching the ground. Fortunately I had given him a copy of Paul Dickerson's "Crewin' For a Biggie" (See Chapter 9) to read the first night out, and he took it all in his stride.

Fran and Ruth were having their problems turning the oversized rig around in the undersized side road, and meanwhile Baird, Hume and Ordway were flashing around the course to Nogales and back to Ryan, far out of sight above, or more likely, miles to the side, on course.

The third and last day, after a particularly coherent and remarkably accurate weather forecast of overdevelopment, my crew chief quietly suggested I take an early take off time and just try to get around the course. (Diplomacy comes with age). I made one of the first takeoffs and, having found a safe thermal to return to, I dashed through the gate at red-line, the air noise being so great I had to have two repeats of "Good Start". I mean to re-read "Soaring Cross Country" to refresh my memory as to why I go through the gate so fast.

Also, this day, I tried to justify my many-splendored Rainco radio by calling the radar advisory service at Tucson International and advising him I was flying over at 10,000 feet.

"Ho Hum, Papa Yankee, squawk transponder code so-and-so."

"Sorry, I'm not transponder equipped." He lost interest in me and went back to unscrambling the DC-10's.

I pressed on into a rain shower, which didn't help my onward and upward progress and landed at a place called Pomarene, near Benson. It must have been a good area - John Baird landed 3 miles away. We invented several interesting and useful tricks for getting a sailplane out of soft sand and de-rigging in a 30 mile wind. Fortunately, I have a patient wife and, more importantly, a strong one. I heard later I got 300 points, but someone else told me that these are automatically issued when you pay your entrance fee.

ACCORDING TO MY CALCULATIONS, I DON'T KNOW WHERE I AM by Dan Halacy, October 1972.

The above remark has been attributed variously to Columbus's navigator, "Wrongway" Corrigan, and an unidentified navigation student in the Air Force during WW2. I can sympathize with them all, and with Wally Raisanen, who had to drive something like 600 miles to retrieve an embarrassed soaring pilot who had covered only 80 miles of a 200 mile triangle. My only excuse is that I couldn't hold up a waterlogged Phoebus in a solid downpour - and our compass sure must need swinging!

Like a lot of others, I couldn't stay aloft on my first tow at Prescott and by the time we replaced a flat tire and got me back into the blue it was after 2:00 pm. But things went well and I made the first turn at Robidoux averaging about 50 mph. Reached 15,000 MSL at one point and wasn't worried at all about completing the task as I headed out on that desolate second leg. However, shortly after I left Valle, at about 11,000, the situation began to deteriorate with great rapidity, as they say. As a matter of fact, not only have I never before flown in that kind of sink, I still don't believe it really exists.

If I had better sense I'd have done a quick 180 and got out of there. But up ahead 81 and 3D were gleefully chasing each other along the course. (I found out later Al Hume (3D) had problems of his own and at times was something less than hilarious).

Matching the needles on the Winter speed-to-fly produced a heady speed and the feeling of nosing straight down into the murk. I couldn't see too well for the Niagara coursing over the canopy and neither could I elude the powerful downward push. When the deluge finally eased up and I could see daylight again, I tried to console myself that at least I was making swift progress over the bleak and forbidding terrain way down there. Only now I suddenly realized it wasn't "way down there" but right below me. I think I have an idea how the astronauts felt on the first letdown to the moon.

Chris Crowl had said that Bishops Lake was landable and that there was a ranch there and probably a phone. I knew I hadn't come that far yet, but maybe

I could stretch it out before contacting terra firma. I was pretty sure I was not going to remain an airborne contestant much longer, so I got on the radio and called anyone who could read my transmission. (Wally and I hadn't been in contact all day, for some reason probably connected with the flat tire?) Pete Petry and Bill Ordway both came to the rescue and word was passed to Wally that Fox Yankee was probably going to land at Bishops Lake.

Working hard at trying to climb in zero sink, I noticed what I was pleased to think was the dry lake ahead and a bit north of my track. It should have been south, but I had deliberately steered left of course so as not to miss the second turnpoint. What a treat to finally see a landable spot, for everything else down there ranged from inhospitable to downright hostile. Still hoping to reach some halfway-promising scraggly clouds farther west, I stayed with the attempt until the last possible minute for getting back to my "dry lake". When I saw it was a vain hope, I radio-ed that I was definitely landing at Bishops Lake. There was the ranch house Chris had promised, at the end of the plainly discernible "lake" outline.

81 told me that Wally had received the call and I headed toward the ranch buildings at max L/D, holding my breath and thinking "up" with every brain cell. It works! About a mile from the ranch I cleared the last fence and just ticked a slight rise with the wheel, then coasted on another half a mile or so on the slight downslope. FY finally sighed to a stop not far from a small band of horses grazing away in great unconcern.

So far so good. I turned off the radio and staked out the Phoebus, hoping that horses don't eat fiberglass. Now to phone Contest Headquarters and wait for my trusty crew to arrive. But there was a strangely deserted feeling about the "ranch". I was a little surprised that no one had galloped out on horseback or astride a jeep to welcome the great white bird from the sky. Then my faith was restored as a carryall truck appeared from behind the buildings. But my greeters turned out to be a band of antelope hunters, wanting only to know if I had spotted any of the beasts from the air!

These kind souls were the essence of helpfulness. First they signed my landing card. Second they informed me not only that this was not Bishops Lake, but also that it was an abandoned ranch about 10 miles north of there! Third, they could not give me a ride to the highway since they were heading the other direction in pursuit of their quarry. In the event that I survived until their return, they would be happy to give me a ride to civilization. Smiling cheerfully, they drove off in a cloud of mud.

I groaned, thinking of the 20 or 30 miles to the highway -- as the Phoebus flies. Visions of hobbling that distance almost made an antelope hunter out of me, but at that moment another truck appeared from the other direction. It was driven by an Indian whose job was hauling feed from a barn to the deserted outfit. In terse, Tonto-fashion, he told me he wasn't going to the highway either, or anywhere near it. He was going back to the home ranch, however, and with some urging reluctantly agreed to take me along. It was obvious that he was leery of types wearing funny blue hats who flew airplanes without engines.

Fifteen rutted, soggy miles later I climbed down and rapped on the door to tell my sad story to a lady who turned out to be Mrs Pat Cain of the Babbit Ranch. Very graciously she let me use the phone (their number is "Anita Two", believe it or not) and soon I was pouring out my sad story to Nancy Hume back at Prescott. By now Wally would be half way down the rough trail to Bishops Lake, expecting to find Fox Yankee and its hapless pilot. "When he calls in tell him I'm sorry about that," I said lamely, as I gave my correct co-ordinates. It was going to be pretty late by the time he reached me, I was thinking. Little did I know how late.

As luck would have it, my faithful Indian companion had to make another trip back to the "Tin House", as the desolate outpost was called. He even drove me clear out to the sailplane, displaying about as much interest in it as the horses did. Maybe he didn't really believe it.

There wasn't much to do then but untape the wings and try to hammer the tiedown stakes deeper into the rocky ground in case the wind came up. By now the rain was a dim memory and a beautiful sunset was taking shape. Long rows of still-working cumulus stretched tantalizingly toward the second turnpoint as I shrugged and trudged back toward the ranch buildings. It was going to get dark eventually, and Wally had better hurry up or...

I killed some time trying to figure out how I could be north of the course and then gave it up and smoked my one cigar while I gazed wistfully toward the east. By the time it got dark I had reached the brilliant conclusion that Wally couldn't possibly cover all those miles in anything less than several hours.

It was chilly by now and I investigated the barn with the thought I could wrap up in feed sacks and keep warm. But the cement floor looked unappealing and I moved on to a small cement block building farther on. I pushed against the door, sure it was locked or nailed shut, but it swung wide. In the feeble light I could make out a gas heater across the room, and in the corner something was humming softly and familiarly. It was a refrigerator. Then I saw a gas mantle hanging from the ceiling. Scrounging around on a table I found some kitchen matches, scratched one and surveyed my haven. The gaslight glowed cheerfully and I saw I was in a kitchen, complete with sink, gas stove, and wonder of wonders, a well stocked pantry! Before long I had brewed up a cup of tea and fixed some sandwiches for a light supper. Take your time, Wally!

It turned out to be a three room place: huge kitchen, a bedroom, and another room that was completely bare. There was also a bathroom of the inside variety, with its own gas lamp, hot and cold water and shower. On the kitchen table was a small library of paperbacks and I selected an Ed McBain mystery and settled down for a leisurely wait to be rescued.

I had positioned myself facing out of the window so I could keep an eye on the road, and when lights appeared I walked nonchalantly out to greet Wally and invite him in for a snack. Only it wasn't Wally, but Rancher Pat Cain, come to relay the news that Wally couldn't make it tonight. Sorry about that.

Pat was a typical hospitable westerner, inviting me to make myself at home (his invitation came several hours late) and lighting up the gas heater, which was thermostatically controlled, of course. His hired hand had quit just the day before, he told me, and that was why the place was deserted. I probably could have gone to work in a nice quiet environment. Instead I thanked Pat and returned to McBain. After that I sacked out on the cot in the bedroom and didn't wake up until the sun came through the windows next morning.

Wally must have spent the night cussing his stupid partner. Unable to negotiate the disastrous road to Bishops Lake, he barely make it back out to Seligman. Next, he rounded up the local Search and Rescue Outfit and got a commitment from one Jim Grisenti to go look for me that night! Finally, Wally called Prescott - and got the word that I was down in another county. By the time

73

he could get back to the rescue boys, they had already left. The air must have been pretty blue up at Bishops Lake that night. If I had known all this machinery was in motion I wouldn't have enjoyed my evening nearly as much.

Meanwhile, back at my ranch. At about 8 am a passing cowboy swung down from his trusty Dodge and left me a thermos of coffee and a sack of chocolate chip cookies. He had seen the Phoebus grazing out in the pasture and had come to investigate. We visited a while and shortly after he drove on, here came Wally and Mike Selser (who by now must have had a pretty dim view of contest soaring as an aerial sport). They had been on the road since six, and Wally was eager to get back to Prescott and take his turn in the blue. You know the rest; we arrived just in time to learn the mission was scrubbed - a particularly fitting term for the gloomy Sunday Prescott delivered for ASA. But we're used to it by now.

The moral? Fly fast and don't land out, I guess. I can't think of anything I would do differently in a similar situation, although it will help to swing the compass when flying over wilderness like that. It was an interesting experience and I'm grateful for good fortune, a good and faithful crew, and the kindness of the Cains and Jim Grisenti, who searched Bishops Lake in the dark for the soaring pilot who wasn't there. Plus the heart warming greeting from 6 year old Eric Raisanen (just back from Prescott Hospital himself for a head cut): "I'm *glad* you got back." So am I, Eric.

GOLD DISTANCE ATTEMPT by John Lincoln, August 1974.

John Lincoln II says his main claim to fame is that it once took him 1500 feet of altitude to refold a map. He was a youthful 23 with just 125 cross country hours when he attempted Gold Distance and landed out. Having found his way to a telephone...

"I looked up Estrella's number having forgotten to take it and called. My crew asked where I was and I gave the usual answer. "Help meeee, I'm lost."

Crew:	"Where are you calling from?"
Me:	"Mr Hildebrandt's farm."
Crew:	"Where is that?"
Me:	"South of Rittenhouse about two miles."
Crew:	"Wait, I don't have a pencil."

Finally the directions were given and I hung up. It was 3:30 pm. I thanked Mr Hildebrandt and asked if I could have a drink of water. He offered me iced tea and I said OK.

"Would you like to see where I planned to fly today?"

"Alright," was his reply.

I got out the map and started to explain all about how to use the chart and my flight course and mileage, when he stopped me. He was a bit annoyed and since he stood about 6'3" or 6'4", I decided to shut up.

"These flies are bothering me," he said, "so I'm going to get my fly swatter."

"OK."

He returned carrying a fly swatter that measured about 6" by 12". Its handle was about 4 feet long but he liked short handled fly swatters and had broken about 2 feet off. As a fly landed on my map he used the swatter full force. I closed my eyes thinking he might miss and kill me instead but his aim was true and when I opened my eyes I saw the remains of a fly scattered over my map.

"That's a helluva swatter," was all I could get up just then. He laughed once and said, "It's a Texas fly swatter," and continued to study the map... fly and all.

A TRAILER BY ~~JANUARY~~ ~~FEBRUARY~~ ~~MARCH~~ APRIL by Paul Dickerson, May 1973.

I chose not to buy the trailer that Bob Wentroff had when I bought his lovely 15 meter Diamant, because it was made of wood - and as some of you know, I think wood is an ignoble material, suitable only for use in tennis racquets and toothpicks. Since wood can't be welded, cut with a torch, or threaded, what good is it? A secondary reason for passing up Bob's well designed trailer might have been that even after selling my Jeep, motorcycle, motorcycle trailer, a set of Michelin tires, a tachometer and a Mercedes engine, I still couldn't really afford the basic ship and had to borrow an altimeter from Fred Arndt for three months.

I was therefore faced with the prospect of building a trailer. This was in mid-October. I immediately began to plan the trailer to end them all - self powered, air conditioned, controlled humidity, electrostatic precipitator to remove that awful fouling dust, three kinds of burglar alarms hooked directly into L. Patrick Gray's office, and an air-ride suspension. Unfortunately, my wife thought that her stretched microbus (Dachwagon) would look a little funny parked across 6 spaces at Smitties so I lowered my goals a bit.

The next plan was an aesthetically pleasing trailer with rounded upper and lower edge (for reduced yawing movement when passing those big semi's) and a streamlined nose to reduce the overall drag. (My Mercedes is a bit more thirsty than it used to be). The only problem was finding someone to bend the 13 or so 1"x1" square tubes into a 60" radius. In November I located a small company in Tempe which could do the job - cheap. We were off and running! The shop foreman called in a week or so to tell me that the first rib was complete and did I want to examine it? I wanted.

The rib was beautiful - smooth, no flattened sides, no gouges, perfect - except that it was bent to a 60" diameter - not a 60" radius. Poor. The chagrined foreman (name withheld to protect the guilty) suggested that I call another upstanding local craftsman and purveyor of fine works. Foreman number 2 agreed to do the job. He would call me with a quote within 48 hours. A week later I called him - oops! He had forgotten - will call back tomorrow! A week later - you guessed it - no call - to hell with him.

Then I saw Herman Stiglmeier's advertisement in the January Soaring magazine - wow - trailers of almost any cross section! A phone call to Herman - sorry - he will be in Hawaii until February 15th. A phone call to Hawaii? That is ridiculous! Besides, I have plenty of time - good ole Fred Arndt is still letting me use his trailer - in addition to his altimeter - by this time I also have Dean Fleming's Friebe (no pun).

So lots of letters back and forth to Hawaii, via Calcutta and Johannesburg. Herman thinks I'm crazy. I think he has no taste. Finally, in late February, my phone rings at work, it's Herman. He says, "I give up. Tell me what shape ribs you want. I'll bend them." He says he knows the difference between radius and diameter and that nobody likes a smart alec. It might take several weeks to make them because his work load had kind of stacked up while he was in Hawaii. (I thought only air conditioner repair men went to Hawaii in January). He said he had a set of standard ribs ready and why didn't I buy them. A check on my fingers showed only 6 weeks till the first contest. OK - send a set of the standard ribs.

Now, two weekends later (approximately 16 man hours) the ribs are riveted to the plywood (ignoble plywood) floor, waiting for the shipment of special pre-painted aluminum skins to arrive from Happy Herman's hula hoop house. I have put in some 200 rivets so far - and only 83 are defective. American Shoe Machinery Co. makes great rivets but watch out for those other guys, theirs are worse than useless.

So far I have spent about $550 on materials. I have everything except hitch, tongue, tires, lights, wires and internal fittings. To this point the trailer has almost assembled itself.

BUY GLASS AND WIN by Pete Petry, November 1974.

After a couple of years of hogging the bottom spots of the contest score sheets, Fran and I thought it would only be fair to give someone else a chance at them. So I bought Art Hurst's Standard Cirrus "UP" when he finished flying it in the Standard Class Nationals at Hobbs. We crewed for Art the last two days and brought it home.

First we took it to the FAA at Scottsdale Airport to be re-licensed. We placed the components in what seemed a logical arrangement and fiddled and sweated to fasten them together, while two Inspectors stood by with folded arms and weak smiles which plainly said, "Sad, really sad." Finally they re-licenced it, apparently assuming it was perfectly safe since we'd never get it together.

After a week of polishing and fussing and Fran becoming convinced I was a coward and would never fly it, I took it out to Turf and finally got it together with Dick Panther's help, and made four flights. When we had it assembled the spoilers were up 1/8" at the inboard ends, and I assumed it was slightly out of rig. On takeoff the spoilers immediately started coming open, so I held the handle forward. They made a whistling noise, plainly audible at the office as I passed, and Bob MacLeod called on the radio to inquire what was going on. This was very frustrating, since I had my left hand on the spoilers and the right hand on the stick, and turning either one loose to pick up the mike caused wild gyrations on tow. So for once I had to forego talking on the radio.

Off tow, I idly wondered why there was $2\frac{1}{2}$" of shiny, oily tube at the front end of the spoiler handle rod. I had a flash of inspiration that perhaps the spoiler handle went even further forward than I was holding it. Sure enough, that locked them in, and the spoilers pulled in flush with the wing surface and there was no more whistle.

Flying it was a real pleasure. Very light on the controls, no tricky characteristics, responsive -- a real treat to fly. I used my usual 1-34 approach pattern, and except for finding I was approaching a little faster than necessary, there were no great differences. The real difference from the 1-34 was not readily apparent from local flights. The increased performance and the difficulty in believing it, is what the rest of this article is really about.

We took the new ship to El Mirage a couple of days early for the Region 12 Contest. I flew the ship with water for the first time, and again there were no surprises. All speeds were increased, although the only place I really noticed it was in the necessity of thermaling faster to avoid a stall.

The first day of the contest contained bad news and good news. The bad news was that after filling one wing tank with water, I flopped the ship over the other way without closing the shut off valve and had 7½ gallons of water in the cockpit before I had sense enough to close the valve or tilt the ship back like it was. Just then the Humes arrived from Phoenix, and even Nancy had the perception to see that it was not the time to talk to me.

Four days after returning from El Mirage I had a flight which I wish I had made four days before the Contest. Four or five of the ASA group flew informally from Estrella to Sells and back. Over Table Mountain on the return, Omer Reed took me in hand. He said his calculator said we could make the airport at 90. I would have agreed we could make it half way back, but started back with him anyway. Pretty soon Omer reported, "Now it says 100." I hung in there. Soon he was calling for 110, 120 and finally red line. We still had to spoiler down to land. If I had this "hand holding" demonstration before El Mirage, I'm sure I could have improved my standing. (You can be sure I now have a final glide computer in the cockpit).

John Baird has always said, "Fly fast and don't land out." I never fully appreciated the real humor of this. They are diametrically opposed. And I now see that contest flying is a balance, and a difficult one to accomplish, between his two injunctions. But just finishing would appear to be number one.

WHY COMPETE? by Bob von Hellens, February 1975.

In August, 1973, Bob Hohanshelt and I were speculating about flying in the ASA contest to be held at Prescott in September. Neither of us had ever competed; my log book indicated 53 hours with no off field landings and only two cross country flights, one of which was a straight glide to Eloy from 9800 feet over Estrella. To the best of my recollection, the decision was made on the basis of "I'll do it if you'll do it" and confirmed with another can of beer.

Once the decision to compete had been made, I began what seemed to be the necessary preparatory work. The possibility of outlanding was not seriously considered, but a ground crew seemed to be expedient during assembly and disassembly; besides, everybody else had one. A husky 17 year old was found who considered the whole thing interesting. Subsequently, I have made sure prior to a contest that the crew can drive a stick shift and pull a trailer. Other preparations were limited to obtaining a current Sectional and a borrowed $9.95 cartridge camera. No camera mount was made as it seemed simple enough to one handedly hold the camera and push the button. Radio, oxygen, emergency kit and more than a quart of water were believed to be non-essential.

We arrived early, found room on the field and assembled my L-Spatz 55 without a hitch. After washing it because everybody else washed their planes, we partook of the culinary delights of breakfast at the local eatery. The flavor had a touch of after taste of someone else's supper, altogether not too bad if one didn't dwell on it. On finishing breakfast, it was still early and it would have been bad form to perch and wait for the Pilot's Meeting to begin. Moreover, it was a good time to meet, talk to and watch the other contestants fuss with their equipment. Why did they stuff more than a vario, ASI and altimeter into their panels?

Finally, it was time. Naturally, I was late for having forgotten to carry pencil and paper and had to sit almost out of earshot. The task for Class B was Drake, an unmarked dirt strip identified only by longitude and latitude and return - a distance of 97 miles. The wind was going to blow from the west and there would be thermals. The Contest Director probably said more but I didn't understand the import or significance of any other information. A hat containing numbered slips of paper was passed and some compassionate person kindly told me that the drawn number would indicate the order in which take-off times were chosen. Here was a first contest decision and I wasn't going to botch it and selected a time in the middle.

The meeting finally broke up and everybody seemed to be very busy with paperwork. I couldn't understand why as I had managed to find the turnpoints during the meeting. In order to appear equally busy, I showed my crew the turnpoints, the straight line projected flight path, the closest roads, and gave him the telephone number of contest headquarters and a dime. This took about 25 seconds and everybody else was still very busy. So as not to appear completely uncomprehending we sauntered off, loaded the camera and polished the canopy again.

After another interminable wait, it was time to pull the plane the half mile to the start grid. On arriving, some officious person told me to strap on my parachute, take a picture, check the controls and sit tight. This seemed very demeaning and shabby treatment of a Contest Pilot, but I got back at him. The L-Spatz, with an occupant, is very hard to maneuver on the ground and it took 4 men and a dainty woman to get the plane and me onto the runway.

Following a series of hand signals backed up by yells, I became hooked to the towplane, which promptly started to stretch the towline as my plane wasn't yet ready to move. It may be well to point out that the L-Spatz has a forward ski which at rest supports about 350 lbs of the 600 lb glider. Necessarily, the friction between the metal shoe and the runway is very high so a very great force is required to initiate movement. It is also a good way of breaking weak tow ropes before one becomes airborne. Once movement commences, a violent forward motion occurs in conjunction with a severe upward pitching. Instinct dictates a reflex action for down elevator which immediately puts the skid back on the ground and the glider stops. Take-off is only accomplished if the tow pilot is either very persistent or oblivious to the whole problem.

Lift off was finally made despite unspoken words of doom and disaster from the spectators and I was fully confident of winning glory and fame. But not for long. The L-Spatz has a tow redline of 65 mph, and I was flying at 75 mph when the tow plane lifted off. I had become used to Las Horvath's tow pilots who would stay at 65 mph until lift off, then very considerately, would slow down to 55-60 mph. After clearing the Prescott runway, we hit turbulence which became worse the higher we climbed and we were still at 75 mph. The "Joy of Soaring", my newly found bible, said to wiggle the rudder as a signal to slow down. The tow pilot must have been ham handed and blind - nothing happened except the wings groaned more and the fabric began to flap in staccato. There was no alternative but to release and hope to reach the airport.

It felt awfully good to fly at a reasonable 40 mph even if at 600 feet and 2 or 3 miles away. A thermal blundered my way and carried me up to 9500 feet (Prescott is at 5000 msl). This seemed like the propitious moment to go through the start gate. As I had no radio, I had been told to begin at the I.P. (whatever that was), fly straight, waggle the wings and cross the start gate at less than 8200 feet. The start maneuver only cost 2500 feet in altitude but the early friendly thermal was relocated and I had become a competing Contest Pilot, racing to Drake. Promptly, I lost track of everyone else and was very much alone.

Paulden was reached and overflown without any serious difficulty, aided to a great extent by a strong rear quartering wind. With the first glimpse of Drake, an inkling of the innate perversity of Contest Directors was suggested - there appeared to be no landable fields close by. Nevertheless, my altitude was 3000 feet AGL and surely I could fly to Drake and make it back beyond the east escarpment of Chino Valley. Drake hove into view neatly in line with my banked left wing but it took two more circles and a two mile drift to wind the camera and take the picture. For those of you who have not had the opportunity, Drake is a very easily recognizable landmark from 2000 feet.

Flying northwest to the second turn point and into a strong quartering headwind at 40 mph can be very sobering but with superior dead reckoning skills an earlier abandoned thermal was encountered. It was recognized by its ragged core which refused to conform to my perfectly circular flight path. At least I was now climbing at almost 300 fpm and refused to leave it until Drake again appeared under my wing. Took another picture from 3500 feet so as not to waste the trip.

Again an assault on the escarpment was made but in a more northerly heading. The terrain suddenly changed to scrub pine and there was little turbulence except from the wind. Something strange and unknown had happened. By bore sighting my flight path, it also became evident that I would miss the escarpment edge by at least -50 feet, not counting the trees. At this point a rational man would have retreated to Drake - I kept on flying and started looking for gullies along the edge. About a mile from the edge, the variometer began creeping up to -100, -50, -25, 0 and finally +25 fpm and then just as smoothly dropped off. On reflection, it must have been mild ridge lift, but whatever, ecstasy reigned as I cleared the edge by 200 feet and entered Chino Valley and landable terrain. A thermal was soon spotted and carried me to 10,500 feet beneath a line of clouds.

This was my first experience with other than sporadically located clouds and it was very exciting to explore in zigzag fashion the differing lift pattern beneath and upwind of the clouds though their bases were many thousand feet above me. After gamboling with the lift surplusage and cruising along the east side of Chino Valley, thoughts of locating the second turn point precipitated. Readily visible Picacho Butte seemed to be across the valley from where the turn point should be so it became my reference. Is it unreasonable to ask for a turn point visible from at least 3000 AGL? My inkling of the nature of the Contest Directors and their genealogy was confirmed. It cost another 500 feet to take the photo (forgot to wind the film again).

Over the hills just south of the turn point a 500 fpm thermal was cored and carried me to 10,000 feet. This is easy. So easy that lesser thermals were discarded until the vario pegged at 1000 fpm. It carried me up to 12,700 feet at which point I broke off for I had no oxygen and had experienced the disabling effects of hypoxia in the Air Force altitude chamber. Nothing takes more character than to deliberately leave 1300 fpm measured, not indicated, lift.

About half way back, somewhere north and east of Jupiter, even sporadic lift ended and despondency replaced euphoria. There was some cloud formation to the west and over forest but nothing ahead nor over landable Chino Valley. Have you ever held a panel discussion with yourself to establish a course of action? Anyway, the cloud formation won and a race was on to get to the cloud generator before the ground got to me. About half way down the glide path a ranch house was spotted a few degrees off at closer range than desired, a cleared area of sorts was located adjacent to the house - an alternate landing field was in hand, as the good book suggests. Very close to setting up a quasi landing pattern, the variometer did its thing again and my wings waggled as a departing gesture to an excited dog. This thermal plus some reduced sink carried me to the hills north of Chino Valley.

Even a pre-solo neophyte has heard or read about blue holes and before me a picture perfect one lay. The clouds were all around the Prescott plateau except for a lonely cloud over Chino Valley. Should I take the sage course to Granite Mountain and cut east to Prescott Airport or fly the straight 11 mile route via the lonely cloud? Clearly, straightest is shortest and a thermal was marked. The thermal was dying and nothing but residual sink remained at 1000 feet AGL or less accompanied by a strong quartering wind. The agony was intense in being so close.

A farmer was harrowing (plowing?) a field and the dust gave a good indication of both wind direction and speed (that's what one is supposed to look for). However, once the decision to land was made, field selection became a necessity. The harrowing farmer's field was too far downwind to make an upwind landing, some of the unimproved terrain looked rough and I was not yet relegated to landing on an athletic field. A sparsely populated trailer court development appeared best as no poles could be seen in one section and it had a road in line with the wind. However, final would have been over power lines (a no-no). Nevertheless, I selected it and approached the power lines at 65 mph with the boards out to provide a climb capability if the power line height had been misjudged. The power lines were cleared without altering the flight path. An unnoticed two foot mound ran down the middle of the road which required a quick bit of sashaying and nothing was hurt or broken, least of all my pride.

The nearest trailer had no phone but the occupant was delighted to see me, handed me a beer in true soaring fashion and thought it a privilege to drive to Prescott Airport three miles away to find my crew.

In Class B for that day, Dick Gorton, the only finisher, flew all the way to Seligman looking for the second turnpoint and apparently photographed the wrong strip. The only other contestant was one of Gordon Dutt's boys who bogged down somewhere close to Drake. Hence, I was given the 1000 points but that was only of incidental satisfaction.

I have continued to compete whenever possible because a contest is one of the few times for which I have enough audacity to ask, cajole, threaten or bribe someone to suffer the discomfort and panic-punctuated-boredom of a ground crew so that I can fly cross country in an effort to meet and best the constantly changing challenges. In answer to the title, I must paraphrase A.E. Slater, of British gliding fame: The world's population is now of two kinds: on the one hand, those who cannot imagine why anyone would fly cross country without an engine when it is so much easier to fly with one; on the other hand, those who know the answer to that question but cannot put it into words.

KEEP THE FAITH, BABY by John Baird, April 1975.

The other day, while in a careless frame of mind, I said that I had an article type subject in mind for Air Currents, and guess what? Ben Stanton (the Editor) heard me and there hasn't been a minute's peace since. So to get myself ready for this season's soaring competition (you'll know why after reading this article) and to get even with Ben, HERE IT COMES...

This article is mostly true, the names have been changed to protect the innocent, and it is about how I tried to improve my soaring last year, the method that I used, that is, and the results. Some of you readers may know that last year it became clear that my flying suffered from a lack of faith. It was not possible to just go off into the strange air with great speed and confidence that the glider would stay away from the ground. Even though others did it and did not hit the ground, when I did go off into the strange air, it was with care and slowness. Faith was required, especially on days when the ground did stay close no matter how hard I pulled on the stick or how loud I yelled. Faith was what I was after last year and the method was to tempt it and then let it be true that positive thinking would win out and good lift would hump out of the sand and rocks and lakes and cattle feeding pens to move the glider at great speed relative to the competitors over the course to victory.

Now, if a lot of the intermediate practice is omitted, and we move to the last contest day of the last contest weekend of the ASA contest for 1974 we will see that the faith thing was still in vogue with my sailplane and me and now with my crew, and we will see that faith and positive thinking is not too swift. I hit the ground the shortest distance out for all of the season for the Open Class thereby earning the Lead C Award, and that flight represented only a slight extension of the degree to which faith was examined as a soaring aid. That flight could be explained in detail, but it is too sad and not good for my preparations for this year.

The good part of the faith practice for my preparations for this year has to do with other more successful flights and the contest at Minden, Nevada, one of the better places in the world. Some of the better flights too were made at Prescott in the spring. On one weekend, I went up with no crew, planning to fly with great care, but the weather was very strong and there was no reason to have a crew. Other pilots and I traded assembly aid, launch aid and the like. At the end of the weekend someone inquired as to the nature of my invisible crew and getting the answer, "Didn't bring any," said, "Boy, does he have faith." It was showing. Flying out of Prescott is a good place to learn faith, it is fun too and there is a soaring operation up there this year.

But on to Minden. On Day One, I won the day against all those pilots that went to the wrong (slow) turnpoint and got a 6th overall. On the second day, I was 3rd overall till they looked at my turnpoint photos. Other than making me sick, this miserable turn of events was another opportunity to practice faith. I had lost over 700 points. The next flight was not too good and there was trouble en route that only faith got me out of; got a 10th daily and moved up to 25th overall. On the fourth day, the photo sickness had gone away and even though I had flown into the trees twice, I got a 4th for the day and moved to 21st overall. Faith was working. It was not such a good day either; many didn't finish. On the 5th day, there was a wave and lots of pilots did not finish; got a 4th and moved to 14th overall. How about that? Yes, how about all that? It turns out that is not too good considering all things, but for me it is better than ever before and it is all the product of faith. (And "winning by not losing"). But the last day is the best of all. I got a first and moved to 9th overall.

It was a problem type day with unreliable thermals, weak waves and lots of wind. That faith really pays off is indicated by the fact that the least number of points I picked up on others in the first ten places is 101. Anyway, since it was the last contest day, it was clear that I wasn't going to get to talk about the flight at the pilots' meeting, or at all. Not true. At the banquet, there was a slot for the day's winner to get up and tell lies. I didn't think anyone really wanted to hear about flights so I said something nice about the great contest and walked away from the place. From the floor came, "Well, how did you do it?" I think it was Dan Schat's wife, who is a doll, which is part of the reason for all this. The faith aspects of the flight are hidden in the following.

On tow we went through an area of lift that felt like a big thermal and gained more than 1,000 feet in it. The tow ended in an area of weak lift, so I went back to the good place, got the gate and approach altitude and went to the gate. It was rough getting under and so the day looked like better than the task indicated. After the gate, I went toward course and some hills and there was only chop and no lift. Can't remember if I started again, or decided that it was a lousy day and to get on with it. It probably took longer to decide that so I probably struggled up, went to the good place and found nothing, then decided on the lousiness, collected faith and then got on with it. The first leg was to Stead Air Force Base and took one over Carson City, along some hills, across Reno, in through a little valley in the lee of a mountain, to Stead, the first turn. So from the gate, I followed some low hills to Carson City with enough altitude to cross to the big hill north of Carson. There was some delayed sink along the way and a glider was circling on the big hill. Went under him, it was Striedieck, and he had no lift so went on.

Faith said Reno is a big airport and there will be lift in the cup in the hills this side of there. Getting to the cup at a little below the hills the thermal appeared between the spoilers and outer wing joint and it was 37 mm in diameter. I centered it though, still full of water out of necessity. And when centered, from nowhere there were two gliders with me. It stopped upgoing at 8,000 feet which is just too low to proceed without faith. I had it. Aimed at the turnpoint, it looked as if there was no more lift, one would have to make a downwind landing. I made some excursions to places which should have shadows, got to the turnpoint with about 1,000 feet AGL. On the way I saw gliders just way too far downwind from course and not climbing very well either. Not for me. Did not have any really good ideas from the first turn so not wanting downwind, I went upwind. The course to the second turnpoint is just about back over Minden and on to Bridgeport.

The task was set to favor the use of wave, if there was any, and otherwise not to get anyone too far downwind away from the mountains. Going upwind from the first turn gets you to a dry lake which is soggy and some low hills, these hills going south get you to Mt. Peavine and on south across a big chink to the Sierra Nevadas, the real mountains. Before I got to the hills by the dry lake, it looked like I was going to land in them but as I got closer, the sink went away, turned to lift and then to a fierce but choppy thermal that gave an average rate of climb of about 1,200 fpm. This had to be true since there were clouds over a similar situation with some bigger hills further north. That is faith. This thermal was going to go up to 15,000 feet and then into the wave for an easy flight. Not true. It stopped at 9,100 feet and with nothing to do but head for the second turn, I did that.

There had to be the good thermal into the wave from Peavine so went there without losing too much and there was no big saving, laborless thermal there. I zigged and zagged, worked some chop for only a waste of time and decided the big thermal was on the other side of the chink. The chink sink was great so I told myself that I could land at the truck stop where the girl servicing vehicles had a nice smile, crossed to the rocks and found another very rough and strong thermal. It took me almost to the tallest local rock and stopped. Ridge soar, it is the only answer and so I did, very close to the rocks and trees, along slopes too shallow for complete comfort but with faith borne of the absolute fact that air does not blow far through rocks. I was getting the idea that the only way to get to Bridgeport was to relax and ridge soar there. After the turbulence on the slopes of Mt. Rose the shores of Lake Tahoe were a joy. Nice view, smooth air and enough lift to cruise at 75 to 80 knots. Going by Minden on the west, I was high enough to see the place and advised honorable crew of my whereabouts in code. Billie stays at the base because that is where she told me to land. It became apparent that it would be difficult to ridge soar all the way to Bridgeport, no hills all the way. So I plan to get as far down as great speed on this course would permit, leave the hills and let me get blown across two valleys to another hill behind which sits the second turn.

I do it and it works even better than planned because of some gain on the hill between the two valleys. Ridge soaring the hell (spelling is right) north of Bridgeport is great sport. If you make it over this rock, it is much shorter than going way around where those other gliders were, and finally, the last spur, and *it has no ridge lift on it*! To get in and out of the turn with any kind of rapidity takes more altitude than these trees have. Found another thermal in a cup, tiptoed in and out (tip toe means fly looking for waves, thermal streets and otherwise minimizing sink), got back to the thermal in the cup at the bottom with two other gliders and dropped the water because it was the last flight of the contest, and I was going to ridge soar all the way back with the wind helping. The trees looked friendly with the wind blowing up the slope through their leaves.

Once on the top of the hell hill, the course home just runs along one continuous range, past a short chink, onto another scalable hill and then down a range of hills that decrease in height and put you off at the airport at Minden. On the way, I ran into strong ridge lift which was a thermal, put on 1,000 feet (not needed) and flew home.

By this time, the flight seemed to be easy, hence slow, so I was just glad to have finished. Hetty said that I was a half hour faster than Bill Ivans, our leader, so I knew that I was not the slowest and that was nice. When I finally found out that I had won, I said, "UP WITH FAITH!"

Now I have to figure out how to rationalize the flight which earned me the Lead C....

TWO LONG FINAL GLIDES by Jim George, June 1975.

This article won the very first Joseph C. Lincoln Award and was subsequently reprinted in SOARING magazine as a tribute to its author, Jim George, after he was killed in a soaring accident.

THE CLAXON HORN ROARED ITS SIGNAL TO SCRAMBLE; A FAST START OF THE JET ENGINES AND A ROLLING TAKE OFF DOWN THE METAL PLANKING RUNWAY AT K-13, SUWON, KOREA. THE DATE, JULY 13, 1952. MY MISSION, TO LEAD A FLIGHT OF FOUR F-86E SABRES TO INTERCEPT MIG 15s ATTACKING OUR F-84 FIGHTER-BOMBERS ON THE YALU RIVER DIVIDING NORTH KOREA AND RED CHINA.

"VECTOR 330, ANGELS 33, BANDIT TRACKS FROM ANTUNG". FROM OUR GROUND CONTROL STATIONS I WAS BEING GIVEN CLIMB INSTRUCTIONS WHILE MAKING "S" TURNS TO ALLOW MY FLIGHT TO JOIN UP. WE WERE TO CLIMB TO 33,000 FEET ON A HEADING OF 330 DEGREES AND COULD EXPECT INTERCEPTION BY MIGs CLIMBING OUT SOUTH FROM THE CHINESE SANCTUARY, ANTUNG AIRFIELD, JUST ACROSS THE YALU RIVER.

TEST FIRING OUR 6-50 CAL MACHINE GUNS AS WE CROSS THE FRONT LINES, WE CLIMBED HIGHER AND HIGHER. "BUZZARD LEAD, YOU'RE CONNING," MY WINGMAN CALLED. "ROGER," THAT IS WHAT I WANTED TO HEAR, ANSWERING HIS CALL. USING A TRICK TOLD ME BY JIM JABARA, I SIGNALED MY WING MAN TO DROP DOWN WITH ME TO ABOUT 2,500 FEET BELOW AND ABOUT 5,000 FEET WIDE OF MY ELEMENT. THERE I COULD BE COVERED FROM ABOVE AND BEHIND AND IN TURN MANEUVER TO PROTECT MY ELEMENT (NUMBERS 3 & 4 SABRES). THE SECRET WAS TO PUT OUR HIGH ELEMENT JUST BELOW THE CONDENSATION LEVEL (WHERE THE JET EXHAUST TURNS TO TRAILING WHITE CLOUDS - CONTRAILS) WHERE THEY WERE NOT CONNING. THUS, ANY ATTACKERS FROM ABOVE WOULD HAVE TO PENETRATE THE CON LAYER AND WE COULD PICK THEM UP EASILY. IT TOOK THE CHINESE A LONG TIME TO FIGURE THAT ONE OUT.

...Slowly the tow ship pulled my Diamant up to the 2,000 foot release altitude. Wagging his wing was the signal to release, I then glided over to the only thermal near the start gate. There nearly 49 other sailplanes circled in weak lift trying to get high enough to make their starts. It was the third day of the 39th United States National Soaring Championships at Minden, Nevada, 1972 - the task, a 189 mile triangle from Minden to Air Sailing to Schurtz to Minden.

Very slowly, each ship would climb up to start gate altitude, make a slow start and return to the same thermal. Looking off to the north on course, I saw a small cu building up east of Mt Rose and right over Reno. This is unusual for this time of day and I knew the time to start was now! Most others were holding back for better conditions, but the strategy of a few would pay off.

By the time I had reached the area north of Virginia City, the build up had become a high thunderstorm and had covered the entire northern first leg. Those behind would never make it through. I was flying just below the thunderstorm, making good time, when suddenly the lift stopped...

CRUISING AT 350 KNOTS AND USING THE BASIC FLIGHT TACTICS THAT BARON VON RICHTHOFEN HAD USED SOME 35 YEARS BEFORE, WE SEARCHED THE SKY SEEKING OUR PREY. THE FINEST RUSSIAN FIGHTER, THE MIG 15. SUDDENLY - "BUZZARD LEADER, BOGIES 4 O'CLOCK HIGH." MY IMMEDIATE VERBAL RESPONSE WAS: "BUZZARD FLIGHT-CADILLAC." IN A FLASH, 4 SETS OF 120 GAL EXTERNAL FUEL TANKS WERE JET-TISONED, FALLING AWAY LIKE EIGHT HUGE BOMBS. SINCE EACH F-86 CARRIED TWO EXTERNAL WING TANKS AND THEY COST THE TAXPAYER ABOUT THE SAME PRICE AS A 1952 CADILLAC - NO BETTER CODE WORD FOR DROPPING THEM. THESE TANKS WOULD END UP AS ROOFS, WALLS, BATHTUBS, YOU NAME IT, ALL FOR THE RESIDENTS OF NORTH KOREA.

NOW I PICKED THEM UP: A FLIGHT OF SIX MIGs DIVING DOWN ON MY TOP ELEMENT. BREAKING HARD TO THEIR RIGHT AS THE MIG LEADER STARTED TO FIRE, MY ELEMENT ESCAPED THE FIRING PASS. AS USUAL, THE MIGs WOULD NOT STAY AROUND TO FIGHT, BUT JUST DIVE ON PAST, KNOWING THEY COULD OUT DIVE US.

NOW THE MIGs PICKED UP ME AND MY WINGMAN, THIS IS WHAT I WANTED. WAITING UNTIL THEY WERE NEARLY IN FIRING RANGE, MY WINGMAN CALLED - "BUZZARD LEADER BREAK HARD RIGHT": INSTINC-TIVELY I HAULED HARD OVER AND PUT 5 G's ON MY SHIP, PULLING UP AT THE SAME TIME. LARGE RED BASKETBALL SIZE FIRE BALLS CAME FLOATING BY ME - THE MIG LEADER WAS PUMPING HIS 20 MM CANNON FIRE INTO MY PROXIMITY. AS I PULLED UP INTO A TIGHT CLIMBING TURN, IT CAUSED THE TWO MIGs TO OVER-SHOOT AND PULL OUT IN FRONT AND BELOW ME. MY TACTICS HAD WORKED AND HE HAD MADE THE FATAL MISTAKE. A HARD HIGH G BARREL ROLL OVER THE TOP, PUT ME RIGHT ON THEIR TAILS.

The thunderstorm blow-off had killed all the lift for miles, no choice but to glide toward the turn point. Lower and lower I glided, suddenly a sunny spot appeared about 10 miles ahead, that should provide a thermal. Arriving with about 700 feet, I had not seen one of the other 52 contestants. As I started to turn in a weak thermal, I was suddenly joined by 4 other sailplanes, all diving for my flashing wings. I had the only thermal around. Climbing away and into the turn point, things improved. Now I was far down wind of the storm and into clear air. Others behind were in trouble as repeated calls for crews to get to assorted fields and pick up their pilot were being received on the radio. They had made their mistake.

Half way down the next leg, I saw a sailplane circling right on course and with this marker, I speeded up to join Dick Schreder and his ASW 17. Looking beyond the next turn point and back toward Minden, I could see a line of thunderstorms built up between me and the finish line...

NOW I HAD A GOOD LOOK AT THE GUY WHO WAS TRYING TO KILL ME. THE MIG 15 WAS PAINTED A BRILLIANT PURPLE ON THE UPPER SURFACES OF THE LITTLE FIGHTER. RED STARS MARKED THE WINGS AND FUSELAGE.

DIVING STRAIGHT FOR THE YALU RIVER AND HIS HOPED FOR SANCTUARY, THE MIG LEADER AND HIS WINGMAN TRIED EVASIVE MANEUVERS TO SHAKE US OFF. MY WINGMAN WAS CALLING "BUZZARD

LEADER, YOU'RE CLEAR." NOW I COULD CONCENTRATE ON CLOSING AND TRACKING. EVERY TURN BY THE MIGs GAVE ME AN ADVANTAGE, AS I COULD CUT HIM OFF IN THE TURN AND CLOSE THE GAP.

MY RADAR GUN SIGHT WAS SHOWING A LOCK-ON AT 2,800 FOOT RANGE, THEN IT WOULD BREAK LOCK AND RANGE OUT. AGAIN, A SERIES OF TWISTING TURNS BY THE MIGs. THE #2 MIG PILOT MUST HAVE BEEN A NEWCOMER, AS HE IS WAY OUT OF POSITION AND NOT DOING HIS LEADER ANY GOOD. ANOTHER LOCK-ON AND I AM ABLE TO TRACK FOR A FEW SECONDS AND FIRE. I CAN SEE THE TRACERS GOING BEHIND THE WINGMAN. THE SOUND OF THE MACHINE GUNS MUST HAVE PANICKED THE MIG WINGMAN, AS HE SNAPROLLS UNDER AND STARTS AN UNCONTROLLED SPIN OUT OF THE FLIGHT.

ANOTHER TURN OF THE MIG LEADER AND I CLOSE TO 1500 FEET - ANOTHER BREAK LOCK BY THE RADAR GUNSIGHT. THE DAMN THING IS UNRELIABLE! SO I TURN OFF THE RADAR FUNCTION OF THE SIGHT AND GO TO A FIXED SIGHT. NOW I AM ON EQUAL TERMS WITH RICHTHOFEN. JUST OLD DUCK HUNTING WINDAGE. PULL LEAD AND FIRE - ONLY AT 450 KNOTS. TRACER BULLETS GO OVER HIS WINGS - TOO MUCH LEAD. EASE OFF - NOW FLECKS OF SILVER FLASHES PECK AT THE PURPLE WINGS. PIECES START RIPPING OFF THE MIG. IT DOESN'T TAKE MUCH TO SPOIL THE CONFIGURATION OF A WING AT .9 MACH. SUDDENLY, THE MIG CANOPY FLASHES BY MY LEFT WING TIP - THIS FOLLOWED BY A HARD INSIDE SNAPROLL - AND THE PURPLE MACHINE DISINTEGRATES.

"BUZZARD LEADER - I GOT BINGO MINUS 4." BAD NEWS - MY WINGMAN HAD JUST ANNOUNCED HE IS 400 LBS OF FUEL BELOW OUR SAFE GET HOME FUEL RESERVE.

The Diamant climbs by Schreder and on into the second turn point. Suddenly, a speedy Libelle comes into my thermal with a high speed chandelle. 7V embellished on its tail - Ray Gimmey (the future champion) had joined me. Into the final turn and on home. Ray flies a little ahead of me and driving hard in hopes of losing me. The blocking thunderstorm is now directly on course for home. 7V thinks he can lose me by pulling up into the bottom edge of the clouds. Might as well use old Ray, so I tuck the Diamant some 15 feet directly behind and below the Libelle. Using Ray as an artificial horizon, I fly instruments on him; knowing he will not turn, just stay on course. It's black inside, but I just keep glued to 7V's empennage.

We break out and Ray does not know I am just behind him. But now it tells - we are on a 50 mile final glide, with a solid line of rain showers and the Pine Nut Mountains between us and the finish line...

CLIMBING BACK UP TO NEAR 30,000 FEET AND HEADING SOUTH TOWARD HOME BASE, MY WINGMAN AND I BEGIN TO SWEAT THE FUEL. WE HAVE SOME 200 MILES TO GO AND EVEN WITH THE PREVAILING TAIL WINDS, WE WON'T MAKE IT. I HAVE 600 LBS. OF FUEL SHOWING - THE AMOUNT WE ARE SUPPOSED TO HAVE ENTERING THE PATTERN AT K-13.

LEVELING OUT, WE THROTTLE BACK TO NEAR IDLE % RPM - THIS GIVES US ABOVE MINIMUM FUEL FLOW, BUT BELOW THE SAFE TAIL

PIPE TEMPERATURE. NOW BEGINS THE LONG FINAL GLIDE HOME. PERHAPS I CAN SHUT DOWN AND DEAD STICK IT DOWN TO A LOWER ALTITUDE AND THEN RESTART THE ENGINE - IT HAS BEEN DONE BEFORE, BUT YOU ARE GAMBLING ON THE ENGINE SEIZING AND IF THAT HAPPENS - THAT'S ALL, SHE WROTE. BETTER TO CHANCE A DEAD STICK AT A LOWER ALTITUDE WHEN THE FUEL RUNS OUT.

GROUND SPEED IS LOOKING GOOD. STARTING THAT GRADUAL DESCENT FROM ABOUT 125 MILES OUT, WE HEAD DOWN THE COAST FOR INCHON HARBOR, JUST IN CASE WE HAVE TO BAIL OUT, OUR NAVY COULD PICK US UP. CROSSING THE LARGE FLEET OF U.S. NAVAL VESSELS, BLACK SMOKE APPEARS BELOW US IN SMALL PUFFS. THOSE DAMN NAVY GUNNERS CAN'T TELL F-86's FROM MIGs. ALL SWEPT WING FIGHTERS LOOK THE SAME TO THEM AND THEY ARE FIRING AT US.

Now Ray Gimmey drops his nose and speeds up to 85 knots to keep on his glide slope. Here is where the Diamant falls away. Gimmey's well watered Libelle has too much L/D for me and I fall lower behind his flight path. Looking up ahead, I see I will just barely clear the Pine Nut Mountain Range. Ray has 1,000 feet on me now and we run into a rain shower.

Beads of rain drops form on the Diamant's wings and down, down, I go. The sink rate is doubled. The mountains are higher than my glide slope. But a sudden break in the showers allows me to see a saddle-back crossing to the right of course. No choice - dive for it and just scrape across the top of a small meadow, almost hitting a herd of wild mustangs. Overhead 7V clears by a high margin and steams onto the finish line some 14 miles away.

Drier air and near zero sink give me new hope. Slowing down, I start a white knuckle glide toward Douglas County Airport and the finish line. Lower and lower I sink; a little zoom, then a little "s" here and there, closer and closer the ground gets. Two miles out and about 800 feet. Thank goodness there are no obstacles en route; I could not clear them. Zero sink - a bubble here - gliding to within a pattern final approach much lower than standard, I cross the threshold with about 25 feet.

Riding ground effect for all it's worth, I have 5,000 feet of runway ahead, with the finish line about two thirds of the way down. Finally, not being able to hold off, we touch down and roll on and on. Fifty feet to go and there is Joyce waiting to catch my wing - just crossing the line under my own energy. We clocked 66.0 for the day. Third place - and we beat Gimmey by .5 mph...

THIRTY MILES OFF I CAN SEE K-13, SUWON AIRFIELD; DOWN TO 90 LBS OF FUEL, I SWEAT. HOW CAN I EXPLAIN THE LOSS OF TWO SHIPS - IN EXCHANGE FOR TWO MIGs? PRESSING ON AND ANGLING FOR A STRAIGHT-IN APPROACH, EASE BACK ON THE POWER - GOT TO LEAVE THE WINGMAN SOMETHING TO PLAY WITH - HOLD THE GEAR, NO FLAPS, GET THE MOST OUT OF THE GLIDE. FUEL 40 LBS, FIELD CLEAR, 1,500 FEET, 2 MILES, CAN JUST BARELY MAKE IT - IF SHE KEEPS RUNNING. "BUZZARD TWO, WE WILL MAKE A FORMATION LANDING, TIGHTEN UP," I CALL.

"K-13 TOWER, TWO FOR A STRAIGHT-IN, LOW ON FUEL, GEAR DOWN AND LOCKED." WE MADE IT, PERFECT TOUCH DOWN AND ROLL OUT.

THE PLANKING UNDER OUR WHEELS REALLY SOUNDED GOOD AS WE ROLLED TOWARD THE TAXI TURN OFF - JUST CLEARING THE RUNWAY; FLAME OUT!

Some pilots fly by faith; others by fear!

TRAVELS WITH DAVE - From the Saga of the Blanik Racing Team by Philip C. Todd, March 1978.

As one of the country's foremost soon-to-be up-and-coming young competition pilots, I was faced with the prospect of spending my first competition season without a ship. Dave Robertson, fellow gliding deviant and soon-to-be up-and-coming young competition pilot, was faced with a similar situation. From this common need sprang the entity which would be known as the Blanik Racing Team.

"There's the airport," Dave announced.
Prescott at last. I watched Juliet, the Club Blanik, sway on her trailer as we made the last turn into the airport. We swung around the line of ships, crews, and families encamped on the grass apron for another weekend of the Arizona State Championship and position the trailer for Juliet's assembly.

"What time is it, Dave?"
"Let's see, the big hand's on... ten thirty-seven."
"Ah well. We miss the Pilots' Meeting again," I said.
"We'd have been alright if you hadn't driven for 10 miles with a flat on the trailer."
"We wouldn't have if you'd noticed it earlier. Come on, let's find out what the task is."

We walked casually through the encampment toward the start gate, mentally noting who was getting ready for lunch and could therefore be expected to provide some sustenance (lunch) soon and also noting idle bodies to help with the herculean task of Blanik assembly.

"Hi, Bob, how's it going?" I called, as Dave and I approached our arch competitor, Bob von Hellens, who was busily engaged wiping fresh dust from the leading edge of his immaculate 1-26. "Destroys laminar flow," he claims.

"Well, glad to see you two finally made it," said Bob cheerfully. "Guess I don't have the sky to myself after all."

"Yeah, you know how it is. Say, what did the weatherman have to say this morning?" asked Dave.

Bob reached into the cockpit to get out his notes from the pilots' meeting. I took the right shoulder, Dave the left.

"Task Prescott, Dewey, Paulden and return, 59.2 miles," I read.
"Thermals 500 fpm to 12K. Start of lift 10:30. Wind SW at 10," read Dave.
"Gee, Dave, I don't know about that," I said, looking at a sky already filled with towering cu's. "What do you think?"

"Well," said Dave, pondering deeply, "start of lift was probably about 9:06 which puts the start of the over-development at 1:14. We'll just have to start late and go like stink."

"Sounds good to me. Thanks, Bob."
We then went in search of help for Juliet's assembly. We have had to assemble and disassemble Juliet sixteen times during the season and on 14 of these

times the wind was blowing over 20 mph. This time was no exception. By the time we had rounded up the necessary extra bodies to assist with the assembly, the wind had increased to 23.2 mph and the cu-nim over the airport was looking awfully dark. About the fifth time we were taking Juliet apart we realized that the job would be greatly simplified if she were pointed into the wind because then the wings wouldn't weigh so much.

As soon as Juliet was assembled, our helpers disappeared into the sagebrush and we began to search for more assistants to help us walk Juliet to the other end of the runway. Because the runway is over 7000 feet long, this task always requires four people; one on the wingtip, one on the tail and two resting in the cockpit. About this time the cu-nim moved east to Mingus Mountain and the wind dropped back below 10 mph. Rumblings from deep down inside caused us to halt our search for helpers and begin the search for sustenance.

Camille asked whether our ground crew could help move the ship to the other end of the runway. Ground crew?

"Oh my! Don't you boys have a ground crew?" she asked.

Now we really had no cause for offense from this statement because Camille was graciously providing us with lunch at that point.

"What's a ground crew?" I asked innocently.

"You know," said Dave. "It's someone who follows you on the ground with the glider trailer so that when you land out you can call them on the radio and they come and get you and help put the glider in the trailer."

"Oh, one of those! No, we don't have one, Camille. It wouldn't do much good, anyway. We don't have a radio either."

"No ground crew and no radio! I don't see how you boys manage!" Camille exclaimed.

"It's easy," said Dave, biting into a ham and swiss on rye. "We never land out."

The first launch was delayed until 1:30 due to the inclement weather. As per our standard strategy of start last/finish first, we were last on the start grid at 2:30. With the reluctant air of two unsuspecting bystanders, we made a leisurely trek to the far end of the runway. From the bottom of the cloud over Mingus Mountain, wisps of rain began to appear.

"Look, it's starting to rain over Mingus," panted one of our helpers as we passed the middle of the runway.

"A little after 1:00, isn't it, Dave?" I asked.

"1:14 as a matter of fact," he replied happily.

Juliet waited patiently for her turn to take the air.

"Come on, Dave. It's almost time," I said as the towplane was turning final.

"Let's make a Le Mans start today!" said Dave.

"What?"

"You know what a..."

"Yeah, I know. All right. Let's go." We sprinted toward Juliet, yelling and screaming at the top of our lungs.

"Hook up the tow rope!"

"Hold the wing tip!"

"Here we come!"

I had lost the toss earlier so I got in back while Dave jumped into the front seat.

"Roll us out!"

"Hook us up!"

"Let's go!"

We continued yelling while fumbling for the seat belts. The towplane stretched out the tow rope and the canopy closed.

"Ready?" called Dave.

"All set!" A new record for time to launch!

Down the long runway we rolled. With the help of the gentle southwest headwind, the towplane staggered into the air before running out of pavement and our climb began. Prescott is 5000 feet above sea level so climbs take a little longer than us lowlanders are used to. Dave and I settled down into the routine of flying, both of us watching intently for all other aircraft in the vicinity. We released from tow and Dave pulled smoothly into a thermal.

"von Hellens is in the gaggle to the north and Kurzman is out to the west," I called cheerfully. 1-26's are so easy to identify.

Despite our best efforts at staying with the lift, the thermal had the gall to up and die on us. We went in search of another. With all those clouds, there must surely be some lift. Sink, too, but that is incidental. We found another thermal and Dave pulled smoothly into it.

"My turn," I called and Dave relinquished the controls. At the proper moment, I wrapped the circle up tight and, of course, we were then properly centered in the lift. "Would you mind moving your chin so I can see the vario? That one in front is the only one which works..."

"Oops, sorry. I think we're going to have to get high and stay high for this one," said Dave, surveying the clouds thoughtfully. "If we start in about 25 minutes there will be a cloud street into and out of the first turn."

"Sounds good to me but that makes the start especially important," I added.

"Right. We need a boomer right after the gate."

We topped out and headed back to the start gate area to hunt for our boomer.

"von Hellens is out there to the west but I lost Kurzman," I said.

"I think he's down to the south a bit. Hasn't started though."

We searched vainly for the boomer we needed. We made a practice run through the start gate to avoid going over the start time interval. We searched further for our boomer and at last the vario betrayed its presence. I pulled up smoothly into the lift.

"This one's yours, Dave."

"Okay, Phil," said Dave as he executed the precise maneuvers necessary to center the lift. It is a truism of flying dual that the pilot not flying always knows exactly where the best lift is and can center a newly found thermal better and faster than the pilot who found it. The joy of this occasion made us break spontaneously into a revision of a current popular song.

"A little bit of lift is better than no lift.

Even a slow lift is better than no lift.

Any kind of lift is better than no lift at all."

Sung, of course, in four part disharmony.

The Prescott Club's trainer came into the thermal a 1000 feet below us. We were already well above the gate altitude. It was time to start. I carefully memorized the clouds so that we could find the vicinity of the thermal again.

"Let's go for it, Dave. We can let the 2-33 mark it for us."

"Good idea. Here we go."

Dave rolled out and put the nose down as we headed for the I.P.

"Traffic?" asked Dave.

"2A to the south. Double Echo making the run now. von Hellens is out to the north. I think he started but he hasn't gone out on course yet."

We rolled into the turn at the I.P.

"Juliet Papa I.P." we yelled in unison at the ground. Like a banshee we streaked through the start gate. I watched the ground carefully. "JP for a start. Three... two... one... mark!" I called. We pulled up smoothly and headed for our thermal. There's the trainer. It's flying straight and level. Sigh.

"About 10° right, Dave. That'll take us back to the same clouds."

"This is it! We're in the race!" cried Dave as the vario swung to an almost indecently high rate of climb. We wrapped it up tight and held on.

"Find Kurzman and von Hellens if you can," said Dave.

"Kurzman is out to the north and von Hellens is out to the east. Looks like he might start."

"Let's hope he isn't watching us. If he follows us soon he could win."

"Yeah. With the handicap, we have to beat him by 12% to win. Hey! Looks like the lift is tapering off."

"'Bout 1,000 below cloudbase," said Dave.

"That street to the turn is just about into position. Let's go. We can climb straight into the turn."

"Up in the air, Junior Birdman. Up in the air..."

"Stop! Enough already! Change channels or something," I cried.

"Awww shucks."

"Sure hope those clouds don't dump on us. They look awfully dark."

"I think we're early enough. This is still just the edge of the system," said Dave.

"Sure hope so."

We cruised toward Dewey at 60 knots in zero sink.

"Look out to the west there, Dave."

"Yeah, pretty clouds today. Look south there toward the Bradshaws."

"Nice. Say, how are you and what's-her-name doing?" I asked.

"Fair. She's getting a little flakey. You want a shot at her?"

"No, Dave, that one's all yours. Good luck."

"You gonna make it to the Club party next weekend?"

"Yeah. Should be a lot of fun. What did they tell you to bring?"

"Chips and dips. You?" asked Dave.

"I volunteered for Egg Fu Yung."

"Far out. Hey, isn't the turnpoint up ahead someplace, Phil?"

"We should be over it in a minute or two. The question is not where is the turnpoint so much as what is the turnpoint. Dewey is only about two miles square."

"Pick a crossroads. After all, you are the official photo evaluator."

"True enough. Let's use that one where the road from the west meets the highway. Here, you take the camera. You're front seat so you get to take the picture," I said.

"Okay, Phil, got the controls?"

"Right, Dave. Okay, here we go." Juliet pirouetted into a perfect wing over.

"Got it!" announced Dave.

"Take several!" I said and Juliet danced through several more gyrations.

"Let's go!"

91

"Right. Watch for von Hellens."

We headed back along the cloud street toward Paulden, the second turnpoint.

"Hey, Dave. Uhh... isn't that rain between us and the turn?" A finger of rain from the storm system over Mingus Mountain stretched across the course line.

"Let's just follow the clouds until the lift weakens. Maybe we won't have to go too far off course to avoid the rain," said Dave.

We plunged on below the darkening clouds, running in weak lift. Soon rain began streaming lightly across the canopy. The lift peaked and then fell to sink. We turned to thread the narrow line of lift at the edge of the rain.

"Dave, won't the rain have an adverse effect on the glide ratio?"

"On a Blanik? Are you kidding?"

"Well, it is supposed to have a laminar flow wing."

"Yeah. So?"

We passed the rain and were once again on course line. We had passed beyond the end of the cloud street and were now racing toward the next cloud when the vario began inching upward.

"Go for it."

"Which side?"

"Take it right."

The vario peaked and we pulled in under a cloud which was developing on the edge of the storm. Far below us a white sailplane appeared.

"Hey, isn't that your uncle down there?"

"Jerry?"

"Yeah. Isn't that Double Echo?"

"Sure enough. Wonder what he's doing way down there."

"Probably looking for lift."

"He's heading back toward the airport now."

"Hope he makes it."

"The lift seems to be only up high."

"Yeah. Let's go. We're getting close to the cloud."

We headed along the course line once again.

"Phil? What say we run the cloud street just to the right there?"

"Sounds like a plan, Dave."

The cloud street stretched 20 miles to the north. A small town was visible at the far end.

"Isn't that town Paulden? The town there at the end of the cloud street?" said Dave.

"Don't know. Take it while I check the map," I said. "The map shows a railroad fork at Paulden. Slip her a bit so I can get a good look ahead... I don't think that matches."

"Where are we, anyway?" asked Dave.

"A lot of help you are."

"Wait a minute. There's a river there and a railroad fork and... There it is!"

"Where?'

"A little behind us and three miles to the left."

"Then what's up ahead?"

"Ash Fork."

"Okay. Here we go."

We peeled out to the left to make a run on Paulden.

"Altitude?" I asked. The working altimeter is in the front seat.

"Eleven five."

"Field's at five and we have to finish above six and we're about eighteen out... We've got a twenty to one final glide going now. Care to chance it?"

"Are you kidding? If we find lift we'll make it."

"Okay. Here's the camera. We're almost to Paulden."

I took the controls and stood Juliet on a wing while Dave snapped the picture. We pointed toward the Prescott airfield and began a long dolphin glide. Dave, since he had the instruments in the front seat, took the controls.

"I wish I had brought my calculator," I said.

"Why? You can't read the numbers in direct sunlight anyway."

"Well, it's difficult but not impossible."

"Try pencil and paper."

"Nag, nag, nag. Altitude?"

"Nine oh," said Dave.

"Ten miles out. That's about 18:1. We may make it yet."

"We have to. There's no more lift."

"It does look rather dead, doesn't it?"

We pressed on through the still air. To the west a large thunderstorm had cut off the afternoon sun and stopped convection.

"Whoops, there's a bump."

"Just a little one. We're through it already," I said.

"It would be nice to make a decent finish today."

"Not like our first one, you mean."

"Phil, we are the only team ever in the history of Arizona soaring to make a rolling finish in both directions intentionally. That in itself is an accomplishment."

"True enough, Dave. But today we know which direction to finish so we only have to go through in one direction."

The airport was drawing slowly nearer. Chino Valley passed below us.

"Five miles out. What's the altitude?" I asked.

"About 7500. I think we've got it made!"

"All right! Go for it!"

The nose went down and the speed went up.

"There's the finish line," I called happily. "Finish west. JP one mile out."

"Say, Phil, where is the finish line?"

"You mean you don't know?"

"Well, not precisely."

"Quick, let me take it. It's right down there. What's the altitude?"

"Six one!"

"Perfect." We swung around the northern corner of the gate in flawless racing form.

"JP for a finish!" we yelled at the ground.

"Sure hope they saw us," I said.

"The way this ship screams at speed they'd have to be deaf to miss us."

"Guess so. Your landing, Dave."

"Okay."

We touched softly and rolled to the end of the runway. Some of the other Club members were there to help us get off the runway and take JP to the tie-down area.

"Did you boys make it all the way round today?" asked Dan.

"Of course," said Dave.

"Why do you ask such a ridiculous question?" I asked.

"You two seem to be the only ones who made it round today. All of the Class A ships landed at Seligman but a lot of them didn't even go."

We quickly tied Juliet down and headed for the finish line, landing card in hand. The sun was slowly sinking behind Granite Mountain to the west. We found the day's contest committee at the finish line.

"Welcome back. How did it go today?" called Dick, the day's Contest Manager.

"Just fine," I said.

Dave turned to Ron who was doing the scoring that day.

"Ron, what was our time?" asked Dave.

"You guys didn't really make it all the way round the course, did you?" asked Ron.

"Of course we did."

"That was a nice finish you boys made today," said Bill, who had been working the finish gate when we came through.

"Thanks, Bill," I said.

"Did you clear the thousand foot minimum altitude?" asked Bill.

"Six one right on the button," said Dave.

"Now then, Ron. About our speed?" I asked.

"Did you guys really make it all the way round?" asked Ron.

"By our turnpoint photos shall we be vindicated," I replied haughtily.

"Well, all right. I'll work it out but I don't think it will count anyway," said Ron.

"You two are the only ones who went out on course. Kurzman, von Hellens and Cutler landed back here. They never left."

"Oh no!" Gloom.

"If you made it all the way round as you claim, your speed was 46.35 mph. But if no one else went out it will be a no contest day," said Ron.

"A no contest day when we just turned in the fastest speed ever recorded in Class B?" I asked incredulously.

"Not only that but Seligman is only 54 miles out so we flew father than anyone in Class A," said Dave.

"It is still a no contest day if you are the only ones who went out on course," said Dick.

And it came to pass that the day was in fact a no contest day but the scribes have taken up the cause and given here these words from the as yet unfinished Saga of the Blanik Racing Team that they who flew with such great skill and cunning farther and faster than all others that day in July might yet achieve some measure of infamy.

AVOIDING THE PARACHUTE OPTION as told by Tracy Tabart, March 1987.

The following incident occurred when the aileron control linkage failed in flight on a Grob 103 Acro. Australian Tracy Tabart landed safely without evacuating - either the plane or his bowels.

There I wuz... being towed to 4000 feet but going through 3,500 I realized that in a matter of seconds the aileron control had diminished to absolutely nothing. Being unable to maintain position behind the towplane, I released and the aircraft began a slow roll to the left. A pull back on the stick to reduce speed proved to be a waste of time because the aircraft was obviously entering a spiral dive. I recovered straight and level flight by using the rudder and its secondary effect.

At this point a decision had to be made, either to bail out or sort it out. (Things have to be pretty crook before I'll jump). My first thoughts were of the quick release couplings coming undone but then I wondered why *both* would do so?

My mind went into the control box behind my seat. (Luckily I was in the back seat). Eight months of working on Grobs suddenly paid off. I could see in my mind's eye the whole layout of linkages behind my head. Releasing my shoulder harness, I reached behind me and pressed in that stupid little button and turned it so the hatch door could be hinged up and I could reach into the box and grasp the main aileron control push rod linkage. With a bloody big sigh of relief I found I had full control back there. By this time I was probably at 2,500 feet but I wasn't looking at the altimeter.

"We have a slight loss of control here," I said to my unsuspecting passenger. "Could you see what aileron control you have?" In a very apprehensive voice he said,

"Er, very little." The front stick was flopping from side to side. I think he got a bit worried then.

"Don't worry," I reassured him. "I've got control in the back here."

I practiced turns with the limited height I had left. I had one hand holding the stick and one arm through the back hatch. It was like riding a bicycle with your hands crossed on the handlebars. I decided on a precautionary high circuit at 1200 feet and wondered how I was going to work the airbrakes. I made a long final knowing it was going to be a hassle. I let go the stick completely and pulled on the airbrakes which resulted in a pitch forward into a steep dive. Adjusting the trim to have another go produced a nice stall at 300 feet. Rehashing it, I moved the trim lever forward and held the stick in the crook of my arm, holding the airbrake with my hand.

This produced the worst landing I've ever achieved but after pushing the aircraft onto the ground at quite a high speed and relying on no elevator control and full wheel brake, I finally ground to a relieved halt.

Afterwards, it occurred to me I could have told the passenger to move the blue lever and operate the airbrake for me. Next time it happens, I think I'll do that."

A CAUTIONARY TALE as told by Joe Carter, June 1987.

Everyone has heard about it by now. During Region 9, Joe Carter (D9) was caught in a microburst and subsequently suffered dehydration and heatstroke. He was retrieved by his sweet wife, Camille, who calls her pilot "Darlin'" in a delicious

Southern accent and would retrieve him from the jaws of hell if necessary. This retrieve must have felt like a practice run.

"I went through the gate early," said Joe when he had recovered from his ordeal. "I could see the build ups to the south east and wanted an early start because of overdevelopment and thunderstorms. I went good to Continental and made the turn about 11,000 feet."

Up ahead Joe could see two storm cells 2 or 3 miles apart. "There was an opening in between that I could see was right down the course line so I started through before it closed off," continued Joe. "By the time I got there it was lightning and it started getting dark above me. Both storms were very dark, almost black, and I was in light rain. I was about 8100 feet at that point. Probably about 4000 above the ground just off the far end of Apache Peak. I was doing about 80 knots and all of a sudden I just hit this tremendous sink. I put the nose down 45° to speed up and I was still doing about 80 knots. The controls became very sloppy, I just couldn't figure out what was going on. The ship wasn't behaving the way it normally should. Very sloppy like it was almost stalled but with 80 knots indicated air speed. The varios were pegged down but I finally got it up to about 120 knots by putting it almost into a vertical dive, then started pulling out of the dive slowly because the ground was coming up pretty fast and I was probably about 200 feet above the terrain.

"I'd already resigned myself to the fact that there was no way I could fly to landable terrain so I figured I'd just have to write the ship off. I hoped I could land it up hill and maybe ground loop it but as I continued gliding toward Benson I found myself just about maintaining altitude above the ground because the ground was sloping off about the same as my glide ratio. I looked at the road to Tombstone as I crossed it but it was dug out the side of the hill so I carried on. I was hoping then I could make it to the river bed which would be sandy and soft. Then I spotted these three abandoned farm fields. Two of them were too short but the third was slightly bigger and it looked pretty flat - the lesser of all the evils.

"At that point I was probably doing about 80 knots and I had maybe 100 or 150 feet altitude. So I just popped up, put the gear down, full flaps, and turned into the field with full spoilers. It was soft and the roll out was very short. I landed diagonally so I'd have the longest part of the field and I stopped about 50 yards short of the fence at the other end."

Asked how he was feeling at that point, Joe admitted to being relieved, "but I had been so busy it hadn't really sunk in to panic or anything." What amazed him most was that he had glided so far. "I measured it on the sectional afterwards and the glide at 200 feet had been for 8.5 miles."

Another ASA member, Paul Dickerson, experienced a microburst sometime ago and said going from red line to stall felt like a rat being tossed by a cat. Joe said his experience was totally different. "It was very much like being in the lee of a wave. It was very smooth. The speed at which I was dropping was incredible. It wasn't turbulent at all."

After he'd landed, Joe was more than a little disoriented. "I didn't have time to look around when I was in the air," he explained, so walked half a mile to a house but there was nobody home. He returned to the ship to relay a radio message. "Then I tried to find the way out to the main road and also to get to a telephone to give Camille specific directions on how to get to me."

While he waited by the road a storm started moving in to the area, and, worried about the ship, he decided to return. "I walked back and about the last half mile it was gusting pretty hard so I started running and that's when I got overheated and dehydrated." By then, Camille was close enough for radio contact and he was able to give her directions.

Joe had taken water with him and had been drinking it too, but with the 104° temperatures, the walking and running, heat stroke was not surprising. "I wasn't really incoherent when she found me," explained Joe, "but I wasn't too clear... It was hard to think about normal things when I was disassembling the ship. I'd forget little minor things that I would normally do without even thinking. I had to concentrate very hard to think of the procedures." It was still that way next morning when they came to rig at El Tiro. "That was when I decided not to fly," said Joe. "My mind just wasn't sharp enough." What Paul calls brain fade.

Asked how he feels about it all now, Joe said, "It's given me great respect for thunderstorms. It didn't scare me off flying but I've flown near my last thunderstorm."

THE DOWAGER QUEEN by Bob Welliever, January 1988.

Every aspect of aviation has its own venerated machine, a particular type of aircraft that seems to stand as a symbol for that phase of flight. The Babe Ruths and the Red Granges of flying machines. To general aviation, it was the J3 Piper Cub. To air transport, the DC3 Gooney Bird. To heavy bombardment, the indestructible B17 Flying Fortress. And to fighter pilots, the romantic P51 Mustang. It matters not that others have broken their records nor that their performance may not measure up to today's competitive standards, they remain the talisman of their own game. Hank Aaron may have hit more homers and O.J. Simpson danced more yardage, but they're still not the Sultan of Swat, or the Gallop'n Ghost.

Soaring too has its Grande Dame, albeit not so well known as her cousins. Go to any soaring field and you'll see at least one SGS 2-33, squatting back on her hockey puck tail wheel with her nose in the air like some offended old dowager who just smelled cigar smoke. Her creator, Schweizer Aircraft Co., never got around to giving her a name - just a model number. Perhaps she was so homely that nobody could come up with a marketable name and keep a straight face at the same time. There's no denying, she's god-awful ugly. To begin with, her nose looks like a cross between W.C. Fields and Jimmy Durante. Her torso is a slab sided triangle that tapers in uninspiring straight lines to a skinny point like the ass end of a Jersey bull. Not for her the slim and gracefully sculptured wings of her modern sisters, but instead mountainous rectangular planks of aluminum, externally reinforced by struts the size of a man's arm. Her skin is a motley mixture of aluminum, fiberglass, and fabric, usually showing signs of frequent plastic surgery. Growing gloriously from the upper surface of her nose are the twin tubes of her pitot/static air system, like 12 inch aluminum whiskers sprouting from a fiberglass wart.

If Schweizer neglected to give her a name, they're the only ones who did. Everyone else who has ever flown her has a pet title. Some call her The Cow, and some The Pig. I've heard her called The Flyin' Outhouse, the Dodo Bird, the Lumber Wagon, and a host of even less delicate titles. One thing's for certain though, if she ain't much for pretty, she's hell for stout.

Schweizer, with its history of designing and building for the military, is noted for its conservative approach to the eternal design question of strength versus performance and/or esthetics. Some very wise people realized that this airplane was going to be used as a primary trainer and by new, low time pilots, and was destined to take one hell of a beating day in and day out. It had to be not only strong, but durable and relatively easy to repair by the average aircraft mechanic, in an average shop, located a thousand miles from the factory with its limitless parts inventory. Besides all that, it must be easy to control, uncomplicated, highly forgiving of error, and above all, free from any of those nasty little habits such as spins, oscillations, ground loops and various other common traits that create widows, orphans and rich plaintiff's lawyers.

Well, they succeeded in spades. Actually, she started life with a different designation number. When she first rolled off the line in Elmira, N.Y., in 1945, she was called the 2-22. Her wings were a lot shorter in those days and her tail feathers looked a bit different in profile. She lacked some of the cockpit esthetics that were to come later, but basically she was the same bird. There are those soulless technocrats who will argue that subsequent changes in wing design so changed her that the 2-22 and 2-33 are different aircraft, and I suppose they're right if you look at a plane in terms of nothing but L/D ratio, aspect ratio and airfoil number. The rest of us incurably romantic slobs still consider her the same old gal who just grew a little and had some cosmetic surgery.

In 1965, Schweizer added eight feet to her wings and gave her a little more rudder to handle the increased yaw. They gussied up the cockpit a bit and lined it with a composition material so you weren't sitting next to the bare steel tubing of the fuselage. Granted, there were enough changes so that the practicalities of licensing, marketing, etc., required that she be given a new designation number. Still, numbers are only numbers, and if we loved her before, we loved her even more now that she could fly a little further and climb a little faster.

Without benefit of a formal survey, I think it's safe to say that 85% to 90% of the licensed glider pilots in the US today took their first glider training and flew their first solo in the Grande Dame. Each time you hear her mentioned as the Cow, the Pig or the Outhouse, if you bother to listen you'll detect a warm note of affection in the reference. Occasionally some low-time, self impressed little snot who has recently graduated to the higher performance ships will make such a reference with a genuinely condescending air, but he's the exception and given a few years to temper his ego and build some memories, his tone too will carry the tenor of old affection. And why not? How many of us don't remember the car in which we learned to drive, or the first time we drove it solo, without Mom or Dad sitting there to keep us out of trouble? Can you forget your first love affair or your first puppy who grew to be your childhood companion?

What's it like to fly the old girl? Well, let's look at a day in the life of Grande Dame N2802H, who goes by her nickname, "Oh Two Hotel". She lives in a typical sailport in the southwest desert country. She doesn't sleep inside, hangar space being at a premium, but spends her nights tied down on the line enduring the discomfort of wind, dust, rain and hail. She gets a bit grimy and her wings show the pimples of several hail storms, but she doesn't seem to mind. Her morning ablutions consist of a canopy cleaning and thorough preflight inspection to see if she survived yesterday's abuse and last night's weather. At 0900 she's pulled out to the launch point and tethered by one wing. She's not the oldest in her family, but neither is she a youngster. Today will be her 8,288th day of flying.

0930: An instructor and student leave the line shack and walk across the gravel to where she sits. The student is a young female physician taking her third lesson. Being bright, enthusiastic, and well coordinated, she's done well in her first two sessions and today she'll be trying her first unassisted take off. The instructor's hands and feet will never be more than an inch from the controls but unless things turn really sour he'll let her correct her own mistakes. A brief review; climb in and button down; tow rope taut and line boy raises the wing; signal the tow pilot and they're off. Well, not quite. When the power comes on in the tow plane the student hasn't anticipated the effect of the tension on the line. The tail slams down onto the runway with a thunderous impact and the whole ship shudders with sound and shock.

It takes a second or two for the student to react during which the plane has started moving. When she does react, she pushes the stick full forward and now the ship rocks forward on its nose skid changing the sound to an ear piercing screech as the steel shoe grates along the gravel like a thousand fingernails on a blackboard. Finally she gets the pitch attitude more or less stabilized. Her concentration has been on the pitch and now comes an ominous WHUMP and a cloud of dust. "Keep your wings level," the instructor tries to keep his voice calm. "You're dragging your left tip on the ground." Finally pitch and bank get under control and by now the ship is ready to fly. Gracefully it lifts from the runway and begins to climb and climb and climb. Twenty feet above the runway and the tow plane is still rolling on the ground! Things are getting critical and the instructor hasn't the time nor temperament to make gentle suggestions. "Not so high," he snaps. "You're going to raise his tail and put his nose in the dirt. Get it back down. NOW." She does - all the way down! The main gear impacts the runway with a sickening thud and for an instant 5 negative G's ripple through every structural component of the ship. What happens? Nothing much. The old girl just bounces back into the air and wallows off after the now airborne tow plane like some happy little puppy following its mama. Another day has begun for Oh Two Hotel.

1015: After having bounced four times on landing, Oh Two Hotel is now resting quietly on the line. Another student is ready, this time a high school senior whose sister had given him a gift certificate for an introduction ride on his birthday. The first ride triggered an emotional response, opening a new dimension of life to him. After some more training and a little experience he's going to be an excellent pilot, but today he's still a student with only 19 dual flights in his log, total a little over 12 hours of air time. He doesn't know it yet, but his instructor is thinking about letting him solo today if things go well. The first two flights are short "pattern shots", and they go well. The air is smooth and wind calm - a perfect day for a first solo flight. After the second landing the instructor climbs out of the back seat and tries to sound casual. "I'm hungry as hell. Why don't you take it around once by yourself while I have a sandwich?"

"Really? You really think I'm ready?"

"Don't you?"

"Yeah, but - Ya Know - I didn't think we were going to do this today."

"We're not - YOU are. And don't bend this bird all up. I've got another lesson at 2 o'clock. Now get on with it before I change my mind."

We could detail the flight but we won't. It was pretty much like all first solos - full of errors for which she gave him time to sort out and correct. He got out of position on tow, stalled in a steep bank while trying to find a thermal, turned on final 20 mph too slow and 150 feet too high, dragged the tail before finally landing 200 feet past the touch down point. He was still moving 20 mph when he let his left wing come down and the old girl slewed to a sideways stop like Quasimodo sliding along the battlement. Those mistakes will come to mind later tonight when he reviews the experience for the umpteenth time, and he'll vow not to make them again, but for now nothing matters except being King of the Mountain. He's on top of Everest and the world is at his feet.

Those weren't the last mistakes he'll make, nor the last time she'll forgive him and he'll fly her many more times before moving up the performance ladder, first to a 1-26, and then on to the sleek fiberglass ships. But years from now when he casually refers to her as a Flying Bathtub, the discerning ear will hear a smile in his voice and know that somewhere in the past was a bright spring morning made even brighter by the smile of a young man and the benign nature of a grand old girl who forgave him his many aeronautical sins and nursed him gently back to earth to fly again another day.

1130: A short demo flight flown by a staff pilot carrying a passenger who is curious to see what it's all about, and may be interested in taking lessons. A short tow and 30 minutes of floating around in weak thermals while the pilot answers all the usual questions such as, "How much will it cost?", "How long will it take?" and "Is it really as safe as they say?"

0200: Another lesson, not much different than the first except that this student touches down without the spoilers, balloons 10 feet in the air and gets confused. Realizing that he should have had some spoiler out at touchdown he now adopts the "better late than never" philosophy and jerks the spoilers full out while the old girl is trying desperately to stay afloat. Even a sweet tempered grandmother has her tolerance threshold and she comes back to earth like a dropped bowling ball, rolls fifty feet and sloughs to a stop.

0330: Her last flight of the day is by a 48 year old realtor on his tenth solo flight. The wind increases after take off and he drifts too far downwind of the field. Ignoring several suitable clearings he doggedly tries to make it back only to realize that with a half mile to go he's already in the valley below the end of the runway. At the last minute he heads for a dirt road leading up the hill and plops down on the steep grade after dragging his left wing through a palo verde tree and decimating a cluster of cholla cactus. By dark the plane has been pulled up the hill and back to her tie down spot. Time enough in the morning to replace the blown tire, touch up the paint and pull several hundred barbed cholla spikes from her fabric belly.

After some early morning surgery she'll fly again tomorrow, and the day after, and the day after that. She's already flown almost a quarter century, and with a little luck and some decent maintenance, she'll go another couple of decades. Children yet unborn may take her on that for ever remembered solo flight, placing her image in their minds for ever.

The Grande Dame isn't coming off the assembly line anymore. Paul Schweizer tells me that in 1986 only two were made, as a result of special orders. I didn't have the heart to ask the cost but I know that building airplanes one at a time has to be an expensive proposition. It's doubtful that any more will be built. So the

100

grand old lady has joined the ranks of the endangered species. Like the rest of the great ones, the birthing is over and only the dying remains. Every year there will be fewer and fewer until some day...

Still, I have a feeling that when the last Cub is decaying in a hangar, and the last Fortress and Mustang have finally gone to their aluminum Valhallas, a weary old 2-33 will still be floating slowly over the desert on a soft evening thermal.

CHAPTER 6 - THE LAS HORVATH CHAPTER

Las Horvath needs little introduction: he made a success of Estrella Sailport and a success of his career as a sailplane pilot. We now reveal yet another talent you did not know he had - that of raconteur.

I MISSED THE BIG ONE by Las Horvath, February 1973.

There goes another beautiful day. The cloud base is over 14,000 AGL and business is booming. Sure looks like it's going to be the same tomorrow. I hate to think about it. Before leaving the sailport I checked tomorrow's schedule carefully. Yup, not a single plane available all day again! How in the world could I get hold of a 1-26? I could probably have somebody take my scheduled flights, but where can I get the 1-26? Oh! You dumb... You have one! The one that has the broken canopy. Hey! That's it!! All I need is a canopy! Let's see now... Elliott Kurzman? No, he wants his 500 km too. Well, I'll just have to start calling the private owners as soon as I get home and hope that one of them will not want to fly tomorrow.

My first call is to the Detwilers. A really long shot; both John and Charlotte are pretty regular at the sailport. I am apologizing, explaining to John that all I really need is his 1-26's canopy so that I can make my Diamond Distance tomorrow.

"You think it's going to be that good?" John asked.

"I do," I said.

"I'll tell you what, Las, we been flying too much lately anyway. Go ahead! Take it, and I wish you lots of luck."

I don't even remember if I said thanks as I am hanging up, I am so happy. (Many thanks, John and Charlotte). Finally I get another chance. Last year I messed it up by loading my 1-26 to the limit and landed a few miles short of the sailport. I covered 306 miles unable to use the weak thermals toward the end of the day. Not tomorrow! Only the bare essentials come with me this time. And I mean BARE.

Beautiful day! We start operations at 9:00 am and the cu's already have begun to pop over the Mogollon Rim to the east of us. A couple of hours and it should be good enough to take off here. Over the Rim it always starts early, but by midday over-development renders it useless. Well, back to business! One of my pilots did not show up. Hmmm... Our time keeper wakes me up. "Las, we have several demos show up. Can you take them?"

"I'd be happy to take them, Jill. May I help you folks?" I asked, thinking to myself, well, goodbye cross country for today. A few minutes later I realized that I could start NOW on that cross country if only I had another pilot to fly demos. The thermals were already good: 200 to 300 fpm... Oh well... us working people have to mind business when we have business. "Next please!"

It's 11 o'clock. Burns me up! I have not even been able to put John's canopy on 41S just in case... I can't believe it! The lost pilot shows up at 11.01 am MST. "My car..." he says. I can't even listen to him as I jump out of the backseat apologizing. "Please excuse me sir! This great young pilot will take good care of you. He'll even let you fly the glider..." and I am running toward John's ship for the canopy.

Exactly 24 minutes later I am on the flight line ready to go! These 24 minutes were just unbelievable. Every able bodied person gave me a hand to get ready for this flight: declaration, camera, barograph, water, food, clothing, maps, radio, wingtip wheels... oh yes, the canopy! Do you ever have a day that is yours? You feel nothing can go wrong? That was just the feeling that came over me as I signaled the tow pilot and waved goodbye to the onlookers.

I always release in the first usable lift, but not today. Today I am going to take a high tow. Finally, at 2700 feet AGL I abruptly pulled the release and made a 90° turn onto my course line. This is insane! No lift, but I'm going. Going at best glide speed steadily losing altitude. I have heard about final glides from release. Well... Why didn't I release at 2200 in that boomer? I don't know. I spotted a swirling dust devil ahead of me. A minute ago I had doubts... Now? The old ticker began to slow down to normal as I approached, checked the rotation of the thermal and lowered the nose with impatience. You little devil you! I hope to get one of you every time I am in trouble today. Reaching it at 1500 feet I rolled in and noted the time to check the rate of climb.

The NE wind was slowly pushing 41S back now as it was climbing. At 7500 feet I said goodbye to the little devil and called Elliot Kurzman (who started about 15 minutes after I did) relaying the information about the thermal I just left. Not much sink, occasional bubble and meticulous handling of controls to follow the speed ring, slowly took me away from the sailport. The next few thermals were progressively better; getting higher and faster. 58 minutes after release I made 30 miles and the altimeter indicated 11,600 feet. My disappointment came at Newman Peak: reached the first cu at 1 pm expecting nice, smooth lift, but it was rougher than a sled ride on a wash board, had very choppy lift under it. However, managed to climb 5400 feet in 10 minutes, then rolled out and lowered the nose.

By this time, the soaring is getting really good. I even have time to look around and enjoy the scenery besides the usual thermal scouting ahead. I always go around the cultivated area if possible, but I can't help but enjoy looking at it. The neatness, the orderliness of the irrigation has a beauty of its own. How man can draw straight lines every mile is beyond me. And of course the desert, with its dry washes, letting you know instantly where the good thermal should be. The rugged, rocky mountains slicing up the flat lands. This is what's so beautiful about cross country flying. Being able to see so much, from such a small platform.

At 2:02 pm I am between Mount Lemmon and the heart of Tucson, looking down from 16,400 feet. The turnpoint (Tombstone Airport) is only a rock throw from here, it seems. Before I reached my turnpoint, two significant things happened. (1) I have reached the highest point in my flight; over 18,000 feet and I'm not even at cloud base. Almost crying, actually forcing myself to level the wings, lower the nose and leave this 1000 fpm lift. (2) Nearing the turnpoint I noticed a black wall approaching from the northeast. DUST STORM! It raced through my mind. Elliot! If he did not close the gap between us since our take off... well, I've got a problem of my own! Can I beat that monster to the turnpoint? Let's go!

At 3:02 pm I'm over Tombstone and leaving a thermal at 16,500 feet. Two minutes later took a single picture of the airport. Monster, you may cover it up now! Checking the time, I realized that the distance for the last hour was 68 miles. Incredible.

Coming back to Tucson things begin to slow up a bit. That dust storm was the signal for the weather to overdevelop all around. I've noticed the snow coming through the vent. My thermometer now shows 24°F, but... it's supposed to be 100° on the ground. The liveliness of the air disappeared. Hooo... slow down, kid. After a long, long glide, finally, east of Tucson, I got a gentle smooth thermal, then nothing again. Heading to Mount Lemmon in the hope of finding something under a few scrawny looking clouds, my altitude slowly was going away. On the ground high winds indicate that a dust storm has moved through, leaving no lift behind.

Desperately looking around I've noticed a little dust devil far in the distance about 45° to my left. I almost yanked the stick out of 41S in my hurried effort to make the turn. It took me an eternity, but I made it. And holy smoke! I mean DUST. Another dust storm from the northeast. The way it looked to me it would go between Tucson and the sailport.

My inside just started to glow. A free ride home? For a few minutes all I could think about was Bill Cleary's flight in the 1971 1-26 Nationals. Riding home on a dust storm and ending up with 50 mph for the 150 mile triangle.

Reaching the leading edge of the dust at 4:40 pm rewarded me with a thermal that put me 11,000 feet higher in 9 minutes. The rest was a child's glide. In front of the dust I was able to cruise from 40 to 90 mph at 12,000 feet altitude keeping the variometer on zero.

Touching on runway 2 at 5:55 pm, it took 6 hours and 23 minutes for the 318 miles out and return for an average speed of 49.82 mph. My third 1-26 Diamond. Oh yes, the title. I did not declare Estrella as a GOAL and I was 150 feet short of Diamond altitude. I missed a 3 Diamond 1-26 flight!!!!

WHERE THE SKY BECOMES THE SEA by Las Horvath, January 1980.

Many times on a cold and windy day, the only activity that makes sense to most of us is one that takes place indoors. Yet some of the most fantastic soaring flights of the year are accomplished on those days. One such memorable day, my son Ken and I left our home in Tempe in the rain, driving winds, and a cloud deck only 600 feet above the ground - not an exciting beginning. But, before the day was over, we had soared above 22,000 feet, gaining 21,200 feet above our low point. Crazy? Not really...

It was early Saturday morning, and our flight school operations at Estrella Sailport were at a standstill because of the dreary weather in Phoenix. As is frequently the case, the rains were concentrated over Phoenix itself, leaving the area around Estrella with strong westerly winds and a few high scattered clouds. Distinctive lens-shaped clouds were stacking up downwind of the Sierra Estrella Mountain, and these lenticulars marked clearly the moist crests of a standing mountain wave. Since Ken had never been up in a wave, we pulled the Janus out of the hangar and prepared for a high altitude flight.

ON YOUR MARK: "Got an extra jacket?"

"Check."

"Mittens?"

"Got 'em right here."

"Oxygen system?"

"Ready!"

GET SET: "Hey, Ken, let's take a barograph, just in case..."

Ken had read my thoughts and this ticking box was already in the plane, ready to record our flight altitudes and duration.

GO!

We were towed aloft by one of our Pawnee towplanes, and released from tow abreast of the highest peak on the "Little Ridge" northwest of the field. Immediately we encountered four knots of lift on the windward side.

"The plan is to search this area of lift," I explained to Ken, "then go down and set a low point. Then we'll come back to this lift, work our way up, and cross the valley to the Sierra Estrella. If the lift there is as strong as this, then we'll jump over to the wave from there."

"First things first," I went on. "We've got to work this little ridge for a while right now." Ridge soaring was not new to Ken, since he'd been flying for several years, but this was his first mountain flight in such a high performance sailplane as the Janus. He took the controls and began the serious work of exploring the lift area. We flew along the windward side of the ridge, tracing a figure eight pattern, and using the deflected wind currents to gain altitude.

Meanwhile, as Ken grins with every foot of altitude he's gained, I plot our descent to a low point. I check the movement of the bushes on the ridge... "Great - they're really moving," I think to myself. "Must be a strong flow at ridge height, and plenty of lift."

"I've got it, Ken," I said, as I took the controls and opened the spoilers to begin the descent toward the north end of the ridge. We cruise past the highest peak, lower than it is at 1500 feet AGL. Soon the altimeter shows 1200 feet, all according to plan, and I continue the descent. Now Ken's grin has dissolved. I can sense the uneasiness he's feeling as he twists his head to look back at the sailport, now some six miles away. I grinned slightly to myself, remembering the times I've had those feelings. "We're almost there, Ken."

The altimeter now slips below 1000 feet, as we whoosh over the Flying A airstrip and make a left diving turn to get down even closer to the ground. The airspeed increases to 150 mph, as I had planned, and we will convert this airspeed to altitude at the end of our run. Whistling along, we level off just above the tops of the trees, holding altitude for a few seconds to let the barograph record the low

105

point. Then, a smooth pull up over the northernmost foothills, and we've regained about 400 feet. We're established in lift of about 2 knots, and in the quiet of that moment, I see Ken's reflection in the canopy - he's smiling again.

It's back to ridge soaring now, flying a pattern similar to a switchback hiking trail, slowly working our way higher. The higher we get, the next higher ridge line I seek, since the strongest lift is found at the ridge height. Finally at 3500 feet, we start east across the valley, heading for Montezuma's Peak on the Sierra Estrella. "Monty" welcomes us with 6 knots of lift, and we quickly climb through 4500 feet.

"All according to plan," I think to myself. "Mountain wave, here we come!" Just in that moment of self-satisfaction, it becomes obvious that we will not be rewarded quite yet. The lift becomes progressively weaker, and we reach what seems to be a stalemate. As we climb now, so very slowly, I think to myself about the times impatience has caused me to land just minutes after having crossed the spine of the Sierra Estrella in search of other mountain waves. "A little longer, Ken, and we'll cross over into the wave," I promise, as much to myself as to him.

The ridge lift has now been reduced to only 1 knot, and we can't wait any longer. If we are going to get into that wave... if we CAN get into that wave, we'll have to try it now. Ever optimistic, I turn downwind toward the lee of the mountain. The tension mounts as the instruments show a vast expanse of sinking air. Sink, sink, and more sink! The vario is firmly pegged at 10 knots down. The altimeter unwinds at an alarming rate, looking like an old fashioned elevator marker showing a quick trip to the basement. We've lost more than a 1,000 feet in a matter of seconds, and decide to head for the pipeline road, hopefully to find this elusive mountain wave... possibly to land.

Ahh... what's this? The altimeter is not unwinding so quickly now. The vario teases me... 9 knots down, 7 knots down, 5 knots, 1 knot, and at last it shows lift. The lift intensifies, the instrument responds, and soon the needle pegs again, this time at 10 knots of lift. Ken, of course, is amazed. He shakes his head from side to side and breaks the silence. "I can't believe this! A minute ago, I thought we were going to land on the road, and now... WOW! It's so silent, so still." In minutes we climb through 5,000 feet, 9,000, up to 12,000 feet, and it's on with the oxygen masks at 12,500.

Suspended, apparently motionless, we hold a position over the pipeline road. Headed into the wind, yet not moving over the ground, the mountain wave caries us up. The silence is overwhelming - conversation is pointless with the oxygen masks on, so we're together, alone, with our own silent thoughts.

What a beautiful sight! Every now and then I glance at the instruments... fascinating... the only thing moving is the altimeter, going up! That sun sure feels good! Hey, we just went by the highest lenticular cloud. From the ground, the sky has never looked so clear, so deep a blue. And the clouds - have they ever looked so brilliantly white? It seems we're suspended over a sea of sorts - waves without sound... time without movement.

Suddenly, we're drawn back to reality by the hissing of our oxygen valves. Gradually, the lift began to top out, the rate of climb decreased. Altitude - 22,600. Net gain - 21,200 feet, nearly 5,000 feet to spare above a Diamond altitude gain!

We began our descent to Estrella, with both Ken and I smiling from ear to ear at what we'd done, and where we'd been. We could see the rain in Phoenix, now reduced to a drizzle, and imagined how sensible it would have been to stay indoors today. And, as we flew through a patch of warm sunshine on our descent, we could hear the barograph ticking off our 22,000 feet of altitude. Crazy? Not really.

THE LONGEST FLIGHT OF MY LIFE by Las Horvath, January 1981.

Ring! Ring!
I glanced at my wrist watch as the phone rang again. 7:00 am - a little early for telephone calls. "Hello?"

"I have a collect call from a Julian Martin, will you accept the charges?'

"Yes, operator." Julian had been using his weather wisdom these past few weeks to help me plan a record flight. What would today's forecast bring? "Well, Julian, what have you got?"

"There's a front coming in, Las; it seems to have quite a lot of energy. Today might be the day you've been waiting for. There are strong winds forecast, and the leading edge is at Yuma, Arizona right now. If you can get 300 feet per minute by 11 this morning, I think you ought to go for it."

"OK, thanks. I'll let you know what happens. Bye, Julian."

"Good luck, Las."

I checked my watch again. 7:05 a.m, Sunday, May 10, 1980. What the watch doesn't tell me is that it is Mother's Day - that I already know. For a month now I've been waiting for a cold front that could give me a good long flight, hopefully a straight distance record in Multiplace. Being in the soaring business at Estrella Sailport, it's often difficult to find a day I'm not scheduled for a local aerobatic or cross country training flight. Now I have the day miraculously free, the cold front is on the doorstep, and it is... Mother's Day. My wife Betty will not be thrilled at all this.

I probably shouldn't go. Well, I'll just go through the motions of getting ready. As I dress, I pick out all the warm clothes I might need, and pack some extra stuff too. Just in case.

Our Estrella crew and I load up the VW bus by 8:00 am. Betty carefully packs in a crate of special Estrella wine we'd received as a gift, and loads boxes of food for our big picnic party that evening.

I can feel a change in the weather - it's not all that subtle. There is something different here, an electric feeling. There's no early morning inversion, but no winds yet either. There is just a feeling of something yet to come. We arrive at Estrella at 9:00 am. I went straight for the phone.

"Harry, this is Las. Do you want to go for a record attempt?"

"Uh, sure, Las. When?" asked Harry.

"Oh, there's a front between Yuma and Estrella. We should take off by 11 this morning."

"OK, I'll be there by 11. See you then."

Betty has heard this conversation. After I hang up, she asks the obvious. "You're really going, aren't you?"

"But, honey, I may not get another chance like this again this year!"

Oh sure, I'd like to have said, "No, it doesn't matter, I'll do it some other day," but I can't. I recalled another time in 1972, when I was scheduled with a student and elected instead to get my third diamond. No amount of explanation could make up for the deed, and I've never seen that student at Estrella since.

107

The weather, the plane, the time and opportunity all spelled TODAY; this time, a record flight. Betty knew all this, and understood.

"But who'll be the life of the party tonight?" she kidded.

The next hour passed quickly, in cleaning and loading the Janus. Food, drinking water, maps, portable radio. Oxygen gear? Of course. Water ballast, plenty of warm clothes, barographs for both the sailplane and the tow ship. The list went on and on.

The wind began to blow; it was not even 10 am and already the horizon was studded with dust devils. "I want to go NOW," I thought to myself, "where the hell is Harry?" Harry's son Tom is one of our line boys and he'd sensed my impatience.

"I'll go," he volunteered, "we don't have to wait for my dad." I smile.

"No, I'll wait till 11, Tom, but thanks." I can tell that Tom will be looking at the clock every minute, and hoping his dad has a flat or something. Harry Alton drives in at 10:58 and calls to me from his car.

"I'll be with you in a minute - have to visit the simulator." As Harry ambles over to that portable compromise to indoor plumbing, the flight line bustles with a flurry of activity.

I say my goodbyes to all, get the Janus in take-off position, and settle into the front pilot compartment. As Harry approaches to claim his spot in the back seat, my heart stops. This man is nuts! He's wearing short sleeves and Bermuda shorts! It we ever do land in the mountains of Colorado, he'll freeze.

"Harry, didn't you bring any warm clothes?"

"Oh, I'll be OK. I'm not cold at all."

At that moment, I was grateful for what ever foresight had made me put extra warm clothes in the back seat.

"OK, Harry, here we go."

At 11 am, Kyle revs up the tow plane. We're about to begin a journey that will take us to who knows where! By prior arrangement, Kyle tows us up to Montezuma's Peak on the Sierra Estrella, and we release at 3,000 feet above the sailport. We ridge soar in the Sierra Estrella gaining about 400 feet. We're slightly above the crest in unremarkable lift. Do we sit and wait for a thermal or chase that little dust devil down wind?

I turn downwind. Crossing the Estrellas, we encounter some turbulent sink - rotor? - but there's no wave forming yet. We just glide at maximum L/D speed, slowly but steadily losing altitude. With full ballast, max L/D occurs at nearly 70 knots, and the tailwind is making our progress over the ground seem pretty good. But the altimeter is winding ominously down. At about 2,000 AGL, we roll into a usable thermal. Not strong, mind you, but useful; 200 fpm is all we're getting, but the wind is really pushing us.

"What are our turnpoints?" asks Harry.

"What turnpoints?" I said absently.

"You know, the turnpoints of the triangle."

"What triangle?"

"For the record, Las. You know, the speed record."

"Uh, Harry, we're going to Denver today. With this wind, we can't go back to Estrella even if I wanted to." I tried to make him see things my way, but Harry was missing the point altogether.

"But it's Mother's Day. Maggie and I were supposed to join another couple for dinner tonight. When you called, I thought we were going on a 500 Km speed triangle."

Mother's Day. "OK, Harry, we can land at Falcon Field and have Kyle tow us back to Estrella instead of trying for Denver." At that point I was thinking... I should have taken Tommy... I should have left at 10... Maybe I just should have stayed put and had that Mother's Day party with Betty... In the midst of my mental should-have list, Harry ventured, "Do you really think we could get to Denver?"

"Well, we might not get quite that far, but we'll get close! With this wind behind us we don't even need very strong thermals."

At about this time, we were well downwind of the last bona-fide airport within reasonable aerotow distance of Estrella. The wind had made the decision for us. On to Denver!

In 30 minutes we were 40 miles from Estrella, entering the Superstition Mountains east of Phoenix. So far the thermals had ranged between 200 and 400 feet per minute, but we could not get above 3,000 AGL because of a wind shear. I quickly assigned Harry the difficult task of locating landable spots. As we were bouncing along between 1800 and 3000 feet over this Godforsaken terrain, I was really glad Harry was with me. The last time I had flown over this area, I'd made myself a promise... "Never again!" But as the years had gone by, I'd forgotten the feeling of having the rocks and cactus in my pants. Well, I was feeling them now! I guess it doesn't matter if you're in a 1-26 or the Janus with its 41:1 L/D.

We approach the Mogollon Rim country, where the ground is a minimum 7,000 MSL. No sweat, when we get to that rim wall, we'll go up for sure. Right on cue, the Janus indeed starts climbing and with the aid of a small thermal, we make it to 9000.

Even with this altitude, I'm no longer uncomfortable as I'd been back in the Superstitions. I'm downright concerned! So far, Harry's done a super job of selecting possible landing spots - now he'll really have to work! I am totally immersed in locating and utilizing lift. I have never entered so many of what I call "suckers' thermals" before in my life; there are lots of clouds, but the lift is really chopped up. Our average altitude is now only 2000 feet above the terrain.

I hesitate to dump our water ballast even though I know I should. But it is only 12:30. Clouds shade almost 100% of the earth below, but northeast of us, it looks definitely better. I'm hoping that we can reach that promise of better lift with the ballast intact.

Harry is picking out the landing fields, and getting ever more creative in his choices. "If you have to, the shores of that little lake look pretty good. They're only 4 or 5 miles from the road." The roads themselves are much too narrow for the Janus, and are lined with trees. Scenic, but not inviting. Ah well, I didn't want to look down anyway.

The average altitude is now down to 1500 AGL. I note that the surface wind direction is a bit different from the direction of cloud movement. Great! If I park in this zero sink, in a few minutes we should be over that sunny ground. Sure enough, the air is starting to feel livelier. "Hey, the vario is moving up!"

As we climb at 100 fpm, I'm thinking, "Soon we'll need all this water in our wings." Three minutes later, I see a swirl of dust about 2 miles northeast of us. Hooray! And we're off toward it. After centering, the Janus is climbing at 500 fpm and all I can do is lean back and enjoy it. Finally, some two hours after take off, we've nailed our first good thermal. We're taking this one to cloudbase. Nine... ten... eleven... twelve thousand feet. Denver, here we come!

"Harry, what was that city?"

"Holbrook, Arizona."

"Holbrook in two hours and five minutes. Not bad, eh?"

The next hour was incredible. At a 12,000 foot cloudbase, we zoomed along at 100 to 110 knots, following the cloud street and taking advantage of the 30 to 40 knot tailwind. I have never seen the real estate move so fast in my life!

"Where are we, Harry?"

"I don't know."

"Would you mind looking at the map?"

"Well, I would if I could, Las, but we don't have a Colorado sectional and we left the Phoenix chart about an hour ago. I've got a jet route chart here, but that's not any help." Oh well. I'm following the clouds, and we're going as far as we can anyway!

Flying now over the Painted Desert in northwestern New Mexico, what a beautiful sight. Reds, yellow, rusty orange, white, rosy pink - name a color and it's there. If we could only film a gorgeous flight like this and show it to the people who are afraid to fly. They'd forget the word fear! We're happy and content. Looking around, we're following nature's incredible highway in this cloud street. But what's this... rain??

The sound is worse than my alarm in the morning as the huge drops go ping-splatt on the wings and canopy. Let's see... yup... we'd better make a right turn and get out of this mess. (And this flight was turning out to be so neat! Drat.)

With this rude awakening, I must look around to assess the weather. Yes, it is rather overdeveloped. We'd better climb as high as we can. We found a 400 fpm thermal and made it to 14,000 MSL. "Harry, you fly over this area all the time for Republic. Any idea where we are now?"

"We're headed for Denver all right, and I think that over there is Farmington."

It would be nice to know for sure. How could I have stashed the wrong map on board? Well, it's obvious we'll have to follow the weather anyway - there's only one way to go with all this overdevelopment in the area.

The ground is wet everywhere; the area must have had a lot of rain fairly recently. Things are definitely slowing down. We're no longer finding any strong lift, and 200 fpm seems like a boomer. There is 100% cloud cover, with snow and rain moving threateningly up from the south. We have a nice smooth ride down to 10,000 feet with barely a ripple. The terrain is ruggedly mountainous with peaks at 9,000 feet and we head for a roll cloud of sorts up ahead. We gain a few hundred feet in that choppy lift, then glide quietly again.

There is too much water everywhere! No more thermals at all. We're down to 9,000 feet when I finally decide to dump the water ballast and we begin to ridge soar. I look down to see a small village with an invitingly big blacktop runway. Should I land?

The wind is blowing against the ridges, but so what? The ridges are 90° to courseline, so ridge soaring is not very practical. Without thermals, how can we go on? Well now, maybe there's a wave. And maybe if there's one, there are more. All those ridges lined up like ripples across the course might work out after all.

110

"Harry, there are some houses in those hills. What do you think - shall we take a chance at jumping ridges? We might make it into the big one somewhere out there. And, if we have to land, at least we'll be close to people."

"OK, let's go, Las. Sounds slick."

We jumped a couple of ridges, then found some very strong lift. Aha! There it is! Or is it? What we've got is 2,000 fpm on one side and we're losing 1,000 fpm on the other. Interesting. At about 300 feet above the peak of the ridge, the lift quits entirely. We find ourselves free-falling, with the Janus' nose pointed down at a 45° angle and no indicated airspeed. Very interesting! The hillside is really coming up fast. At what looks like about 6 feet above the tree tops, the Janus finally decides that the better part of valor here is to fly again. Now that was about as close I ever would want it! The back seat is very quiet.

As I work the Janus closer to the big mountain, the lift gets better. Pretty soon we are looking some 1,000 feet down at the peak that had almost consumed us. It had lost its hold on us. Now we are really moving. At 14,500 MSL, we were ridge soaring - a new experience for me. We could turn downwind and glide a long way, but there is a snow shower on the lee side of our ridge. One scare is enough for today!

For 20 minutes, we followed the ridge to the south, and managed to get around the snow shower. We crossed the mountain crest and found not wave but turbulent lift which we used to climb back to 14,500 feet. Then we continued the downwind dash. After crossing a large flat marshland, we reached the foothills of a 14,000 foot mountain. The altimeter shows us at 8,000 feet, probably some 700 or 800 feet above the valley floor. We work weak lift of only 50 fpm, the air as smooth as silk, and find ourselves getting colder.

At 9,000 feet, we spot five golden eagles. They're ridge soaring quietly, minding their own business and looking at this big white intruder. Four of them move away, but the fifth approaches. Power radiates from this beautiful bird, and he glances over as if to say, "I was here first, you know. Bug off!" His majesty was telling me to stay away and I held my distance.

At 10,000 feet the snow level started. The mountain became frightening; wind howling, snow boiling off it. The slope looked like a cauldron of churning winter storm. Happy Mother's Day, Mother Nature! On each successive turn, we had to bear upwind, because of the strong drift which would otherwise slam us into the slope. The peak was a brilliant white as we climbed past it showing 500 fpm.

Soon we were at cloudbase, now 15,000 MSL, and guess who was climbing into the clouds just off our right wingtip... none other than our golden eagle friend. We turned downwind once more, and I sense that the day is coming to an end. Crossing one more mountain, we find the long awaited wave some 2 miles past the crest. It is a silky smooth climb at 700 fpm. Apparently, this last mountain wants to be nice to us, but it is too late. The sun is setting; we must quit the climb and look for a landing place.

We spot a city in the distance, and I aim for it. Harry soon declares this town to be Pueblo, Colorado. As we circle over the airport with enough altitude to flat glide another 100 miles, Harry calls the tower.

"Pueblo Tower, Glider 468F. Just arrived from Phoenix, Arizona. Request landing instructions." All's quiet. After some long seconds,

"Uh, glider uh, 68F, say again from where?"

We touched down at 8:08 local time, and the whole airport came out to see this magnificent soaring machine that could waft along for the 563 course miles we'd flown. We secured the ship, answered the obligatory questions, and walked rather stiffly up to the operations building. It was time for the phone calls.

Harry had a bit of explaining to do and I wanted to let my Estrella gang know their fearless leader had set a new National record.

Ring! Ring!

"This is Estrella Sailport," a voice answered the phone.

"I have a collect call from Las Horvath, will you accept the charges?"

"Well, I guess so. He's the one who pays the phone bills."

This was not exactly the enthusiasm I had expected.

"How's the party going there?" I asked.

"Really good. Lincoln and Mitchell got their Diamond Altitudes today, so we're pretty happy. This is one of the best parties we've ever had! Kinda too bad you missed all the wine and everything, Las. Oh, by the way, where are you?"

"Pueblo, Colorado."

"Oh, well, that's far enough, right? Gotta go - the party's just getting good out there. Here's Betty."

"Hi, Las, where are you?"

"Pueblo, Colorado. Happy Mother's Day!"

"Oh, thanks. Say, what have you got planned for Father's Day?"

CHAPTER 7 - WALLY RAISANEN, BARNSTORMER

Wally Raisanen is a sailplane barnstormer at heart. He loves to simply take off and surprise himself (and his wife) as to where he'll end up. Wally joined ASA in 1970 and now has 2000 hours in his log book. You can trace his progress as a pilot through his writing.

FLYING, WALKING, THINKING AND TALKING by Wally Raisanen, September 1972.

Diamond Distance! The pull of that elusive goal was irresistible, so, crew or no crew, on July 3, 1972, I started out on a 318 mile triangle. Estrella, Avra Valley, and Mohawk Junction were my turnpoints. The 25 mph wind against the long leg over the rough, roadless Papago Indian Reservation didn't concern me, since I would be flying it in the strongest part of the day.

Weak conditions in the early part of the day, coupled with a late start, made it easy for me to decide against filling the ballast tanks. I pulled on my boots, filled a canteen, and left my wife and kids in the pool at Estrella. Jeri made me promise to call in periodically to let her know my position. Arizona Soaring's radio has an outdoor speaker so she could hear me, even if she didn't plan to answer.

Thermal activity began a little late for this time of year with the first dust devils visible at about 11:30. I got launched about 11:45, immediately got into a good thermal and started out down the course line. I worked five thermals between 3,000 and 6,000 MSL in the 72 miles down to Avra Valley. It was an uneventful trip while somewhat slow. After I made my turnpoint picture at Avra I got into a thermal right over the field, climbed to about 7,000, shot another photo just for insurance, and headed off towards the west. Just short of the Silver Bell mountains I hooked my first good thermal of the day, up to about 11,000 feet. I worked four 11,000 foot thermals between Avra and the Gila Bend area. I had to make a small detour to avoid the gunnery range where two groups of four fighters each were practicing strafing attacks in the desert near the abandoned Luke auxiliary south of Gila Bend. I got a little bit low avoiding them and was never again able to get up to the altitudes I had been getting coming across the Indian country.

The day was wearing on. The wind was working about 30 miles an hour against me, and I got to the Gila Bend area about 4 o'clock. From there to Dateland I followed the highway, never getting above 6,000 and having to work some very marginal thermals, which wasted more time. I made my turnpoint picture at Mohawk, got into a nice thermal in the Mohawk Mountains and climbed up to about 8,000 feet. As I coasted back downwind I noticed that the dust that had been blowing near Gila Bend was no longer visible, indicating the wind had died down. It was now about 6 o'clock and I knew with the altitude I had that I had to work two more thermals to make it. I was worried that the day would run out on me but I thought if I could get those two thermals when I needed them, I could make it and land about 7:30.

I found the first thermal 10 miles west of Gila Bend. It was a beautiful thermal. Very smooth, that took me up to 8,000 feet again. I started a final glide from there, recording my altitude and position on the chart. As I passed Gila Bend I realized I was just barely going to clear the 2,500 foot Maricopa Mountains, which are about 20 miles west of Estrella. I could see the field and hangar at Estrella this whole time. I hit some heavy sink as I passed Gila Bend, but by flying fast and by pulling up in the light bubbles I was able to maintain my altitude over the Maricopa Mountain tops.

As I approached the Maricopa Mountains I realized I was not going to make it without finding another thermal, but I was hopeful of either working a little bit of ridge lift or some thermal off the Maricopa Mountains. Unfortunately I hit a patch of heavy sink just as I approached the mountains and had to dive right on the rocks in order to get over them. As I approached the mountains I found some very patchy and extremely turbulent lift just off the rocks. I was clearing the rocks by only 50 or 100 feet and jumping up and down violently. I couldn't work this stuff because I was afraid of stalling and I didn't have enough altitude to recover from a stall, so I slipped through a little pass in the mountains pretty much despairing of making it. I knew Turnbow had made a field just past those mountains which would give me a safe place to land. I coasted down behind them as the lee curl pushed me down and at the last minute I dropped the wheel and made a steep right turn, diving close to the ground and dropped it into Turnbow's field.

I was not overly concerned even though I had been calling in on the radio periodically and had never received a reply for I felt certain I would be picked up on the road and I'd be able to get into Estrella and aero tow the sailplane back. I didn't know the field radio wasn't working that day.

I pushed the ship off to the side of the field, tied one wing down with a stake, and tied the other wingtip to a big barrel cactus. I picked up an apple, my maps, the remaining water, and headed for the road. It was still daylight. I noticed I had landed at exactly 7 o'clock. It was very hot. The peak temperature that day, I later found out, was over 110°. It must still have been over 100° as I started walking down the road. I knew I was 8 miles from Mobile. The lack of water started to concern me after I had walked the first half hour and drunk it all and hadn't seen a single car going in either direction. I was starting to get a little sore from walking and I kept going. After I finished the first hour I stopped and rested. I estimated I had covered about 4 miles the first hour but I knew I couldn't make that pace very much longer because my hip joints were getting very sore. I rested for 5 minutes and started off again. I passed a couple of cows on the road and had some fleeting thoughts about capturing one of them and riding it in to Estrella, but I couldn't get close enough to them to do a thing about it.

By then I was perspiring profusely and very conscious of my lack of water. The second hour I really got sore. My left foot blistered badly, my hip joints were aching, I was wringing wet from perspiration, and all I could think about was water. I thought about beer, pop, coolers, waterfalls, swimming pools, showers; my mind was constantly on water. After the second hour of walking it was quite dark. I started to get a little bit panicky because if I got to Mobile and there was no water there I was going to be through for the night and I didn't know whether I could survive through to the next day without any water.

I knew it was going to be bad news in any case. I was really getting irritated now because I still hadn't seen a car going in either direction. The clear desert air enabled me to clearly see the lights of houses at Mobile several miles away and as I trudged along the gravel road they didn't seem to get any closer. I made up my mind to stop and rest every 15 minutes, but when I stopped I got so dizzy and sick to my stomach that I was afraid I wouldn't be able to get going again, so rather than stopping to rest, I walked more slowly. For some reason my pace would pick up automatically after a few minutes of slow walking and I would be steaming down the road again.

By now I was aching all over. I was very worried about my wife because I knew she had left Estrella some time before and would be sitting at home thinking that I had crashed and killed myself. There was nothing I could do, however, so I kept going. As I approached the lights of Mobile I had alternate visions of seeing light coming out of building windows indicating the presence of people and moments when I knew they were just reflections of shiny objects. But the closer I got the more I realized that I was going to make it if there was water there. I soon noticed that the Mobile school was the prominent building I had been watching for the last 15 or 20 minutes. After three hours of walking, at about 10 o'clock, I finally walked into the schoolyard. Fortunately there was an outdoor faucet on the side of the building, so after chasing away some big fat frogs and unhooking the hose, I filled up my canteen with warm water and started guzzling it. Now the problem was to get home.

There were two school buses in the yard, but the high chain link fence all around the schoolyard was locked and there was no way to get the buses out. There was no sign of human habitation. Everything was locked up tighter than a drum. It was another 8 miles or so to Estrella and a telephone. There were houses up on the hillside to the north, but they looked like they were two or three miles away and the way my hip joints were aching I knew I couldn't make another two or three miles that night. Finally I did the only thing I could do. I pulled the screen off an office window, pushed the window open, stood on a box, reached way in, and opened the front door. Fortunately there was a telephone in the office so the first thing I did was call Jeri. She was crying when she answered the phone and my throat was so dry, despite having drunk about a quart of water in the last five minutes, that my voice was very hoarse and she knew I was in bad shape. She was so relieved to have heard from me it didn't matter. After I hung up I went into the school nurse's office and put some alcohol and Bandaids on my blisters and put my boots back on. Then I had some time to think about what had happened to me.

In retrospect I had made some terribly stupid mistakes. The first one was flying off across the desert in the hottest part of the year with only a quart of water. No one should fly across this country without at least a gallon of water in the ship that he can carry away with him. If that cannot be arranged, then at least fly with the ballast tanks full so you can stay with the plane, sleep overnight, and have somebody come and get you next day. Without water you have had it.

The desert survival course indicates that if you don't move around but stay in one place, a gallon of water will hold you two days. If you walk, a gallon of water will hold you one day. From then on, you're dying of dehydration. As an example, a young man, 21 years old, presumably in good shape, got his car stuck in the desert on 4th of July. He tried to walk out without water. He made 10 miles and died. I walked out 9 miles with essentially no water. If it hadn't been night time I would have been in real trouble. I weighed myself in the nurse's office at the school and found I had lost 10 pounds in 3 hours. That's about 1½ gallons of water weight. You don't have another gallon to spare. Hallucinations caused by dehydration would have set in within another two hours of walking.

Another stupid mistake I made was overflying Gila Bend Municipal Airport, knowing full well I wasn't going to make it to Estrella. Hoping to find another thermal at 7 o'clock at night is futile. I could have landed at Gila Bend at 6.30, got to a phone immediately, and been aero-towed out in plenty of daylight.

Another warning I would like to give is that no one should fly cross country in the Arizona deserts without heavy walking shoes or boots. I was wearing a pair of heavy cowboy boots which permitted me to hike nine miles in three hours. If I had been flying in sandals or light street shoes I would have been in bad trouble.

Fortunately I knew exactly where I was and there was a smooth, graded road going directly from where I landed to where I wanted to be. If I had to walk cross-country or on a cattle track in unknown country I could easily have gotten lost, disoriented, and died out there. If you land away and don't know exactly where you are or have a very clear road that you *know* goes to where you want to go, stay with the plane. It is the most visible thing in sight. A landed glider in the desert can be seen for 50 or 60 miles from a search plane. A man walking alone, or worse, lying down collapsed under a palo verde tree, is almost invisible. Stay with the plane if you don't know exactly where you are going and that help and water are available there.

Desert flying adds many exciting dimensions to cross country soaring. Thermals to 20,000 feet, clear air, dust devils, scenery and spectacular sunsets all contribute to the thrills of diamond hunting in the southwest. Dangers lurk in profusion as well, but by application of enlightened common sense, risk can be minimized. The lesson of this flight is clear: start early, fly fast and carry plenty of water.

THE FIRST ANNUAL "SOAR YOUR ARSE OFF REGATTA" (Or Another Vulgar Downwind Dash) by Wally Raisanen, July 1979.

PROLOGUE: When the phone rang and Paul Dickerson explained the scheme that he and our avuncular ASA President had cooked up, I at first thought it was some kind of gag designed to harass the mothers about their prospects for Father's Day.

After some questions, however, I concluded he was serious.

"Fly to Texas?" I said. "You're kidding!"

"No I'm not -- Hohanshelt thinks he's a cross country pilot now and he wants to fly to Texas," Paul claimed.

"Well. Why not?" I said. I was willing and, after all, it's Father's Day.

We all agreed to get an early start on Sunday, so on Saturday, Eric and I went out to Estrella, assembled the Cirrus, and then I took him and his girlfriend up in the Blanik. She got sick. I hope Eric learned an indelible lesson from that: gliders and girlfriends just don't mix.

DENOUEMENT: Sunday dawned bright, clear, cool and windy. Five of us met at the Sailport, to be joined by five soaring gypsies from California, on their way to Las Cruces and Taos. (They even brought their own towplane). After admiring some of the most beautifully built homebuilts I have ever seen, being prepped by some of the most beautifully built crew I have ever seen, I talked the California contingent into taking off first and testing the conditions. "Oscar Lima" took off first at 9:50, and rapidly climbed to over 7,000 over the big ridge. When I heard that, I said to Eric, "TIME TO GO!" And off I went at 10:30.

I worked a series of 400 fpm dust devils downwind toward Chandler, while waiting for 19, 28, and 5Z to launch. I heard 1X getting ready too. Thermal tops were only 3,000 above the ground, but getting stronger as I passed Casa Grande airport. I got low at Picacho Reservoir, but a dust devil there took me up to 8,000 at an average rate of climb of 900 fpm!

The Californians were fretting about the wind behind me, so I checked the Tucson ATIS - 27 knots at 220°! I could see the mine tailings being blown across the valley south of Tucson, with dust rising over the mountains downwind.

After working some ridge lift off Newman Peak, and a line of bubbles downwind of Marana, a giant dust devil took me up to 10,000 at 1,000 fpm average. I sort of slid out of the top of the thermal into a 300 fpm wave lift band downwind of the Tucson Mountains. I worked the wave up to 12,000 and headed out for Mica Mountain, where I could see rotor clouds over the Redington Valley beyond.

The lift approaching the mountain was extremely bumpy and hard to work, so I called Paul in 19 and said, "I'm going into the lee of the mountain, and I don't know what's going to happen!" I lost 2,000 feet in two minutes, flying at 120 knots through rough air, and wound up too low to work the rotor, which was then above me. The turbulent air sustained me as I slid down the valley toward Benson and some clouds.

A beautiful cloud street from Benson past Wilcox provided 4 to 6 knot lift as I dolphined back up to 12,000. I watched the white alkali dust rising off the Wilcox Playa in great streamers, zooming up to merge with the cu's over Dos Cabezas.

A quick conference on the radio revealed the startling fact that our average cross country speed was only 15 knots faster than the 30 knot gale we were riding. A little reflection brought the realization that returning to Estrella was all but impossible. I passed the word that Eric was to go home, I would not be returning that day.

The cloud streets pointed toward Oklahoma City, but a glance at the Albuquerque Sectional showed a big restricted zone in the way. Something about atomic bomb testing areas or whatever. I decided to forget Lordsburg and return and head for El Paso.

117

I crossed Wilcox to work the ridge lift along the Catalinas, getting up to 12,000 at the southeast end of the ridge, and I turned downwind toward an enormous dust devil stretching from the farms at San Simon almost up to the cu's above. Strong sink again in the valley, but 7 and 9 knot thermals up to the cloudbase, now at 13,000+.

The courseline passed south of Deming, and the Florida Mountains. Lines of cu's at about 30° to course extended as far as the eye could see, way into Texas. Dickerson and Hohanshelt were at Lordsburg, taking a turnpoint picture. 1X was approaching, while 5Z, not having a radio, turned back. (I found out later that he got back to Estrella somehow. I wouldn't have believed it then!) The California crew was far behind, but one of them did finally get to Lordsburg.

28 and 1X landed at Lordsburg, probably to save retrieve time, and Paul was talking about landing at Deming, as he didn't like the look of the weather ahead. Since I was about 30 miles farther on, and didn't want to head into Texas without someone to interpret for me, I worked hard at telling him about all the cu's I could see ahead, and he decided to carry on.

After a lot of unwieldy scrambling around with the maps, I set Pecos, Texas, as a tentative goal. Paul said the state distance record was about 420 miles, so anything beyond El Paso would break it.

The air ahead was definitely moist, with blue haze up to cloudbase. The clouds were father apart too, and I could hear Paul getting low in the valley east of Deming. Since he had flown off his map, I tried to pick landing spots for him as I headed for some clouds near the Mexican border. Some good dust devils in the sun south of the border looked tempting, but I decided to stay legal in the high cirrus shade on the US side.

After being as low as 800 feet above a small ranch, Paul reported getting back up, so I pressed on to El Paso, arriving over the city in a strong thermal that carried me up to 14,300, the high for the day. It was only 4 o'clock, and the wind was still 25 knots at 250°.

Paul exclaimed, "Do you realize we can fly for 3 more hours!" After some struggle with a relief bottle, he decided to press on into the unknown. I set "Mile High" airport near Sierra Blanca as an intermediate goal, should things not work out, and continued to point out landing spots to Paul as I progressed past Fabens down I-10. We exclaimed over the beauty of the eroded red and green terrain below.

Paul tried to explain things to the El Paso FSS, since his crew was following, but hadn't been heard from since Tucson. I don't think the FSS ever really understood that we had flown dead stick from Phoenix!

The day was definitely dying as we approached Van Horn, steadily losing altitude. Paul decided to land there, but I was 4,000 feet over the ground, so I pressed on. If I could get one more thermal, I could make Pecos before dark. I dropped my water ballast in a street of zero sink under some straggly cloud remnants, and headed for the freeway. Landing out there in the boonies would mean an interminable search!

Flying at minimum sink, drifting with the wind, I searched for a landable spot, and finally picked out a service road at a railroad stop called "Boracho", which is Mexican for "drunk". (Appropriate but unlikely in a dry county!) Miraculously, just as Paul was reporting downwind at Van Horn, I flew into a weak evening thermal, smooth as glass. I trimmed the ship to circle at 45 knots and it flew itself up to 10,000, taking at least 20 minutes to do so. It was so smooth that I concentrated on the chart, making out a final glide to Pecos, 45 miles away in the deepening gloom of the evening.

That was the slowest final glide of my life, shivering in the shade and ticking off the miles. I called the airport Unicom, and got a nice old lady who couldn't believe I was actually going to land there. I made the field with 2,000 feet to spare, and picked out a landing approach that would put me right in front of the little operations building. As I rolled to a stop, there stood an old couple looking for all the world like "American Gothic" by Grant Wood. The old man strolled up and, in an incomparable west Texas accent said, "Yah'll waunt sum gazoleeen, bowah?"

EPILOGUE: It turned out that Pecos is 519 Great Circle miles from Estrella, beating both the Standard and Unlimited Class State Soaring Records by 100 miles. At an average wind speed of 25 knots, just being in the air for 8½ hours added 210 miles to the distance made good; I really flew 310 miles at 35 miles per hour, and got blown another 210. Talk about your vulgar downwind dash!

It took my valiant son and wife 12 hours to get me the next day. And it took us two days to get back, against the wind! A pair of long-dreamed-of diamond earrings soothed the pain for Jeri, and Eric thought it was fun. So did I - I'm already looking forward to next year's S.Y.A.O. Regatta!

HOW IT LOOKED FROM THE GROUND by Paul Dickerson.

It was left to Paul to report the subsequent pain and expense of retrieval.

Early in the day, I radio-ed my crew, son Charles and Mark Arndt, that I intended to proceed to the east as far as I could go. I had left messages for them at several flight service stations along the way and was confident that they would be along within a few hours. Wally, on the other hand, was, as usual, flying without a crew. So, when he finally landed, in great trepidation he called Jeri to solicit a retrieve. The conversation went something like this.

"Hello, dear. This is Wally."
"Are you gonna be late for dinner again? We have company, you know."
"Well, yes, I may be a little bit late."
"When will you be here?"
"Well... You're gonna have to come get me."
"I suppose you're down by Tucson some place..."
"Not exactly. I'm a little east of there."
"East? Further away than Tucson? You mean Benson?"
"Well, actually, a little east of there."
"Surely you're not all the way to Lordsburg?"
"Well, actually, a little east of there."
"Why don't you just tell me where you are."
"Well, actually, I'm in Pecos."
"Where the hell is Pecos?"
"Well, actually, it's about 150 miles east of El Paso."
"You mean west of El Paso."
"No. I mean east of El Paso."
"Expletive Deleted. Why don't you just take a bus back?"

Well, anyway, it went on like this for a little while. Finally, Wally prevailed upon Jeri to come and pick him up but she refused to leave until dawn the next morning. My crew arrived midnight Sunday night. We spent the night in a hotel, and next morning got up at dawn, retrieved the glider and launched for home.

We stopped at Deming for gas and sure enough, as luck would have it, there was Jeri and Eric headed east. We visited with them a little bit. She said she was really having a good time, she was enjoying seeing the desert a little bit and was looking forward to seeing Wally sometime in the next 7 or 8 hours.

We departed and arrived back in Phoenix 4 o'clock or so Monday afternoon. Jeri and Eric proceeded to the east and recovered Wally that afternoon. Wally was ready for an immediate departure, to arrive back in Phoenix about midnight. However, Jeri had other ideas. She said, "As long as we've come this far, why don't we have a little vacation."

So they toured the scenic west Texas and New Mexico border, hitting such hot spots as Juarez, Carlsbad Caverns and Santa Fe. Jeri said she really enjoyed the trip to Sante Fe because there is, among other things for tourists to do, some wonderful jewelry stores in Santa Fe.

Wally, in his gratitude, and without any coercion from Jeri (I'm told), offered to buy Jeri the set of diamond earrings that she had wanted for so long. So as it worked out, a good time was had by all. Wally had a good flight, they had a good vacation, and nice pair of trinkets with which to remember it by.

BARNSTORMING IN A SAILPLANE by Wally Raisanen (2E) and John Baird (6F), July 1984.

It all began when Paul Dickerson (19) casually mentioned his plan to fly from Carefree Airport to Moriarty (30 miles east of Albuquerque) on the last weekend in May. Tows would be available there for the flight back the next day. 2E was preparing to put new tail numbers on his recently acquired Ventus and Paul had dropped over to help. During the conversation, he recalled a barnstorming venture he and John Baird (6F) had made last year, flying from Carefree to Las Vegas, camping out at the airport, and getting a tow to return the next day. No crews were involved, the whole idea was to emulate the barnstormers of old, who ventured out wherever their fancy might suggest, dealing with life and the weather as they found it. The concept was very appealing, and 2E allowed as how he would be interested to go along, and so they agreed to try it.

They met at Carefree early on May 26. 2E had spent several hours excitedly planning the event, as had 19. Both had studied the possible courses, 2E favoring a direct route to keep the already long course (340 miles) to a minimum, while 19 preferred a routing that emphasized airport access to minimize problems should a landout be necessary. 6F uses WAC charts, to be able to see the big picture, and proposed an adaptive approach to course selection. All three were equipped with extra water, sleeping bags, minimal food, and toys. (6F had a plinking pistol, 2E had a turgid book on philosophy and 19 had his hiking boots). During the brief wait for a tow pilot (the regular man overslept and a replacement was recruited from Turf Soaring, 20 miles away), the three would-be barnstormers agreed not to race, but to help each other find lift. Nobody bothered with a weather forecast, generally agreeing that they were unreliable at best, and an unnecessary distraction. All three have come to the opinion that the best weather information is gleaned by getting into the air and doing one's own research.

2E launched first, at 10:55. It was his first flight from Carefree and he was appalled at the total lack of suitable escape routes should a problem appear early in the tow. The only likely spot was a golf course liberally studded with sand traps and granite boulders bigger than semi-trailers. Fortunately, all went well and he released in weak lift 1500 feet above the airport, soon to be passed by 6F and 19 who towed farther into the mountains, and somewhat higher. As 2E struggled to climb, he drifted with the wind into the mountains northeast of the field, and soon found improved lift. 6F had climbed to the top of the inversion at 9,000 MSL and headed to the next mountain ridge, finding little. As he got low, 19 and 2E topped out at 9500 and left down course in search of lift over the ridge tops. Working bubbles, they soon found themselves over the west edge of the Verde Valley, while 6F was struggling to the south near Mount Ord. Finding little there, he crossed the Verde Valley to the foothills on the east side where he worked for 18 minutes in delayed sink before locating a thermal that got him high enough to see over the top of the mesa. The trio was learning more about the weather. 19 pressed on across the valley, headed for Gisela, south of Payson. 2E shifted north along the cliffs on the west side, and found a nice thermal, climbing to 10,500 MSL before crossing the valley, so was 1500 feet above 19 when they met in the high ground between Payson and Gisela. 2E climbed a little, and pressed on over Diamond Peak to spot lift on the way to the next chosen landing spot near Young, called Waldrip Airport.

19 was unable to climb and had to work his way south into the lower ground. 6F advised working close to the canyon walls, as this stratagem had enabled him to get away from a similar trap, and he was now proceeding toward Waldrip. Unfortunately, 19 found nothing and announced that he was committed to a landing at a farm near Gisela. A series of relays via WK over Carefree arranged a retrieve for 19, who was safely on the ground, but bitterly disappointed in this turn of events. Now the trio was a duo and had learned even more about the weather; there was a good chance they had started a little too soon.

6F and 2E met in a 7 knot thermal over the pine covered canyons NE of Waldrip, 2E spoilering down to the level of the mini-Nimbus. After a brief conference, they agreed to head north to the cu's now visible over the Mogollon Rim past Heber. Working several pine-scented thermals, the pair arrived at Heber at 11,000 MSL and soon were climbing at 8 to 18 knots over the spectacular Painted Desert between Heber and Holbrook. Cloud bases were near 18,000 and a street extended eastward as far as could be seen, at least 200 miles.

2E was carrying less ballast than 6F, and generally found himself higher. Keeping visual contact was difficult, as the cu's were about 18 to 20 miles apart, and of course selection varied. Frequent radioed descriptions of the ground features was required to establish location.

"Six Fox, you see that round thing on the ground?"

"You mean that agricultural thing?"

"Yeah. I'm over it. Where are you?"

"Coming."

"OK - Whoops!" 2E was startled more than once to suddenly see 6F flash by, having been totally invisible for the last 30 or 40 minutes.

St. Johns, New Mexico, passed below about 3:00 after a lengthy debate as to its correct identity.

"Six Fox, I'm not exactly sure of our location, maybe we should follow the road for a while."

"I think that's Springerville down there."

"No, we must be further north than that. Maybe it's St. Johns."

"I don't know. Maybe it's Black Rock."

"No, it's St. Johns."

"Yeah, it's St.Johns."

By now they were getting out of radio range of the departure point, so a last status report was relayed via YU over Carefree, and the pair started across an enormous blue hole between St. Johns and the next feasible landing spot, King Ranch south of Zuni. Even from 10,000 feet above the ground, the terrain below was awe inspiring and forbidding. Very few roads, even fewer flat spots, and colorful geological formations spread in an endless array in all directions.

"King Ranch must be in that high valley up ahead."

"I don't know, it's the right heading."

"I don't see any strip, maybe it's that grass field by the ranch house."

A foreign voice on the radio said, "Ye're mighty close to the King Ranch. Keep coming!" 2E thought, who is that? Only the sight of a new cloud street ahead gave courage to press on.

Arriving at the clouds in the Tularosa Mountains about 4000 feet AGL, the pair once again gained comfortable height over a lake embedded in a pine forest, and studded with weekend boaters. They proceeded along the cloudstreet in a northeasterly direction, somewhat uncertain as to their true location. They agreed to meet over a remarkable object on the ground, a Y shaped array of circular dish antennas, later identified as a deep-space radio telescope located in the Plains of San Agustin. Using five year old charts, they found no mention of this incredible landmark on the map, so no location information was forthcoming at this time.

Soon the radio chatter from Moriarty was heard, as was conversation from another Ventus flying from El Paso to Las Cruces. 2E had previously contacted both the Albuquerque Soaring Club at Moriarty, and the New Mexico Soaring Ranch north of there, as to the best place to obtain a tow. The advice at that time was to use the commercial operator, to avoid insurance problems with the club operation. Re-checking by radio brought a forcefully friendly instruction that Moriarty was the place to go. Fortunately, 6F had in the meantime identified the town below as Magdalena, some 60 miles south of their presumed location. Staying west of the brown ribbon of the Rio Grande to Belen, the two raced off on final glide past Mosca (Fly?) Peak at the northern toe of the Manzano Mountains, over Chilili, and on to a landing at Moriarty.

Ken Harper, Leo Doyal, Dan Gallacini, and several others of the Club helped with moving the planes across the soft infield to a pair of tie-downs. Both had landed with ballast, to save hassle the next day, but 2E had to dump his to extricate the Ventus from a gopher hole, creating a giant mud puddle. They soon learned the reason for the suggestion that Moriarty was the place to land. Apparently, a demo ride in a Blanik at the New Mexico Soaring Ranch had ended in a crash, destroying several gliders, their only towplane, and killing the passenger. This sobering news put a damper on things, and everyone hurriedly completed their preparations for the night.

Soon, the barnstormers were checked into a local motel, and on their way to Estancia, NM, where a fine prime rib dinner at the Co-op Feed Store (!) put everyone in a mellow mood. The locals informed the barnstormers that their arrival was most unexpected, as the local weather had been wet, with a low cloud base and little lift, until 3:00 pm. Apparently the two had been chasing a cold front all day, unaware of the weather conditions ahead.

Sunday dawned bright and clear, with no wind. The 10 to 15 knot wind from the west had greatly aided the trek, but posed a fair problem for the return. Optimistically, they discussed making a three day jaunt of the trip, going to El Paso, and back to Phoenix on Monday, but cooler heads prevailed, and it was agreed that an early launch and a direct route back were the best plan. This plan was reinforced by the local weather forecast which called for 22 knot winds from the west and a weak cold front crossing the course line at the state border.

An excellent breakfast at El Comedor in Moriarty put everyone in an optimistic mood. True to the forecast, by the time water ballast was reloaded, and the planes staged, the wind had returned at 15 to 20 knots. As soon as a dust devil appeared, 2E launched. Off tow at 10:55 am (9:55 Phoenix time), 2 knot lift topped out 3000 feet above the field. 6F was soon launched and the two spent 45 minutes bobbing up and down over the airport, trying to penetrate against the wind. Then lift improved, and 2E rode a breaking bubble to 15,000 MSL (9,000 AGL), calling out increasing rates of climb. When lift reached 6 knots, 6F joined him.

"Six Fox, if you are not climbing, I suggest we press on."

The two headed for the 7,000 foot pass to Albuquerque and the Rio Grande valley. Flying at max L/D through silky smooth air, 2E passed over 6F who had gone faster, and was now desperately low over the lowest point in the I-40 pass between the Sandia Mountains and the Manzanos. Struggling over the ridge, 6F dropped into the valley, directly in line with the main takeoff runway at Albuquerque International, whose controllers were somewhat unsympathetic with the plight of gliders.

"Take a heading of 260°."

"I've got to find some LIFT!" (Click).

Finding no lift, 2E pressed on across the city, heading for the cu's a few miles west of the Rio Grand near Alameda. Arriving below the clouds about 1000 feet above the low mesa just west of the river, 2E worked narrow, turbulent ribbons of lift, searching for the thermals feeding the clouds, now about two miles directly overhead.

The lift got more organized and stronger as altitude was gained, and soon 2E was climbing at over 10 knots, with occasional bursts up to 20 knots. He watched anxiously as 6F struggled far below, still very low, but now west of the river, and in striking distance of the good lift. 2E lost sight of his partner as he climbed to 18,000 feet, and orbited under the clouds a few minutes waiting for his friend. A microphone problem blocked attempts at communication and the two separately wondering what happened to the other, and considered whether to land or press on alone. Suddenly, they spotted each other near cloudbase, and with radios once again working, joyfully agreed to follow the cloud street which was aligned with I-40 past Mount Taylor and on towards Gallup. Cruising at 14,000 MSL, in a contemplative mood, 6F said,

"I was reflecting on how awful it would have been if we had hit the ground at Albuquerque."

"Awful doesn't begin to describe the magnitude of terribleness like that."

Following a more northerly route past Grants, NM, over beautiful Blue Water Lake, across the desert, cruising at 90 to 100 knots under a cloudstreet directly on course, life was at its zenith. The wind seemed somewhat abated at altitude, and ground speed had been averaging about 80 knots once the clouds were reached. Skirting a blue hole near the Petrified Forest, a band of clouds appeared on the horizon ahead, developing cu-nims marking the northern edge.

"It looks like that cold front is up ahead."

"Let's go around the southern end of the clouds, there are cu-nim on the northern edge."

"OK."

Changing course southward at Holbrook, contact with WK at Carefree arranged for crew to come up from Scottsdale, with a planned landing at 4:30. Leaving the clouds at the Mogollon Rim near Payson, the 50 mile final glide was uneventful, and the tired but jubilant pair met to shake hands and share a welcome cool one in the heat of the desert where the great adventure began only the day before.

Relating their tale to Woody Woods and Dieter Loeper at Carefree while waiting for the crew to arrive, it seemed hard to believe that such a short time had passed, so many were the sights and struggles packed into the last 48 hours. The spirit of barnstorming lives on, and the rewards of adventure and fond friendships are there for the taking.

THE INCREDIBLE SOARING SAFARI by Wally Raisanen, July 1987.

"Hello?"

"Wally, this is Paul. Would you be interested in a cross country soaring safari?"

"Sure. What is it?"

"The Tucson Soaring Club has authorized us to take one of their towplanes for a week, and three of us are going to tour Utah, Colorado, and New Mexico, and we thought we would like you to come along."

"Sounds great, count me in!"

I discovered that the scheduled dates coincided with a meeting I was supposed to attend in Boston, but I managed to bow out, semi-gracefully, and agreed to go. The plan was to take four sailplanes, one tow plane and pilot, and one crew car and trailer with two crewmen. Team flying was the order of the day, no racing. If one person landed, everyone else was obligated to land at the same place (assuming it was an airport) to simplify tow procedures and lodging logistics. If someone got low, everyone else was to orbit, to stay together. We were to use a line abreast formation to maximize the probability of finding lift. I thought this would be a nice break from my usual routine of all-out racing, and a wonderful opportunity to see some fabulous western scenery.

We finalized our plans during the week of the 1987 Region 9 contest at El Tiro, Tucson. The participants were to be myself (2E) and Paul Dickerson (19) flying Venti, John Baird (6F) Mini-Nimbus, and Steve Fahrner (EU) in his venerable but fast Speed Astir. Crew members were my son, Eric, and Dennis Haworth.

We gathered at Turf Soaring, north of Phoenix, early on Sunday, June 14. We sent the crew ahead to Kingman at 9:00 am, and launched at 11:00. Our tentative goal was the glider FBO at Boulder City, Nevada, about 150 miles away. It took us an hour of scratching at release altitude to work our way up the southern slope of the Bradshaw Mountains, where we contacted 7 to 9 knot lift under strong cumulus clouds. "Ahh, we have broken the surly bonds..." from 19 echoed the general feeling of relief.

From our rendezvous at 14,000 feet over Crown King, Arizona we set out past Prescott in wide bands of lift under the clouds. 19 and 6F were flying very fast, with EU and 2E trailing. While the leaders thermaled in strong lift, the followers dolphined along, generally winding up in the same place at the same altitude. 19 got a little low as the group approached Kingman, and 6F got very low crossing I-40 near Seligman.

"Where are you guys?" came the plaintive cry.

"We're orbiting north of the highway, under the cu, at 15,000. We'll wait for you here, come on."

"I don't see you!"

"Well, I don't see you either!"

A lengthy exchange of radioed steering commands followed.

"Oh, there you are." 6F rapidly climbed to cloudbase, and we set off northward towards the Grand Canyon.

"19 ground, where are you?"

"Just leaving Kingman."

"Proceed to St. George, Utah."

"Roger, proceeding to St. George."

This was the last we were to hear from them until much later in the day. The course crossed the western end of the Grand Canyon, where the brown waters of the Colorado merged with the turquoise blue of Lake Mead. Dirt strips at Pearce Ferry and an unnamed mesa high above the river were the only landable spots in view. 19 wanted to take the cautious route to the west, but was persuaded that our 7000 foot terrain clearance was sufficient to safely take the scenic route.

Cameras were busy as we orbited at cloud base over the river, then on to the north towards St. George. The group separated again, with 19 speeding ahead, and the rest following. 6F loitered behind, working every thermal. As we approached the red rock cliffs between St. George and Hurricane, the group was spread over 15 miles of spectacular scenery. 2E edged close to a thundershower east of Hurricane, and rapidly climbed in rain to cloudbase. Radio conversation resulted in a decision to continue to Cedar City, about 60 miles to the north, and the crew was contacted as they left Las Vegas to continue to that location. The strip at Hurricane Mesa was a visual guide post, easy to identify as it ran right to the edge of a 200 foot red cliff.

"We can make Provo, easy"

"Yeah, but the crew is three hours behind us"

"Okay, let's land at Cedar City".

The airport manager there seemed extremely co-operative on the radio, cementing our decision to make that our first stop. We landed at 4:00 pm, and quickly tied down the ships, none too soon, as the downwash from the storm quickly made things hectic on the ground. We spent the next hour sitting on the ships tail booms, waiting out a 40 mph blow. Gordon Jewett, the airport manager, arranged an airline discount at a local motel, and free transportation thereto. We raised the ground crew from the motel on the hand held radio at 7:00 pm as they rolled into town, and Bob Link showed up in the Super Cub 24Y shortly thereafter.

The next morning was brilliantly clear but very windy, and a visit to the local FSS verified strong SW winds all day. The FSS was learning to use its newly acquired collection of computer gear, and showed us high resolution cloud pictures updated every 45 minutes by satellite, but couldn't provide any soaring intelligence. In fact, they were unable to predict the local high temperature! We were introduced to Doc Sigfrid, a local vet who has a towplane and was eager to talk to some fellow glider enthusiasts. We enjoyed a picnic in a city park, and generally lazed away the day. The next day would probably be much better, as we would be in the unstable air following the cold front.

And so it proved. The wind was light and variable on the ground, and 25 to 45 knots down course at altitude. We launched at 10:30 in 2 knot lift, and climbed the mountains to the east towards developing cu. We met over the town at 15,000 feet, and headed towards our goal of Grand Junction, Colorado. The group scattered again following spectacular red cliffs and green pine slopes past the Bryan Head ski area. Lift was extremely far apart, and we got low over the 10,000 foot mountain range, north of Cedar City. Our original plan was to stay on the windward side of the ridge, but 2E spotted a developing cu in the next valley to the east, and everyone streaked over the ridge. After some thrashing, good lift was found, and we found ourselves at 17,000 MSL, headed for Colorado. Once again, we were spread over 25 miles of high desert.

"6 Fox, where are you?"

"I am over a lake."

"What's your altitude?"

"Seven thousand."

"Seven thousand! How the heck did you get there?" (The ground is at six thousand). Immediately, the other three converged on the lake, looking for 6F. As we got low, searching for him, he called again.

"I am southeast of the lake, orbiting at 17,000." 19's laconic Texas accent filled the air with,

"Ahhh - I believe we have a communications problem here."

"6 Fox, do you have your oxygen on?"

"YESSS!"

We eventually rejoined and proceeded to Wayne Wonderland (!) and across the colorful desert past Green River and along the Book Cliffs escarpment to Grand Junction. We conferred with the ground crew and agreed on a destination of Garfield County airport, near Rifle, Colorado. A fire near the airport showed a 90 degree crosswind, verified by 24 Yankee. We landed without incident, and ferried our gear to Glenwood Springs, where we spent an enjoyable evening soaking in the natural hot springs. A planning session rejected Owl Canyon Gliderport near Fort Collins as our next goal, due to the early overdevelopment between Granby and Boulder. We decided to fly to Taos, to participate in the Taos Soaring Fiesta, which had started the day before. "Yeah, let's terrorize the natives!" We were getting a little cocky at that point.

Cumulus began developing in the high country at 8:00 am and had formed within 25 miles of us by 9:00, so we launched under scattered weak cu at 10:00 am, and promptly all landed. It appeared that the valley was developing later than the high country all around. A moment of excitement was provided by EU who ground looped on landing, neatly pirouetting between a landing light and a VASI box. It turned out he had forgotten to pull the tape off his port wing vent, and dumped only one wing. That was the last day anyone flew with water ballast, and reduced the cockiness quotient considerably. We relaunched at noon, and quickly climbed to 17,000 feet, heading southeast across the 14,000 foot mountains near Aspen. The formidable snow covered terrain surrounding pine forested valleys led to not a little apprehension, and we worked every thermal to stay near cloudbase. 2E forged ahead, impatient with any lift weaker than 5 knots. He led the group to McClure Pass, where 19 and 6F got low. Eventually, good lift was found, and the chastened group headed towards Crested Butte airport in a tight gaggle. It was hard to concentrate on flying while viewing the incredible scenery. Brilliant blue and white frozen lakes nestled between snow fields and yellowish scree slopes, provided visual contrast to the deep blue of the sky and the deeper green of the forests. Off in the distance lay the snow-capped Sangre de Cristos (Blood of Christ), named for the reddish glow they give off at sunset. 12 knot thermals under cumulus streets kept our altitude well above 17,000 MSL. The outside air temperature was 12°F, causing some shivering in the cockpit, and sticky controls.

"It's a good thing we decided to fly dry, we'd have been frozen solid by now!"

The route over Blanca Peak and the Sangre de Cristos led directly to Taos, and our ground crew and towplane were ahead of us, so we pressed on, once again separating into individual flights. 2E reported battery problems, and went off the air. Final glide checks showed a 10 knot headwind, which complicated the lowering glide past Questa and Molybdenum, but ridge lift around the southern end of the mountain, and convergence lift across the alluvium to Taos airport brought everyone in high and hot.

The friendly attitude of the Taos area pilots and the beauty of the town made it hard to leave, but the towplane had to be back on Saturday so we made plans to fly to Gallup, NM or Holbrook, AZ the next day. The weather looked fabulous, with a slight hint of cirrus on the southern horizon, and we were filled with optimism as we launched at noon. We had a little trouble getting high, so met over the Taos Pueblo and headed south along the mountains towards Santa Fe. The crew was well ahead, with instructions to wait at Gallup. The lift over the mountains was very choppy, with 7 knots up and 4 knots down on every circle. We stayed close together, calling lift whenever found, and we were barely able to stay level with the peaks. Lift was mostly bubbles, and being a few hundred feet low in the gaggle meant no climb. 19 was well below us, and got lower and lower as we proceeded south. Approaching Santa Fe, we worked weak choppy lift over a ski area until everyone was at 12,000, and we tiptoed across the Rio Grande valley towards Los Alamos airport, at 7,200 feet. We worked weak bubbles at 8,500 to 9,000 near Los Alamos before getting up to 12,000 again. 6F nearly landed, but managed to get up on the tree covered slopes of Redondo Peak. Headwinds of 15 to 20 knots had greatly slowed our ground speed, and we vainly tried to contact the crew to get them to hold. It took us two hours to pass Santa Fe, and we flew at max L/D towards some good cu visible west of Albuquerque. All got to 1500 above the ground at Rio Puerco (Pork River) where good lift to 14,000 allowed some time to eat a late lunch and replan our destination. It was getting late, and with the headwind, it appeared that Gallup was not possible, so we agreed to land at Grants, NM. Arriving there, we had 24 Yankee check out the runway. He reported a 20 knot crosswind, and we agreed that a landing there was not safe, so we pressed onward to the next strip, at Thoreau. This proved to be behind a locked gate, as verified by the ground crew, who we were finally able to raise on the radio. (The Gallup airport is in a hollow, blocking VHF radio communications.) 2E pressed on along the redrock escarpment north of I-40, and found weak ridge lift and thermal bubbles sufficient to limp into Gallup, where the runway was aligned into the wind.

"Keep coming, guys, there is help along the way!" The low sun made finding the airport a problem, but all made it in safely at 8:00 pm. "We are finally learning to work together."

"Yeah, that radio conference on landing spots produced good decisions, and no excessive argumentation."

"Let's hope the weather improves tomorrow, this has been a long, tough day."

"Amen!"

Today, the goal is home. After launching at noon, the towplane headed for Tucson, and the crew was well ahead, so we formed up at the top of the airport thermal (12,500 MSL), and headed west along the freeway. Long bands of weak lift along the dry wash following the interstate helped, but thermals were widely spaced, and we were in constant danger of landing. Just when things would get desperate, the welcome cry of "Turning!" would be heard, and all would converge on the lucky pilot. In this manner we proceeded past each available strip on course. Sanders, Petrified Forest, Taylor at Snowflake, Arizona, Mogollon, Pleasant Valley at Young, and finally Payson, where our crew waited. It was generally agreed that we should not go further, but 2E found a 5 knotter just over the end of the Payson runway, and a hop over the Mazatzal Wilderness seemed possible.

"I'll hold here to mark it. Come on."

"I see you, go on."

"OK."

We made it back into Carefree airport, near our homes at Scottsdale, at 4:00 pm, while EU proceeded to Turf where his truck and trailer awaited. On the ground, enjoying the hospitality of the crew at Carefree SkyRanch, we marvelled at the fact that we had made our goal each day, with no landouts or other mishaps. The scenery, camaraderie, shared pride in achievement, and overall good fun made the scary moments fade in our memory. It was truly a soaring odyssey, and we eagerly began discussing a repeat next year.

SOARING COMPETITION IN THE 21ST CENTURY by Wally Raisanen

Gentlemen:

After my first competition flight with your new "Copilot", I am so impressed with its performance, that I have compiled my impressions of the flight for your advertising program. (For those of you who have not been informed of the details, the Cambridge "Copilot" is an electronic system that consists of two parts. The sensor system copies all communications between the ARSA radar and mode C transponders within 100 miles of itself, keeping track of the altitude and position of each aircraft. By calculating the changes in altitude and position of each communicating aircraft, it determines the type of aircraft (powered or glider), its flight mode (cruising or thermaling), its present and average cross-country speed and climb rate, and its ground track relative to the terrain. The "expert" system is a computer program written in Prolog that advises the pilot, based on over 10,000 expert rules, on the best speed and course to fly.)

"Aah, Copilot, didn't we go a little over redline there on that start?"

I'M AFRAID SO SIR, YOU EXCEEDED MY SUGGESTED ENTRY ALTITUDE BY 100 FEET.

"Hmpf, must have been a thermal in the IP."

I SUGGEST A RIGHT COURSE DEVIATION TO ONE FIVE ZERO.

"Explain."

NINE SHIPS THAT STARTED EARLIER SHOW BETTER LIFT OVER THE HIGH TERRAIN THAN OVER THE VALLEY.

"I'm heading for Newman Peak. There is always a good one there."

TWO SHIPS ARE THERMALING OVER NEWMAN PEAK. AVERAGE CLIMB FOUR KNOTS. INDICATIONS OF LIFT STREET DOWNWIND OF HIGH GROUND TO THE SOUTH.

"Explain."

FOUR SHIPS THERMALING INDIVIDUALLY LINED UP DOWNWIND OF 3200 FOOT HILL TO THE SOUTH. CRUISE PERFORMANCE INDICATES ZERO SINK FOR EXTENDED DISTANCES. LEADERS AVERAGE SPEED 75 KNOTS.

"Okay, we'll try it."

THANK YOU, SIR.

The auto-trim system kept my speed at the optimum value for the sink encountered, and the lift ahead. I was surprised at the speed, as I normally fly quite a bit faster, but I had confidence in the computer at this point.

Suddenly the collision-avoidance alarm came on and the stick-shaker began pounding my hand to the left. I pushed to relieve the pressure on the stick and did a left-right coupled Dutch roll at redline speed!

"What was that!" No response from "Copilot". Remembering my training, I took a deep breath and said "Explain".

A SHIP 100 METERS BEHIND US SUDDENLY ACCELERATED. EMERGENCY SAFETY MANEUVER FOR CLEARANCE.

"Where is he now?"

FIVE O'CLOCK, SAME ALTITUDE, 1000 METERS.

Craning my neck and maneuvering slightly, I spotted the glider. Damned leeches! "Aah, Copilot, that was a good one. Why didn't we stop to climb. Explain."

LIFT STREET AHEAD. CROSS COUNTRY SPEED TWO KNOTS FASTER BY DOLPHIN MANEUVER AS COMPARED TO CLIMB/CRUISE MANEUVER.

"I don't see anyone ahead. When did you identify that lift street?"

MOST RECENT UPDATE TWENTY TWO MINUTES AGO.

"It better still be there," I muttered. No response. "Aah, Copilot, confidence of forecast."

LIFT FORECAST CONFIDENCE SIXTY THREE PERCENT.

"Aah, Copilot, explain alternate tactical plan."

IF LIFT NOT FOUND IN THREE MINUTES, DEVIATE TO SILVER BELL MOUNTAIN, REDUCE SPEED TO SIXTY KNOTS, ARRIVE AT PROBABLE THERMAL WITH FOUR HUNDRED FEET GROUND CLEARANCE, DEVIATE TO EL TIRO AIRPORT AT TWENTY SEVEN HUNDRED FEET.

"Aah, Copilot, has anyone made the first turn yet?"

AFFIRMATIVE.

"Aah, Copilot, list turnpoint photo altitudes."

129

MAXIMUM TWELVE THOUSAND, MINIMUM FOUR THOUSAND, AVERAGE SEVEN THOUSAND.

"Aah, Copilot, are we gaining on the leaders?"

NO SIR. Dammit!

"Aah, Copilot, explain task tactical plan."

LIFT ON SECOND LEG FORTY PERCENT STRONGER THAN FIRST LEG. WE WILL EXCEED LEADERS AVERAGE SPEED ON SECOND LEG AND THIRD LEG. ESTIMATED TASK SPEED NINETY THREE KNOTS. ESTIMATED WINNING MARGIN THREE MINUTES, TWENTY SECONDS.

"Aah, Copilot, are the ships behind gaining on us?"

SEVEN YET TO START. TWELVE ON COURSE. ONE GAINING ON US. SPEED ONE HUNDRED TWELVE PERCENT OF OURS.

"Aah, Copilot, explain winning strategy over ships behind us."

WEATHER FORECAST INDICATES LIFT WILL FALL OFF BEFORE THEY COMPLETE TASK. ESTIMATED WINNING MARGIN ONE MINUTE TEN SECONDS.

"Confidence?"

MARGIN ESTIMATE CONFIDENCE THIRTY PERCENT.

"Explain low value of confidence."

WEATHER FORECASTING FOR THE FIRST THREE DAYS OF CONTEST IN FIRST QUARTILE OF RELIABILITY. LIFT FALLOFF BASED ON FORECAST HIGH CIRRUS. PLEASE UPDATE PILOT CLOUD OBSERVATION.

"Aah, right. No cumulus, high cirrus on western horizon, estimate distance one hundred miles. Aah, Copilot, winning margin estimate and confidence, please."

MARGIN ONE MINUTE TEN SECONDS, CONFIDENCE FIFTY PERCENT, STANDARD DEVIATION TWENTY SECONDS. PLEASE UPDATE CLOUD OBSERVATIONS MORE FREQUENTLY.

Well, needless to say, I was really impressed at that point. As we passed a number of competitors on the second leg, I was more impressed. We beat the second place finisher by about a minute, and almost everyone that started behind us landed out on the third leg, as the thickening cirrus blanked out the lift. As a final touch, the "Copilot" reminded me to recharge that battery! Thanks for a wonderful product.

Now, if I can only figure out how to keep Dickerson from buying one.

Technical Note: While this little story seems like science fiction of the wildest order, it is based on existing technology. Expert systems are in use today for tasks ranging from fault diagnosis of industrial processes to analysis of geological data to predict the presence and concentration of minerals in the ground. Two way verbal communication with computers has been demonstrated by IBM, Kurzweil, and others. The FAA computers calculate position, altitude, and course predictions based on radar transponder data. Putting all this capability into a battery powered system light enough for glider application is a daunting prospect, but will undoubtedly be done before the year 2000.

IT CAN NEVER BE BETTER THAN THIS by Wally Raisanen, March 1986.

Joe Lincoln once wrote about a flight in which, after a great struggle low in the Verde Valley, he finally achieved maneuvering height above the Mogollon Rim and could see cumulus clouds for 200 miles to the east and his goal of Sante Fe. "...that great laughing-light feeling in the chest when you know you've got it made." That's what I think of as a great moment. A moment so vivid in the mind that even as it is happening, some part of you knows that you will never forget it, that it will be a part of your life for ever.

I would like to share with you one of my great moments in soaring. I want to do this because it is still so intensely thrilling to me that it is too big to keep it to myself. I hope too that broader knowledge of the special experiences that are available through soaring will serve to awaken the interest of others, and add to the ranks.

It is late in the afternoon in the fall of 1981, and I have just returned to Estrella after a practice flight to Wickenburg. As I complete my mock racing finish, I think how nice it would be if Eric (my 15 year old son) were in the air now. By radio Betty Horvath verifies that he is indeed flying a 2-33, so I pull up in lift over the runway and begin to climb, hoping to share a flight at the end of the day. The thermal quickly develops strength and I automatically steepen the angle of bank. The audio variometer is singing now, as the Cirrus climbs more rapidly. 7 knots, then 8 on the averager, and as I pass 6,000 feet I begin a more intense scan for other craft. Suddenly, in my peripheral vision, I spot a trainer just above me, wheeling in giant circles. As I slow and open out my circle to intercept, I see Eric waving a greeting from the trainer!

To teach him something about gaggle flying, I very deliberately space myself directly across the thermal from him, in his circle radius, and at his speed. (Fathers can't help it, everything is a lesson). I am concentrating so hard on the maneuver at first I miss it, but suddenly a huge bird sweeps into my consciousness. A golden eagle has the thermal centered, and is climbing up between us. For a magic moment, eagle, father and son pass through the shimmering golden light of the Arizona evening, a majestically rotating disc in the dance of flight, sharing the smooth power of nature and the special feeling that comes from a perfect balance of force, means, intent and action. Awestruck, I think to myself, "It can never be better than this."

The eagle outclimbs us, sets his wings and is off for an eerie far away in the mountains. I peel out of the thermal in a spiral dive to build the energy for an exuberant series of wingovers, and Eric slowly descends to touch down just as the sun falls behind the horizon.

CHAPTER 8 - THE BOB HOHANSHELT CHAPTER

Bob Hohanshelt writes better than he flies! His love of soaring was tempered somewhat after the loss of his much loved partner and friend, Tom Madigan. Bob has been President of ASA twice: he has almost 1000 hours in his log book and easily five times that amount in the garage.

A LETTER TO THE EDITOR OF AIR CURRENTS FROM BOB HOHANSHELT ON THE SERIOUS SUBJECT OF BEING OVERWEIGHT, February 1975.

Dear Sir:

A great many pious letters to the Editor have appeared recently in both your journal and in Soaring magazine concerning aircraft which are flown at greater than certificated gross weights. Many of the older designs suffer from this problem due to the production airframe differing from the original planned weight and the tedious process required for a manufacturer to re-certify and possibly redesign the aircraft for a higher gross weight. Until quite recently, nearly all gliders were over gross when flown by a normal size, healthy adult male (even the 170 pounds average used by the Military for aircrew members becomes 192 pounds when parachutes are worn.)

Realizing that my own ship was just a tad over the certified limit, I undertook an investigation to see how I could get within the limits. I have tabulated a few of the components which could be eliminated to achieve this worthy goal.

ITEM	WT(lbs)	JUSTIFICATION
Oxygen bottle	18	I seldom get high enough to need it.
Oxygen regulator	4	No value without bottle.
Oxygen Mask	2	No value without regulator.
Radio	3	It seldom works anyway.
Battery	4	No value without radio. (It was always dead anyway).

Survival gear	4	I'll just have to stop landing out.
Survival water	9	No value if I'm not going to land out.
Variometer	1	The only thing in the panel not required by FAA.
Instrument panel	1	No need for a big panel with only 2 instruments.
Seat cushion	3	I won't be up long without a variometer.
Charts & Glide Calculator	½	I won't need these because I refuse to fly without a seat cushion.

The total of the preceding items results in a 49½ pounds possible reduction in gross weight which is still 22½ short of the amount required to meet the limits of my ship. I have never carried any lead bars, bags of pennies or other ballast in the ship, and a wooden bird does not like water in any form, including ballast. A parachute is required by the rules so the only practical solution is to force the pilot to reduce his own weight by an additional 22½ pounds.

Now the very idea of a diet is repugnant to me and particularly a diet devoid of that particular elixir brewed in Tumwater, Washington. In fact, I'd give up flying first. I therefore took the only reasonable course under the circumstances, and sold my beloved K-6 to a 140 pound elf who may be able to figure out a way to fly it and still be under the certified gross weight.

I have replaced the ship with a Nugget which is certified for a 300 pound cockpit load and still carries 200 pounds of water. It also sports an experimental certificate so no serious problems should occur if a couple hundred extra pounds of water is desired.

The object of this rambling letter is simply to point out that not everyone has *intentionally* caused the gross weight of his ship to exceed the certified limits, yet there is a legal "out" for those who do. The idea of weighing each ship prior to takeoff sounds okay on paper, but three additional volunteers are required and volunteers are not knocking each other down rushing to get the existing jobs of start gate, start window, timer, contest manager, competition director, etc.

The logical solution would simply be to ask each pilot to certify that he has added no ballast which would cause him to exceed the certified limits for his aircraft. I always picture glider pilots as a fairly honorable lot who are quite capable of performing within the honor system if it is agreed that flying with excess ballast is contrary to the rules.

It should be remembered that unlike other forms of racing, few people will retire solely on the prize money offered for winning an ASA contest or regionals. It would also be a shame to let soaring contests sink to the level of yacht racing where nearly every race is protested and a participant's legal ability in interpreting the rules is more important than his sailing ability.

In closing, I would advise the ASA to review the total impact of any constrictive change such as weighing gliders prior to launch. It does not require a crystal ball to see the start line becoming a swamp as pilots dump ballast down to legal limits, or long delays occurring as underweight pilots send their crews for another half cup to bring the weight up to the limit. A pilot who has had to remove his variometer and seat cushions is not going to be very happy even if the scales were calibrated yesterday by the National Bureau of Standards and every pilot possesses a valid copy of his operating limitations certified by the Director of the

FAA. He might even be a bit obdurate if he hasn't had an Oly in the last six months. Let's face it, it is hard to stop at being just a little bit chicken!
Sincerely, R.O. Hohanshelt.

THE PRICE OF HIGHER PERFORMANCE OR HOW TO TRADE A FEW HOURS OF SPARE TIME FOR A NICE NEW SHIP, A Saga by Bob Hohanshelt, December, 1976.

The need for a new ship had been obvious from the time I had moved to Arizona, bringing my venerable K-6. The ship was beginning to take on the character of a prune as the dry Arizona air appropriated every molecule of moisture remaining in the aging wooden structure. My wife steadfastly refused to consider moving back to San Diego just to prevent further shrinkage and also explained (with her confused wifely priorities) that I could not afford to buy a new bird like all the big kids have. In September 1974, I discovered that the prototype Nugget, damaged during the 1971 Nationals after only five flights, might be available to the right party.

My work required that I make a trip to the Los Angeles area sometime during the next several weeks, so I decided to visit the factory the next time I was conveniently in the area. It only required a small amount of reorganization of my plans to make it "convenient" to be in Los Angeles the next morning.

I was unable to visit the factory until after dark, where the ship was carefully examined with the aid of a pen cell flashlight. The fuselage was residing, alone and dejected, behind the factory. The canopy was missing and the cockpit was full of leaves, rags, old paint cans and a couple hundred pounds of rainwater. The aft tail cone was broken in the area of the numbers and the bottom of the rudder was smashed as might be expected from a severe ground loop. The cockpit appointments and controls were scattered everywhere. Some major portion of the landing gear was missing since the ship rested precariously on half-open gear doors. It was love at first sight! I turned off the flashlight and told myself the big globs on the fuselage surfaces were not the result of some careless workman using this proud beauty to clean out paint brushes, but simply some cosmetic blemishes undoubtedly caused by a careless sparrow.

The wings and horizontal tail surfaces were stored inside the factory where a more careful inspection revealed only a few minor dents and creases on the right wing and tail feathers. The left wing had about 3 feet of damaged skin at the root and a slight bend in the spar fitting as a result of the ground loop. The spar itself was undamaged and true, so the replacement of a few feet of skin and a few ribs did not appear to be an insurmountable task. The prototype wing differed slightly from production wings which meant that I would have to make the ribs from scratch. I had never built a metal rib before, but then I had never attempted bonding metal either, and the whole airplane was a bonded structure, so a little thing like ribs did not bother me. Jack Laister could not locate any plans or drawings for the prototype and the differences between it and the production ships were extensive, so the reconstruction job would involve a lot of "eyeball engineering".

Negotiations were quickly completed. I simply told Jack, "I've got to have it. How much will you take?" After that dreary business with the local banker, I was the proud owner of two sailplanes (you can't be a collector if you have only one!) All that remained was to bring my proud possession home and "correct a few cosmetic blemishes".

Nearly a month passed before Bob von Hellens, my son and I, complete with a K-6 trailer full of sponge rubber pads, would attempt to bring the Nugget home. The plan was beautiful; to spend Friday night at Tom Madigan's house in San Diego, arrive in Los Angeles by 8:00 am Saturday to allow all morning for the ship to be leisurely loaded, return to San Diego for an afternoon barbecue, a good night's sleep, and on to Phoenix by mid-afternoon Sunday. Tom, my ex-partner in the K-6, would even go to Los Angeles with us to help load the bird in the trailer.

The execution of the plan is where the problems began. Car trouble in Jacumba resulted in a thirty mile tow job to a service station where the mechanic had gone home for the weekend. A panic call to Tom ensued and a mere three hours later we were transferring trailer hitches and lights over to his car. The waiting time was spent giving free mechanical advice to fifteen or twenty helpless travelers who also found this service station as a haven in the night. We finally arrived at Tom's house for our "good night's sleep" around 3:30 in the morning and were awake again by six for the trip to Los Angeles. We arrived at the Laister factory a little tired, but a very anticipant group. This was all changed as we viewed my new prize in the light of day. Apparently, someone really had cleaned out paint brushes on my fuselage.

It required four hours of hard labor to get the entire airplane settled in the trailer amidst large chunks of foam, a couple hundred feet of rope and various chunks of 2 x 4's. The loading was complicated by Bob threatening something about "torts" and "lawsuits" each time he got a tiny scratch from the loose chunks of torn aluminum. He also kept bleeding all over the ship.

We arrived in San Diego in time to drop off the trailer, skip the barbecue, rent a tow bar and proceed again to Jacumba to retrieve the car. The return trip to San Diego with my heavy Olds in the tow of a light Chevy station wagon was a very sobering experience. That night it was only one o'clock when we got to bed. The following day was spent giving the Olds a new set of head gaskets in Tom's driveway and then leisurely driving back to Phoenix. We were slipping back into our old ways, since we didn't arrive home until 3:30 Monday morning.

The following two months were spent getting the garage organized (that means pushing all your family's junk over to the side so you can get in the door) and getting the K-6 tidy so it could be put on the market. It had already become obvious that there wasn't enough time in the day to repair one ship while flying and maintaining the other. The K-6 would simply have to go. The period was also spent completely stripping the fuselage interior of the Nugget and designing jigs and fixtures to effect the fuselage repair.

The major damage in the tail cone area proved to be a very simple repair. Stringers were spliced and approximately 4 feet of skin was replaced in the damaged area. Pre-rolled skins were obtained from Jack Laister and a simple doublet was bonded and riveted at each joint. After weeks of trying to figure out how to do it, the actual repair only took a few days. The rudder and horizontal tail feathers also proved to be simple tasks. When I had repaired spruce and plywood aircraft in the past, a degree of skill and patience was required to fit and glue respectable scarf joints. Bonded aluminum repairs are so simple they can be done by the village idiot and still produce a joint which is stronger than the original material.

Many hours were spent trying to design a proper seat in the cockpit and I finally gave up and bought a complete seat from the factory. New rudder pedals of my own design were fabricated and installed. The missing component in the landing gear proved to be a common motorcycle shock absorber which was available locally.

This period also saw a hole cut into the tip of the nose to incorporate a large diameter ventilation tube. Considerable filling of the nose area with microballoons and resin was accomplished to give the ship a more pleasing contour.

The damaged wing would pose a different problem. The bent spar fitting was attached to the spar by 48 bolts in addition to epoxy glue and, naturally, the glue covered each bolt head and was in each thread. I expected a two month project to remove the fitting for straightening or replacement. Any damage to the fitting during removal would mean a sizable machine shop bill to duplicate the part without drawings. I enlisted the help of our plastic engineers at work and these specialists suggested an exotic chemical which might dissolve the epoxy bond. Unfortunately, it was only available in 55 gallon drums, had to be shipped from Ohio, cost $36 a quart, and was so dangerous that you get could cancer of the eye just from reading the label. One of the lowly plastic lab technicians suggested that I might also try plain old paint remover. Paint remover caused the epoxy bond to dissolve overnight. The fitting was easily straightened and tested at the factory. The wing skins and flap repairs did not pose any particular problem after having made a similar repair on the fuselage. (It sounds easy if you say it fast!) I was able to get a fine piece of pre-bent skin for the wing from Arnie Jurn so I didn't even have to bend or roll any skins.

A new canopy was acquired from the factory over the Easter weekend. I managed to trim the canopy and cut it into fixed and removable halves without any major cracks. However, I now have an appreciation of the stresses a brain surgeon encounters. The canopy was bonded into place and the fuselage filled and contoured to fit the canopy.

By this time, the ship was ready for primer. I attempted to locate white epoxy primer locally. The stuff the paint store said was "off-white" turned out to be an obscene yellow suitable only for power planes. A panic telephone call to the factory produced 4 gallons of the world's finest white primer. This was duly applied to the entire ship. Sanding and contouring was planned but by this time, mid-June had arrived and the garage had become unbearable, so a set of numbers was painted on the primed ship and the FAA notified that I was ready for their inspection. I reasoned that I had been working on the ship for nearly 10 months and had expended about 900 hours of my spare time on the project and thought I was 98.7% complete, so why not go ahead and fly it? The final clean up would only require a few days and I might as well fly it first.

By July 26 we were ready for the first flight. Tom Madigan had agreed to drive over to hold my hand and bring my newly acquired trailer from California. The Manual For Test Pilots clearly indicates a good night's sleep should precede the "Big Day" but Tom, true to form, didn't arrive until about 3:00 am. The ship was eventually loaded in the trailer, transported to Estrella and rigged. The lack of sleep may have made me a little irritable, but it prevented me from becoming as nervous as I felt like becoming. By the time we had rigged the ship, Tom was not speaking to me, Dorothy was talking alimony and my children were telling me what I could do with the Nugget.

Finally, around 1 o'clock we were hooked up and towed to 3000 feet for an uneventful 45 minute flight. To quote Joe Lincoln, "Never was an event I've looked forward to so long been such a disappointment." The cockpit was noisy due to the many air leaks I had neglected to seal. The flaps were fairly ineffective because I had ignored Jack Laister's advice and had not replaced the flap drive mechanism. The rudder pedals (my own design) proved to be very poorly laid out. The air vent in the nose seemed incapable of passing anything except a tremendous amount of noise. The stick was located such that full aileron control was impossible due to my legs getting in the way. And to top off everything, I had forgotten to even try retracting the gear.

A couple of hours were spent adjusting the elevator to give more stick room and readjusting the wing attachment to eliminate an interference problem. The ship was then ready for another try. This flight was considerably better except for a few strange sounds which were caused by a loose flap drive which was the result of readjustment of the wing. This time I remembered to retract the gear after only 30 minutes of thermaling. I also discovered a few more discrepancies. The wheel brake didn't work very well; the Venturi caused the variometer to be erratic. The ship was excessively nose heavy so my arm was cramped from pulling back after only 30 minutes in the air. It was time to go back to the drawing board. It might take more than a couple of days to accomplish all of the clean up required.

A new flap drive was designed and the stick was moved a few inches forward to give more room. A 15 pound block of lead was installed and later increased to 25 pounds to bring the C.G. closer to the correct spot. The rudder was sealed to improve sensitivity. The radio and battery were installed. A water dump valve was installed and the tank sealed to allow water to be carried. A minor redesign of the rudder pedals made them adequate although still far from ideal. A restrictor was added to the Venturi to dampen the variometer but this proved to be unsatisfactory and was eventually scrapped along with the Venturi. A new cable was installed on the wheel brake but this also proved to be unsuccessful and was eventually replaced by a hydraulic brake system.

Perhaps I should pause at this point in the narrative and admit that the ship was not totally without redeeming virtues. Once I got the C.G. back where it belonged, the ship began to display superb handling qualities, nearly the equal of my beloved K-6, and, of course, it is more than just a little bit faster. The wings only weigh 105 pounds each and rig independently to the fuselage so rigging would only be a two man (two person?) operation if I ever get around to building a wing tip stand. The cockpit is spacious, although a little spartan without any upholstery or the other niceties of a production design, but I couldn't figure how these things could improve performance, so I left them out.

The Nugget uses flaps for glide-path control and these were not too effective on the early flights, so I began to long for the super dive brakes of my K-6. A few months work improving the hinge and redesigning the linkage has corrected all the ills and I now prefer flaps for every condition except when flying fast under a big black cloud. The flaps also have the added advantage of providing something for your left hand to do when you're not holding maps and you tire of fondling your rosary.

When I returned home after the initial flight tests, I made a list of about 20 important items which should be cared for in the immediate future. Nearly 18 months have passed since those early flights and the list seems to grow longer with each flight. I never seem to get around to building the ground handling goodies like wing stands or a fixture for stowing the horizontal tail in the trailer. I have probably spent 400 to 500 hours designing flap-aileron interconnects, including many hours studying the way it is done on other ships, yet I still have not located a satisfactory scheme or installed even an unsatisfactory one in the ship. I have, however, managed to seal the canopy, design and install a comfortable seat and install a water dump valve linkage. I have also designed, fabricated, installed, tested and scrapped at least six flap drive linkages before arriving at the current configuration which, conceptually, borders on the brilliant.

The project is presently far from complete, but I estimate only 500 to 1000 man hours are required to finish the ship, depending a lot on how soon I discover a really good scheme for flap-aileron interconnects. It has required just about all of my spare time (and quite a bit of Bob von Hellens') for the past two years. At least it has been two years since I had the time to mow the lawn or fix the washing machine or any number of other tasks I have not been too diligent about recently. Of course, not every moment was spent productively - many hours were spent trying to figure out how to do each task or trying to figure out what the next task was. Some hours were even spent with a cool beverage in my hand admiring the last task.

In retrospect, I would advise anyone who is contemplating a project of this type as a means to own a modern competitive sailplane for a 1-26 investment, to reflect a moment before jumping in with both feet. Consider, instead, enrolling in dental school - it could be a lot less work, take less time, possibly cost less money and when you become an orthodontist, you can order a brand new glider from Rainco with your increased buying power. You also won't have to go through life with epoxy all over your hands and in your hair or sit up all night typing your stupid saga.

ASA PILOT HANDICAPS - A SCORING SYSTEM PROPOSAL by Bob Hohanshelt, February 1978.

A new soaring season is upon us and I feel it is appropriate to review the recent experience of awarding contest points for a pilot handicap. The system we tried a few seasons ago contained several flaws and some people were even a little vocal about their lack of whole-hearted enthusiasm toward the scheme. The basic premise of the system seemed to award points with the connotation, "He sure did well today - considering what a lousy pilot he is."

Now I will be the first to admit that I am not as good a pilot as John Baird, Bill Ordway, Jerry Robertson, or 50 to 60 other Arizona pilots. However, the previous handicap scheme addressed itself only to the symptom while ignoring the disease. I have attempted to analyze my own situation and I feel I can isolate my problem pretty well but whether my disease is part of a soaring plague or not would require privileged information from other pilots which is not currently available. I am beginning to suspect, however, that my own situation is not entirely unique.

The basic reason John Baird et al are better pilots than me is that I never seem to get an opportunity to practice. Now this in itself is not so enlightening so we must explore why I don't go flying more frequently. The problem is primarily with my wife, Dorothy. I do not wish to give anyone the wrong idea because I definitely don't want to get a new one (inflation has hit alimony even harder than German fiberglass). A wife is also an ideal crew chief since she is the only person who will keep looking for you if you land out. (A partner will quit looking as soon as he finds the ship - he may even hope you are never found). Dorothy has many attributes but she also has an affliction which, to put it delicately, is similar to the "King Midas Touch" only everything she touches does not turn to gold. No, definitely not gold!

Dorothy recently borrowed our son's car to go to the local 7-11 and upon her return the car required a new alternator, starter, battery, water pump and radiator. The automatic transmission was also in doubt but it had been replaced recently so it represented only a warranty repair. Are you beginning to get the picture?

I have long ago forgiven her for dropping the K-6 wing in the driveway, for tipping over the Nugget wing in the trailer, for letting the fuselage fall over in the garage, and for polishing my canopy with engine oil. These were all honest mistakes and I was totally to blame for letting her get close to my glider. My problem involves leaving her home all day where she has an entire house to vent her affliction. On a quiet weekday afternoon she can generate more work than the entire Maytag service corps could repair in a week. I expect that somewhere in ASA is a capitalist with so many blue chips that he can afford to call an appliance repairman, perhaps even so rich he can call a plumber to unstop a drain - but I can assure you he is not a Motorola engineer. Around our house these tasks must be accommodated by the ace glider pilot. Even a superior pilot cannot remain in top contention when he has spent every waking hour for the last 8 weeks trying to repair a washing machine.

The object of this monologue is to propose a handicap scoring system where the handicap is based upon the number of "Honey Do's" accomplished since the close of the last season. The idea would be to score points for being a domestic good guy and combine these points with your daily contest score to arrive at a composite score. I have submitted the following list as an example of the scoreable tasks and typical scores:

TASK DESCRIPTION **	SCORE
Change a hard-to-reach light bulb	$\frac{1}{2}$
Fix a leaky faucet (new-fangled type only)	1
Fix a broken door chime	1
Clean up the yard	1
Clean up the pool	1
Clean up the garage	10
Paint your glider	0
Paint someone else's glider (as part of garage clean up only)	2
Paint a room	2
Paint the outside of your house	15
Repair the crew car	0
Repair your wife's car	5
Overhaul the pool filter	10

Overhaul the water heater	10
Unclog a stubborn drain	10
Repair the clothes drier	10
Repair the washing machine	10
Repair the oven	10
Repair the range	10
Repair or replace the garbage disposal	10
Repair the furnace or air conditioner	10
Repair the dishwasher	10
Fix the damn dishwasher	25
Fix the bloody thing again	50
Try to fix it one more time	100
Remove dishwasher from bottom of pool, replace arcadia door & install new dishwasher	250

BONUS POINTS

Travel out of state to visit relatives on a soarable weekend	100
Invite relatives to visit you during peak of soaring season	200

Note** All faulty conditions must have existed for at least 90 days to qualify for points. If you have attempted a repair within 90 days, have been unsuccessful and later effected a repair after 90 days, score half the normal points. All repairs accomplished prior to 90 days indicate that you are a "Goody-Two-Shoes" and lack sufficient character to become a good soaring pilot.

While I am sure the list is far from complete and the membership may wish to contribute additional items for consideration, I must confess that I terminated the list when I discovered my handicap was greater than 1000 points. It is theoretically possible that someone may still beat me by being a better pilot and having a good handicap but this seems highly unlikely because the good pilots always seem to be able to get their priorities right and don't have to put up with all of this domestic foolishness.

THE ODD COUPLE by Bob Hohanshelt, July 1980.

Several years ago when I immigrated to Arizona, I was surprised at the small number of glider partnerships active in the state. The vast majority of aircraft were privately owned, and crewing was accomplished primarily by pilots' wives. This appears to have been a mutually rewarding experience since the wives normally spent a very pleasant day in the outdoors, complaining to each other of their sorry lot and telling lies about their mates' soaring prowess.

This situation was in great contrast to my experience in California, where crewing was accomplished by a partner who heckled over the radio and prayed you would fall down so it would be his turn to fly. Excessive kibitzing was occasionally rewarded by the fallen aviator consuming all the cold beverage while the heckler tried his hand at soaring. It was common practice for the partner who was to fly last to encourage the first pilot to launch before conditions were soarable, which resulted in a very short first flight, and the airplane was his for the rest of the day. Of course, the pilot who was to fly first attempted to delay his take off until he could cut the heart out of the day, leaving his partner with a picturesque but quiet tow at sunset. I could not understand the Arizonan's lack of appreciation for the joys of joint ownership.

My own partnership had endured for nine years and included three aircraft, all of which we still owned when the partnership dissolved. My ex-partner, Tom Madigan, has continued his propensity to collect aircraft and currently owns three ships and has custody of a fourth - the LK which was our first acquisition.

I believe Neil Simon had been spying on Tom and me when he wrote The Odd Couple. Of course, he changed the location from California to New York to protect the innocent, and eliminated the glider association to give the program greater appeal. Still, there is little doubt which of us was the sensitive, articulate, bon vivant character Felix Unger, and who was the disorganized, unkempt and unscrupulous Oscar Madison. How this partnership should endure for so long has been a source of amazement to us both.

I found that when flying with a partner, our treks to the sailport were more frequent and more pleasant than subsequent private ownership. It is easier to talk yourself out of going flying than it is to upset someone else's plans, and you may suspect in the back of your mind that if you don't go, he may take the ship anyway and fly all day long. Over the years, I have spent the time while waiting for my turn to fly contemplating the variables which result in a good partnership.

I have heard horror stories of partnerships which are formed between complete strangers who have nothing in common except a financial arrangement. These arrangements are doomed from the beginning, since choosing a partner should be approached with the same care as choosing a wife. A marital misunderstanding can usually be resolved by treat or coercion, but telling your partner that you must have your way or you're going home to Mother seldom brings the desired results. It is also considered ungentlemanly to kiss and make-up.

A solid partnership should consider the financial positions, occupations, and soaring aspirations of both parties, as well as mutual temperaments.

Financial equality is a must if squire-servant relationships are to be avoided. It is embarrassing to have your children go barefoot in order for you to pay your half of the new air data computer that your partner purchased with his pocket change. It is equally difficult to decide which aircraft to buy if you were planning on a used 1-26 and your partner has his heart set on a carbon Janus. The only practical method of handling finances is to agree in the beginning on how the initial funds will be raised, the details of periodic support and the precise method of dissolving the partnership.

Strong consideration should be given to your potential partner's occupation. Dentists make terrible partners since they are reluctant to return to work on Mondays with epoxy on their hands and paint under their fingernails, so you could end up doing all the work. Brain surgeons and concert pianists are also inclined to fits of temper when you smash their fingers during the rigging exercise. Engineers, obviously, make the best partners although one should beware electrical engineers, since they are unable to resist the temptation of tinkering with electric variometers and radios. Show me a glider owned by an electrical engineer, and I'll show you a ship where only the PZL is working. Show me a glider owned by two electrical engineers, and even the trailer lights won't work.

Careful consideration should be given to the soaring aspirations of the partners. Successful partnerships can be formed by up to four parties if only the badge and recreational flying is considered. The ideal number of partners, however, remains two since this eliminates any democratic process and all decisions are made by mutual agreement. Two-way partnerships can be quite successful where one pilot desires to fly in competition and the other wishes to fly for recreation. Successful partnerships between competition pilots are rare, since the competition season must be rationed between the two pilots, and neither flies as much as he would really desire. Additionally, the grounded pilot is considered prime material for contest officiating. It is especially loathsome to be stuck with a ground job while your partner soars.

A practical example of the careful selection of a partner is my own case. A couple of days after reporting for employment with my fresh Electrical Engineering diploma, I discovered a soaring calendar hanging above a neighbor's desk. (Also an electrical engineer). As a means of introduction, I asked the calendar's owner if he was familiar with a local glider which had appeared in the Soaring classifieds. His reply was, "Yeah! Want to go half on it?" That particular aircraft was sold before we could drive across town to see it. But, after such careful preparation for a partnership, we decided to explore the market and eventually purchased, sight unseen, an LK residing in far off Pueblo, Colorado. My new partner graciously allowed me to drive with my family to Colorado to retrieve our purchase while he flew to Massachusetts to acquire a bride. Our reunion in California involved the introduction of both his new wife and our new glider. After a quick handshake, Tom and I disappeared into the garage where we spent the next nine years. Thousands of hours of toil were expended resurrecting the war weary wreck from Colorado into the finest LK in the country (although we never did get the radio or trailer lights working properly).

Our Damon and Pythias relationship grew to the point where Tom could not stand the pain of my shame for slightly scratching the LK in a tiny bit of a hard landing (he called it a crash!) and he unselfishly erased all my remorse by nearly destroying our brand new K-6 on a rock pile. There were mutterings amongst our wives about us jealously smashing our toys so that no one could play, but I was fully aware of Tom's unselfish motivation. We returned to the garage for a few more years, and both ships were presently repaired to like-new condition.

It should be obvious to the reader by now, that sharing a glider is rather like sharing a wife: (1) It is only rarely successful between two very good friends and should never be attempted between strangers. (2) Threesomes are out, since you can never reach agreement on who gets to do what. (3) It becomes an orgy with four or more, and you'll never get to do anything.

Still, it should be obvious that two partners can share a glider which is twice as good as they could individually afford. I have often wondered if the same would be true of wives?

CHAPTER 9 - CREWING: ART OR SCIENCE?

RETRIEVE IN 1949 by Nancy Ordway

We thought this crewing was a snap, with food stops and soft music on the car radio, especially when we saw what we thought was the TG-3 near Inyokern. We drove out there expecting to greet our pilots only to find that what had landed was not a TG-3; it wasn't even a glider. We had stupidly followed a power plane all the way to Inyokern Airport.

The trip to the airport cost us some time and it was getting late, so we pulled into a gas station in Inyokern to have our trailer lights hooked up, a small detail our pilots had neglected to take care of. The poor station attendant couldn't figure out the Ordway/Smith wiring system, so he finally sold us a battery operated lantern affair which he hung on the rear of the trailer, and we headed north again.

By now it was dark and we knew that Bill and Smitty had landed, but still no message when we called (pre-arranged) Claremont. So we continued driving toward Bishop -- and ran smack into a cow. The lights of an oncoming car had momentarily blinded Helen who was at the wheel, and she hadn't seen the cow standing in the road. When we got out of the car the poor creature was lying on her side, and we walked closer to see if she was alive or dead. Suddenly she stood up, scaring us so that we ran half way back to Inyokern. By the time we'd calmed down, the cow had walked off the road and back to her pasture, apparently none the worse for wear.

The same could not be said for the car, Smitty's car incidentally. The whole front end was smashed in, but it ran. So we continued driving north until, and this is really embarrassing, we ran out of gas. In all the excitement of following power planes and hooking up trailer lights, we'd forgotten to gas up. But luckily we weren't stranded for long. A passing motorist took pity on us and towed us back to Inyokern, his car pulling our car pulling the glider trailer. There we found the accident with the cow had done more than crumple the hood of the car. The radiator was pushed against the fan.

So what were we going to do now? We called Claremont and found out that Bill and Smitty had landed and were waiting for us at Little Lake, some 25 miles up the road. Should we have the fan fixed, without Smitty's okay and causing us further delay? Or should we try to drive the car without the cooling system? Our hero, who had towed us to Inyokern, rescued us again. He drove us to Little Lake where we finally got together with Bill and Smitty about midnight at an all-night cafe. Smitty was not quite so happy to see us when he found out about his car. But he put on a brave face and we all drove back to Inyokern... again.

The two pilots had not had an easy time of it either. They had landed about 10 miles from Little Lake in some brush, damaging one wing of the ship. Then they'd walked to the highway, waiting in vain for a ride. Not until they brought the stabilizer out to the road with them did they get picked up, so they hadn't reached Little Lake until 10:00, some six hours after they'd landed.

Back in Inyokern we said goodbye to our friend who had done so much to help us and decided to drive the car the way it was, bent fan and all. Although we were pulling the trailer, it was late at night and had cooled off considerably, so we figured we could make it.

We found the glider all right and had lots of fun dismantling it and carrying it out to the road between 3:00 and 4:00 in the morning. Then began the long trip home, creeping along about 35 miles an hour so that the car wouldn't heat up. Long before we reached El Mirage, it heated up anyway, so we left the trailer and drove to the next gas station, about 30 miles away, for some minor repairs. A mechanic pushed the radiator away from the fan and sold us a new fan belt, and we were on our way again -- back up the highway to retrieve the trailered glider. By the time we finally drove into El Mirage, it was close to noon, and we were a tired, hot, sorry-looking group.

The last thing I remember about the trip was Smitty driving away from the sailport with the hood of his car tied down. He wasn't out of sight before the rope broke and the hood flew up and completely covered the windshield, putting a quick stop to his trip home.

WHEN A GUY MARRIES by a coward named N. Cog Nita, April 1958.

Air Currents' Editor Joe Lincoln found this article in Texas Soaring Association's Spirals magazine and reproduced it in Air Currents with great relish.

Most soaring pilots can be characterized by one set of descriptions. Not so their wives! In almost every case it would be fair to say that a glider pilot shows the same progression of symptoms from the time the bug first bites him until he is a nationally or internationally known gliding figure. Where glider pilots all fit neatly into the same pattern, wives do not! For practical purposes wives can be divided into 5 groups. It is often difficult, and sometimes impossible, to determine into just which category an unmarried girl will fall.

There are a few wives who take up soaring as enthusiastically as their husbands. They may take on the same symptoms of an honest-to-goodness glider pilot and progress through the same stages. However, their final aspiration ends with owning and flying a high performance ship jointly with their husbands. This type of wife is even more rare than the whooping crane and the possibility of a guy marrying one is so remote that it is mentioned only for the sake of rounding out the curve. There is little danger of the species becoming extinct in view of the fact that it hardly exists.

The second category is almost as rare as the first, but a few cases are known to exist. The wife marries soaring and lives every moment for soaring and soaring talk. She will crew willingly. She insists on going wherever hubby goes and being in the middle of all the know. She can identify sailplanes on sight and sometimes prides herself on being able to quote details of ships that even veteran pilots do not know. She will sand hubby's dream ship and actually enjoys running errands. She feels that every wife who does not feel as she does is a traitor to her own husband.

Then there is the wife who resents her husband's soaring interests. She fights him at every turn and begrudges every hour and every dollar that hubby spends on soaring. If he spends $2 on Sunday, she feels it is her due to go out on Monday and spend $4 on herself. She considers herself a martyr and thus expects reparations for time and money spent on soaring. If hubby is the silent type, his friends quite often do not even know he has a wife and he accepts his persecution in silence without benefit of sympathy.

Next comes the wife who wears the pants. This type is generally not easily recognized in the courtship stage. She plays a part and plays it well until he slips that ring on her finger. Simultaneously, she slips a noose on the poor unsuspecting soul and tethers him to the back door. If he is ever seen again, it is purely by accident and he just happened to be shopping for groceries in the same store you are. If someone ever happens to mention his name, and asks whatever happened to so-and-so, the likely reply is, "Oh, he married out of soaring." And that is that!

Last comes the wife that goes along with the game. She realizes that soaring is hubby's first love and she is the second and tries to make the best of it. Through the years she grows to like soaring people and soaring talk and will allow hubby to do most anything so long as she can be allowed a nominal amount of freedom to go to church on Sunday morning. She doesn't mind taking the kids to the airport and wrestling with them, but she appreciates a choice of whether she will or won't go every Sunday. She can generally be counted on to help with the social end and admits she doesn't know one ship from another - except for the Pratt Reads and those she recognizes because they are the "fat" ones. She is familiar with soaring terms of L/D and glide ratio but she probably couldn't tell you what they meant. There are generally a few of these in every club and they seem to enjoy life in spite of soaring.

Not all wives fit neatly into one category. One may have symptoms of one kind one weekend and another kind the next week. Or they may be of a mixed variety. Let it suffice to say that before a glider guider marries a girl he should at least try to imagine what kind of wife he is getting. If she prefers a book - any book - to his friends, he should beware. She may take the book to the airport with her after she says "I do" but then again she may prefer to read it at home while hubby mows the yard and washes the dishes.

CREWIN' FOR A BIGGIE by Paul Dickerson, September 1971.

"It's only 500 miles of desert driving to El Mirage," Bill Ordway said, "and besides that, we'll be there in no time since we can drive at least 55 miles per hour. And besides that, you'll get lots of fresh air, see lots of new countryside, and you'll get to meet some famous pilots like Obershaw, Fellner, and maybe even Manfred Sczesny. You'll really like crewing."

Sensing that I was still somewhat reluctant to agree to spend 5 days driving 2,500 miles in a pick up truck with a 30 foot long 3,000 pound trailer, Bill said,

"Tell you what I'm gonna do -- I'm gonna buy you one hamburger a day and throw in all the Dr. Pepper you can drink." Well, with an offer like that it was certain that I would be crewing for Bill in the Regional Contest at El Mirage, California, during the two weekends prior to Labor Day. And crew I did!

The first day (August 28) dawned bright and early as we rolled out of the sack to assemble the glider. We got up at 6:00 am and by 8:45 am we had the wings on, so Bill went to the Pilots' Meeting which surprisingly lasted until just after we had finished cleaning the canopy and washing the bottom surface of the wings. Bill had drawn an early take-off time, so we rolled the ship out to the line where, with only minor problems, Bill finally got airborne. Things went pretty smoothly except when I walked into the wing as a blond lady in a pink bikini flowed by. I later decided that there were either lots of pink bikinis or else she was the alfalfa inspector because every time I turned around -- there she was.

"Stay on 123.3," Bill had said, "until I go through the gate, then switch to 123.5." So, I found a convenient spot, coincidentally close to the kitchen where I dispatched the assistant crew chief, and settled down to wait for my hero's start. After a few minutes, I saw him come boiling through the gate at about Mach 0.181 and 2900 feet AGL. Wow! What a start! I'll bet Al Leffler wishes he had a BG-12. The officials apparently weren't so impressed. "Bad Try, 81." So, I watched my leader turn his ship around for a second start -- a little lower and a little slower. But again -- "Bad try, 81." I began to hope nobody would notice who I was crewing for. But my fears were unfounded, as on the third try my sterling "piloto" flashed through the gate, scattering spectators, and received a rousing cheer from the officials.

"He made it."

"81 made a good start."

"Hey -- did you guys hear? 81 made it through."

So, with a lump in my throat (dry hamburger) and a Dr. Pepper in my hand, we entered the trailer race. A.J. Foyt of car racing fame and a good Texan from Houston, once was quoted as saying, "If your pucker string ain't drawed up tight, you ain't going fast enough!" I have raced bicycles, soap boxes, cars, boats, and motorcycles, and I can tell you that those are tame compared to trailer racing. I snatched more doughnuts out of the seat in 3 hours than I did in 20 years of prior racing. But we persevered and gave Bill all we had for 3 hours. Unfortunately, I later found out that the pilot's score is not based on the average speed of the glider and trailer together. In fact, I never did find out how the officials score the crews' average speed -- but it must have been important in some way.

After several hours of wheel-to-wheel competition in what will next year be named the El Mirage 500, I discovered that the real purpose of the crew is to fetch the damned glider out of some bug-infested field while the "piloto" describes to his admiring wife (or girlfriend) the skill and cunning required to beat the competition to this beautiful landing spot only 123 miles short of the goal.

Well, once I began to get the big picture, things went a lot better. In fact, I managed to distinguish myself the very first day. I was the only one to forget to turn in a crew card and thus received the only lemon award of the opening day. But I was subsequently outdone by a glory-hunting Phoenix pilot who performed so outstandingly it was necessary to design a special award for the occasion.

The second contest day was pretty uneventful except that we learned to know and love a pilot (who will remain nameless but will be referred to as 7 Beta), who directed his crew from point to point, (usually at about one mile intervals) with a human relations philosophy that would have made Captain Bligh pea green with envy. The "Outstanding Communication of the Day Award", however, has to go to the Crew Chief of 3 Delta (or was she the Assistant Crew Chief? I never could decide). It was approximately 1600 hours when our radio brought us the following exchange:

"3 Delta ground, 3 Delta, I'm at 12,000 feet over Tehachapi."

Male Voice:	"3 Delta, 3 Delta Ground, Roger."
Female Voice:	"Al Honey, I'm so proud of you."
3 Delta:	"Say Again."
3D Ground: (Pause)	"I'm proud of you." (Clipped).
3 Delta:	"Say again please."

3D Ground, more pause "Never mind."

We never did find out who 3 Delta Ground was, but she sure was proud of her pilot. Almost everybody got home that day, so we all got an early start to Phoenix.

On the following Saturday, (September 4), we were once again assembling our bird, wondering what excitement the day would bring. Happily, we weren't disappointed. One of the better known Phoenix pilots, who, unlike myself, had yet to distinguish himself, began to have radio problems on his way back from the day's single turnpoint. He could receive but could not transmit. After a frustrating hour of clicking his boom mike, the ever-alert crew chief said,

"3 Delta, if you can hear me, click your mike 3 times."

"Click, click, click." It isn't hard to imagine the confusion that followed.

"3 Delta, are you west of Apple Valley? One click yes, two clicks no."

"Click."

"Are you west of Rabbit Dry Lake?"

"Click." Then the crew chief got suspicious.

"3 Delta, what is the last digit in your area code?"

...Silence... 3 Delta had forgotten his area code.

This kind of nonsense went on for an hour or so while everybody became thoroughly confused. Nevertheless, 3 Delta winged his way back to El Mirage, and after landing, began debugging the radio. Due to his superior electronic ability, the pilot of 3 Delta proceeded directly to the heart of the problem - peanut butter in the boom mike. Despite the best efforts of his crew and Phoenix associates, word of this unfortunate incident somehow leaked to the Contest Officials and the 3 Delta pilot was presented the First (and hopefully Last) Annual Peanut Butter Award.

The task on Sunday was a prescribed area distance. This was the task the crew had been waiting for - the opportunity to tour scenic eastern California. Everything went smoothly except that we made a wrong turn at Barstow and ended up holding at Essex instead of Baker - only 175 road miles from where we were supposed to be. But we finally found our pilot, who had landed at Harvard, disassembled the ship and returned to El Mirage. The "Crew of the Day" Award should have gone to the team that was sighted 40 miles west of Essex only an hour before their pilot landed at Stovepipe Wells.

After giving everyone time to assemble their ships on Labor Day, the officials canceled the day's competition due to rain. Thus, the contest ended and we folded our tent and slipped away into the gathering rainstorm. It was an experience I'll never forget. Lots of beautiful ships, lots of flying stories (I don't believe any of them), and lots of laughs. Crewing in a contest is surely the next best thing to flying in one.

THE UNIQUE WAY IN WHICH MARIO CROSINA DE-RIGGED DURING THE OPEN CLASS NATIONALS AT EL MIRAGE IN 1976 by Paul Dickerson.

Mario is a hotblooded Italian who is, coincidentally enough, married to a hot blooded Italian woman named Maria. They live in the Bay Area and came to Arizona a few times in the late 70's for Region 9 Contests. Mario had a habit of getting himself into worse messes than anybody I ever heard of.

One of the best happened at El Mirage during a Nationals. He was flying at quite a disadvantage in this contest for two reasons. First of all, this was his first Nationals, so far as I know, and secondly he was flying a Nugget which even at its best was only a mediocre 15 meter airplane and was certainly no competition for the Nimbus 2's that were flying at the time.

The contest tasks were long and arduous, even for the big airplanes, with the result that Mario had landed out more times than he had gotten back in this particular contest. Maria had about had her fill of all this, and I don't think she liked crewing at El Mirage anyway. It is just possible that after 5 or 6 landouts out of 8 or 9 days, her pilot was not in as good spirits as he might otherwise have been.

As it turned out, poor old Mario had landed out again on the very last day at some ungodly place called Rabbit Dry Lake or some place similar. I agreed to go with Maria to retrieve him because it was not clear whether the dry lake would support the car or not. Consequently we were prepared to push the glider for some distance.

As we got closer and closer to Rabbit Dry Lake, Maria had agitated herself into a high density ball of aggravation. She was indeed not happy with another trip out to the wastelands east of El Mirage. As the lake and then the glider came into view, she reached the height of her anger when she discovered that he was not on the lake-near-the-road but on the far lake beyond the lake-near-the-road. There was some question indeed whether or not we could reach him with the car.

"I kill him! I'll kill him! I'll kill him, I'llkillhim!" she said, pounding her fist on the steering wheel. As we approached we could see there were tracks on the lake and thought perhaps we could drive across to him. As we got closer we discovered that he had begun the de-rigging procedure in advance of our arrival, obviously out of deference to Maria so that we could get the ship in the trailer and back to civilization in the minimum amount of time.

148

As we drove up beside the glider, Maria's mood changed from anger to horror as she discovered the wing lying on the ground had a protruding pair of feet that obviously belonged to Mario who couldn't get out from underneath it.

"My Gosh! He's been killed!" she said. "He's wrecked the airplane landing and he's been killed." Then a voice came out from under the wing saying,

"Dammit, Maria, will you quit yellin' and get this wing off o' me." Which we did.

After discovering that he was not only not dead but wasn't even hurt, we cautiously asked how it was that he happened to be lying on the ground with his airplane wing plonked on top of him. It turned out that, as mentioned earlier, he had anticipated the possibility that Maria might be in a bad humor and anxious to get back to civilization. He therefore had begun de-rigging the airplane. He had removed the wing tape, the control actuation pins and finally had loosened by partially removing but not completely removing the two spar pins on the left wing.

Thus having done as much disassembly as he could do, he settled under the shade of the wing to await Maria's arrival. He was beginning to enjoy himself, freed from the knowledge that he was going to have to get out and do this again tomorrow (since this was the last day) when a dust devil ripped its way across the dry lake, rocked the airplane back and forth, finished loosening the wings and dropped one on top of him. He said he believed he had been knocked unconscious for a few minutes but came to smothered by this large, stiff, aluminum blanket which he was not able to remove as he was flat on his back and could not bring his arms into play.

After struggling for several minutes, he decided to make the best of a bad situation and simply wait until someone came to help him. Maria was not amused by this story saying that she was more angry than ever. I subsequently advised Mario that he would probably be better off, should the circumstances repeat themselves, to just go ahead and die than have to endure the trip back to civilization with his wife.

SWEET REVENGE by Paul Dickerson.

This is the story of a truly wonderful joke played on a pilot who had landed out by his crew. The pilot in this case was Bob Gravance and the crew chief getting even with him for unknown past sins was his son, Jack.

The setting is the El Mirage high desert area in the early 70's. Bob Gravance was on a long cross country in the hottest period of the high desert summer, mid-August, when he hit the ground at Darwin which is truly one of the garden spots of the Death Valley area. It is rumored that there was at one time two live plants in the city Darwin. Inspection today, however, does not reveal any evidence to substantiate this.

Bob landed his ASW-12 on the local strip and through the usual comedy of errors and bad communications managed to establish a link with his ground crew who was back at El Mirage in the swimming pool. Now I'm sure it's not true, but the story was told that the pilot was surly as he addressed his crew, wondering why they were standing there in their wet bathing suits while he was suffering from beer withdrawal in Darwin, some 3 to 4 hours away.

Well, as it happened, in his younger days as a crew chief, Jack Gravance suffered many of the defects that our own modern day crew chiefs suffer from, and that is a lack of proper humility, a lack of understanding of the agitation a pilot feels when he lands out, and a sensitivity to being yelled at. It's unreasonable that they should act that way but it's reality and one needs to address reality.

Bob, however, failed to address reality and Jack and his friends hatched a plan to get even. They launched immediately from El Mirage in their old pick up truck with the ASW-12 trailer. However, rather than the usual arrival at the airport, beer in hand, trailer behind, ready to retrieve pilot and aircraft, they stopped about 5 miles from the airport, disconnected the trailer and left it in a parking lot. Thus, when they arrived at the airport to retrieve the now-steaming pilot, they did not have the trailer with them.

As they rolled to a stop, an agitated Bob Gravance launched out from the shade beneath his airplane wing which was the only shade within 150 miles of Darwin. Jack had an open can of beer, frosty and cold, hanging out the window ready to hand to his father, when his father said,

"Expletive Deleted, you forgot the trailer!"

So in mock surprise, horror on his face, Jack said,

"My Gosh! You're right. I'll go get it. Stand by." So he took the beer back inside the car, rolled up the window, made a dusty 180° turn and roared off in the direction he had come, leaving his father agitated because not only did he now have a 6 hour wait for the trailer to get back, he still didn't have a cold beer.

With some difficulty, the crew managed to keep the car on the road and disappeared into the distance at high speed. As soon as they were out of sight they pulled off the side of the road until they recovered their composure sufficiently to safely drive an automobile. After a further mile or two, they recovered the glider trailer, and returned to the airport to recover a properly humiliated hot and thirsty pilot.

GLORIA! GLORIA! WHEREFORE ART THOU, GLORIA? by Judy Lincoln, September 1978.

That Friday had been an obviously super day for soaring. Not merely cloud streets, but a veritable cumulus freeway extended from the White Tanks on up the Bradshaws. Prescott, Flagstaff, the Canyon and points north were arranged like roadside rest areas along the way. And so the decision was made. Not Winslow for us that weekend - John would instead fly his Grand Canyon and return flight from Estrella. I would be the intrepid crew.

Our Saturday morning preparations went without a hitch. Washing, taping, and watering have become a ritual to impress any efficiency expert - right down to the careful timing of the peanut butter and jelly sandwich ten minutes before the J-john trek. Undaunted by the persistent and advancing cirrus, and the lack of cu's locally, John took off at 12:45 with slim encouragement from John Detwiler. CD has just spent some twenty minutes notching the barograph and regaining release altitude for a Diamond Distance attempt. And so the Johns went their separate ways: CD headed for his first turn at Ryan, and IF sauntered north for the Canyon.

In the artificial calm that settles in after take off and before the crew is summoned, I consoled myself by recalling that no news is good news. Except, of course, when he's too low to transmit over a mole hill, or the battery's dead, or there's no phone or trace of civilization anywhere near where he's landed. Such a vivid imagination!

When news did come, it was via EE at 21,000 MSL; he relayed that IF was down at Luke 2. Suddenly, I wished we'd gone to Winslow. I wished I were warming a booth in that Mexican Restaurant on the field, and that John, too, could be at 21,000 feet. It turned out that Jerry Robertson was ensconced in an Air West machine - fortunately! If things had been that incredible at Winslow, the retrieve of IF would surely have been an exercise in clenched jaws and blue language.

I dallied in leaving the field. I was torn between watching Dick Elliott's first flight in his new Pik, which was also our old Pik, and dutifully fetching John. On the one hand, Dick is one of my all time favorite people - I can clearly recall his first solo in June of 1975. And here he was, now a full-fledged old timer in the sport, proud new partner in the Pik. I felt oddly maternal about the whole thing.

Of course, on the other hand, dear John was out there at Luke 2, probably sweltering under a wing, rationing his water. 2 o'clock in the afternoon is a bad time to be downed at an abandoned military field. I could see him now, salty with sweat and wishing only for the arrival of his devoted wife. Oh Dick, old friend, have a super flight - you've long since left the nest, and I'm off on a mission of mercy.

Meanwhile, John Detwiler in CD was on his second leg, returning from Ryan and pushing on toward Wickenburg. As I sped up Maricopa Road with saintly perseverance and visions of my suffering John, CD relayed that I should go to Gloria's place, near 163rd Avenue and Grand. My foot jerked off the floored gas pedal. Why was I hurrying to meet this "Gloria"?

"Say there, CD, just who is Gloria?"

"Uh, IF Ground, Gloria's place is - uh on the left side of the road, right near an Exxon Station. There's a red and yellow sign - you can't miss it. It's a bar, and there's a - uh - trailer parked next door. Hey - be on the look out for the sign that says "Massage". Ha."

"Gee, thanks, CD."

This was obviously a situation that called for expediency. Desert survival is a matter of common sense and saving your strength. Gloria's Place probably was not. I stomped down on the gas pedal and charged onward with a renewed sense of urgency. Carrie Nation, zealous prohibitionist that you were, did you ever rush headlong into Gloria's, perchance?

As I streaked past Sun City, I thought or hoped that maybe Gloria was in fact a Sun Citizen. Of course! She was a retired WAC! She'd served her country well in WW2 as an army nurse. In fact, she still put in part time hours at Boswell Hospital. A nice grandmotherly woman, this Gloria.

That fantasy waned as I pressed on past Surprise and El Mirage. It occurred to me that "Surprise" was so apropos! What ever Gloria's Place was, and who ever Gloria herself might be, I'd sneak in, yell a blood curdling "Surprise!" and watch everybody scatter. At last I had a plan.

I finally saw it. Exxon station, house trailer, gaudy sign. So this was Gloria's Place...

"Uh, CD, you still there?"

"IF Ground, CD's gotcha. I'm between the White Tanks and Wickenburg. Doing OK."

"Good for you, CD, I just found Gloria's place."

"Well, honk the horn and see how long it takes him to come out."

"Gee, thanks, CD."

I decided the "Surprise" routine might be a bit much, so I took CD's advice and leaned impatiently on the horn. John bounded out immediately, a rickety screen door slamming behind him. Was that a shadowy figure still in the doorway? Waving? Was that Gloria? Was anyone really there? The who ever or what ever it was, was gone.

The retrieve continued, somewhat more quietly than normal, I thought. Oh, we talked about the hole between the White Tanks and the Bradshaws. We called CD, told him we were rooting for him and to keep us advised. John had to do some creative fence un-mending to get our rig through to the overgrown runway, which is complete with bushes and trees. We de-rigged and got underway.

We re-mended the fence, and bounced along the lumpy driveway back to Grand Avenue. I'd had time to think about it all, and reached the rational decision that Gloria's was, at worst, just a diner and bar after all. And being on the outskirts of everywhere, the owners simply lived in that trailer. It was, after all, a nice trailer...

"Say, John, I've got some cokes here. Let's get some ice at Gloria's..." I suggested.

"No ice at Gloria's," he said.

"Well, we could just get some cold cans of pop, or a couple of beers..."

"No cold cans at Gloria's."

Cryptic, John, very cryptic. I didn't feel brave enough to pursue that line of questioning. I do, however, see more clearly now the merit of the drive and chase method of crewing. The complete crew really never should be more than a half hour's drive from her downed pilot. Desert survival is one thing, but Gloria's Place and the enigma therein - well, you just never know...

THEY ALSO SERVE WHO ONLY STAND AND WAIT by Trish Durbin, August 1981.

Recently there was an advertisement in a glider club's newsletter where some brave but misguided soul offered her services as weekend crew. "Poor child," I shuddered, "she knows not what she does." Although I do not know this optimist personally, I have taken it upon myself to enlighten her, hoping she sees my words of wisdom printed here.

As crew, your duties are not confined to weekends. You stagger home on Sunday night from a weekend's soaring and unload the ice chests, cool boxes, thermally-insulated water containers, pump pots and empty yoghurt cartons. You dispose of the disgusting congealed messes reposing in the far corners of your precious Tupperware, and get around to washing them up or cramming them in the dishwasher on Monday. Maybe Tuesday is a respite, but by Wednesday you are again pondering the ever-present problem of what food to take, and desperately trying to think of something original and interesting that will remain recognizable throughout a weekend spent in rapidly warming ice boxes. Even McDonalds' marketing drive has not brought their 30 billion hamburgers to the outer reaches of civilization frequented by glider pilots. Thursday you shop, and Friday you have an orgy of baking, creating a quiche and a pizza from virtually the same ingredients, and checking stocks of canned soft drinks for flying hours and beer for afterwards.

Apart from this, you will be called upon to produce a never-ending supply of *clean* rags (T-shirts are best, but to maintain sufficient supplies of old T-shirts, you'd also need to maintain a football team). You are the bestower of multifarious gifts such as space blankets and snake bite kits at Christmas and birthdays. You drive the local bookstore crazy by ordering all sorts of obscure titles they've never heard of and wouldn't dream of keeping in stock. ("You don't mean *hang* gliding, do you? Are you sure?")

It seems to me that Crew has so much to do with wings in this life, she will surely merit them in the next. She is the lucky one that gets to take the full weight of the wings while her pilot yells things like, "Forward! Forward - not so much! Back a bit. Right. Now up and down. More up and down. O.K. Fore and aft. More fore and aft! That's lovely!" If he yelled those things anywhere but an airfield, he'd get arrested.

So you've lovingly washed the wings and held them level as they fill with water while your pilot is doing bigger and better things. You've made the sandwiches, polished the canopy, generally titivated the whole plane, and run between the cockpit and the trailer (parked a minimum of 50 yards away) at least ten times when the Resident Expert comes by and intones, "These wings are filthy. They ought to be washed." Well, he's chosen the wrong damn day of the month to come casting aspersions on your wing washing, but you content yourself with a baleful glower at his retreating back because, after all, he is an expert and all advice is gratefully received by your pilot. So you make a bit of noise with the bucket and slosh the water around while your pilot's back is turned. Then you swipe at the wings once more with a damp, and by now probably gritty cloth, just for the look of the thing.

When you finally get the glider to the launch point the Expert runs a discerning hand over your leading edges and pronounces them excellent, and you alone have the satisfaction of knowing that even Great Experts bullshit sometimes. (It should be noted here that pilots have a fetish about having their wings washed, the way lesser men have fetishes about having their ears tickled or their backs rubbed. It has been my observation that if "the wife" isn't around to do it, it doesn't get done. Like tickling, wing washing is apparently something you cannot do for yourself.)

So. You've fed and watered him and done his positive checks, and the 98 other things that fall to your lot, and it's time to get the ship on the launch pad. He pushes and you're supposed to steer, but as you need eyes in the back of your head to do this, and no one ever tells you where you're actually supposed to be going, even this part should not be underestimated.

Once you've got your pilot ensconced in the cockpit, sprinted 300 yards back to the trailer for his hat, offered up the straps for strapping in, tucked his two granola bars into the side pocket in case he lands out, checked that he's got his radio paraphernalia round his neck, the tube for his water bottle conveniently placed, the barograph ON, nothing loose in the back, kissed him goodbye in case you never see him again, put the canopy on, told him three times the tail dolly is OFF, and no, dear, you won't forget to take it back to the trailer, and reached in through the window to give his arm a loving squeeze in case he really does kill himself this time, and finally seen him launched, then your day *really* begins.

You are no doubt by this time bursting to use the facilities (if there are any, or a local bush if there aren't), dying for a drink, and yearning for a bit of shade (the foregoing procedures having been carried out in temperatures approaching 100°). But it is not to be - not yet! First priorities are to rescue the tail dolly and go back to the car and wait for the radio check he'll need immediately he comes off tow. So you sit in the car, which already resembles an inferno, knowing there's not going to be any shade until two o'clock, and you hate to put on any suntan oil because the blowing sand will stick to it like sparkle on a Christmas card. You cast anxious looks at the facilities (or the bush) and wonder if there's time for a desperate dash before he comes off tow. You curse yourself for not having gone as soon as he was launched - there would have been time. Eventually you can tell by the change of note in the towplane's engine that he has released, and sure enough after a few more moments he calls in for his radio check. "Receiving you loud and clear," you say, drop the microphone and run. Blessed relief.

After that, you come back, take a deep breath, and survey the scene. All is chaos. You try to get things shipshape. You put the lids back on the ice chests, having inadvertently left them off when rummaging through them for the pilot's lunch. You put the tail dolly and the wing stands and the bucket and all the other associated equipment into the *front* of the trailer, as instructed, in case you have to tow it empty. This has something to do with tung weight, or tongue weight, or maybe even tun weight. One of life's mysteries, anyway. The only sort we wives are expert on is the Long Wait.

Now you can sit down and relax. You set out a chair or a lounger, place a drink, Sunday newspapers, your library book, letter-writing equipment, and pen in convenient proximity, adjust your sunhat to a jaunty angle, and luxuriously lie back. By jove, you've earned this! Suddenly the radio crackles into life and you hear your call signed uttered with an urgency that suggests your pilot is going down in flames. You leap to you feet, knock over your drink, bruise your leg on the lounger, and grab the radio to reply. Your call sign again and then, "I'm at 7,000 feet and I'm leaving the field, heading south toward the goal."

"Roger," you say, forgetting the call sign.

Was that all? Oh well, you're glad conditions are already good enough to give him 7,000 feet and that he's going to get another crack at Diamond Goal today. (Three attempts so far, all very good, but not quite good enough). Mind you, four attempts in two consecutive weekends is a bit keen, even dedicated, but what else is there to do in Arizona anyway? Your pilot is always so reasonable during the week. "Well, what else do you want to *do*? *Say* what you want to do, and we'll do it." In the week, you yearn for that Diamond as much as he does, but sitting here all on your own you can think of a hundred and one other things you could be doing, together too! That's when you look around and discover a merry little dust devil has come by during your radio conversation and made off with the Sunday newspapers.

You start to wonder if it's lunch time yet. Pilots profess to know all about Murphy's Law but there is one law they know nothing about: "It is impossible to diet on an airfield." It's perfectly possible at home in the kitchen when you are preparing the weekend's food. In addition to all manner of goodies for the pilot, plus an ice chest of cold beer for either celebration or condolence afterward, you also pack pineapple and cottage cheese for yourself. However, at the gliderport, as lunch time approaches, either the hunger pangs are too devastating to contemplate such meager fare or the cottage cheese has gone runny in the heat or the pineapple tastes fizzy and has gone off too.

Or else you've forgotten the plastic plates, spoons and forks; cottage cheese eaten with a credit card just doesn't taste the same. So you get to thinking about the pizza and cans you brought for your pilot and consume vast quantities of that instead. If, by a supreme effort of will, perseverance and fortitude, you have stayed with the wilting lettuce leaves and a whole cherry tomato, Murphy's Law then dictates you will later fall in with other wifely crews for a game of Scrabble and consume inordinate portions of their tortilla chips and Mexican Salsa Dip. Which makes you thirsty so you have to have another can. More calories.

Some hours have now passed and you are yearning for your afternoon cup of tea. (British instincts.) A decent cup of tea is an impossibility in America anyway, but in the midst of the Arizona desert, forget it!

Your pilot has been out of radio distance for some time now, so you are confident he has at least got within photographing distance of the turnpoint. You look at your watch and you know in another half hour he should be back within radio range. You are trying to contain your excitement and stop yourself from thinking, "He's done it! He must have!" too early. You are practically keeping him aloft by an effort of will all on your own by this stage.

It is not until the shadows are lengthening and you are beginning to think fondly of your dinner that you hear your call sign over the P.A. loudspeakers. Your heart sinks, as your pilot must have done, and not exclusively because a phone call means he's down. It always coincides with one of the following: (a) you are in the loo, or (b) you are at a riveting place in your library book and can't wait to find out what happens next, or (c) you are heavily involved in a game of Scrabble and at your next turn you can put down a really demon seven-letter word across two triple scores and get a bonus of 50 points. It is a physical impossibility for your pilot to call in at any other time. The P.A. calls again, and inexorably adds, "Your pilot is on the phone."

You hasten to the office, and the minute you hear his voice, he has you in the palm of his hand. He has flown 100 miles, photographed the turnpoint, and flown 70 miles back. He was at 13,000 feet and then got in an area of unbelievable sink and went down at a 1000 feet a minute. He was over the saguaro cactus forests at the time, with no landing strip in sight, so he put the ship down on a 2'6" wide gravel path, ground looped it 180° around a cactus, and has badly scratched a wing.

You could weep. You could take it worse than he seems to. You would do anything if only... You would drive across deserts and over mountains for this guy, and being in Arizona, that's exactly what you do!

The mean temperature is now 105°F in the shade (that's not mean, that's evil!) and you set off into the unknown to bravely go where no wife has gone before. You've got your directions and the area chart and a road map. (He says use the chart, it's easier, but you know it ain't!) And you've got yourself to the freeway a couple of times before - so why are you hyperventilating like this? So you start talking to yourself. It's either that or chewing gum, and you haven't any gum because you used it all up when you were hyperventilating on a retrieve yesterday.

You tell yourself politely you wish your pilot had fixed the car's air conditioning - 105° is a bit much. You also mention that going on a retrieve in England would be far less hazardous. Here in Arizona, there's nobody about and nothing for miles. You might see a friendly face en route, but you're afraid to stop and check if you're on the right road because he's probably got a gun in his belt and a can of Mace up his sleeve. (You know perfectly well everybody but everybody is armed in America).

So you plough on and after two hours on the freeway you see the signpost your pilot said to look for. Here you head west, deeper and deeper into the saguaro cactus forest, intrepid and alone, with only those weird, almost human-shaped cacti for company. After 25 miles of this, during which time you have been repeating your call sign into the radio, you begin to wonder where on earth you are going to end up. The sun is setting and it's very, very beautiful but you know darkness comes quickly after sunset here and you wonder what you'll do if you haven't found him by dark.

All the way over here you've been thinking about the pilot you love, envisaging him sitting disconsolate and dejected by his damaged plane, dwelling on his mistakes and watching the thermals go by. You plan what you will say to him by way of comfort, and do a mental check on the contents of the ice chests. Plenty of cool beer and pizza, and some watermelon too. Poor darling will be starving by now. And thirsty. You hope his water has lasted alright. You feel a bit guilty for complaining about the lack of air conditioning and reflect that 105° might be bad but he's been stuck out in the blazing sun for nearly three hours with no shade whatsoever. At least you are in a moving car with the windows open.

At last, at last and at last - the radio gives an answering crackle. You hear his dear voice, distant and wavering, but you've made contact! "Hello, darling!" you cry with a fine disregard for the sanctity of the airwaves in general and channel 123.3 in particular. "Are you alright?"

"Yes, I'm fine," he answers, sounding considerably happier than you'd anticipated. It must be delight at knowing you are at hand, you think fondly. "The whole village is waiting for you," he says, and chuckles.

Chuckles? Three hours in the blazing heat with no food or extra water and a damaged wing and he's *chuckling*?

It's a tiny copper mining community. As you approach the mine workings, there's a whistle, a shout and a wave. A man runs across from his front yard and points you in the right direction. (You're pretty easy to recognize when you're towing a big box with a bump on the top). Someone else in a pickup truck calls for you to follow him. You go back down the rough track and there before you is a panoramic view of Arizona in the sunset, a sailplane sitting nonchalantly beneath a cactus, a hoard of village children busy fingerprinting the canopy, and your pilot with a great big grin on his face.

"Hello," he says. "I've had a lovely time. They've given me some Pepsi and fried chicken, and lots of beer. And one guy asked me if I wanted an auto tow, and a lady let me use her phone..."

"Oh, good," you say. "I'm sorry you didn't quite get back, darling. That was bad luck."

"That's alright," he says, "I mentioned at work I might not be in on Monday. I think I'll try again tomorrow."

DURBIN'S DIAMOND - HOW IT LOOKED FROM THE GROUND by Trish Durbin, July 1985.

The weekend started off with an ill omen. As we were about to leave, we realized neither of us had any cash, as usual. A detour via the bank was necessary, but as we pulled away, feeling rich once more, we discovered a flat tire on the glider trailer. Inevitably, the spare was housed in the bowels of the trailer itself. So, there we were at Thunderbird and 19th, with the fuselage out in the bank parking lot, making a major spectacle of ourselves. We didn't dare leave Phoenix without buying another spare, just in case Golf Yankee landed out and a lengthy retrieve gave lightning every opportunity to strike twice.

So instead of arriving early at Estrella as planned, in plenty of time to get the ship and our act together, we staggered in when it was too hot to even contemplate rigging. We contented ourselves with playing spot-the-call-sign on homecoming ships completing the final day of the Region 9 Contest and relaxed at the Awards Dinner/Barbecue afterwards.

Although next morning found us rigging the ship and filling the wings with water - always a lengthy procedure with the Mickey Mouse methods employed - what we were really doing was preparing to land out. My pilot filled in the forms, photographed his declaration and loaded a barograph in the exceedingly unlikely event that the impossible happened and he actually completed Diamond Distance at his first attempt. We concentrated more on making sure he had a warm shirt and spare water, a sandwich to eat in case it took me a long time to reach him, and various instructions for me on how and how not to go about finding him.

Once he'd launched and was on his way, I tore myself from the radio to enjoy a much needed but hasty shower in the bunkhouse. Ah, bliss. I was perturbed to discover when I got back on the air, however, that Golf Yankee had only covered 35 miles and was finding nothing but weak lift. I was glad we'd left the car and trailer hitched up.

A message to say he was polishing rocks at Silver Bell brought back dire memories of May, 1981, when I'd retrieved him from a 2'6" wide path near the mine and been sufficiently inspired to write about the exasperation, desperation, elation and jubilation of that experieence. Not again, Golf Yankee, pleeeeeeease.

Gradually the day strengthened. He was at 8,800 feet. Then 12,000 feet. This was better. Bless your little cotton socks, I said. Those nearby laughed. An English expression, undoubtedly. Passersby enquired how he was doing. It was no doubt a casual enquiry, but they got a blow by blow account, his precise position, his altitude, my interpretation of his frame of mind, the concern that he might not be drinking enough water... My paranoia seemed to involve them too and pretty soon there was a group of us, cowering in the 105° shade, awaiting his every transmission. Lunch time came and the group disintegrated except for one other sailplane owner whose partner was also attempting Diamond Distance that day, but had declared a different task. Hotel Tango 4 Ground and I set up camp for a lengthy vigil.

By this time, Golf Yankee was out of radio range and Echo Uniform was relaying radio messages. Bless your little cotton socks too, Echo Uniform. And your funny hat flaps. Golf Yankee has photographed the turnpoint and is heading home!! Hotel Tango 4 Ground narrowly escapes getting hugged at this juncture. I manage to contain my enthusiasm with the reflection that Golf Yankee will be telling himself he's only half started. Whereas I know he's half finished! At last he's back within radio range, although I can hear from his voice he's lower than he cares to be. Then there's a long period of silence. This means he's busy working every shred of lift, with no time to call me on the radio. Don't forget to take the tail dolly when you leave, I remind myself. I have to sit on my hands to stop myself touching the microphone. Walk away from it completely as the minutes tick by. I yearn to call and ask if he's OK. What are you DOING, Golf Yankee?

It's not until I'm seriously contemplating digging a hole in the sand and sticking my head in it that he nonchalantly calls to let me know he's at 13,000 feet. Euphoria! Then I hear him calling El Tiro to ask what their surface winds are and I know I'll never find El Tiro on my own. You can't possibly land at El Tiro, Golf Yankee, get your rudder out of there!

At 6:07 he's back on the air to say he's 25 miles out and "on a sort of final glide". How can he do that to me? What's a *sort* of final glide? At 6:16 he's 5 miles out. The adrenalin is foaming in my veins until I deliberately and cruelly remind myself more experienced pilots than him have landed less than 2 miles out. Just the wrong side of the airport fence would ruin it all. Don't count your chickens until they've landed, I tell myself severely. Las Horvath comes by.

"Where is he?" he wants to know.

"Five miles out."

"Vot are you standing there for then? You should be vaiting for him with the tail dolly."

I grab the cold beer and the tail dolly, quite unable to decide which is the more important at this stage, and race for Runway 3. He always comes in on Runway 3. Then I hear Golf Yankee on the radio and have to race back again. I know I'm running around like a chicken with its head cut off but that's about how I feel. He's one mile out and wanting to know if the circuit is clear. I answer him completely incoherently and race back. I set off down Runway 3. (He always lands on Runway 3). I'm at least ten feet off the ground and could meet him in the air by this time.

Then we see him, careening across the sky with water streaming out behind him like smoke, victory in every line. Las is filming it on video; an enthusiastic stranger is happy snapping with his Polaroid. Someone else is alarmed to see this airplane dumping fuel. My eyes fixed on his red wing tips, I stumble further down Runway 3 until Las gently points out he's coming in on Runway 2. (Typical). Oblivious of rattlesnakes and tarantulas, I change runways, running with the tail dolly weighing me down, sweat pouring unheeded down every limb, and the cold beer clutched doggedly in my hand. My glasses fall off, I drop everything, and Las calmly films Golf Yankee coming in to land with my rear end weaving about in the foreground, gathering up my belongings. I plunge onward, dump the tail dolly and take the canopy from weary hands. After 6 hours and 49 minutes in the cockpit, it isn't surprising that Golf Yankee looks more exhausted than triumphant. I probably look the same. After all, I've flown every inch of the way with him.

SOARING FOR DIAMONDS, CREWING FOR PEANUTS by Trish Durbin, March 1988.

Oh-oh. It's soaring contest time again. Time to unwrap the bird, flex your muscles, dig out the tail dolly. And watch your pilot insinuate himself once more into the good graces of his crew. You.

Most glider pilots either turn their crews into wives by marrying them, or their wives into crew by shouting at them. The only qualifications required of a good crew are abject obedience at all times, an ability to immediately understand completely incomprehensible instructions and a complete disregard for all creature comforts. (Like showers). It is preferable if you marry your pilot for his body or his money. If you marry him for his company or his conversation, you are likely to be discontented.

I've been crewing now for about six years, a novice by some folks' standard, but it sure feels like a long time. I still maintain I was lured into crewing for my first contest under false pretenses. The blurb said,"And for your crew there will be swimming, horseback riding and ball games during the soaring contest." Oh goody, I though, a vacation! Now, with the wisdom of hindsight and bitter experience, my only question is, just *when* did the organizers envisage we were going to avail ourselves of these magnificent recreational opportunities?

A "normal" contest day starts at 6 or 6.30 a.m. and your pilot wants his O.J. or his coffee to get him started. Then it's down to the tiedown area to check out the plane, wash the dust and bugs from its wings, fill up with water, polish the canopy, connect the battery, do the positive checks, make sure the drinking water is stowed and accessible, etcetera, etcetera, etcetera. Before you can say "Standard Class Champion" it's 9 o'clock and your pilot is ready for his breakfast. So you hunt around for that and prepare his in-flight sandwich while he eats. Then you wash up while he takes a leisurely half hour over his ablutions and you rush into the pilots' meting with wash-day red hands and no shower.

After the pilot's meeting, and plotting plans of campaign on charts, it's back to the plane for the final attentions and titivations you last enjoyed when you were a bride, and then it's time to get the ship out to the grid. You supply your pilot with his in-flight fodder, grab the Gatorade and wait for the sniffer plane to stay up and the lift to start. This takes hours but make the most of it, it's the lull before the storm, and it's certainly no time to be thinking about swimming or horseback riding.

The moment they give the word to launch, it's all hell let loose. Tow planes roar, dust rises and line boys scurry back and forth in apparent confusion. It reminds you of the scene in "The Battle of Britain" where they scramble an entire squadron in four minutes. There's a surfeit of adrenalin all down the line and the soaring blood pressures would make any thermal envious.

Once they've launched (including the re-lights), after all that tension you're glad to see the back of them but you grab the now empty Gatorade bottle, and, perversely, you race back to your radio to hear your pilot go through the gate and write down the time he gets his Good Start.

Maybe this is the bit where they bring on the horses? But how can you?? Manning a radio is the soaring equivalent of having one boot nailed to the floor, and if the portable radio doesn't have sufficient range, you are tethered to your vehicle by the radio's umbilical cord like a goat to a post. (Manning a radio on horse back isn't really practical. For a start, where would you put the antenna?)

The old hands nonchalantly strip off (well, almost) to sunbathe or swim, secure in the knowledge that their pilots will not only get back but probably create a few new records at the same time. We novices sit poised for action, microphone in one hand, paper and pen in the other, tow vehicle ignition keys at the ready, confident that we'll be called out on a retrieve and tensely marking our pilot's progress on the chart so we'll know where to head for when the inevitable happens.

Later, when your pilot has either amazed you and himself and flown home, or you've gone out and retrieved him, you're allowed to wash the bugs off the leading edges while he hands in his flight card and films, and swaps fisherman's tales with the other pilots. Of Diamonds that got away because of failed barographs, disallowed traces, camera malfunctions and other Acts of God.

And then, of course, it's dinner time and all the barbecues come out, the air redolent with One Match starter fluid. Evenings are nice during soaring contests. A quiet time for camaraderie and laughter, for a drink with friends, sharing and getting by without the things you forgot to bring with you.

Toward the end of the week, your pilot is getting tired and maybe - perish the thought - even irritable. He begins to look as if you built him from a kit. The tension of who lies where in the ratings, the pressure of maintaining a ship to perfection with no facilities and not enough tools, begins to tell. A late retrieve the day before means putting the plane together in a rush next morning. Instead of thanking you nicely for his coffee, he mutters, "There's enough grounds in here for a divorce." You read somewhere you must not permit domestic strife before a flight so you bite your tongue and content yourself with the happy idea of wrapping his in-flight sandwich in plastic wrap instead of the usual aluminum foil. Let's see him unravel *that* while he's centering a thermal.

Eventually, and yet too soon, it's the final hectic day and the Awards Dinner. Come evening, as the fires die down, the results are in and the tasks are done, you cast your mind back over the events of the week and you're still wondering, "When *was* I supposed to go horse back riding?"

HOW SOARING REALLY STARTED by Trish Durbin, June 1985.

Way back in the beginning of time, man was lonely and bored. He rarely bothered doing any chores, being totally incapable of perceiving that his cave was the pits and really in need of a good clean. He spent most of his time sitting on his backside, drinking beer and watching the pterodactyls fly past. (Birds with feathers hadn't been invented yet, which is why aircraft don't have feathers, even to this day). The pterodactyls were fun to watch; quite thrilling, in fact, but it certainly hadn't occurred to Man to attempt anything similar.

Then one day Woman happened along, looking good and happily going about her business. It really hit her in the eye what a mess Man's cave was in, so she set about tidying up the place. Then she had to rinse through a couple of animal skins because she only had three to her name; one to wear, one ready to put on and one in the wash. (She was behind in her routine because of cleaning up Man's chaotic cave).

160

By then it was supper time, so she set about preparing a good dinner from leftovers, since Man had been "too busy" watching pterodactyls that day to go hunting. After that she washed up the flint dishes, dried them and put them all away. By that time there was nothing left of the evening, and the next day she got up and started all over again. By the sixth day she had gotten into a bit of a routine and managed to finish up early, so on the seventh day she was able to sit down and put her feet up.

Now, seeing her relaxing for five minutes really bugged Man, and after a week or two of that he got to figuring he was really being sold short on Sundays. How come Woman was sitting around on that day, and not looking after him like she did Monday through Saturday? Admittedly, they ate as well as they always did, if not better, and it all got cleared up just the same. Even though other things got left, it didn't actually make that much difference to his comfort, if he was really honest with himself. But dammit, it just didn't seem right!

What was needed, Man fell to thinking, was to find something to keep her occupied that could only be done on Sundays. It would be even better, he realized, if it was something that could occasionally be done on other days of the week as well, especially Saturdays, but it had to be something that was more or less obligatory on Sundays.

Lying in his usual position, his eye fell once more on the pterodactyls, wheeling and dealing in the sky and just having a grand old time. It occurred to Man that if he could do that too, and had some wings himself, Woman could do all her other chores during the week and he could kid her along that it was her job to wash the wings on Sundays. The more he thought about it, the better he liked the idea.

It was obvious from the start that if he did get a pair of wings, he couldn't use them in the neighborhood of the cave; he'd have to lug them out to some remote and distant spot. That way, Woman would have to pack up enough food to keep them going while they were gone. Better yet, if he told her he wanted to use his wings and party with the pterodactyls on Saturdays *and* Sundays, that would involve Woman in even more work and maybe wipe out her weekends entirely. Great!

So he worked on a few ideas and pretty soon had a workable model that emulated the pterodactyls tolerably well for wing span, dihedral, swept tail volume, center of gravity and a bunch of other stuff. It flew pretty well and Man decided to call it The Goods because he was sure it was going to deliver. Another bonus was that, whereas the pterodactyls ate any insects they encountered when they flew, Man's version plastered the insects onto the wings and make them look yukko. Man landed, noticed this phenomenon, and went off to convince Woman it was her job to wash off the bugs.

Woman, however, was nowhere near as dumb as Man thought she was, and told him if he wanted The Goods' wings cleaned, there was the palm leaf bucket, there was the coconut fiber cloth, there was the pond, and to go right ahead and do it himself. Sundays were her day off, and she sat right down and put her feet up.

Man was pretty choked up about this turn of events, but he was danged if he was going to let Woman see that. He took off again and flew without washing off the bugs, but they made more difference than he realized, slowed him down a heck of a lot and increased his sink. So much so, in fact, that he landed out a long way from base, and had to push and pull and lug The Goods all the way back on his own. Woman saw him coming and watched him getting nearer just to the right of her big toe.

Trouble was, now he'd gotten started on this soaring, Man found he liked it. Too much to give it up, in fact. So the next weekend he took off once more, despite grungy wings, and had a great time but still landed out a long way from home. Knowing full well it was Woman's fault, resenting her attitude, Man sat down on a rock, lonely, incensed and exhausted, thinking that what he desperately needed was a Goods' Crew, when who should saunter by but Woman. In spite of himself, he was really glad to see her.

"Hi!" he said, hauling himself vertical. "Howya doin'?"

"I'm doin' real good," Woman replied, and he could see she spoke the truth. She looked cool and rested, freshly showered from the waterfall, a clean animal skin clinging provocatively to one tanned shoulder.

"Wish I could say the same," Man muttered sheepishly. She looked at him. "What I need here," he continued, "is some help. It'd make a big difference. I'd sure..." The words seemed to stick in his throat. "I'd sure appreciate it."

"Great!" she said, picking up the coconut fiber cloth and sloshing it around in the palm leaf bucket. "You only had to admit you *needed* me, and show a bit of appreciation, and I'd be happy to help."

And that's the true story of how Man got hooked on soaring in the first place and how Woman got conned into crewing for him.

CHAPTER 10 - OTHER PEOPLE'S STORIES

OVER-COFFEED? by Anna Hutchinson.

T'was a Mid West Meet at Frankfurt, Michigan, in 1938 and there was a rip-roaring wind whipping across Lake Michigan and up over the sand dunes. The forecast held promise of a steady two day blow. To Dick Randolph this was an opportunity to try for a duration record and preparations were made accordingly. Since there would be no moon that night it was arranged with the people living at the edge of the dunes to turn their porch lights on, and friends and officials built huge bonfires at the turning points.

It started to get dark after about 7 hours in the air and the wind was still pushing up over the dunes. Dick was real prepared for the big sit: he'd brought along a bottle of caffeine tablets, of which he took a few at a time. After a few more hours, he figured he had it made and this breeze was good for the night, so he polished off the rest of the tablets. Around mid-night, after being in the air for over twelve hours, the wind suddenly died dead.

As he gradually sank lower he could be heard shouting for the crews to douse the fires, they were so bright they were blinding him. When he got below the dunes it was so dark he couldn't see the beach but could make out the white edge where the surf was breaking. Using this as a guide he was able to follow the contour of the beach, but was gliding far down into an unfamiliar area. He was quite low now and there was no way of judging height. He held the stick in a set position, put his arm across his face, braced himself against the panel and waited.

Soon he heard the wheel roll and felt the ship stop as if on a feather. Boy! Was he beat? He got out of the ship, and remembers vaguely wondering, as he staggered up the beach, why didn't the wing tip go down when he stopped? Anyhow, he informed everyone that everything was alright and they would retrieve the ship in the morning.

When they returned next morning they were confronted by an unbelievable sight. The ship was resting in the only clear spot in the area, the wingtips were perfectly balanced on two hummocks of sand, and completely surrounded by debris, tree trunks, old pieces of highway, wrecks, rocks, etc. Apparently when Dick got out of the ship and staggered away he zigged at the zigs and zagged at the zags and in the darkness he was under the illusion he was walking on a perfectly clear and level beach.

In addition to all this, he became a familiar sight in town, roaming the streets for days and nights, walking off that dose of caffeine tablets.

DID YOU EVER SEE A DREAM WALKING? heard at Elmira by Anna Hutchinson.

During one of the very early Elmira contests, there was a contestant whom everyone called "Flourpants", the literal translation of his German surname. Well, Flourpants had an argument between his Haller Hawk sailplane and the terrain. The friction caused a little damage around a wingtip, calling for a little repair work. The usual situation: work most of the night to repair the ship, and hope-to-get-enough-sleep-to-be-able-to-fly-tomorrow routine took place.

His cot was one of sixteen jammed side by side into a small upstairs room in the Rhodes farm house (this was before Harris Hill buildings were thought of). Most of the occupants were from Akron, Ohio, "The Gas House Gang of Gliding". Getting in and out of bed in these conditions necessitated walking on the cots, sometimes avoiding the occupants. But nobody seemed to mind, least of all Flourpants, this particular morning. He slept undisturbed through cot-hopping, hurdling, and whooping of the noisy Akron glider gang.

Someone suddenly became aware of this calm and serene figure in the midst of chaos and brought it to everyone's attention. Someone else expressed pity that Flourpants should miss one of those superb "Rhodes" breakfasts. Another suggested that he wouldn't have to miss anything, they could carry him down to breakfast with them.

With unanimous approval, the still sleeping figure of Flourpants was hoisted from his cot and juggled down the narrow staircase which opens directly into the dining room. Everybody, and there were about 40 men, women and children, burst into laughter as the group emerged. A chair was set onto an empty table and the limp, still sleeping form of Flourpants was lifted up onto it. The people were still howling as somebody flicked a little water in his face and he finally started to wake up.

Suddenly he became aware of the laughter. He stared incredulously at the crowd which was practically in hysterics by now, then looking down at himself clad in carelessly-repaired pajamas, he became ashen white as the blood drained from his face in shocked disbelief that he was living this nightmare.

Just as suddenly the color came back to his face, he stood up, smiled, and announced solemnly to the group before him, "This is a dream. These things only happen in dreams," stepped down from the table, went back upstairs to bed and to sleep again. To this day Flourpants still isn't quite certain if he just talked in his sleep or whether it really did happen.

BLOW HARD by Lyle Maxey, as told by Anna Hutchinson.

One of my flights during the 1956 Nationals terminated at Garnet, Kansas, a little farm town about 50 miles from Kansas City. The Editor of the weekly newspaper came out to the airport to interview me. He showed interest in soaring in general, but he seemed particularly impressed with my description of the flight. After talking for sometime, we said goodbye and he left for town.

About 45 minutes later he returned with one of the local citizens in tow. The newcomer gave the ship his personal analytical inspection and then demanded a complete recap of my story. When I'd finished he said, "You mean to tell me you flew this here contraption all the way from Grand Prairie without no motor?"

I allowed modestly as how that was about the size of it. He stepped closer and with an air of emphatic finality he boomed, "Bull shit, there ain't no wind that strong!"

THE LONG TOW by Ken Bradford. From Zero Sink, Orange County Soaring Assoc.

Last month we reported that, when accepting delivery of the Club's new 2-33, Dave and Karl Jessop left some parts on the runway at Tehachapi. This month they left a whole glider - including the pilot.

As the story goes, the brothers happily took off from Orange County Airport for Tehachapi to tow in Karl's brand new 2-33 with Dave's 172. And in due time arrived (110 miles). After the check out, and amid happy goodbyes, they saddled up for the long tow home, Karl comfortable in the glider on his donut cushion, Dave in the Cessna. Come the takeoff and Karl was just wobbling down the runway when all bedlam broke loose - it sounded like his brand new glider was falling apart. Was the wheel gone? Was a strut dragging? Karl didn't look. He released fast and pulled off.

After his heart got back in place, he climbed out to survey the wreckage as everybody rushed up. Look they did, and found - nothing. It seems the rear window was not secured before takeoff and started banging the wing. With a few choice words, Karl locked and taped the latch and saddled up again.

But where was brother Dave? Nobody told him about the unhook, and by this time he was a speck on the horizon doing a masterful job of pulling the tow rope all the way to Elsinore (125 miles) while brother Karl had fits in Tehachapi.

After he recovered, Karl placed a call to Florence at Skylark Field, asking her to break the news to Dave when he arrived - which he did after two hours at 60 mph. He rolled up to the gas pump, got out and scanned around for Karl, with that, "Now what the H---'s he up to" expression.

At this point, Florence walked up - grinning - to give him the jolt and broke up completely - as Dave gasped and staggered back against the Cessna. And made a few remarks reserved for mashed fingers or barked shins. We can't print it here. But it was too late to go back for Karl so he flew to Orange County and tied down.

Meanwhile, back at the glider factory, Karl had calmed down long enough to take a tow to 2000, found a good one, and was soon at 10,000 - headed for home. After all, he thought, it had been done. And he would "have" brother Dave from then on.

165

But Karl ran out of day around El Mirage so put in for the night. Placed some calls for Dave, who by this time was on the job taking care of his air conditioner business. So dawned a new day and Dave lit out as soon as he could and flew back to Tehachapi (110 miles). When they told him where Karl was, his hat really hit the ground - so hard the boys at 4000 feet felt it. So it was back in the Cessna where he firewalled everything and got the STOL out of there for 60 miles to El Mirage. Where brother Karl was looking in the wrong direction and didn't see him come in.

So, the brothers were reunited and after they stopped yelling at each other, Karl settled on his donut ready to go again. So did the brothers hook up and go peacefully fading off into the sky? Was this the end of their problems? Not yet!

Karl was ready to go but Dave was there jumping up and down. He didn't have time to make the long tow... he had to get back on the job... his customers were sweating!

So Karl climbed wearily out and it was full bore back to Orange County (70 miles) where Dave got out and on the job while Karl flew over to Skylark (35 miles), picked up Ray Brown (a real tow pilot), and then back to El Mirage (75 miles) where, after carefully adjusting the rear view mirror, they towed off for Skylark (75 miles) and arrived late Thursday. Whereupon the '33 was tied down and Karl flew the Cessna 172 back to Orange County (35 miles). Wheuuu!

This adds up to 730 airline miles of flying to get the new bird 110 miles and qualifies them for the Royal Order of the Cast Iron Tow Rope.

A BIKLE OUTLANDING From THE THERMAL, February 1958, an excerpt from the inaugural address of Bob Smith, newly elected President of SCSA.

Many of the best stories that originate at our soaring contests never seem to get into print. I would like to tell you one of them. This is a story Paul Bikle told about the flight he made at the last National Contest when he flew to Cape May, New Jersey. I have only heard this story once some months ago. I hope Paul will forgive me if some of the details are not absolutely correct and I embellish them a little.

Paul landed on a Marine training post parade ground and after due course of military routine, he was taken to the Officer of the Day and allowed to call his retrieving crew. The Officer of the Day questioned him as to when his crew would arrive and pick him up. When Paul told him 8 or 9 o'clock, he was quite perturbed. He apologized for appearing inhospitable but he had an important engagement that evening and would have to stay on the post as long as Paul was there. Could the ship be moved outside the gate some way? Paul told him if he could get some manpower he could move it.

They went out on the parade ground and the officer talked with a sergeant who was drilling a group of men. The sergeant marched the men to the ship. With Paul's assistance, they placed the marines along the leading edge of the wing at close intervals and put a few along the trailing edge, stabilizer and fuselage. Each man put one hand under the ship and, on a command from the drill sergeant, "Lift ship, Ho! Forward march!", they marched off across the parade ground with the sailplane a foot or so off the ground. I bet at this moment Paul thought, "This is the best glide angle this ship ever had!"

166

When they reached a point opposite the gate, the sergeant gave a command of "Left flank - March!" and without changing the attitude of the ship, they abruptly changed direction 90° without slowing down. And while Paul held his breath they passed through the gate with inches to spare. At the entrance to the Post there was a little park with a monument, trees and a grass covered clearing big enough for the ship, where they set it down. Later, when the ground crew arrived, one of the crew members looked at the trees, monument, fence and little patch of grass, and then asked Paul, "How in the world did you manage to land in here?"

DEAR SOARING MAGAZINE EDITOR... Author Unknown, Air Currents, June 1974.

This letter is in answer to your plea in Soaring Magazine to report all "long" soaring flights for publication purposes. A brief description of the flight is as follows:

After I read Mr Katinszky's account of his record breaking flight, I immediately realized the importance of advance planning. So, on the morning of October 11, on my way to the soaring site, I planned everything to the most minute detail. To give you an example, even such a small thing as releasing from tow prior to the completion of the first 360° (opposite to that of the towplane) was not overlooked.

My declared goal, Banning, (35 miles), may seem to you as much too modest, but considering the fact that this was not my first attempt, I didn't think so. To tell the truth, this is the third attempt, and the farmlands en route to Banning should have bumper crops this year judging from the amount of sweat I dropped over them. Also, I was fully aware of the possible scorn of my fellow club members if I set my sights on a more ambitious project without a trailer. Anyway, I curtailed my urge to break Al Parkers' record.

After arriving at Elsinore's Skylark Field at the break of dawn, (11:00 am), I set about the methodical task of preparing my hot little ship, a 10 year old 1-26, for the ordeal.

Again, no details were overlooked. I even remembered to unhook the tiedown chains before pulling "Sweetheart" to the take off line. Small items, such as chewing gum, (Spearmint, of course, knowing that spearmint gives you that extra lift), application forms for badge awards, etc., were carefully stowed away in the tiny cockpit. (I must admit here I made a small mistake that I discovered one hour and 25 minutes and 8 miles out on course; I forgot to pack a map.)

On the take off line, the towpilot and plane all set to go, the usual last minute arrangements had to be made, such as disconnecting the tow line, dragging Sweetheart a quarter mile back to the hangar to put air into the nearly flat tire, then drag the ship back to the takeoff line, find the towpilot who by now was having lunch, etc... as I said before, not even the most minute details were overlooked.

Thanks to fifteen years of flying experience - I was tossed out of class once some years ago - I managed to keep my cool and by 12:50 pm I was airborne and was listening to the sweet, familiar sounds of the towrope snapping taut and going slack again.

Right after release, (Aha! You thought I would forget!) I made the second mistake of the afternoon. The thermal I released in turned out to be one of the puny variety and I had to struggle some 15 minutes to reach 5,000 feet. This was much too long a time to spend in one thermal (as it turned out, I didn't; I spent most of the time out of it) when you had a goal like Banning in mind.

Nevertheless, I was on my way singing happily... "to follow that star-r-r-r, no matter how hopeless (?), no matter how far-r-r-r." (Some pilots talk to themselves. I sing.) Soon I made the first long (2 mile) elegant glide across the airport in the direction of Banning.

Just as I was getting to "...how hopeless..." again, I was rudely interrupted by a line of B-52's climbing out of March Air Force Base, right in front of Sweetheart's nose. I don't have to tell you that this was no time to argue about FAA priorities! I decided that discretion was the better part of valor and got the ---- out of there.

As soon as my heart slowed down to about 1,000 beats per minute, I concentrated on finding new lift. Sure enough, just a mile or so ahead I spotted a dust devil that carried me up to 8,000 feet and over Sun City.

With altitude like that under me I began to relax once again ("...to follow that star-r-r-r...") and proceeded toward the Hemet/Ryan airport. I even found time to look around. Little farms swam slowly into sight and disappeared under the right wing. (Possibly there were some to my left also, but when I look down on the left, I get dizzy).

As Sweetheart sailed silently over the landing site of one of my previous attempts, I had an unexplainable, triumphant feeling come over me. ("...To dream the impossible dream, to...") Today I will make it! (Not in 700 feet a minute down you won't, pay attention!)

Down to 3,000 feet (and back to sweaty palms). Surely this is the time for that gum with the "extra lift". Here she comes, up we go again. From 9,000 feet the ground looks so alien. (Boy! I wish I had that map along!)

Now let me see, that must be the ridge I have to cross just before Banning. But so soon? (It's now 3:00 pm, and I'm not at all sure that I could have made it in such a short time). That must be it! It has to be! If not... well, let's try anyway. ("...No matter how hopeless... etc.")

Down to 4,000 feet, still singing, but my throat is getting sore, and my ---- too. Careful now! Was that a nibble? A smooth 180° to the right (I told you about the left, didn't I?) and sink all around. Another 180° and sure enough, another nibble. Holding at 4,000, let's try it again. From here I can see a city over the ridge. Banning? (Sure wish I had that map!)

Phew! The day must be wearing on, this thermal yielded only 2,000 feet. High enough, though, to make it across the ridge. ("...to run where the brave do not go-o-o-o.") Oops! What in the heaven was that? A shudder and we are in "green air" again and going up. This turned out to be the strongest thermal of the day. (How did I luck into this one?) Wow! 10,000 feet! From here the town below (Banning?) disappeared in the haze. Who cares? With so much altitude to spare I could make another of those elegant glides to the right, through that pass. (Have I ever told you about my left?)

Here we go! ("...To dream the impossible...") 45 minutes and 6,000 feet later over the pass I can see an airport sprawling on the white expanse of sand below. (Banning? I sure wish I had that map). Let's make a couple of lazy passes over the control tower. (Anybody home?) Down to 2,000 feet and even without a map I can tell that this isn't Banning. What if I get a red light from the tower? (Don't think, just keep singing.)

Down to 1,000 feet. At last! They have spotted me, and there is the green light. (Today we are landing on a runway, Sweetheart!) As we roll past the tower a huge sign grins at us: "Welcome To Palm Springs". (Yeah! But 3 hours and 35 minutes for 60 miles?)

THE CHINESE FINGER LOCK by Charlie Spratt, Sailplane Racing News.

Now here's a good one! Seems that a chap wanted to increase his personal duration in his 1-26. Like his bladder was not large enough for hours in the sky. He designed a relief tube to extend along his left and down the bottom of the fuselage next to the 1-26 wheel. The upper end was attached to a condom, so that he was "plumbed in" all of the time.

The test flight was OK but the landing was another matter. The tube near the wheel caught in the axle which began winding the tube. The condom acted like a Chinese finger lock. Your eyes should be watering about now. They say his certainly were!

After the rollout, he did not jump out of the cockpit. Friends went over to help him push the bird off the runway. They opened the cockpit and the pilot weakly said, "Could you roll it back a bit?" They say he couldn't stand for a week.

THE SILVER SEA SCROLLS by Phil Thorndyke. Wind & Wings, September 1980.

The following scrolls were recovered from a recent archaeological dig, along with a number of other artifacts, in a stratum of unusually fine dust. Inscriptions on the artifacts indicate that the region was ruled by a powerful king name Schweizer and his queen, Elmira, NY. The scrolls are thought to be the work of a nomadic tribe from whom are descended the Elsinords, Elmiragites, Hemetians, and Crystalanians, together with the Perrisites. The scrolls are presented here in the order of their discovery, since the actual chronological order has not yet been determined.

SCROLL NUMBER 6: When it comes to pass that a place to fly is to be chosen, thou shalt choose a place where lift is plenty. Ye shall know such places by these signs: that the earth shall be devoid of all that comforts man, these things being trees, grass, and all other green things: water, food, shade, and places of rest; and all other things which alleviate suffering. There shalt thou make thy camp. And thou shalt proclaim thine own place best, and shall denounce all other places as bad.

SCROLL NUMBER 21: Now it came to pass that when the season of heat was upon the land, the AGCAscians did go forth from beside the cool sea and went into the deserts, for such was their way. And they journeyed into a place where lift was plenty.

And lo, there were great numbers of gliders upon the firmament and in the heavens. The first among these did have the appearance of whalefishes; and their wings were above and were supported by pillars, and between the pillars sat a wise man and before the wise man sat a scholar. And where a man measures four cubits, his allotted space was three cubits, and his knees were beside his ears.

169

The second among these were of lesser size, and there were no pillars beneath the wings, and he who sat beneath the cover of crystal was alone. And when he made the parts of the glider to move, shrieks and moans did come from within. And his number was one, one score and six.

Of the others which there were, one had the body of a tadpole, the wings of a moth, and the weight of an elephant. Others were of the color of polished iron, and when others circled upon their left, these did circle upon their right. Some were of trees and cloth, and others were of the light metal. Still others did have the appearance of fine pottery and flapped their wings when they went.

Lastly were those which went upon three wheels. And there was a great noise with them, and a whirlwind did go before them. And they turned not when they went, but went straight. And some did have a rope behind them, and they did extract many pieces of silver from the glider pilots, and did lead them through the descending air.

And of all the machines in that place, the lord of each machine did proclaim his to be the best, and did denounce all the others.

SCROLL NUMBER 193: If, having assembled thy machine, there shall approach a vast multitude shouting, "How much did it cost?", then knowest thou that the spectators have come, and they shall be a plague on thee. And if they hinder thy toil of preparation with questions, thou shalt restrain thy anger and answer as possible, for verily they know not that thou hast answered these questions an hundred score and seven times before. But, if a man layeth his hand upon thy canopy, or lean himself to rest upon thy glider, or in any manner defile thy leading edges, then shalt thou loose thy sword upon him, for he is an abomination and shall not be spared.

SCROLL NUMBER 92: Lo, there were gathered upon the plane a multitude of gliders and glider chariots. And on the first morning the people gathered in the temple of the aircraft. And the king of tasks did stand before them, and spake unto them, commanding that they should go forth from the lakes unto the Torrable Zone and from thence unto the hills of the Chankly Bore ere they returneth. And there arose a great cry from those assembled, and there was a great wailing and gnashing of teeth, for the journey would lead them through the Bad Places.

Then did come forth the Prophet of the Winds and spake falsely unto them. Then did they cast lots to find who among them would go first, and who second, and so on unto the last of their number. And having done this, the people went forth from the temple, and girded up their loins. And when the gliders were assembled, the signal was given and they were cast into the air.

And it came to pass that those who harkened unto the false prophet fell to earth against their will, and their wrath was terrible to behold. And they did tear their hair and beat their breasts and blasphemed greatly. But when the inhabitants of the land came unto them saying, "Lo, hath the wind forsaken thee?" those who had fallen said, "Yea, verily, it is so," for they were trespassers in that land, and were in sore need of telephones.

But those who followed the paths of lift did not fall by the wayside, and their Coors runneth over, and they rejoiced, for their points were many. And the morning and the evening were the first day.

170

DESIDERATA from Free Flight, publication of the Soaring Association of Canada.

DESIDERATA was originally found in the map pocket of an old 2-22 and dated 1954.

Go placidly amid the noise of the towplanes and remember what peace there is in the silence at 5,000 feet. As far as possible without surrender be on good terms with the tow pilot. Speak your truth quietly and clearly; and listen to others, even the dull and ignorant; they too have their good flights. Avoid loud and aggressive persons, they are vexations when you are preparing to fly. If you compare yourself to others, you may become vain or bitter, for there always will be novices or diamond pilots around. Enjoy your achievements as well as your plans, keep trying for that next badge leg. Exercise caution in competition for contest pilots are full of trickery. But let this not blind you to what virtue there is; many pilots striving for higher altitude get help from others already in lift. Be yourself. Especially do not feign affectation. Neither be cynical about lift; for in the face of sink and poor landing areas, it is perennial as the grass. Take kindly the counsel of the years, gracefully surrendering the things of youth. Let the younger club members push the gliders to the flight line. Nurture strength of spirit to shield you when lift fails. But do not distress yourself with poor forecasts, many fears are born of fatigue and loneliness in the cockpit. Beyond a wholesome discipline, be gentle with the controls. You are a child of the universe, no less than the power pilots and jet jockeys; you have a right to some airspace. And whether or not it is clear to you, no doubt the universe is unfolding as it should. Therefore, be at peace with the C.F.I., whatever you conceive him to be, and whatever your labors and aspirations this season, in the noisy confusion of the hangar or on the flight line, keep peace with your fellow pilots. With all its sham, drudgery and broken dreams, it is still a beautiful sport. Be careful. Soar to be happy.

CHAPTER 11 - HISTORY OF THE ARIZONA SOARING ASSOCIATION.

The Arizona Soaring Association is unique. Although it began as a club in the accepted sense of the word, it has ultimately become an association of contest pilots with an annual contest series that is the envy of many. The Club's history was the original reason for this book. In addition to being an unusual Club from which other Clubs might care to learn (from our mistakes as well as our triumphs!) ASA mirrors general progress in the sport of soaring. National events such as the on-going fight with the FAA over airspace are reflected here. This history has been principally compiled from 33 years of Air Currents newsletters. This left me very much at the mercy of newsletter editors. Some were superb, others were not quite so dedicated, informative or accurate!   *Trish Durbin.*

The first recorded soaring flight to take place in Arizona was made by Peter Riedel, a German, on June 21, 1939. Peter flew a two place Kranich from Winslow, near Flagstaff, to Magdalena, New Mexico, and reached altitudes of almost 18,000 feet ASL. His maps were road maps prepared by Standard Oil and Shell and merely showed a few second rate roads. He may have been the first but he certainly wasn't the last pilot to take off in shirt sleeves with no food and just a gallon of water, anticipating only a short ride.

In an article entitled "Soaring In Arizona", which appeared in Arizona Highways dated July 1967, (price 50 cents!) Joe Lincoln reports Riedel's flight in detail. He also tells how the Southwest Soaring Club, forerunner of the Arizona Soaring Association, started.

"At 8 o'clock on the night of June 9, 1941," wrote Lincoln, "Lewin B. Barringer presided at the first meeting of the Southwest Soaring Club, held in the workshop of Phoenix Junior College. Barringer was holder of the World Two Place Altitude Soaring Record (14,960 feet), former holder of the American Single Place Distance Record and was one of only three Americans at that time to hold the Golden C. He was also author of "Flight Without Power" which became the textbook for the Army

Glider Training Command. Finally, he was the first paid manager of the Soaring Society of America. Adrian and Fred Riggins were present at the meeting, as was Don Stone, then of Phoenix Junior College and later for many years the principal of West Phoenix High School. The highlight of the meeting was Barringer's revelation that a Cinema II training sailplane was being ordered from Frankfort Sailplane Company of Joliet, Illinois.

Delivery of the Cinema II was promised for July so in the meantime Fred Riggins and Don Stone took the opportunity to get some initial glider training with autotow at Glendale in California. Fred was called up for military service before he finished his training - it was 1941 - but Don continued and qualified for Arizona glider license Number 1.

When the Cinema II arrived, flight training operations were set up at Thunderbird Field No. 1 north of Glendale, Arizona. Autotows and training were regular events for the next five or six months, until on December 7, 1941 news of Pearl Harbor was received shortly before noon and civilians had to leave the field since it was a military installation.

Consequently, in early 1942 the operation moved to Cactus Field on 16th Street in Phoenix, and graduated to a winch for launching. Training continued until the Army bought the glider, presumably because of the war effort and not because the Club had put it up for sale. "Later on," wrote Joe, "the operation moved again to an auxiliary field west-northwest of Mesa's Falcon Field, on a strip just north of the canal. Here flying went on until early 1946 with a Baby Albatross and a war surplus Laister-Kaufmann sailplane."

Unfortunately, in March 1946 there was an accident which not only killed the pilot but also killed soaring in Arizona for nine years. Joe's writing seems to belie suppressed anger at such crass stupidity. "One blustery Sunday morning in March of 1946, Mr. Stone instructed at the field. Because of the wind he stopped flying at noon and went home.

"That afternoon one of the members of the club talked his friends into giving him a tow in the Baby Albatross. This was done against the advice of some of the members present. An automobile tow began, and the Baby Albatross climbed sharply to an altitude of approximately 400 feet. Evidently the pilot was unable to release the tow cable. People in the tow car felt a tremendous jerk and they released the cable from their end, but it was too late. Some of the fuselage was pulled out of the sailplane and apparently a wing came off. The aircraft fell to the ground like a rock. The dead pilot had two packed parachutes in the back of his car but had refused to use them because he wanted to be as light as possible."

Joe goes on to mention a group in Mesa with a two place sailplane whose interest subsequently dried up, and an interim club operating on the west side of Phoenix that stopped almost as soon as it started. The Southwest Soaring Club's five years had "ended with a fatal crash, like so much early American soaring, where enthusiasm outran knowledge, caution and careful training."

During the war there was a glider training operation at an air base near Wickenburg, under the auspices of Loy Clingman. And in the early summer of 1946 Robert Sparling came to Prescott. Bob's name was to pop up over and over again and continues to do so. He enjoyed some apparently alarming flights with Dick Johnson.

After the war, glider training began at Paradise Airport on 19th Avenue. Bill Ralston and Earl Pylant had taken over that field in 1946. Loy Clingman, suffering from what Joe Lincoln referred to as a chronic lack of students in Wickenburg, brought down one of his three gliders. "He and Earl Pylant were both good mechanics," reports Joe. "They worked out a public address system which was installed in this glider. It was powered by a gasoline-driven generator. They checked out Bill Ralston as a tow pilot, and, flying an old Piper Cub with an 85-horsepower Continental engine, he spent many hours towing this barking monstrosity over Phoenix. Bill Ralston went around selling advertising for this unique medium and, although he reports it was a business disaster, there was one political campaign during which they had good success. Often they were airborne for hours at a time, exhorting people to vote for their candidate who was keeping this oddly assorted team of aircraft flying."

Loy Clingman subsequently brought his other two gliders from Wickenburg and a school flourished at Paradise for some eighteen months before it was closed down for lack of students. "This was one of the very few soaring schools in the country approved to give glider ratings under the GI Bill," wrote Loy later. "A number of students were given ratings, mostly under the Bill, so after that potential was pretty well used up, I, having grown accustomed to eating fairly regularly and wishing to keep the habit, decided to sell my sailplanes and towplane and went back to teaching school."

For some years there was a little desultory gliding achieved here and there, for a while at Tucson and Marana Air Field, but nothing very major happened until Don Barnard arrived on the scene. Born in 1911 in Portland, Oregon, Don's love of flying began when he saw a flying circus of World War One planes in 1918.

Don wasn't long in Phoenix before rumors of a glider put him in touch with Jerry Hopf, who owned a TG-3, and Roy Graves with a Cinema. Soon Don and Roy were on their way to El Mirage to pick up a Laister-Kaufmann for Don and from there on it wasn't long before the Arizona Soaring Association was born.

It was Don Barnard who taught Joe Lincoln to fly sailplanes. Joe speaks of him with enormous affection in his Arizona Highways article. "In Arizona, several previous efforts to get soaring started had come and gone. The spark of interest was turned into a flame in 1955 when Don Barnard came over from California. He crystallized local interest, became one of the founders of the Arizona Soaring Association, and its chief instructor. Weekends and some weekdays he was out at the airport - deeply tanned, slender as Mahatma Ghandi, with the face and moustache of a British Air Force Officer, and a deep musical voice. He was everything in soaring: teacher, disciplinarian, humorist, errand runner, poet and pilot."

It was a major highlight when the ASA team won the February 1956 Mid-Winter Meet at Torrey Pines in San Diego. "This was the first time the Stanley L. Peterson trophy has been out of state," crowed Don, wearing his Editor's hat. "Congratulations to our team Don Barnard, Fred Daams, Marjy Crowl, Roy Graves, Jerry Hopf, William Rogers and Jerry Robertson. Looks like we might get the trophy again next year if we continue to show the same enthusiasm next winter that we had then." They didn't. The event was postponed because of the weather.

By September 1956 the Arizona Soaring Association was one year old and going strong. They were operating out of Falcon Field, just north of Mesa, but would later admit, when they moved to pastures new, that they had always felt unwelcome there. Finding a permanent home was an on-going preoccupation.

That month they issued their very first monthly bulletin, so new it did not yet have a name, and were offering a prize to attract suggestions. With Don Barnard as editor, the newsletter was newsy, stimulating and, on occasion, quite stern! More than once, Don started off, "Now look, fellows..." Membership was $12 a year and it took a 2-cent stamp to mail the newsletter.

With Don as Editor, Joseph C. Lincoln became president. Joe was already an American Soaring Champion, having won C Class in the 1956 Nationals, and held a plaque to prove it. He was also holder of the Arizona Altitude Record having flown to 13,100 feet that June. Roy Smoots earned an Endurance Record with a 5 hour 13 minute flight in September. They had a large membership and were achieving great things.

Their inspiration was a love of flying but their primary aim was to spread the word and to get as many other "fellows" in the air as possible and to C standard. They were indefatigable in their efforts to promote soaring. They took a booth at the Arizona State Fair in November 1956 and handed out 400 leaflets promoting soaring and their rapidly growing Association.

In October 1956, President Joe Lincoln promoted soaring in a remarkably generous and effective manner. "News Flash," wrote Don Barnard in his second issue of the newsletter. "Joe Lincoln has bought Herman Stiglemier's Pratt Read, and it is without a doubt the finest Pratt Read in the country, with its molded glass enclosure and fiberglass pod (which) puts it in a class of its own. Joe is forming a Club around it. He says he is going to take in 14 fellows at $100 per membership. Here fellows is what you have been waiting for and wanting - a chance to get in cheap on a real top performing two seater... Hats off to Joe!"

In December, the Luke Aero Club based at Luke Field put on an airshow and invited ASA to be there. "We can haul passengers all day," wrote Don, "and there is to be a contest during the day, spot landings, ribbon cutting, etc., so it will be a good chance for us to sell soaring and the ASA. We want all the members we can to come out. There will be a lot of help needed and if everyone pitches in we are sure some new members can be signed up."

In February 1957 ASA was visited by KPOK radio, which interviewed three members. Don Barnard wrote, "They also asked us to phone them the winter contest results as soon as we could. Chuck Schmid took care of this and he reported it was on the air 3 minutes after he phoned it in." That same month they were invited by the Apache Prop Spinners to come to Williams Air Force Base and "sell soaring" at the air show there. In June they had a display in the library.

They were justifiably proud of their accomplishments during their second year of flying. "20 students solo-ed; 8 private licenses issued; 2 commercials; 9 C pins earned; 1 Silver C completed; 1 pilot earning two legs on Silver C - duration and distance; over 500 airplane tows made and approximately 300 hours of soaring completed. With our good fall soaring weather coming up we will have a lot more to add to these totals."

All this was quite remarkable in view of the fact that they had very few sailplanes at their disposal and great difficulty in scrounging up a tow plane. Flying was limited to one hour per person and there was always somebody else awaiting their turn. It seems the only ships they had were privately owned, but cheerfully regarded by one and all as Club property. Undeterred, in January 1957 they announced the commencement of contest flying.

"Yes," ran Don's Editorial, "that's what you've all been asking for - when are we going to have a contest - so your Board of Directors approved it at their last meeting and this is the good news." The Winter Contest started Saturday January 12, 1957 and ran for four consecutive weekends. Points were to be awarded in several categories: Altitude, Endurance, Spot Landing, Bomb Dropping and Ribbon Cutting.

The first Contest went well and began on schedule despite a lack of co-operation from the weather. Joe Lincoln and Don Barnard tied for first on ribbon cuts, each making 7. Don also nosed out Kenny Bawden on the bomb drop with 72 feet 10 inches. Joe Lincoln won the duration by a hairy 10 minutes.

The brief series was supported by six contestants and a small but faithful audience. A great time was had by all but it revealed "without a doubt that we must have more ground help and officials to conduct a meet. For the contestants to have to help in the measuring, scoring and timing was just too much to ask."

They certainly enjoyed their contest flying and set off for the 1957 Torrey Pines Meet to defend their trophy. William A. Rogers III crewed for Joe Lincoln and although Joe landed on the beach and was retrieved by aerotow, Bill didn't get off lightly.

After a lot of complicated borrowing of ships and fixing of trailers, Bill Rogers wrote, "On our way at last! Chuck, Sally and I left Chandler about 11:00 pm. Everything went smoothly all the way to Yuma where Joe Lincoln was to have left word with the local police for us. In Yuma a police car pulled along side us to say someone was waiting for us at City Hall. It was Kenny, LK, family and all. We had breakfast, then pulled into California and slept awhile along the road."

By sun up on Friday they were off again and arrived at a deserted Torrey Pines. After finding a motel and a shower they returned to the cliff top to discover Joe Lincoln had arrived with his Baby Albatross, Don Barnard, Jerry Robertson and Dave had brought in Don's Cinema. Four ships from the ASA at Torrey Pines, they noted with enormous satisfaction.

After a little flying, despite a lack of wind and a cable break, they tied down the ships for the night. "Saturday morning was cold and showed signs of being wet. More ships had come in during the night but had not been assembled. The wind was parallel to the ridge, expected to hold that way for 36 hours, and the weather began to get nastier. After a hurried consultation of SCSA officials operating the meet, it was postponed for two weeks. We started to take the ships apart but heard a rumor of a possible shift in the wind so we stopped. During the morning Gus Briegleb arrived with the BG-12, Vic Swierkowski with the Mitchell Nimbus III, and Stan Hall with the Cherokee II." Ray Parker was also there with the Tiny Mite.

"After lunch the BG-12 was on its way home, but a weak wind was now coming into the ridge. We put the Pratt Read back together and made a few tows... Before winch tows stopped, Joe Lincoln in the Baby had joined the "Beach Combers", the first of our members to join this year. He was airplane towed off the beach."

In March ASA was on the move again. Still looking for a permanent home, they were invited by the Apache Prop Spinners at Williams field to set up operations at Rittenhouse, probably as a result of the fine work they had done at the Williams airshow the previous month. "It is a beautiful field," wrote Don Barnard excitedly, "with *four* paved runways, one 7,000 feet long and we can stretch it to about 11,000 feet, which is just what we have been looking for to get in our auto tows. All the other runways are over 4,000 feet, so we will be able to pick the one into the wind. No more tailwind or up-hill takeoffs. There is a nice building on the field which we have been offered the use of for our meetings. There are rest rooms, a kitchen for cooking up goodies, and a shop which we can use."

The Willie Club said they had all the tiedowns ASA could need and the offer included 6,000 feet of wire for auto tows. It came just as the new management at Falcon Field began imposing almost punitive rates so it was truly felt to be "in the nick of time".

Their euphoria was tempered slightly by an accident to the Pratt Read in early March. "The flight was a failure," reported the uncompromising Joe Lincoln in a piece entitled Cactus Clipper (See Ch.2). Chuck Schmid had landed out in rough country during a Silver Distance attempt and been retrieved by no less than four club members, four kids, a boy they picked up en route and two dogs. Crewing seemed to be a mass production and joint effort in those days. Everyone went along for the ride if not the flight.

Plans were immediately implemented to get George Lauman's BG-6 together at the Rittenhouse workshop. George said anyone who works on the ship gets to fly it in proportion to the time spent on production. Even though it was privately owned, the BG-6 was obviously considered to be "our ship", a club ship. "Lauman is writing Gus Briegleb for the plans for the BG-6 and BG-7 with the taper wings. We plan to finish up the ship as it is with the straight wings, the utility BG-6, and while it is flying we'll build up the 7 wings. The BG-6 complete, ready to fly, is supposed to weigh only 210 pounds. After the 7 wings are finished we might use the 6 wings for a primary which can be built up with metal tubing open frame fuselage. Some fun..."

Meanwhile the Pratt Read was still undergoing repair. It was moved from Paradise Airport to Fred Daams' home and they were requesting help with it. Fred Daams was a wonderful craftsman having started with model airplanes as a young boy and worked his way up to the real thing. He was to be offered a job in aircraft repair on the strength of the superb work he did on the Pratt Read.

In May 1957 an article by Derek Van Dyke appeared entitled "The Barograph Blues". Joe Lincoln must have borrowed this title years later for a piece in his book, "On Quiet Wings", since Derek's piece was entirely different but told with similar self-deprecating humor. (See Ch.5) Flying magazine for June 1957 was loaded with soaring articles which made ASA members feel good and "recognized".

Encouragingly, a tiny Club in Tucson, formed the previous year with the aid of Don Barnard, was burgeoning nicely. They were even flying their own TG-3. However, rumors were circulating of an accident. Arizona's SSA Governor, George Lauman, received a report written by Thomas Stoops, Tucson's President. "Cause: not definitely known but best guess - too much sun and not enough water, resulting in either complete blackout or at least enough to seriously affect judgement..."

ASA was flying Saturdays, Sundays and holidays and the editor was boasting in the newsletter that the ASA now had its own sailplane, the completed BG-6. Ken Bawden established an official ASA altitude record of 11,500 feet in the ship. He had no warm clothing and a quarter of an inch of ice on his leading edges.

Joe Lincoln flew the 24th Nationals at Elmira in August with Jerry Robertson as his crew and in September Joe came home and demolished Ken's altitude record with a thermal climb to 15,250 feet. September brought sad news and glad news: Don Barnard quit as Editor of the newsletter but Joe Lincoln, retiring as President, took it on. Don could not resign without publishing one of his little homilies. "...and now it's up to you members to get behind Joe and get those articles in to him. Good stories are what makes a good bulletin. George (Lauman, the Assistant Editor) and I have had a rough time on some issues this last year for the want of articles and I hope you will give Joe more support. Let's all get in and make this the best bulletin in the country."

That September was their second full year of operation and they looked back over the two years at the September Annual General Meeting. The romance with Rittenhouse continued: "We have a site with excellent runways, a shaded lounge, cold drinks and coffee, workshop space, and the beginnings of a large sailplane shelter. Best of all we are welcomed at the site instead of being tolerated and sneered at."

Despite that, however, they were still seeking their own permanent home. "The chief thing I hoped to accomplish during my term (as President)," summed up Joe, "was to secure a permanent site for the group. Hunting land for this purpose is time consuming and frustrating as Don Barnard, Derek Van Dyke and George Lauman well know. We have an excellent site at Rittenhouse for soaring but it is distant, out of the way, and we should keep looking for our own place. Many of you remember what a change it was over Falcon where we were unwelcome."

A rather negative mood prevailed at that meeting. Being even more uncompromising than usual, Joe mourned the fact that membership had not increased at anything like a satisfactory pace and faced the even more unpalatable fact that "our safety record is bad". He referred to "my affair with the Baby", which was caused by inattentive flying, the Pratt-Read landing "which, in the hands of a lesser pilot than Chuck Schmid could have been a very bad one," and the Tucson crash "which barely missed tragedy." Joe obviously regarded all three as utterly unforgivable.

The final bombshell at that meeting was the announcement that the Club's towplane, actually owned by Don Barnard, had been sold so they were going to have to provide their own. They were hoping to acquire a PT-23.

The very next month it was suddenly announced they would be leaving Rittenhouse and would be taking up "permanent residence" at Turf Paradise air strip, "our best site to date". There was a cafeteria just 200 yards from the west end of the strip, and it was much nearer civilization than Rittenhouse. George Lauman and Ted Riggins seem to have done most of the footwork in arranging the move and members were told they must thank George personally when they saw him.

A Committee comprised of Charles Schmid, Marcel Godinat and Ted Riggins set up new Field Operating Rules and Regulations which demanded, amongst other things, **"automatic and instant obedience."**

A new note of optimism crept in. "Things are looking up for Arizona Soaring," crowed the new editor, after reminding members Turf was predominantly a race track and they must be careful not to frighten the horses. "We now have a contract towplane, and a standby for emergencies. The TG-3 and the Baby are already at Turf Paradise, the Pratt Read will be flying in a few more days." They were actively seeking a club two-place ship. "Clay Hartman has ordered a new Mitchell Nimbus III kit which is on the way, and Ruth Petry has come to Phoenix and will soon bring out her LK." The advent of Ruth Petry was to mean more than anyone could possibly dream at that stage.

178

In January 1958 disappointment was in store. They had been working hard to repair the Pratt-Read. Someone had flown to California to collect the door in December and they were relishing the thought of earning new badges in the new ship. It went through its annual inspection and although the fabric was a little weak, it passed. Unfortunately, further examination after the inspector departed revealed that the only place the fabric had been tested was the only place it could have passed. The rest was shot. With ten months gone, it was tempting to stagger on with dangerous fabric but they eventually decided to recover it.

There was some good news however. They received free publicity in the Air Force Reserve Center magazine, "The AR Carousel" and also in "Aero Trading Post", a new publication. And they were congratulating Joe Lincoln on being elected to the Board of SSA.

In June 1958 the ASA "at long long last" got two sailplanes into the air at one time over Prescott, the site from which Dick Johnson set his national two-place distance record. This must have been the first of what was to become an annual safari to Prescott for the summer, thus avoiding Phoenix' temperatures.

The same month they were extolling the virtues of the winch, claiming 335 flights and altitudes of 8000 feet after 800 to 1200 foot winch launches. At 50 cents a launch they were well pleased with themselves and it was just as well since in the same issue of Air Currents they reported two tow planes down. The Super Cub that had been available to them was involved in an accident and shortly afterwards their Travelair's engine quit during a tow. Marcel Godinat was the glider pilot being towed and made a 90° left turn and a safe landing. The Travelair landed off the end of the Paradise Airport runway, damaged both gears, sustained some fuselage damage and broke the lower wing. Undaunted, Chet Howard, the tow pilot, promised he would rebuild it.

The Club year ran from October through September so in September 1958 Joe Lincoln looked back over 3 years of Club life and pronounced himself satisfied. They had made good progress during their third year, he said, with a new operations site, a club ship and several members entering contests, including the 25th Nationals and several regional contests.

About this time, a young fellow named Bill Ordway appeared in Tucson to work for one of the aircraft companies there and was planning to bring along his TG-3. Bill had placed 4th in the two-place contest at the 25th Nationals so he was readily accepted. Air Currents' Editor was extremely pleased by his appearance and, assuming rather a lot, said, "What with a Waco primary and now a TG-3 available," Tucson would soon be turning out contest pilots.

Club members suddenly seemed to be whizzing back and forth between New York and Phoenix, towing "new" sailplanes and unmatched trailers. Ruth Petry, now the Club's indispensable tow pilot, went home to Ithaca for a 4 week vacation and brought back a Franklin PS-2 utility glider on her LK trailer, which enabled Bob Sparling to start a club in Prescott. She also ferried the Club's BG-7 wings from El Mirage on Bob Hawke's Bowlus trailer and Joe Lincoln moved Ruth's LK from New York on his 1-23 trailer. No doubt there were excellent reasons for all this!

The new President, Ken Bawden, then announced a decision to make a new winch. If he had known in October 1958 that his precious winch would not be winching until March 1963, he might have been less enthusiastic, but the ongoing progress - and just as frequent lack there of - made interesting reading throughout the next five years.

In October Joe Lincoln retired as Newsletter Editor and was replaced by Derek Van Dyke with George Lauman as Managing Editor. In December Ken Bawden brought along three new souls and gave them introductory flights. One of them was John Ryan who was to do great things in ASA and enjoy an illustrious soaring career. There was great excitement that month since 19th Avenue was paved which meant members could drive out to Turf Paradise on paved road all the way, except for the final quarter mile access road.

The Tucson Club was struggling for air and just about holding its own. Serge T. Winkler wrote at the end of that year that Bill Ordway's TG-3 had not yet made it to Tucson so he had bought a flyable 1-19 from Jim Carlin in Palm Springs. The trailer seemed to be in better shape than the sailplane and would go "70 mph on the highway without swaying an inch". Tom Stoop had donated an old 1948 Packard for a tow car which was reported as doing a fine job towing the 1-19 at Marana 2 (Rillito). There were about 8 active members and they had enjoyed about 30 tows although there had been no soaring. Tom was awaiting struts to fit on his "flying chair" (a Waco Primary). Their arrival would mean a complement of two ships which emboldened Winkler to ask for notification of the next ASA contest!

A shopping list of needed parts for the new winch, and the usual unheeded request for help with the building thereof, was published in Air Currents. They were also searching for telegraph poles - they neglected to mention why - but the big news of January 1959 was that Joe Lincoln had placed an order for a Schweizer 2-22C as a gift for the Club. It truly was extremely generous of him and his incentive was to attract new members.

Paul Schweizer telegraphed promptly in February that the new sailplane was ready for shipment but he advised against motor transport due to flooding and snow on the midwest highways. They opted for rail transportation and prepared to "sweat it out until word comes through from the depot that there is a big crate on the platform, please come and get it the hell out of the way."

In 1959 several new ships came to the valley. Marcel Godinat brought over a German LO and somebody else bought a Waco UPF 7 that was modified and equipped with a 300 HP Lycoming and a Hamilton Standard constant speed prop. They were still hoping for a second tow ship and the observation that the intense sun was doing the new 2-22 no good whatsoever had members aspiring to a new hangar. They asked Bob Drake at Turf Paradise if they could store equipment under the grandstand. Mr Drake told them while he had no objection, the grandstand seemed to lure young boys who might find the added temptation of some exciting airplanes irresistible.

Consequently, Ruth Petry organized the removal of the 2-22 from its tie down at Turf Paradise to Joe Lincoln's hangar-cum-garage. Ruth towed John Ryan in the 2-22 very early one morning at first light. He cut loose at 2,000 feet and slid the ship into the field behind Joe's home very quietly. Ruth "tippy-toed in at that height so as not to disturb Joe's neighbors so early in the morning." Next day they made another early start and dismantled the ship, removing a fence and carrying the wings and fuselage thirty yards to the "hangar". Immediately after this escapade, Ruth Petry was congratulated on her organizational abilities and elected President.

On Saturday November 28, 1959 a new airport opened - Deer Valley. ASA took part in the opening ceremonies even though they could not know then that Deer Valley would eventually become their home for a while. "The ceremony served to introduce the public to the new, million dollar Deer Valley Airport 15 miles north of downtown Phoenix on the Black Canyon highway. This newest airport in Arizona has a mile long paved runway with an extra mile now under construction."

ASA was represented by Joe Lincoln and his 1-23, John Ryan's 1-23 was used in the main hangar as a static display, and the 2-22 was flown by Don Barnard. Ruth Petry served a rigorous day as the official explainer in the hangar where she gave out copies of both ASA and SSA literature to the public. Jim Turnbow joined Master of Ceremonies Art Linkletter to explain just what was going on as the flight demonstrations were given.

"Joe Lincoln was towed aloft to 3,000 feet by Derek Van Dyke in the Waco. At that point a role of useful tissue was jettisoned and Joe proceeded to gyrate through the sky reducing the paper to confetti and the viewing public to awed silence at the maneuverability of the glider. While the tow was being carried out, Don Barnard and Fred Daams put on a demonstration of an auto tow with the 2-22. Using 1500 feet of wire and towing the length of the runway at 50 mph, Don managed to reach 1200 feet. From that altitude, he put in a masterful demonstration of glider guiding which impressed the crowd, ending up with a landing to a spot near the wind tee.

"The opportunity to take part in the opening was very much appreciated and was well worth while. Many of the public who were observers promised to come by for flights at Turf Paradise. We should get some new members out of this."

It was ironic that as a new airport opened and members were cavorting happily in their natural habitat, the Editor, Derek van Dyke, was expressing concern about air space. In an Editorial in his November, 1959 issue, Derek wrote, "Roughly speaking, there are about one hundred thousand square miles of surface area in the state of Arizona. By projecting this land area upwards for another ten miles, theoretically there are one million cubic miles of space involved. Now, best beloved, one million is still a large number no matter what Washington would accustom you to thinking. But what I'm driving at is that here in Arizona the usable airspace which is allocable to all aircraft, both those that reside here and those only passing through, is a considerable chunk.

"At least, to me it was a considerable chunk until the other day when I had a talk with the air traffic control boys at Sky Harbor. For the information of those of you who have believed that there is lots of airspace over Arizona, it just ain't so. For example: we have in our State two large Air Force training bases, one SAC base, one Naval base used by the Marines, one Army missile testing base, and three main airways. Oh yes, there are two special jet airways crossing the State, and a special corridor established within which the Air Force practices aerial refueling. Are you beginning to see the picture?

"Best beloved, it is no longer a matter of shrinking airspace; it has done shrunk."

Getting new members was another cause for real concern. "During the past year," wrote a discouraged Editor, "in spite of the gift of the 2-22, there have only been two new C pilots hatched. At this rate the 2-22 will rot apart before we get even a dozen C pilots into the air." Apathy and despondence seemed to be setting in. In April the Editor was lamenting a sailplane pilot's dependency on tow planes and reported a letter asking about winches featured in Vultures magazine in Detroit, which was answered with a "most complete set of drawings." ASA was in need of someone who could work with the drawings and a welding torch and who had the incentive to "ramrod the project to the end." $3 tows, particularly during the winter months, were cripplingly expensive and the new winch was becoming an obsession.

Fortunately, on April 1, 1960 John Ryan gave the club a much needed boost to morale by getting his Diamond Altitude at 35,100 feet ASL in wave over Bishop in the Pratt Read. Ruth Petry towed him to 11,100 ASL and the feat was reported in the newspaper. John was very modest and insisted his success was due to the effort and support of half a dozen people. They started early, at 5:30 am, but he did not launch until late morning. At the edge of the rotor cloud the turbulence was of the magnitude of 5 to 6 G's and -4 G's with rates of climb in excess of 2,000 feet a minute. At 11,160 ASL there was a sudden bump followed by a smooth upsurge.

The other high spot of that month - April - was two new members at the meeting, known only as Stanton and Northness, who offered to take a look at the Vulture winch plans and the hope of ramrodding the project to completion. This made them "more welcome than the flowers in spring... and an answer to your editor's prayers."

A "fine Editorial" written by Gil Wilson in the June issue of Flying magazine led the Editor of Air Currents to speculate, "Maybe the time is not too distant when we can expect the general public to begin to accept us." He went on to castigate his fellow members that they had all been lax in selling soaring "to our own brethren, the power pilots. If nothing else," he continued, "it seems to me that light plane pilots would be interested in the art of soaring for the lessons it teaches which would make powered flying more enjoyable and safer."

The Club moved to Prescott for the summer as usual and had some fine flights, taking the LK to 10,100 feet, an LO-50 to 18,900 feet and a pilot with no jacket or oxygen taking the 2-22 to 17,200. Bill Ordway came up from Tucson with his TG-3 and made an 8 hour "hop" from Prescott to the little town of Alamo. He was trying for his third Diamond (distance).

"After passing Las Vegas, Bill flew off his charts and more or less navigated from a road map. Alamo is just outside the area which is part of the Atomic Energy Commission and Air Force area and is not very settled. In fact, after the sun went down, there wasn't a light to be seen anywhere. It was a lonesome feeling. In the morning, he gathered his canteens, fruit juice and parachute and started walking for a road intersection he had spotted from the air." After 10 miles a prospector came by and gave Bill a lift to Alamo, 50 miles away, from whence Bill called his crew.

Meanwhile, the Club had readied two aircraft to go out and search for him so were glad when he finally called in to report both pilot and ship OK. What he neglected to mention, and what was to be a closely guarded secret for several years, was that he had flown over a secret atomic bomb testing area.

New member Northness soon reported encouraging progress with the winch and a second winch, not too far from completion, was discovered at Prescott.

Prescott as a site was getting a little bit busy. In June several members were set up and ready to launch by 9:00 am but takeoffs were delayed until 11:00 am "because of the heavy traffic at Love field occasioned by the search operations being carried on by the Army and CAP as well as the early morning departures of several slurry-loaded tankers fighting the fire in the North Kaibab National Forest."

A search for a soaring site near Yarnell, 90 miles northwest of Phoenix, was initiated. The site originally chosen from a map turned out to be "discouragingly rocky but there are other sites in the immediate vicinity and George is not one to be daunted by a few rocks."

On October 21, 1960 ASA was on the move again, having been granted permission to operate out of Deer Valley airport. This was luxury compared to Turf Paradise and they were exhorted to go to extraordinary lengths to maintain their welcome. "We must conduct our operation so that it causes no interference with the present flying being done at Deer Valley. Automobiles and people must stay off the active runways and taxiways... In flight we must be extra careful to follow the prescribed traffic pattern and unless absolutely necessary, we must not take advantage of the fact that sailplanes and gliders have the right-of-way over powered aircraft. When getting ready for an aerotow, all preparations must be done off to the side of the active runway and the only thing that should be left to do after the sailplane has been pushed out onto the runway is the actual connecting of the tow rope. 30 seconds should be ample time for the runway to be obstructed..."

The demand for members' cooperation was not limited to operations. "In return for the privilege of using the Deer Valley facilities, we should endeavour to spend such money as we can with the management of the airport." The restaurant was to be used by pilots and their families, the tow plane was already renting hangar space, and gas and oil were to be purchased there.

Membership was still disastrously low and there was another homily about using the 2-22 a minimum of 100 hours a year to avoid running it at a loss. New ships seemed to be appearing daily, however. John Ryan became President and referred to "our flying equipment, the 2-22". For himself John ordered a Sisu 1, with a 41 to 1 glide ratio at 62 mph. Jim Turnbow brought a beautiful red and yellow LK from Texas and "four of our soaringest members" clubbed together and bought a much needed tow plane, an Aeronca with a 150 HP engine and a climbing prop. Ruth Petry helped five junior ASA members acquire a ship, a Schweizer 1-19. Part of the fun was getting the ship into flying shape.

By June of 1961, just nine months after they'd moved there, Deer Valley was reported as being horrendously busy. "Our operations at Deer Valley Airport are becoming more and more delayed and complicated due to the increasingly heavy power traffic." It was the same in Prescott too, where they went every summer. "Prescott is an ideal cool spot for summer operations and although we are tolerated there, traffic is increasing and at times this field is virtually closed to our operations." Yarnell and Peeples Valley were reported as going all out to locate and build an airport for primary use as a soaring site but with the capability of handling up to twin-engined aircraft.

The area was searched by jeep and on horseback and a meeting was held by the Yarnell-Peeples Valley Chamber of Commerce, addressed by George Lauman and attended by the Yavapai County Engineer, a Yavapai County Supervisor and the State Aviation Director who said the State could match county funds up to $5,000 per year for the construction. The site could offer 6,000 feet of runways and if developed, we would have "a regional soaring center and a probable location for future National Soaring Contests... a sport center that could well become internationally famous."

Meanwhile, Joe Lincoln was elected to the Helms Hall of Fame for his all round good sportsmanship, his participation in and service to soaring, and his distance flight in 1960 of 455 miles from Prescott, Arizona, to Variadero, New

Mexico, the second longest soaring flight in America. He was also awarded the Lewin B. Barringer Trophy for that same flight.

Toward the end of that year, 1961, the embryo winch was moved to George Lauman's new operations site at Litchfield Park and, as always, help was solicited. This was probably when Bob Wister stepped into the breach. As a carrot, the Beardsley strip, owned by Sperry, was offered for winch launches, provided they could obtain their own insurance.

Enthusiasm did seem to be on the wane once more. The existing officers were asked to serve a fifteen month term in order to bring the Club year into line with the calendar year. No one seemed inclined to be Editor so they designated an "Editor of the Month" to "ease the burden and not overwork any member unduly." It also meant a rather lack lustre Air Currents.

Sometime during December 1961 an article on soaring appeared in the Arizona Republic's Sunday supplement, Arizona Days and Ways, which brought out several interested spectators, some of whom were persuaded to take an "indoctrination flight." Auto towing was planned at Sperry's Beardsley strip until the advent of the long-awaited winch.

In January 1962 Phoenix was chosen as the site of the Winter Meeting of the Directors of the Soaring Society of America. It was felt to be something of an honor and ASA members were busy arranging accommodations, transportation and a special dinner at the Safari in Scottsdale, where they enjoyed steaks at $4.50 a head.

In April they were reporting magnificent soaring conditions in northern Arizona, bewailing the unfortunate fact that the LO was down for refinishing. "We all know the summer conditions... but how about the winter? In Northern Arizona, winter is not the time to dismantle the ship and recover it. This is the time for wave soaring. In early February 1962 we in Prescott saw standing waves in the lee of all our major mountains practically all day, and even saw them in the night, with the moon shining between the layers of lenticular clouds. On February 9th, before the greatest cold front of the year, we observed standing waves which remained four hours. These were directly North of Prescott. The following day, Saturday, (a good day for soaring), the same conditions appeared. Any soaring pilot with any experience could have gained the altitude required for Gold C or even Diamond C... On this day from 0900 to 1600 you could observe lenticulars, sometimes two and three superimposed, while in the other direction the sky was a clean, deep blue. Between 1600 and night there were waves coming and going alternately at one point or another continuously."

Marcel Godinat was on his soapbox, reporting the increasing demand for sailplanes in the US, regretting the imports from Europe and mourning the fact that the sailplane business was "going the way of the automobile, with the foreign car taking the best share of the market. Why is the trend continuing in spite of import duties and the high cost of shipping, crating and insurance?" demanded Marcel. He felt as a group ASA should encourage sailplane construction and perceived early that fiberglass was to be soaring's salvation. "Schreder is on the right track with his HP-10 kit which uses a very economical metal honeycomb construction for his wing surface, also permitting the advantage of laminar flow. The Prue Standard is another modern design with good ideas. It is all metal and has very good performance.

"Metal, however, is not the only answer," he continued. "The new Canadian ship, the Viking 104, built completely of fiberglass, should also be favorably considered, especially by us in Arizona. The problems of wooden high performance ships in the arid Arizona climate are numerous and serious. The wood alternately shrinks and swells in the changing humidity, changing the section shapes, destroying laminar flow, and weakening the structure at any point where it is bonded to metal, as it is for root fittings and control surface hinges. Fiberglass is also very easy to work with, permitting the use of molds and forms for quantity production. Witness the tremendous growth of the boat building industry after the coming of fiberglass construction. The advantages are little maintenance, little deterioration and long life."

Meanwhile, the pursuit of parts for the winch was taking on the appearance of a treasure hunt. Earl Goodman had come up with several more items including a radiator and battery. "We are also pleased (and astonished) to report that, after sitting around for nearly three years, the engine started and ran perfectly on the first try."

ASA started a regular ground school in Phoenix College Club Room and a list of Arizona State Records was published, three of which were held by Joe Lincoln, one by Marcel Godinat, the multi-place Distance by Dick Johnson and Bob Sparling, and the Senior Altitude Gain by Ken Bawden. There were no Junior Records.

John Ryan was SSA Regional Director for Arizona and referred to "our enviable safety record" which made a change. He won the Nationals in 1962, held at El Mirage, and there was much rejoicing in the Valley. Dick Johnson, in an Adastra, was hard on his heels in second place just 17 points behind him. This Nationals was written up in the November 1962 issue of Flying Magazine and referred to as "the hottest and closest fought contest". It even merited a mention in Aviation Week and Space Technology in the November 12 issue. And an ASA member had won!

The gilt was slightly knocked off their gingerbread when an accident befell the 2-22. "The ship was landed short of the take-off area and while a car was being driven to the landing area to retrieve, the pilot got out of the ship and attempted to move it clear of the runway. A gust of wind lifted the ship about 15 feet in the air and it landed on its right wing, damaging the right aileron. When the fuselage hit the ground the wheel broke, due to side load. There was also damage to the wheel housing structure when some tubing was bent. The left wing then hit the ground, with resultant damage to the left tip and aileron." Parts had to be obtained from Schweizer and the 2-22 was out of commission for some time and sorely missed. The incident marred the Club's "perfect no claim insurance record" which was also rather sad.

The search for a permanent soaring site continued and in October 1962 they found the ideal place. "Who will want to go to Torrey Pines once the Aubrey Cliffs are developed?" crowed Rickie Meyer. "These cliffs, located near Seligman, could bring fame to ASA because of the remarkable ridge soaring which could be attained there.

"On October 6, 1962, Don Harrell and Chuck Doty sized up this excellent soaring site. It juts almost vertically for 1100 feet above the valley at the Seligman end and then gradually increases to 1300 to 1400 feet at the Colorado River end. There are two sets of cliffs. The one closest to Seligman is about 11 miles long, followed by a break for a half mile with a small valley leading off to the east. The cliffs start again and run for about 13 more miles. These cliffs make ridge soaring possible for 24 miles without a turn and make out-of-state locations seem like anthills."

By January 1963 it had been established the land belonged to Boregas Land and Cattle Company of San Francisco. The Company was sympathetic to the ASA cause and gave permission to soar the Cliffs provided they had their own liability insurance. "Shall we set a date for a soaring expedition?" asked the author. Mysteriously, the Aubrey Cliffs were never mentioned again.

In March 1963 it fell to Ruth Petry, who in addition to all the towing and a multitude of other jobs as well, was Editor of the Month, to announce that the WINCH WAS WINCHING!!! It should have been headlines but it was buried deep on the back page. When Ruth asked Bob Wister for a news item on the winch, he growled and said the item should consist of a greasy fingerprint. However, it was reported that in spite of various trials and tribulations, the winch was definitely winching. "Highest tow so far has been 1200 feet, and that was on a day with little wind. A little more testing and the winch should be all set." Ruth, as sole tow pilot, was entitled to be pleased!

News of the 2-22 was less encouraging. The ship was moved to Pete Miller's shop for wing repair but the fabric on the fuselage was discovered to be in such poor condition it was doubtful the ship would pass its annual in May. A quote for recovering came to $200 more than the total in the 2-22 savings account. "The ASA-ers went into a huddle (5 of them) and in less than 10 minutes had floated a bond issue of eight shares at $25 each, with five shares sold on the spot."

By April it was ready to fly again and in great demand. A recall panel was made, a fluorescent red square to be placed at the take-off area to remind pilots their time was up and that some other "eager, hot-handed, forgetful pilot" was eagerly awaiting his turn. Constant reminders beseeching pilots to glance back at the strip once in a while began to appear regularly in Air Currents.

Charges were $3 per hour plus $4 for a 2000 foot tow. "Might I point out," wrote Bob Wister sternly, "a commercial operation charges $8 per hour for a 1-26 plus the tow from $2.50 to $5. Our rules are not currently reflecting good economic sense." Addressing another subject, Bob went on, "We sorely need to research lift areas other than within bicycle distance of home. My winch will be available for tow at interesting sites throughout the state by arrangement. None of these are anticipated as airport locations. We have to look to the future when we might be excluded from the valley due to congestion."

There were 19 sailplanes and one towplane in ASA at that time, one of which - the 2-22 - was owned by the Club, 3 owned by Bob Sparling in Prescott and one by Reynald Hartman in Benson. 8 of the 19 were on the ground and being worked on or re-built. Even the towplane was privately owned, jointly by John Ryan, Clay Hartman and Joe Lincoln. Arrangements were being made for another tow plane to be available at Deer Valley, both at weekends and midweek.

1963 was a good year for ships. Bob Sparling acquired a "new" Franklin and brought it down from Prescott to Phoenix to get it licensed. The ship had never been issued an airworthiness certificate, having been built before they were required. Due to lack of specifications, the Franklin had to be licensed experimental. Consequently, Prescott had the oldest new ship in existence. "It had had a complete recover job," wrote the Editor of the Month, "with Ceconite on the wings, Grade A on the fuselage and - hear this - mattress fabric around the front and bottom of the cockpit area. If that doesn't keep out the cactus, they'd better try steer hide!"

Joe Lincoln was also back in the air. His 1-23, Cirro-Q, had been damaged in the 1962 Nationals at El Mirage but it was reported as being repaired at last and Joe was flying once more.

ASA members found more fame in the May 3, 1964 issue of the Arizona Republic's Sunday Supplement, Arizona Days and Ways. There was a big spread about ASA and their operations at Deer Valley written by Lyle Neatham. It made a noticeable difference to the Club since they had more visitors than usual during the two subsequent weekends.

In June of that year a contingent of ASA members moved en bloc to McCook, Nebraska, for the Nationals, hosted by The Nebraska Soaring Association "which consisted of six brave men". Along with 48 other pilots, John Ryan and Joe Lincoln were going to compete, a multitude of ASA-ers went along to crew, spectate and promote. Dick Johnson won the Nationals in his Skylark 4. John Ryan and his Sisu "18" took 15th place: Joe Lincoln's contest number "34" turned out to be strangely prophetic since he and his 1-23D finished 34th.

John Ryan may not have placed as high as he'd hoped but he enjoyed a victory of a different kind at that Nationals. He was elected President of the SSA for 1965 at the Director's Meeting held in McCook. Maybe this increased his resolve to do better next year - he promptly sold the Sisu to Jerry Robertson and ordered a Sisu 1A for next season.

That year kit planes began to be popular and two arrived in the valley. Harry Robertson began work on his HP-11 and George Breeland stunned his neighbors by taking delivery of "a monstrous crate which had the whole neighborhood wondering what was in it."

In August, 1964 the little Tucson Club was mentioned in passing and referred to as being "now inactive". Meanwhile, Odessa, Texas, was declared the place to be. Three new world records were obtained between July 23 and August 6. Wally Scott flew his Ka6-CR 505 miles for a new international goal record, Al Parker flew his Sisu 1A 644 miles and took the free distance record and George Moffat broke his own world speed record for the 300 Km. triangle and made 75 mph in his HP-8.

The following January it was announced that in conjunction with the FAA and the Air Force, the SSA was conducting high altitude training courses throughout the entire United States. The cost of the course was $5 and limited to pilots with a minimum Silver C qualification. ASA-ers were keen to take advantage of this opportunity and Chuck Doty was put in charge of arrangements.

There was quite a bit of enthusiasm in the Club at that time and they even began Wednesday afternoon flying. They also made a safari to Marana 1 Air Field in the shadow of Picacho Peak in January. "All that runway and no traffic!" wrote the Editor of the Month in awe. It must have felt wonderful after Deer Valley where traffic was getting perilously heavy. Bob Wister brought his winch and two local Eloy crop dusters rigged a tow hook on their Pawnee and "tried their first stint of towing." A high time was had by all and everyone went home saying, "Boy, if we only had a place like this 30 minutes from Phoenix."

The Board didn't mess about waiting for people to volunteer in those days. The President assigned people and told them it was their responsibility to resolve things "if you cannot, for any valid reason, serve as assigned." After which a list of no less than seven committees appeared, with most members on all of them, democratically arranged so the Chairman of one was at the bottom of the pile on another.

A recently arrived Al Hume was to chair the Scientific Committee which was assigned the gargantuan task of keeping "an accurate account of any and all records of flights of members of this organization." Other Committees were the Education Committee, the Membership Committee, Auto Tow and Winch Operations Committee, Task Flight Committee, Field Operations Committee, and last but by no means least, a Newsletter Committee. Just to round things off, a reporter and two officers were appointed, an FAA Regulations Reporter, a Film Procurement Officer and an Aircraft Readiness Officer. We are not told whether this lumbering system was a success but it seems not to have been repeated in subsequent years.

Enthusiasm and activity were certainly at an all time high. "The last two months have been the busiest ever for ASA," wrote Editor of the Month Ruth Petry. "So busy that no one has had time to sit down and write up the Club activities." They made another safari to the abandoned field at Picacho, Wednesday flying continued, Al Hume solo-ed on Valentine's Day and Tom Root had a heady day when he solo-ed power in the morning and the 2-22 in the afternoon. New sailplanes were arriving regularly. Al Hume bought a 1-26, Joe Lincoln took delivery of a 2-32 and Bill Ordway, moving to Phoenix, put in an order for a BG-12. New members were also flourishing and the hourly rate on the Club 2-22 went from $3 to $6.

That year the U.S. Nationals were held in Adrian, Michigan and John Ryan's new Sisu 1A took him to 19th place out of 69 pilots. Official permission was received for the Arizona Soaring Association to conduct its soaring activities at Prescott Municipal Airport, subject to two pages of conditions and, as usual, having their own insurance.

In October the Club recommenced auto towing. Charlie Rockwell, Bob Wister, John Clark and Don Santee got together to "unroll 1500 feet of wire from the roll of approximately 5000 feet of club wire that Bob (Wister) had used on his winch in the past. "This procedure required several hours, three Nicopressed splices and several beers to complete. Next day we added a ring to both ends of the wire properly Nicopressed in place. Don Santee contributed a new 4 foot parachute from a fragmentation bomb (fortunately the bomb was no longer attached) which we secured to the sailplane end of the tow wire. To the canopy of the chute we fastened 4 feet of 5/16 sisal rope as a weak link to which we in turn attached another ring for the sailplane hook up." They then had a fine time testing their handiwork and enjoyed several launches apiece.

By mid-1965 another Club was stirring at Ryan Field in Tucson. Captain Jerry Davis from Barksdale Air Force Base wrote to say he and another fellow had purchased a 2-22C. "Just as we were getting the Club started," wrote Jerry, "we were both shipped out on temporary duty so things are a bit slow right now. Myles Ruggenberg has been down there and checked out several of the pilots on auto tow." He warned ASA-ers to "get cracking or the Tucson Club would soon show them up."

At the end of the year, 1965, the ASA-ers certainly did get cracking. More new ships appeared. Don Santee brought his Ka-8 over from Oregon, and covered it in Bob Wister's workshop. Bill Ordway flew his new BG-12 for the first time that October. And Robbie Roe bought Bob Sparling's old Laister-Kaufmann, its fabric crisp and tattered from ten years of neglect, that was to make him famous in soaring before he even got it off the ground.

According to Joe Lincoln in his Arizona Highways article in July 1967, Robbie Roe was a highly experienced instrument pilot and had done some towing at Harris Hill in Elmira. Robbie began work on his "new" LK and was fortunate enough to have assistance from Dr. James Turnbow, called "Doc" by his friends, an engineering professor at ASU. "In mid-May, 1966," wrote Joe, enjoying himself immensely, "the wings of this LK were moved into the living room of the Roe house in Paradise Valley. A new era in Arizona soaring was then born.

"The presence of those wings in the living room had a strange and unpredictable effect upon guests of the Roes' and over the whole neighborhood. Cars were seen to drive by very slowly; then, after disappearing down the street, they would turn around and drive by the house again, even slower than before. The postman, who always previously had been content to put his mail in the mailbox out on the road, came up to the house one day and rang the bell. "I keep thinking that's an *airplane* in there. Is it?" he asked Robbie's wife, Chashie.

"One of the sheriff's cars was seen going by the house with steadily increasing frequency. Each time it went by it seemed to be moving slower than the time before. Finally the car nosed rather timidly into the driveway, where the deputy parked and turned his radio up to a volume that could be heard a mile away. The deputy walked up to the Roes' front door. "I thought there was an airplane in there. Then I saw the N numbers on it, and I was almost sure, but I wanted to make real sure. Is that really what it is?"

"Work on the wings carried on through the hot summer months. The young Roes were always playing Tijuana Taxi (on their record player). Rob Roe had planned on calling his new bird some elegant name like "Gull" or "Cirrus", a moniker that would signify the lonely grandeur and exaltation of the sky. But, as the summer wore on, a vague apprehension grew. His beautiful sailplane had picked up the name of Tijuana Taxi.

"People kept dropping in - some to help; some to be astonished; some to admire; some to be appalled. Gallons and gallons of iced tea were served. The air-cooled atmosphere was a pleasant mixture of conversation, the unending strains of Tijuana Taxi and the mixed smells of glue, airplane dope, iced tea, lacquer thinner and sawdust.

"This whole plan was really very practical," explained Rob Roe in the calm didactic tones of an engineer. "We had very good temperature and humidity control." His wife was not quite so enthusiastic. "The air conditioning system also did a great job of wafting the scent of lacquer thinner all through the house," commented Chashie.

"Late one night Chashie came staggering out of the bedroom, pretty mad. "Stop that smell," she demanded. Rob apologized and excused himself by explaining he'd thought she was asleep. Later the same night, Bob Roe Jr. came out of his bedroom, a little red-eyed and gray. "Dad, will you please stop that drill. I've got to get some sleep!"

"The work went on happily. In mid-August the wings were removed from the living room and the fuselage moved in. "In September the fuselage was moved into the living room," said Mrs Roe.

"Yes, I had it here for a little while, but then in late September, we took the fuselage over to Harry's place, where it was sprayed along with the wings," Mr Roe said.

"It came back into the living room in early December," said Mrs Roe.

"Yes, we had it back in here for some final work. It was here just a little while."

"It stayed through Christmas."

"At last the work was done," ended Joe in a congratulatory tone. "Rob Roe had one triumphant comment about his experience:

"A new precedent has been set. No longer is it necessary for a man to freeze in winter and boil all summer, working on his sailplane out in the garage." Thus, Rob Roe became the first man in Arizona to become famous in soaring before really getting airborne. He had a sailplane in his living room for 7 months and he is still married."

In December, the ASA found itself assisting Slim Barnard Enterprises of Los Angeles in shooting footage for several movie and TV projects, two of which involved sailplanes. Harry Robertson was pilot. Most of the photography was done at Wickenburg but they came to Deer Valley for the aerial shots. Bob Wister, Joe Perkins, Doc Turnbow and Ruth Petry turned out to help assemble the Sisu and get it in the air. Shots of a take-off, a pattern and a landing were taken from the ground. Then Don Rooks arrived with a Stearman for the aerial shots. With the photographer in the rear cockpit, the Stearman followed the Champ and Sisu on a tow to 4,000 feet, quite cozily at times. After Harry released they followed him even more cozily as he floated back to the ground.

On the Saturday, the faithful crew took the Sisu to the Remuda Ranch at Wickenburg where the ground shots were made. "We haven't heard the full story yet," wrote the Editor of the Month, "but apparently one of the shots the photographers had in mind was *launching the Sisu by horse!* They were persuaded to settle for a retrieve by horse. Harry has asked for a copy of the footage to be shown at a future ASA meeting."

Their fame seemed to grow daily. George Bromley's Gold Altitude Flight, made the previous May when he had to make three climbs (the last with spoilers out) to make a continuous barograph trace, was published in Soaring Magazine. The trace was subsequently used in an advertisement for a non-clogging barograph ink put out by Ontaero Inc. of Canada.

With all this heady success they became more ambitious. In 1964 the SSA had put out a list of rules for obtaining State Soaring Records and these were reproduced in Air Currents in February 1966. Editor of the Month, Jean Doty, who was to remain Editor for the next four years, spurred them on. "There are NO records for Arizona," she told them, with a fine disregard for the achievements of her predecessors. "The gate is wide open and the sky's the limit."

They rented an additional tow plane for Deer Valley and made several field trips, notably to Ryan Field near Tucson and to Wickenburg, where the "field has recently been improved and the full time FBO is anxious to have us come up and fly." There were no less than 22 privately owned ships in the Club at that time, including a 1-19, a 1-23, two 1-26's, a 2-22 and a 2-32, and five LK's, amongst others. Don Santee finished building his Ka-8 which was no mean achievement. Harry Robertson was getting a new Phoebus and looking for a partner to buy in with him for $2,000 to $2,500.

The Club was still growing in expertise as well as in numbers. John Ryan and Joe Lincoln were the only members with three Diamonds; Bill Ordway had one - Goal - and everyone else was still concentrating on Silver and Gold.

Plans were afoot to hold a contest and it was to be called, "The First Arizona Soaring Regatta." If they had read a few old issues of Air Currents, they would have known it was not the first by any means! It was to be held on two dates, May 15 and May 22, at Deer Valley airport, a three class event with separate tasks for high, medium and low performance sailplanes. Arizona Days & Ways featured the event over five pages of its June 26 issue, having sent a reporter and a photographer on both days. It was a great success, despite several off field landings, and, sounding slightly surprised, they reported no aircraft or property were damaged. John Ryan won Class A and Charlie Rockwell just beat Al Hume in Class B. A Second Annual Regatta was quickly mooted.

Their expansion and increased expertise led President Rockwell, who was a professional photographer and provided many great pictures for the front of Air Currents throughout the early 1960's, to appoint George Breeland to form a committee to find and develop a permanent site for ASA. "As the Phoenix area expands and air space around existing airports becomes more crowded with power traffic, a gliderport of our own somewhere on the periphery seems to be the next logical step if we are to have continued freedom to fly," wrote Charlie, and urged everyone to scout around and cudgel their brains for a suitable site.

The problem was solved temporarily by their annual move to Prescott for the summer. Al Hume completed his Silver C with a flight to Seligman, never below 10,000 feet. Having made his goal, he soared the area for two hours waiting for his crew to arrive. Bill Ordway caused a stir by flying to Flagstaff and back. A Flagstaff radio station reported a news item about a "mystery glider" that had appeared from nowhere and disappeared again. How sinister!

Charlie Rockwell had an interesting flight out of Prescott and wrote it up for Air Currents under the title, "The Day The Sky Went Up." He was flying what everyone then called a Lilly-Spatz and Al Hume had launched earlier, falling back down without encountering a bump. "Later, Lilly-Spatz and I joined a group of vultures south of the airport. A large cumulus was building over Prescott and another near Seligman. At 10,000 feet I headed southwest under black clouds. By the time I reached the other side of town I had only 2,500 feet over the ground and met the only sink of the day - 1500 down. This forced me to turn back toward the airport... Flying along showing 200 to 300 up, I turned south under the black stuff with my rate of climb going to 500 to 800 up. At 11,000, heading down a canyon of clear air, I found myself between two large build ups and going up at 1500 feet per minute.

"At this point the first fleeting thought of dark danger entered my mind. I shot up past cloud base to nearly 13,000 and actually had to look down on both sides at about a 30° angle to see cloud base on both sides. Pushing the stick forward I was doing 60 knots and still going up. Before me a small wisp of vapor appeared. In five seconds the air all around me had turned to vapor and I could no longer see the ground or anything else. The black cloud of fear was again tapping on the door of consciousness. Holding the airspeed at 45 knots, I attempted no corrections of rudder or ailerons. In about 20 seconds I broke out into clear air but was still going up. I pulled spoilers full open and stopped going up for about 30 seconds. I was then in clear air over Skull Valley. I started up again at 1200 fpm with spoilers on.

"At this point I was more than concerned. I passed the Franklin, which was also struggling to get down. About 10 miles southwest of the field I was finally able to descend to 9000 feet. Turning toward Prescott I again hit that hellish lift. Turning back I descended to 7500 feet and headed toward the airport which was about 8 miles away. At first I was in extreme turbulence and holding altitude. Then all smoothed out and I was aware that the wind at airport altitude had shifted 180 degrees and was blowing at a fair clip. My approach was straight in and land. All the others came down within the next 10 minutes and everyone had a tale to tell. Prescott is an interesting place to fly in August."

The Club was discussing whether or not to buy a 1-26 and published the financial pros and cons. They printed financial projections for three years which prophesied the expense as being $1500 a year, but added darkly, "That's if there is no major damage and no trailer problems."

Joe Lincoln bettered his own Open, Multi-place distance record during the sojourn at Prescott. He had declared Sante Fe, New Mexico, but bad weather forced him down east of Grants at Laguna. He still achieved 293 miles and a new state record.

Prescott that year had had its successes and its failures, both eventful and frustrating, and they returned to Deer Valley in September with mixed feelings. A windstorm promptly damaged the 2-22 and George Breeland, Chairman and sole member of the Soaring Site Committee, surveyed a site out at Beardsley with Ruth Petry but it turned out not to be *the* place.

In January 1967 Al Hume became President and a permanent site was sought with renewed vigor. About fifteen visitors were reported at Deer Valley, "probably as a result of the article in National Geographic." Joe Lincoln made a 502 mile flight on April 30 which, subject to paperwork, was a new national two place distance record. With his son Bruce as a passenger, he flew from Prescott to Tucumcari in New Mexico.

The Second Annual Soaring Regatta was planned for May but was suddenly postponed at the eleventh hour because of several problems, one of which was "...your astute contest director set a couple of turn points in Luke's air traffic pattern." Pilots who were scheduled to fly canceled out for various reasons, mostly flu and hayfever. Thirdly, the weather guessers called for a 25 knot wind so the whole thing was canceled and the 25 knot wind turned out to be about 5 knots. They planned to make a field trip and hold the contest away from home.

Also in May, the early evangelical recruitment drive for new members seemed to have waned, and was replaced by new members "being carefully screened" and the Board checking out the "desirability of new members." Approval took from 30 to 60 days. Maybe this was due to a member overload: the list of privately owned ships now spread over one and a half pages.

In August 1967 the first ever commercial operation came to the valley. Loy Clingman wrote, "As many of you have heard, there is a commercial soaring operation underway in the valley. I'll be conducting my Baboquivari Soaring School, initially at least at Deer Valley Airport." Clingman had been an SSA Governor for Arizona in the early fifties, and had operated a soaring school at the former Paradise Airport on N. 19th Avenue in conjunction with the power school run by

Bill Ralston and Earl Pylant. He had been a sixth grade teacher most of the interim but he was happy to be back in soaring.

Loy was operating a Schweizer 2-22C purchased from Michiana Soaring Society in Indiana, and was awaiting delivery of a new 1-26 and a new 2-33. He intended to offer instruction, rentals, "and (hopefully) sales", and also promised to cooperate fully with ASA.

In September the Second Annual ASA Soaring Contest finally was held. The weather was booming, permitting winner Jerry Robertson to fly 327 miles to Albuquerque. Bill Ordway and Al Hume each came second in their classes, flying 234 miles and 192 miles respectively. Bill Staley obliged by acting as Contest Manager, as he had the previous year, and was remarkably professional about it. Meanwhile, at the SSA Annual Summer Directors Meeting, a new class was being added for contests - Standard Class.

Things seemed to be going inordinately well. ASA members could now boast 12 Diamonds between them and two new clubs looked possible, one in Tucson (again) and one in Wickenburg. The Tucson group bought a 2-33 from Loy Clingman and really got going. (This was the beginning of TuSC as we know it today). Loy's commercial outfit, Baboquivari, moved to Buckeye and hired a tow pilot by the name of Roy Coulliette. The enterprise seemed to be going well, operating Saturdays and Sundays, with a 2-22C and a brand new 1-26 which was "available for the advanced fliers." Rates were $8 solo and $13 for dual in the 2-22 and $9 for the 1-26. ASA members instructed and they were averaging 40 tows a weekend. The operation later moved to Chandler and came under the ownership of Roy.

Bill Ordway took over from Al Hume as President and Joe Lincoln was appointed Chairman of a new Soaring Site Committee. Not only were they seeking a permanent soaring site, they had been leading a somewhat nomadic existence as far as Club meetings were concerned, and were also in need of a permanent Club room. Members were enjoying lots of safaris and visited Wickenburg, Tucson, Flagstaff and Eloy that year.

In 1968 Jean Doty was still beavering away as Editor, and reported the birth of the ignominious Lead C award which still strikes terror into the hearts of ASA members today.

"Among the more interesting exploits of our Club pilots which we feel should have public recognition are those occasional short approaches which result in some extemporaneously brilliant maneuvers both astonishing to the pilot and edifying to onlookers. Consequently, ideas contributed by several Club members have resulted in a suitable medal, the Lead C.

"The first winner, if I may use that term, was Mr Bill Dickinson who qualified for the Lead C on a recent weekend in Prescott. Near the end of a pleasant local flight in the 1-19, Mr Dickinson, with the help of a brisk headwind, managed to extend his downwind leg to a point where he could miss the field entirely and land in a pasture on the far side of the railroad track. This was accomplished with such unusual finesse that he was chosen as first recipient of the medal by acclamation. Under the rules set up, Mr Dickinson will hold the Lead C until it is awarded to another pilot who turns in an equally astounding performance.

"This handsome medal was designed and engraved by Joe Vest of Prescott on a lead blank supplied by Bernie Skalniak. The gooney bird is shown approaching the runway through typical Prescott terrain, including the railroad track. It is three and three quarter inches in diameter, one half inch thick and weighs two pounds two ounces. (Mr Dickinson suggested a secondary award to be given to the recipient who can wear the Lead C longest without being bent over double). It is on a lanyard made of part of the tow rope used on the famous flight and attached with a staple from a nearby fence of sad memory.

"ASA proudly salutes all of its members who contributed to the establishment of this new award as well as the first holder, who wears his new honor with an appropriately modest blush."

Jean was also very good about including national and international soaring news. In March of that year, she reported Karl Striedieck claimed a new world soaring record of 472 miles out and return flight from Eaglesville, Pa., to Mountain Grove, Va. and return. The following month, April, "the soaring world was shaken" when James E. Yates III, aged 32 of Chule Vista, Ca., flew 681 miles from California to Texas in a Schweizer 2-32. He was probably feeling a little shaken himself after 10 hours in the cockpit and an average speed of 68 mph.

Not to be outdone, Bob Wister proposed a soaring safari. "Requirements: enthusiastic X-country pilots; faithful crews; a three day weekend. First day - soar from Deer Valley to Wickenburg Municipal. Stay overnight. Second day - soar to Prescott. Stay overnight. Third day - soar home to Deer Valley. Anybody interested?" Yes, Joe Lincoln was interested, and wrote a Letter to the Editor.

"I would like to run up the red danger flag about Bob Wister's proposal for a soaring safari. The idea is fine but I don't think anyone flying in Arizona has had a great deal more cross country experience than I have and I have not yet soared from Phoenix to Prescott. It would be possible to do this safely, but should only be undertaken by a pilot of long experience." Joe went on to recommend other safer routes, and said the plan was inadvisable.

Bob Wister seemed to take offense at this and replied somewhat waspishly in the Letters to the Editor column the following month. "Sir or Ma'am (as the case may be): Those who would not fly over hills should hark to the actions of a sea captain. To achieve his mission, he does not heed the ocean floor over which he travels. In fact, the condition of the floor is unknown to him. He travels in preference to the most auspicious currents and weather at his level.

"We have reason to observe the terrain over which we travel, but there is an erroneous attitude towards mountains. Heed the words of our Lord MacCready: Book 1957, Chapter Jan-Feb, Page 11 - first through last verse: To sum up he saith, "Go thou to the hills and thereat find the first and the last and the most abundant of that which ye seek. Those who would go fly in the flat places between the hills shall abide there, frequently, with a wailing and gnashing of teeth, saying why hast thou forsaken me short of my goal?" The letter was signed, "Yours for more red flags, Robert B. Wister." The controversy died a natural death when the Club made its summer move to Prescott in June.

In May of 1968, the name of Nancy Hume appeared for the first time in the Editorial slot of Air Currents. At first, Nancy was merely standing in for Jean Doty who was completing the indexing of Soaring magazine and enjoying a well earned vacation. Nancy humbly confessed she had no hope of duplicating Jean's fine job as editor, and apologized in advance for her own lousy spelling.

However, Nancy did more than duplicate Jean's fine work. Air Currents took on a new sparkle and although Jean resumed the harness of office for another year, Nancy had done such a great job, her card was marked, and when Jean retired,

Nancy took over in September 1969. It was fortunate she did not then know just how long she was to reign!

Things seemed to jog along happily enough for sometime then. They visited Flagstaff, after an enthusiastic and tempting description from Dorothy Ward. She wrote of "our fabulous waves over the Peaks. The lenticular clouds have just been like a picture book. Also, we have our new "gliderport" ready. It's a hard packed dirt strip, 6,000 feet long and 75 feet wide. We have good secure cable tie downs. I have landed several times on it and we really are thrilled with it. We are having power run in this week. There is a water line there which we can tap into the first week in May. We have a flight shack lined up and as soon as temperatures permit we are putting a 30 foot wide strip, 1500 feet long, of hard surface on both ends. Any weekend any of your members would like to come up, we would love to have them. We get 1500 to 2000 foot tows from our winch depending on the wind. We do not have a tow plane. Our peculiar position up on this plateau and the proximity of the Peaks make us our own weather manufacturer... Lots of camping facilities and no one to bother us."

Bill Staley then wrote a rather heavy piece about crewing with lots of stern advice he obviously expected everyone to follow to the letter. One gets the impression he was not over enamored with crewing, despite his introduction, "Crewing - a nasty word? No, not if approached as another important part of the sport of soaring." In the middle of the article he says, "When the flight is terminated, either by reaching the destination or being forced down, the worst part is almost over." His instructions on arrival at the landing site were to "be sure that all is well with the pilot and ship, and then begin to wrap up the paper work." Crews were instructed to ensure the pilot had not forgotten to get his landing forms signed and to put the barograph in a safe place to be opened later. Bill himself had made the mistake of opening Bill Ordway's Diamond Distance barograph in a moving vehicle. The trace was scraped when the car hit a bump, so he was able to offer "a word to the wise - DON'T."

The Board finally bit the bullet and bought the long-considered 1-26. After some work on the trailer, both ship and trailer were reported to be in excellent condition. Another Contest was held in September. It was to be on two consecutive weekends and the fee, which included 3 tows at $4 each and a $5 entry fee, amounted to $17.

ASA was now planning to buy its own towplane and Ruth Petry burst into print with some amusing hints on how to behave during a tow. "The tow pilot likes to know who is in the sailplane and the type of flight," she wrote. "We have several types of tow, such as The Great Grandmother Special, for passengers who haven't been up before, no banks over 15°." Then there was the Student Training Flight tow, long straight runs for slipstream practice, gentle or moderate turns. Finally she was offering The Thermal Hunting Tow in which the tow pilot tries to locate a good thermal and may circle in large thermals with a glider on tow.

In April 1969 Bob Hurni was reported to have flown his five hour duration Silver Badge Leg in the Club 1-26 "at the Estrella Gliderport." This was the first mention of Estrella, and very casual it was too. Other flights and badge attempts "out of Estrella" were also mentioned, including one from Bernie Skalniak who also made his five hour duration flight there. "Estrella Sailport I thought was a good place to try," wrote Bernie. "Several legs had been made there in just the past few weeks by our members, and after all the good things I've heard of the place I was anxious to see it and fly there." However, with the annual move to Prescott, Estrella had to be put on hold until they returned in September.

Memorial Day weekend turned out to be the day several ASA members had been waiting for, especially Al Hume, Bill Ordway and Curt Bradley, all of whom flew to Albuquerque. "The ensuing preparations were absolutely frantic," wrote Al Hume, "particularly trying to smoke the barograph in a brisk wind." It was finally done "at the expense of several near grass fires and a little soot on the car ceiling." Bill Ordway wrote up the flight too and referred to "Baron Von Hume in his 1-26. I think he believes he's got a Phoebus and pushes along accordingly."

On June 24 the National Soaring Championships began in Marfa, Texas, with John Ryan and Jerry Robertson competing and Chuck Doty and Bob Hurni crewing for them. Paul Bikle and John Ryan planned to fly in from Estrella but "after some judicious peering into the sky they allowed as how the weather didn't really look all that good" and had to drive over. Ryan and Robertson, each flying a Phoebus, placed 17th and 18th respectively. Joe Lincoln wrote up the contest for Soaring magazine. With appetites thoroughly whetted, Bill Staley, Bill Ordway, Curt Bradley, Al Hume and Bill Dickinson drove to Marfa for one of the Contest weekends and arrived in time to witness two rest days.

Meanwhile, Gold Badge holder Number 217, Neil Armstrong, was landing on the moon. He sent a telegram to the participants saying, "Please convey my best wishes to all my friends at Marfa. Good lift and good fortune to all competitors. I wish I could join you. There is only one thing I would rather be doing: fortunately, I am. All the best."

In September 1969 Air Currents' Editor Jean Doty retired after three and a half years, having taken her turn as Editor of the Month in February 1966 and simply not stopped, and Nancy Hume took over. She re-introduced herself with a reminder that she could not spell and a confession that grammar was occasionally a problem. "Therefore," she wrote in her first Editorial, "I have employed a copy reader - my husband... Please direct any complaints to my better half. It will be his fault!" Sometimes the new Editor also lost the ability to count and became confused about page numbering. More than once she sent out the newsletter with a blank page and cheerfully told her readers, "Have a free paper airplane on me!"

Her first issue was a bumper issue since she bullied and harrassed several pilots into writing reports of the 4th Annual ASA Contest out of Prescott. Woody Payne, flying his first contest, started off making "yoyo-like progress" and ended up landing out in the Arizona State University's Flagstaff sports stadium. "My final approach took me across a large parking lot behind the stadium and between it and the parking lot. As I skimmed over the fence, another lower fence suddenly appeared before me. (I'm still convinced the little people ran out and erected this some time while I was on base or final!)" This necessitated abbreviating his landing plans but he managed it safely. "As I opened the canopy, I was immediately descended upon by dozens of children who had been playing in a field nearby, together with coaches, campus police and assorted students who wanted to see the "crash". Everyone was quite friendly and the campus police were very helpful in keeping the plane from becoming a piece of playground equipment. After a few minutes of answering questions pertaining to the fate of the engine ("It obviously fell off," one child observed), an officer cleared the area and took me to a phone so I could call my crew."

Dick Townsend retrieved Woody and he arrived home to discover his wife had heard all about it via various news media and had been receiving "a raft of telephone calls from well wishers, publicity seekers, television studios, radio commentators, people hoping I hadn't crashed and a few wishing I had."

Bill Ordway won the A Class of that contest, modestly attributing his success to "good fortune in hitting the right cycle" despite having been "sloshing through a storm" and "not having flown in such rain or flinched at near lightning bolts for a long time." Al Hume won B Class and, in typical pilot fashion, wrote his report berating himself for what he should have done rather than being satisfied with what he did.

Tucson Club was obviously flourishing since they ordered a Blanik from Fred Arndt, Blanik dealer. They held a ridge camp at the Rocking K Ranch, which was located near a ridge for winter soaring. In December their 1-26 was severely damaged when the wind took advantage of a missing safety pin in the wing tie-down bolt. A new club was being formed in Yuma and boasted 13 members. They bought the Flagstaff 2-22 and were on the look out for a 1-26. They were also promising a pilot to represent them in the next ASA Contest and started producing their own magazine, Towline. Flagstaff and Prescott Clubs were still in existence too, though reporting little news. This meant there was at that time a total of six soaring clubs in Arizona.

In November 1969, now that ASA pilots had left Prescott and were back in the valley, Las and Stephan Horvath of Estrella were offering a service to call anyone interested in riding the wave and notify them when such conditions looked like developing. ASA-ers smelled Diamonds!

Also in the November 1969 Air Currents, there was a brief two-line entry that presaged great things. "The Board further discussed Estrella Sailport. More information will be given to the membership at the November 24 meeting." It was a shame it was all done verbally because there is no record of what was said but it seems safe to assume the discussion pertained to a move to Estrella, and adopting the site as the Club's home base.

ASA would never be quite the same again. As Paul Dickerson observed when he became President three years later in 1973, "The objectives during the early days of the ASA were crystal clear: provide gliders, instructors, tow planes and pilots, and a place to fly. For many years, ASA ran the only glider operation in Maricopa County." For many years, in fact, ASA operated in the same way virtually all clubs in the United States did. "Then," continued Dickerson, "ASA sold the towplane to the new commercial operation and agreed to cease all training operations. Thus, ASA no longer provided soaring facilities for the valley. Since that time, ASA has not had a clear set of objectives."

It was true. However, one of the advantages of having no objectives is that one can simply relax and enjoy oneself and that was pretty much what they did! ASA was no longer a club in the accepted sense but an association of ship-owning would-be contest pilots.

Members had occasional twinges of bad conscience that they weren't bringing new, young pilots into the fold, and occasionally someone would display a sailplane somewhere or give a talk to a group of youngsters. However, the trade off was that existing pilots who might otherwise never attempt cross country, were encouraged to participate in ASA Contests, using the two Club sailplanes if necessary. Once bitten by the bug, they were keen to get their own ships.

Nine years down the road, in 1978, Paul Schweizer was to say that the Arizona Soaring Association had the highest number of SSA members per capita in the United States. Club contests prepared pilots for Regional, National, and even International contest levels and, without benefit of a demographic survey, it is probably true to say Arizona has the largest number of contest pilots per capita as well. If the Board could have known this when they were nervously making the decision to adopt Estrella as their official "home" in 1969, they could have proceeded with confidence.

In January 1970 it became official. "ASA moved to Estrella and from the reports, the flying has been great for this time of the year." There was wave on February 14 to celebrate. Each pilot was responsible for learning field operating rules from the Estrella Sailport operators and everyone was put on his honor to faithfully record flight time in the logs and to pay up promptly and accurately. Stephan Horvath attended one of the monthly meetings to show a film on ridge and wave soaring and showed a map marked with badge routes with Estrella as the starting point.

Despite Estrella having become ASA's permanent new home, the Club continued to enjoy safaris to other airfields. That spring there was an informal fun contest at Gila Bend, exceedingly well supported. "Who was the wise guy that invited the Yuma Club to Gila Bend?" complained Alex Stuart. "That fine group not only exhibited an unfair amount of soaring ability, spot landing accuracy par excellence and bomb dropping persistence, but also general enthusiasm and fellowship seldom experienced by those of us who made an appearance." The ten Yuma members brought along their own tow plane, a 2-33 and Al Hume's 1-26 which they had purchased.

Tucson also was there, with 10 or 12 members who brought their Ka-6, a 1-26 and a Phoebus. ASA contributed 2 tow planes, one of which was Joe Lincoln's 180, with Clay Hartman and Don Barnard acting as tow pilots, the Blanik, 2 Austrias, a Tern, a 2-22, 1-26 and a daily overflight by John Ryan. It was certainly a weekend to remember: the Gila Bend newspaper gave the event front page coverage and several spectators took rides, including the Vice Mayor.

Just 50 years after the discovery of thermal type lift during the late 1920's in Germany, Arizona pilots and sailplanes were certainly becoming more sophisticated. Badges, contests and records were the order of the day. Three Arizonans in three Phoebus C's planned to fly the Region 12 Championships at El Mirage that May - John Ryan, Jerry Robertson, and Bob Brooks of Tucson. The Internationals that year would be flown by 87 sailplanes, 42 Open Class and 45 Standard Class, by pilots representing 29 countries. The US representatives were to be George Moffat in a Nimbus, Wally Scott in an ASW-12, AJ Smith in an LS-1, Rudy Allemann in a Standard Libelle and Dick Johnson would be team manager.

ASA was having fund raising drives and raffling radios for the International team fund and talk of all these contests inspired them to again plan their own Annual Contest in September at Prescott. Tucson, Yuma and Flagstaff Clubs were sending pilots and it promised to be their biggest contest yet.

Records were important too. State records or personal records were great achievements. John Ryan flew from Estrella to Esperanza for a flight of 405 miles. Betty Horvath earned her Gold Altitude at 13,875 feet and her 5 hour duration flight on May 18 in a 2-33. Signe Horvath, Stephan's wife, completed her Silver Badge in a 1-26, also on May 18, with Silver Distance to Arizona City and Gold

Altitude to 14,675 feet during the same flight. Grant Norman set a new Junior State Record for gain and absolute altitude at 14,875 feet in a 2-33 the same day, which must have been a boomer.

Not to be outdone, Las Horvath took off in a 1-26D and took Diamond Altitude to 18,720 feet, a gain of 16,780 feet, which would set a new State Record for Open Class. During that flight he just happened to fly to Tucson and back, 200 miles, in approximately 2 hrs and 50 minutes, and modestly said it was just a question of being in the right place at the right time.

Sundry other A,B,C and Silver Badges were also earned that weekend. As the Editor said with masterful understatement, it was some day. Four new State Records were applied for. Alex Stuart wrote a cheerful piece about the resulting celebration, a runway party attended by about 30 people who "braved the Horvath sense of humor and the cool night air", amongst whom were several Estrella regulars and, "of course, the Hungarian Air Force."

Also in May, Joe Lincoln soared 405 miles to earn the World Multiplace Out and Return record. He released at Sante Fe, New Mexico, soaring 202½ miles north to a pre-designated turnpoint at Salida, Colorado and back to Sante Fe. His total flight time was 7.5 hours, giving an average speed of 54 mph. Joe's passenger in his 2-32, Cibola, was Chris Crowl. (See Ch.2)

Chris Crowl was a regular instructor at Baboquivari, which was now under the ownership of Roy Coulliette and providing a regular column for Air Currents. Estrella also contributed a regular column and that summer Stephan Horvath, its author, was talking seriously about holding the Region 9 Contest there for the first time.

That summer Stephan Horvath flew his first major contest and took second place in the 1-26 Nationals at Hobbs. (Las missed them and chose to spend some of the time in hospital instead). After one retrieve and a 200 mile drive home, they discovered the turtledeck cover had blown off or fallen off en route. They searched the hardware stores next morning for an "adequate covering" and came up with one square yard of linoleum which they braced on the ship with aluminum strips and tape. "We received many comments the next morning - mostly on how pretty it looked."

The 1970 World Soaring Contest at Marfa, Texas turned out to be something of a financial embarrassment later on. It was subsequently announced the contest had gone $12,721 in debt. "Granted somebody goofed," wrote the Air Currents' editor. "Granted, somebody didn't plan properly. However, that isn't the issue now. The bills must be paid, the SSA is responsible to see that they are despite having more than met their original commitment before the Championships." Everyone was reminded *we* are the SSA and exhorted to send a check for the price of one tow. Meanwhile, Estrella was going from strength to strength. The Board polled all ASA members as to where they wished to fly the next ASA Contest and Estrella was the spot favored by the majority. The 1-26 Association held their 7th Annual North American Soaring Championships there and a permanent start gate was planned, to be built according to SSA specifications and available for use by everyone.

Clarke Masters, a Captain for American Airlines and pilot of Boeing 707's, opened a "small, fun-type commercial soaring operation near Mingus Mountain near Prescott" with a new 150 hp Citabria, a new 1-26D and a 2-33. Named Sun 'n Cu, a progress report showed business was going well and 12 students had already been solo-ed. The site boasted "two well paved runways, 6800 and 4400 feet in length, field elevation a little over 5,000 feet, mountains on the east, south and west, pine tree fragrance in the air, a golf course surrounding the field and fantastic soaring."

Fantastic soaring was not Prescott's exclusive prerogative however. Also that summer three new World Records were flown and claimed. A double flight made by Ben Greene and Wally Scott of 720 miles, each in a single place Schleicher ASW-12, for which they released from tow just 13 minutes apart over Odessa, Texas, and landed side by side in Columbus, Nebraska after some 9 hours flying and average speeds of almost 80 mph, allowed them to claim the World Soaring Distance Record. On the same day - July 26 - Irving Prue flew 71 mph in the multi-place speed 100 km triangle category in a Prue 2, an all metal ship he had designed and constructed himself. The day before, July 25, Ross Briegleb flew his Diamant 18 around a 100 km triangle for a single place speed record of 89 mph.

At the change of the year ASA published a roster. There were 49 members and most of the names appeared regularly in connection with flying activities. They were all extremely active. Having ordered a Standard Cirrus in November 1970, Bill Ordway began advertising his BG-12, built by Kenny Briegleb, with wings just re-finished, and including trailer, parachute, oxygen, "normal" instruments plus a PZL variometer. (Note that date.) They sold off the 2-22 which had been bought for ASA by Joe Lincoln 12 years earlier in 1959. Nancy Hume, who was at Estrella when the ship made its last flight, felt as if she were losing a member of the family, "even to a lump in her throat."

Bill Dickinson wrote a moving piece entitled, "In Memory" specially for the occasion. "On February 5, 1971, Harry Robertson and his family slipped our 2-22 across the border from Arizona where she was placed in the hands of a man in the hills of Western New Mexico. No voices of protest have been heard. No words of scorn printed. Such is the way of man...

"Goodbye, beautiful bird! Thank you for your powerful and searching wings; for protecting me from myself. Thank you for allowing me to know the joy and freedom of flight. Fly on beautiful bird! You who are made of patch and paste, steel and tape, your beauty is in the joy you bring. Fly on for ever!"

In early 1971, Joe Lincoln was planning a trip to Colorado in pursuit of 100, 300 and 500 Km speed records. In March he expected delivery of a pair of new wings for his 2-32, Cibola. The Editor teased, "Joe Lincoln is the only sailplane pilot I know with two of everything - two radios, two barographs, two sailplanes and now two sets of wings." In June, Joe became the proud father of twins!

Also in February, 1971, Roy Coulliette moved his Baboquivari base of operations from Chandler to the airport at Turf Paradise at 19th Avenue and Bell Road, "just 15 miles north of Phoenix." It was to be known as Turf Sailport and offered "a paved strip on which to take off and land and also an area cleared for landing next to it." The operation owned two 2-33's, two 1-26's and one towplane. Plans to purchase a second towplane were also featured in the move.

In April, the Club bought new radio equipment for its 1-26 but in May it was reported that "Due to a landing accident the 1-26 will be out of commission for a while." May produced more than the usual quota of excitement. The May general meeting was addressed by a pretty young airline stewardess describing how she survived a 737 crash, Bill Ordway was *still* advertising his BG-12, a 1-23 disintegrated at 18,000 feet at the PASCO wave camp, and 40 pilots had signed up to enter the 1-26 Nationals Contest at Estrella.

In June, Bill Ordway nobly took over as guest newsletter editor to give Nancy a well earned rest. It wasn't that noble since he delegated everything, the typing to his secretary and the duplicating back to Nancy! Drunk with power, he wrote an excellent editorial suggesting a six month contest series. "So how about six contest weekends," he wrote, "one a month, starting in April and ending in September? That would be at least 12 contest days. A pilot's (or team's) best eight days would be scored." The concept was not too far removed from the original Contest Series adopted by Don Barnard in 1957. History was repeating itself. ASA adopted Bill's suggestion and the practice continues to this day. (Thanks, Bill!)

Bill's suggestion was provoked by disappointing weather at the Sixth Annual ASA Contest in Prescott which had brought *snow* in May and gale force winds for the exact 72 hours of the meet. Bill had won the Contest but as Editor could not congratulate himself too heartily.

Commercial soaring sites were also booming: Roy Coulliette had acquired his second tow plane and the owner of Turf Airport was building hangars to rent at reasonable rates. Sun 'n Cu near Mingus Mountain near Prescott was increasing its staff and its complement of airplanes, and Estrella had now received 43 entries from pilots for the 1971 1-26 Nationals.

Speaking of 1-26's, the Board decided to sell the Club's damaged 1-26 and bought one from Phil Fry to get airborne again without delay. The new ship was to be jealously guarded and new rules and new rates were produced. It was reported as being constantly busy and was well equipped with all instruments, radio and oxygen.

Woody Payne made headlines in the local press for landing on a golf course near Flagstaff but his luck was not completely out that month. He and Wally Raisanen planned to attend the Regionals at El Mirage, flipped a coin and Woody won the flying, Wally the crewing. Bill Ordway could have loaned the loser his BG-12. It was *still* being advertised. Three new ships were awaited in the Valley: Bill Ordway's Cirrus, John Ryan's Nimbus and Al Hume's Cirrus were on their way and expected to arrive in the States in January. They could hardly wait: there was wave at Estrella on December 6. John Baird and John Spealman plucked Diamond Altitude from its smooth confines and Dale Donaho took two State records.

Earlier, Nancy Hume had produced the biggest booboo of a lengthy career and announced the long awaited publication of Joe's now famous soaring anthology as Joe's new book, "Unquiet Wings". No matter: a special award of recognition was created for Nancy in 1971 for the sterling job she was doing.

There was sad news too that November. Mark Masters, son of Clark Masters at Sun 'n Cu, was killed in a soaring accident. ASA extended its deepest sympathy and said, "Many, many people, old, young and in between, are saddened by his death."

This was suddenly a period of transition for soaring in Arizona. Clark Masters closed down Sun 'n Cu, with much of his equipment being sold to Turf Sailport, and, the same month, the Northern Arizona Soaring Club in Flagstaff closed down. Wayne Ward wrote, "Sad greetings from Northern Arizona Soaring. It is with regret I have to inform you of the dissolution of the Soaring Club in Flagstaff. Due to a lack of new interest and insurance rates, we are forced to sell our equipment and disband the Club." He went on to offer the 1967 Schwiezer 2-33 and an HP-ll, "both excellent buys at $5,000 each."

While Arizona soaring was being refined, the arts were well represented too. Woody Payne held a one-man exhibition at the Art Wagon Galleries in Scottsdale at which all paintings were soaring-oriented. And, excitingly, Joe Lincoln's book, "On Quiet Wings", was expected off the presses any minute, to be followed by two others in the fall and a fourth the following year. "Soaring For Diamonds" had sold out after three printings.

Flying, however, was still the thing. More wave was enjoyed over Estrella in April, and Wally Raisanen, Bill Ordway, Jim Westcott, Phil Fry, Don Ford and Jim Turnbow took Diamond Altitudes. Wally and Bill threw in a couple of state records for good measure and Bill Ordway was now the proud owner of 3 Diamonds in all. ASA pilots were doing well for themselves and 4 had been seeded and accepted for the 1972 Standard Class Nationals, Al Hume, Bill Ordway, Jerry Robertson and Pete Williams. In May, Las Horvath made his epic flight from Estrella to Tombstone, the first out and return flight in history in a 1-26 for Diamond Distance. He wrote up this triumph in typical glider pilot style, as a lament, declaring if only he'd done this, he would have achieved that. (See Ch.6)

Turf created its own fun at Deer Valley's disused eastern end of the runway with some auto tows during April. "When we returned the rented pick-up, we left the agent shaking his head, wondering how we could possibly have used over 7 gallons of gasoline to go less than 50 miles. With an eye to the future, we left him with the riddle still unsolved."

There was great excitement in May when the Smirnoff Sailplane Derby landed at Turf on May 1 and took off from there on May 2. The winner that year was Wally Scott, with Paul Bikle second and ASA's very own John Ryan third.

While the ASA Contest Series continued, and sites far and wide included Parker, Springerville and Prescott, no one was tempted by the May International Baja Soaring Fiesta in Mexico. Chuck Warner of Yuma sent details to ASA. "Mexican auto insurance is recommended... If sailplanes have collision and liability cover, it's easy to extend this to Mexico for the weekend... Proof of citizenship must be shown... We will have a place to park aircraft Friday night... they will have guards on hand to protect the ships from vandals... When the ships move from Mexicali to Laguna Salada, there will be a police escort through town for all the ships..." However, it seems no one was reassured by his optimism and there were no takers in ASA.

Bill Ordway placed 12th that year in the Third Standard Class Nationals at Marfa, Texas. The event "proved beyond any doubt that Standard Class competition has become widely accepted in this country," wrote Bill, "and is attracting top competition pilots. Even with 65 slots to fill, there was a sizeable waiting list for the Marfa contest this year. This was fortunate, for it was exhausted by opening day as previously-entered pilots had to drop out for various reasons.

"This is a healthy change from a very few years ago when many pilots viewed Standard Class Competition as sort of second rate." Bill had a ball in his new Cirrus, of which there were 20 at the contest, beaten (in quantity) only by the Libelle, of which there were 26. Tom Beltz won in a Cirrus and Wally Scott came second, also in a Cirrus.

Al Hume and Nancy weren't overly delighted with their flying performance at the Nationals, but had a ball anyway. "We met several Texas ranchers (via outlandings)," wrote Nancy. "One such ranch (built in 1914) (and loaded with outstanding antiques), fed us margaritas (it was too late in the day for a restart) and later entertained us with a polo match on the ranch." Now that's what you'd call a retrieve!

Flying in Prescott was available once more, John and Charlotte Detwiler, both pilots, joined ASA, Pete Petry got his Gold Altitude at Prescott, Bill Ordway, Al Hume, Pete Petry and Jim George were to represent Arizona at the Region 12 Championships at El Mirage in August and ASA had a new author, President Dan Halacy. "Soaring" was a hard cover selling at $3.95, with beautiful color photographs on every page taken by Jim Tallon, and a picture of Foxtrot Yankee being flown by Wally Raisanen on the cover. A copy was duly presented by the Humes to a local boys school, which was received with much enthusiasm.

The rest of the world was going crazy getting records. Betsy Howell of Illinois and Helen Dick of San Diego leapfrogged each other all summer, bettering records one after the other. Joe Lincoln's World Multi-Place Out and Return Soaring record was toppled by Edward Makula of Warsaw, Poland, who was claiming a 441 mile flight out of Minden, Nevada, on August 8, 1972, in an Italian Caproni A-21 with ASA member John Serafin as a passenger.

In July, Wally Raisanen had a traumatic outlanding during a Diamond Distance attempt from Estrella, via Avra Valley, Mohawk Junction and return. (See Ch.7) Happily, Wally's enthusiasm was not dampened. The very next issue carried an article by him describing a cross country soaring board game, and trying to sell it. "This publication has a very strange advertising structure," he wrote. "I phoned the editor to ask to put in an advertisement for Soaring X-C, and ended up being persuaded to write an article about it."

Dan Halacy wrote the obligatory President's Report at year's end and was justifiably proud of the 1972 Contest Series. "A total of 37 contestants flew in Class A and Class B on 23 contest days, a performance dimmed only by the damnable fact that Tucson took both first place trophies!"

The following year, Paul Dickerson became President. 1973 began with the advent of a brand new format for Air Currents. It had a magnificent new cover and almost impossible-to-read contents. There was much ...continued on page all-over-the-place... and bits of stories squashed in where ever they could be persuaded to fit. The designer can only have been a logistics expert or an engineer. It left we lesser mortals utterly confused and often wondering how somebody's soaring adventure ended. John and Char Detwiler took on the Editor's job: Nancy was suffering from burnout and retired to rest on her laurels - for a little while, at least.

In March they had an exciting weekend at Turf when the new Swiss-made Pilatus B4 was delivered. It was "flight tested" for a total of 14 hours aloft by 18 pilots. The person who wrote Turf Notes in those days, (probably Jean Engelke) was a very good writer, and told readers, "At one point, Bill (Engelke) spoke for all those who flew her: given a brisk radio-reminder (by the next pilot in line) that his allotted hour was almost at an end, we heard a half minute of silence while we watched the B4 rack a little tighter, climb a little faster, then a low, possessive growl from Bill: "I feel like Jesse James!"

Soaring was featured in Sports Illustrated magazine dated 15th April, 1973, complete with pictures, water colors and an article on the Joy of Soaring. Jim George wrote excitedly to forewarn Air Currents readers of this upcoming acknowledgement of the passion of their lives, and said, "I know for sure it has a shot of my Diamant and I think Ryan and Chases' ships."

Also in April, a public address system was installed at Estrella, the dirt road to the sailport was flooded and The Rumor That It Was To Be Paved officially began. (Fifteen years later the work was actually started and is now complete! A toxic waste dump (non-nuclear) to be built in the vicinity has brought us 21 miles of paved road twixt Maricopa and Mobile at a projected cost of $2,474,167).

Woodson and Margaret Woods were very formally listed as New Members and duly welcomed to the Club. (We were to know them as Woody and Maggie). Woody was the first paying customer to get a Diamond out of Estrella. He had come over from Hawaii, where you don't get a whole lot of cross country flying, and discovered Estrella for himself. He flew Diamond Distance on the Wednesday and Diamond Goal on the Friday. "The main reason I stayed up was because I was totally intimidated by the Arizona desert and too scared to land!" confessed Woody. He fell in love with Arizona and decided to relocate here.

That particular issue of Air Currents (April) had Crews and Crewing for its theme, and contained a very serious article by Chuck Doty entitled Organized Crewing. After an appropriately serious introduction, the checklist started off, "Before Going To The Field: 1. Get the crew together, and make sure they are ready to go, with breakfast eaten and personal gear, (sunhats, glasses, etc.)" There was also an item written by Jim George about keeping it brief on the radio which covered 3 pages.

For some time then, Air Currents carried largely technical articles which may or may not be out of date by now but are not appropriate here. They were enlivened by a contribution entitled "A Double Whammy" by Paul Eskew, who absolutely amazed himself by winning two consecutive days of contest flying. The secret of his success, he decided, lay in the facts that "(1) I was out of radio contact with my crew and therefore did not have to worry about where they were and what they were doing. (2) They would have killed me if I had landed out. (3) My radio was not transmitting but was receiving and the things that I heard gave me the impression that everyone else was smoking around the course at about 80 mph. (4) I was lucky and stumbled into some fantastic soaring conditions."

Paul ended by giving credit where it was due. "My thanks to Roy Coulliette, who let me borrow his crummiest, most beat up 1-26, to John Lincoln and Josh Voynick, my trusty faithful crew and especially to Bill Ordway who let me borrow his car for crewing. If you've ever seen John Lincoln's driving, you'll know what a big favor that was."

A roster printed that year listed 78 members, including a young man by the name of Robert von Hellens, and in July they were querying whether there were any tangible benefits to being a Chapter of the SSA since it involved so much administrative work. Lloyd Licher, Executive Director of the SSA, replied fully in the August issue, listing benefits which in some ways gave ASA's doubts more credence! The response from the Editors indicated they remained unconvinced, but ASA continued its chapter affiliation.

Turf Soaring School then had a great idea, the benefits of which we still enjoy today. "Turf Soaring School, in conjunction with the ASA, is establishing a series of 3 annual awards for soaring excellence... We would like to ask the assistance of the entire ASA membership in helping us decide on the 3 categories and on the way in which the yearly winners should be determined."

Their generosity did not stop there. They then designated one of their 1-26's a Club Ship. Roy Coulliette was being congratulated on his five thousandth flight

("There must be a thermal up there somewhere, Roy!" they said, somewhat unkindly) and commiserated with over the loss of his favorite hat. "He had taken a more than moderately attractive young woman for an Intro flight only to discover two things at altitude. (1) He had an airsick passenger on his hands and (2) he had no sicsac. So Roy, extending gallantry beyond the call of duty, passed forward his favorite hat. End of hat? Ah, no - there are line boys to take care of disagreeable laundry chores, and so, having supervised the washing of his hat and its laying out to dry on a bush in the field next door, Roy took to the air again.

"Enters another character, an older student who had spent a few winter weeks hard at flight and who had solo-ed against the pressure of time and classic case of nerves. Student had said reluctant goodbyes and was leaving immediately for New England. From 2000 feet Roy watched in disbelief as the student rushed to the bush, snatched the still-damp hat and departed eastward behind a large plume of dust. Neither hat nor student has been heard from since..."

Elliott Kurzman also came in for congratulation. He won the Estrella trophy for 1973 with a 384 mile flight in a 1-26 from Estrella to Elko, Nevada via Parker, Az. This was the third longest flight to have been made in a 1-26 and served to complete Elliott's diamond badge, making him the sixth pilot ever to complete his diamonds in a 1-26. Also at Estrella, Las was planning an air show in November with glider and power aerobatics, final glides, paper cutting and parachuting.

Las had a busy November that year. Despite his now-excellent command of the English language, you could almost hear his strong Hungarian accent in his writing since he still tended to muddle his tenses a little. "I have gone to this year's Schweizer Dealers' Meeting with great anticipation: finally I'll fly the 1-35. For a year now I have been hearing how great, how fast, how slow, how small, how light, how it climbed, how it pulled away. Well... I did not fly it! It's hard to believe how long the line was."

Not flying it didn't stop Las from falling in love with the little ship. "The ship is beautiful, incredibly small," wrote Las. "The FAA tests for certification are about done and production is being set up. In 1974 about 60 will be produced." Arizona Soaring would get 2 or 3 of them.

In a moment of expansiveness and well-being brought on by his evening glass of sherry, Bill Ordway offered - and then had to deliver - a story on the 1973 Open Nationals in which he came 46th out of 70 pilots. He mercilessly condemned himself (as only a glider pilot can) for not using the weather properly, pushing too hard, not pushing hard enough and generally blowing it. Jim George wound up 5th and Al Hume came 9th.

Wally Raisanen rose to the top and became President in 1974 and the name of Lincoln once more was listed on the masthead as an Editor of Air Currents, this time Joe's son, John. The new year brought a change of newsletter format which was a blessed relief. Air Currents could once more be read in straightforward fashion instead of in the manner of a maniacal Chinese Arab doing aerobatics.

An impressive list of new policies appeared in the February 1974 issue, including plans to purchase and provide more sailplanes, maintain closer liaison with the Tucson Club to promote mutual understanding, joint activities and share costs. There was much concern about the Club's accident record and a promise to publish a monthly analysis of accidents.

A midair collision at Estrella in March was one of the first incidents to provide an object lesson. "Two air force student pilots stationed at Williams Air

Force Base decided to go flying at Estrella on a Sunday afternoon," wrote Arnie Jurn. "Both pilots rented Schwiezer 1-26's only to return with $1500 damage to the wings of both sailplanes. Nobody saw the accident except for the two persons involved. Both pilots had been previously involved in formation flight training in jet aircraft which is a lot different from a 1-26.

"Las contemplated only allowing one of the two pilots in the air at one time, which leads me to believe these pilots probably were over-confident about their ability to fly sailplanes. Las mentioned he does not allow cameras in his singleplace sailplanes. Flying is a full time responsibility and cannot be sidetracked by such matters as picture taking (except turnpoints). Las believes that the accident happened as the result of one pilot trying to take pictures of the other." Arnie's conclusion was that the two pilots were fortunate to have survived the incident and that Las, as the operator, was left with the most difficult part of the problem.

In April, it was announced because of the energy crisis and gas shortage, the Contest Committee had decided to hold all contest days at Estrella with tasks kept short to reduce the need for ground crews to drive cross country. Tasks tight to the airfield would be flown twice.

There was a fly-in at Turf which promised "flying will continue until everyone has landed", after which a barbecue potluck was attended by some 200 people, and in April a Good Old Days Fly-in was planned at Eloy with tows at $2 each! The travel embargo due to gas shortages was temporarily forgotten and a great time was had by all. Ron Eaton wrote up the piece and rather unsportingly reported on his wife's first attempt at crewing. "Being that this was Kathy's first crewing experience, and being that she has a very poor sense of direction, I initiated our first radio conversation which will go in our scrapbook.

"65 to 65 ground." Long pause.

"65 ground."

"65 ground, what's your position?" (Natural concern since I didn't want to lose a wife, 3 children, our camper and a Genave ground radio). Short pause.

"I'm just behind Nancy." (Ordway). Much chuckling in the cockpit of 65.

"81 ground to 65. *We're* between Maricopa and Casa Grand."

Paul Dickerson then went all technical on us and took a 12 page look at Glider Performance, complete with mathematical formulae, graphs, charts and diagrams. It was impressive and no doubt of enormous value - to other engineers. His good intentions and spirit of pure helpfulness fell foul of Joe Lincoln, however, who responded with a Letter to the Editor. "There was a time when soaring was completely dominated by mathematicians, engineers and scientists. Then in 1970 the soaring world was turned upside down when the World Championships were won by George Moffat in the Open Class and Helmut Reichmann in Standard Class. George Moffat is an English teacher. Helmut Reichmann is a biology and gymnastics teacher.

"This letter is not meant to run down the engineering look at glider performance gotten up by Paul Dickerson in the last issue of Air Currents but in case there are non-engineer pilots who find such hieroglyphics as incomprehensible as I do, they should not despair." With unfortunate timing, another of Paul's articles appeared in the same issue, this time an engineer's look at water ballast.

Meanwhile, the Club's 1-26, 454, (which is still very much with us), had been given a new coat of paint. It was now white "with a sassy grass green trim".

Everyone was threatened, "there is to be no tape anywhere on our ship at any time."

After its inauguration, the new Board quickly realized it had inherited a commitment from its predecessors to sponsor and run the very first Region 9 Contest in 1974. Previously, Region 9 had been hosted at Roswell, New Mexico (in 1968) and for several years at Waverly West, Fort Collins, Colorado. Wally Raisanen was designated Contest Manager and given $600 as his initial operations budget.

It was a resounding success. Billie Baird wrote up the event and did a fine job but ended up saying, "This was my first contest in a long time as a spectator and if I'd known I was going to write this article I would have spectated more and played bridge less." Dan Halacy also wrote up the event as a participant in the July issue and reported enjoying "every scratching minute of every harrowing day."

Tom Brandes and John Ryan took turns at 1st and 2nd places all week, and the final score sheet showed Tom Brandes in 1st place, John Ryan 2nd, Jim George 3rd, Bill Ivans 4th and Woody Woods 5th. Hume, Ordway and Dickerson were 8th, 9th and 13th respectively. Carson Gilmer (39) came 6th and had driven all the way from Texas to compete. He wrote a delightful thank you letter to the Contest Manager afterwards saying he had flown in the last two Standard Nationals and four Regionals "and your Region 9 Contest was the best run of the lot... You and your staff are to be commended for the way the thing came off."

The social activity in those days was remarkable. Nancy Hume had been Social Secretary ever since her retirement as Editor and only relinquished the position to Nancy Ordway in 1974. In July they had a Hawaiian Luau at the Petry's home, who provided "house, pool, wine and colorful leis," the latter having been blown down on the Friday night. "It looked for a while like they would be blown down again Saturday night, and rained on besides, but the weatherman upstairs knew better than to rain on a bunch of soaring pilots and the party was saved." Paul Dickerson introduced himself to someone else's friends, Beate and Peter Pardon.

"Dickerson here."

"Pardon."

(Louder): "I'm Dickerson."

"Pardon."

Someone finally explained things to Paul so Peter did have time to meet some of the other guests.

The 1974 Standard Nationals was held at Hobbs, New Mexico that year, and Al Hume's write up of the event contained a fascinating early description of the place. "Hobbs is half way up the Texas panhandle, just a few miles over the border into New Mexico. The land is quite flat, gently rolling, about half farm land and half low scrub with a generous sprinkling of oil wells. The elevation varies slowly from 4,000 feet at Hobbs to about 2,500 feet at Snyder, 130 miles to the east. There is not a hill in the whole area, and a few dry lakes serve as the only prominent landmarks. From the air almost every small town looks alike and it is easy to get lost if you don't constantly check your location.

"The contest was held at a World War II Air Base with the usual dilapidated hangars. The runways, however, were in reasonably good shape and the facilities adequate. Amazingly, the affair was sponsored by the 12 member Hobbs Soaring Society. They did, however, have more help from several other clubs, particularly the one from Albuquerque, so that everything went off in pretty good order. Hal

Lattimore was Contest Director but the weather was always too good for him to call one of his favorites - a distance task of some sort. Pilot meetings were held in the most sumptuous quarters by far I've ever seen - a small circular theater/auditorium in a nearby Junior College complete with tables for the pilots, projection facilities, and a good PA system, a raised railed area for crews and spectators, and air conditioning."

Al went on to say the weather was absolutely fabulous and the top 10 places were filled by familiar names - Dick Johnson, Tom Beltz, Johnny Byrd, Ross Briegleb, Ray Gimmey, Karl Striedieck, Tom Brandes, Wally Scott, George Moffat, and John Brittingham.

Meanwhile, Paul Dickerson wrote up the Region 12 contest which was well supported by ASA members, including Fred Arndt, John Baird and Jim George in Open Class, Al Hume, Hartmut Karmann, Bill Ordway, Pete Petry and Paul himself in Standard Class.

Owens won the Standard Class in a Libelle H301B (with locked flaps) and Tom Brandes won the Open in a 604. Herman Stiglmeier was something of a philosopher as well as Contest Director. At each day's pilots' meeting he awarded a bag of Fritos to the pilot in last position and a can of beer to the winner with instructions to share the snack as well as various flying secrets.

A Letter to the Editor that appeared in the October issue of Soaring magazine from Wally Scott dealt with the vexing question of pilots flying in contests at gross weights in excess of maximum certificated. This provoked considerable debate, with Pete Petry outlining the situation in Air Currents and inviting members' comments. "The specific question under discussion," explained Pete, "was whether ASA should take a stand on the matter in our ASA Contests and any regional contest we may sponsor, or wait and see what action SSA will take."

The problem of weighing and the expense of scales was aired. Joe Lincoln wrote complaining about this Russian Roulette and suggesting we regulate ourselves before a government agency did it for us. Bob Von Hellens wrote expressing his concern and Bob Hohanshelt wrote expressing a wicked sense of humor. (See Ch.8)

John had managed his year as Editor most capably in the family tradition but retired with apparent relief having learned some truths along the way. "(1) There are articles sent in that are of good quality. (2) There are not many who contribute without being asked. (3) Many who are asked 2 or 3 times never send anything anyway. (4) A very small per cent of the membership ever does anything for the magazine.

Ben E. Stanton took on the Editor's role for 1975 but modestly confessed, "I am new to soaring and do not have the technical background which will enable me to write any original material." It was therefore imperative, he said, "that the membership provide the means and the material." Judging from John's previous comments, the future did not look hopeful.

Comfortingly, however, in Ben's February issue, a small item appeared in the nether regions of the back page that was to presage great things. "Although her arm is still too sore from twisting (for her to write anything for this month's issue), Nancy Hume has offered to develop a monthly column for the newsletter. The title is still under consideration but the contents will cover all those little personal happenings among the soaring fraternity, or at least all that are fit to print. Because of her naturally shy and retiring nature, Nancy asks that the members keep her informed of what's going on around the circuit. This is especially important during the next month, until husband Al puts her back to crewing."

The title of Nancy's new column was to be "Pardon My Squelch" and was enjoyed off and on by Air Currents' readers for 10 years. Even today, members still ask me, as current Editor, if I can't possibly persuade Mrs. Hume to produce some more squelch just occasionally. The answer, sadly, is always No. (So far, anyway).

Nancy's fun was followed by a very stern note from the Board stating that, "The Arizona Soaring Association believes that the generally accepted practice of finishing a sailplane race at very high speeds at very low altitudes (less than 20 feet) is potentially detrimental to the sport and has, therefore, taken specific action to discourage this type of finish. It is a fact that during such finishes, there is a higher than normal risk that longitudinal control oscillations greater than the ground clearance will be induced by flutter, gusts, pilot inattention or pilot induced oscillations combined with the high speed and close ground proximity." Pilots were to desist forthwith.

On March 22 1975, Ron Eaton flew the Estrella wave to an altitude of 27,000 feet and claimed a gain of 22,700, which was pretty heady stuff, and still stands as a record today.

In May of that year, President Pete Petry had the sad task of announcing to a shocked membership that Joseph Colville Lincoln had passed away.

"On May 19, 1975 not only the ASA membership, but our counterparts all over the world, lost an ardent participant in that special communion known as soaring. For twenty years Joe Lincoln enthusiastically pursued that unique relationship of man and air that almost seems to suggest some ancient connection between ourselves and the birds. The nature of this relationship is so intuitive and personal that the vast majority of men can only guess at its meaning. To me, Joe's greatest gift was the rare ability to communicate something of this inner meaning to a wider group of men by his books and articles on which he spent so much time, thought and reflective care.

"But as we deeply feel our loss, we should be grateful that we had the pleasure and privilege of knowing Joe and of having him here in the ASA for the years that were given him. He will be missed and remembered as we carry on in the sport he so loved."

Lloyd Licher, Executive Director of the Soaring Society of America, announced the news to the U.S. Soaring Community. "We regret to report that one of our most devoted enthusiasts, Joseph C. Lincoln, passed away on May 19. A malignant brain tumor discovered just three months ago grew to claim his life, which had spanned only 52 years. He leaves his wife, Dorothy, two young twin daughters and four older children."

Licher continued his obituary with the suggestion that instead of flowers people make contributions to the National Soaring Museum as a memorial to Joe, since he had shown such an interest in the Museum and was its primary benefactor. He went on to list Joe's soaring achievements, his records and his sailplanes, his latest being a Nimbus II for single place record attempts but which he was unable to use before the onset of his illness. Like the ASA President, Licher set greatest store by Joe's writing.

"It was his writing about his soaring experiences that was unique and helped others identify with him," wrote the Executive Director. "In addition to his books there were many classic articles in Soaring magazine, including Beginner's Luck,

Flight to Variadero, The Retrieve and The Walk Out. Then he wrote the reports of the 1969 Nationals and the 1970 World Championships at Marfa, Texas. He was very generous to SSA and to soaring in many ways. We who were fortunate enough to know him will feel his loss greatly."

There was very little to be said after that, but the Editor used a brilliantly clever piece written by Jim George entitled, "Two Final Glides" (See Ch.5) that subsequently won the very first Joseph C. Lincoln Award, later set up in memory of Joe. It pointed up the differences between military flying and soaring flight and Joe Lincoln would have loved it. It was fitting that Joe's Memorial Award should go, that first time, to a fellow ASA member.

Later, Jim George struck again with a very formal letter, a veritable parody of indignation, taking Mr William A. Ordway severely to task for abusing his position in the capacity of Director of Arizona's Department of Transportation. Assuming Mr Ordway to also be in charge of ADOT's publication, Arizona Aviation, Mr George demanded to know how he could permit the inclusion in the calendar of the 6th Annual U.S. Standard Class Soaring Championships at Nevada and omit "the real" Open Class National Championships at Hobbs, the 42nd such event. Mr George could only conclude Mr Ordway was a blind zealot about smaller wingspans, due, obviously, to an inferiority complex.

Taking this in the spirit in which it was intended, Mr Ordway replied with an apology for taking so long to answer his nasty letter, but his spare time had been "devoted to getting my beautiful Standard class ship ready for the big Standard Class National Soaring Championships at Minden." He further added that failure to mention the little Open Class get together at Hobbs must have been a staff oversight.

The Nationals Contest at Minden was a great success, although the weather was a little unpredictable, and ended with Ross Briegleb, Tom Beltz and Ray Gimmey hogging the top spots. Al Hume took 23rd position and said he'd learned more about soaring in the last six days than in the previous ten years. Maybe as a punishment for earlier sins, Bill Ordway was condemned to 42nd place, a very telling position since it was the 42nd Open Nationals he had omitted to mention in his ADOT publication.

Not to be outdone, Arizona's Second Region 9 Championship went off extremely well in June. "As George Moffatt led the Smirnoff pack from California to Turf sailport," wrote Dan Halacy, "35 Open and Standard Class pilots kicked off the 1975 Region 9 meet at Estrella." Dick Townsend was Contest Manager and Fred Arndt was Competition Director. "Fair to middling soaring weather stimulated tasks as long as 322 miles, and speeds in the 80 mph bracket for both classes. Temperatures of 110° worked hardships on ground troops and gave pilots added incentive to get high and stay that way."

On the final day, "five Open Class ships shot across the line in 14 seconds, giving spectators a treat and scorers a treatment." Brooks, Baird and Ryan took the top 3 Open places, Horvath, Karmann and Hume in Standard. "After medal presentations and helpful explanations from winners as to how they had done it," ended Dan, "all those still able to get about convened in nearby Tempe for a gala dinner. It was a tribute to their endurance in the sweltering week of desert sun that 125 were on hand to swap war stories and promises of a different outcome next year."

In early July, ASA suddenly sprouted a new Blanik. It was "a low-time, very clean 2 year old bought from a private owner in Caddo Mills, Texas for $9,950 including all spares but no trailer. (ASA will build a trailer soon)," wrote Char Detwiler, Arizona Governor and Record Keeper. The ship was to live at Turf and cross country flights "from remote places" and introductory rides for family, friends and "influential persons (such as FAA personnel)" were all to be encouraged. "Properly used," finished Charlotte, "the Blanik can be the most effective tool we have for promoting soaring."

It was brilliant timing for in the same issue it was announced that the Club 1-26 had sustained fuselage and wing damage in an off field landing. Plans were afoot to have repairs made and the ship flying again "in short order".

According to Nancy Hume's Pardon My Squelch column, the ASA trip to Prescott in August of that year was terrific for crews and a real bummer for pilots, due to poor weather conditions. Nancy Hume did not attend but super sleuth Nancy Ordway did and reported back to HQ (Hume Quarters) how people spend their time when grounded. "Ron Eaton played bridge. Pete Petry spent the weekend with a calculator trying to figure how long it would take a person to free fall from a plane at a specific altitude. Bill Ordway took a nap. Billie Baird combed Snooky and got enough hair to make another dog." And Nancy Ordway spies on people!

In September Nancy Hume reported on the 1975 Region 12 Championship at El Mirage, California. "The weather was not particularly good and required a fair bit of scratching during the 5 day meet. A number of Arizona pilots participated in the event including Jim George, Bill Ordway, John Baird, Pete Petry, Paul Dickerson and Al Hume. "I had planned to list the top 10 in each class," wrote Nancy, "but I can't find the final score sheet. I suspect Tuffet stuffed it under the refrigerator - a favorite pastime for him."

"I'm sorry to report Paul Dickerson's 19 will be out of commission for the winter because of a landing mishap during the contest. Pete Petry had a couple of fun outlandings. The first involved landing on a dike - 10 feet high on each side and 10 feet wide. He said that from the air it looked like a runway. Ahem, remember folks, he is a 747 Captain!"

There was lots more in this vein, but Nancy ended on a somber note, letting everyone know that Lloyd and Rose Marie Licher had recently made a trip to Arizona to transfer from Prescott to Litchfield the sailplanes and other pieces of soaring equipment which Joe Lincoln had willed to SSA.

Everyone, it seemed, was anxious to remember Joe. Pete Petry, ASA's President, had written to Lawrence Wood, SSA's President, in the matter of a permanent memorial. After expressing the feelings of the members of the Club, Pete ended, "We realize that many issues will be considered in the matter of a memorial to Mr Lincoln, however, it is the feeling of the Arizona Soaring Association that those of us who knew Joe well do have a responsibility to interpret his wishes in this matter as we see them. It is our intention to be constructive and encourage the management of SSA in the establishment of an appropriate memorial."

Suddenly, it was Christmas 1975 and Pete Petry had the pleasant task of looking back over a very satisfying year. He was able to congratulate everyone involved with the successful running of the second Region 9 contest, mentioned the purchase of the Blanik and went on to boast of progress on a new trailer. "A trailer is nearly completed with the expert help of Paul Dickerson, Fred Arndt, Bob von

211

Hellens, Bob Hohanshelt, and others, including the Old Dike-Lander, who was only trusted to steer straight (my specialty), in this case to the parts store and back, while the experts glued the parts together with a torch.

"The 1-26 was bent and straightened. The ASA Contests, organized by Al Michelis, were a great success, as was the Awards Banquet with a new ASA high point reached by Betty Horvath's arranging for a belly dancer. Progress, it's wonderful. Our members flew, bragged, lied, rehashed, and rationalized through another season of the world's most fascinating sport."

After thanking many other officers, helpers and members in his own delightfully eloquent and humorous way, Pete ended by asking, "What is ASA all about? I think last Saturday gave a good example. Six members met for a fiberglass-and-chilli party... to help a fellow ASA-er repair his damaged bird. Hard, critical work, freely given, and a perfect example of our interest, cohesion, and mutual help in the sport and art of soaring - the true purpose of ASA."

In the January 1976 newsletter, they announced all the new officers. However, there was a horrible gap where the Publications Editor's name should be. Mercifully, by the next issue, Bob von Hellens had stepped into the breach and all was well.

Being an efficient fellow, Bob included all sorts of things no one else had seen fit to include hithertofore. He had Monthly Meeting Announcements, Notices, New Members (that month it was Russ and Bonnie MacAnerny), Board Meeting Minutes and Financial Reports. Bob was also the first to mention that the Blanik was "normally tied down at Estrella Sailport." The 1-26 remained at Turf.

At the Boards' first Board Meeting in 1976 they discussed sponsoring the Region 9 contest again that year. Possible sites for the meet were also discussed. It was felt another year's experience in sponsoring contests was desirable should Arizona apply for a Nationals in future years. Great things were planned even then.

Dick Townsend reported from that Meeting that "we again reviewed the aims and activities of ASA and decided we are doing lots of things right. So we don't plan any big changes, but intend to promote the positive."

They were still on the watch for new members - some of the time! A static display of sailplanes was planned for two upcoming airshows that year as a means of promoting soaring. Volunteers were needed to babysit the ships and answer dumb questions. Unfortunately this was subsequently cancelled because it was later learned both Estrella and Turf would be giving sailplane displays and space would cost $25. They decided instead to compile a list of members prepared to speak at civic clubs, schools and similar organizations where converts might be found.

The Region 9 Contest was anticipated with great pleasure, the ASA Series would take pilots to Turf, Ryan, Prescott and Estrella, the apres flying parties continued, the 5th Annual Smirnoff Derby was coming through Turf again in May and everyone was invited. However, there was one somewhat ominous change - the introduction of handicaps.

Messrs. John Baird, Al Hume and Jerry Robertson had been appointed to work out a new handicap system "for determining the ASA Contest Series Champion." The System was subsequently felt to be in need of some refining but it was decided to run it for that season to establish all the problems, and then have a big sort out afterwards. At least one third of the Club was concerned: a membership survey revealed 30.4% members were competition pilots, 29.1% were active and 40.5% were non-active.

Air Currents in April, May and June 1976 were special contest issues and contained, among other delights, the now famous interview by Bob von Hellens of Las Horvath on Thoughts and Techniques of Contest Flying.

In April, TuSC's Andy Gordon (YR) flew from Tucson to Van Horn, Texas, via Las Cruces for a straight line flight of 384.85 miles, a goal record which has not yet been toppled. In May, John Baird was reported to be conducting a one-man public relations program for soaring at Motorola and had appeared on the cover of the house magazine. Also in May, ASA was still trying to collect outstanding dues, which was a bit off to say the least!

In July the Blanik went back to Turf again in an attempt to increase usage from 10 hours in May and 7 hours in June, which wasn't sufficient to justify the investment. It was, as Paul Dickerson said, in heavy sink. Competition pilots made a safari to Winslow, to try out the facility and the area as a possible contest site and several ASA-ers flew the Region 12 Contest at California City. Bob Brooks had the greatest claim to fame for landing out in Death Valley on a dry lake accessible only by 4 wheel drive and as a result, spent the night there, and all next day as well.

"Bob and BX are fine," wrote Nancy Hume, "but he recommends all pilots carry a space blanket in their plane. It was quite cold at night in the valley and he said it helped. He had a little residue water in his wings which also came in handy.

"A change in wind direction created the problems for Bob which ultimately led to his landing on the dry lake. There were some worrisome times involved in Bob's experience. A spotter plane landed on the dry lake beside BX but returned to California City to report that the plane was there but no pilot. He had tried to walk out of Death Valley by road to no avail, but walked 11 miles. By midday, when Bob and BX were again spotted together, a tow plane was sent in to tow them out. During the tow out, the tow plane crashed, injuring the pilot though fortunately not seriously. Bob relanded on the dry lake OK. Soon after, a 4 wheel drive vehicle from the Sheriff's Department appeared and took the injured pilot to hospital. Bob remained with his plane until a 4 wheel drive vehicle arrived with his trailer about 9:00 pm.

"And then," as Nancy Hume said, "there was Kansas." Al Hume wrote up the weather (windy - 20 to 30 knots every day); pilot experiences (those who pushed hard - Wally Scott, John Brittingham - went down on days when others got back); general stuff (92 contestants, a record, and 4 ships damaged); tasks and unusual flying experiences. So it was left to Nancy to tell the world all the important things. Al finished 26th which wasn't too shabby at all.

In September that year - 1976 - the Arizona Soaring Association was celebrating its 20th Anniversary. "During its growth," wrote the Editor with justifiable pride, "ASA has encouraged and contributed to the development of pilots whose skills are equalled by few and the list of pilots continues to grow. The Association initiated a contest series many years ago which is still envied by much larger and many older similar organizations. It has conducted regional contests which were run with efficiency not evident at many national and international contests - many of the innovations developed at our regionals were subsequently adopted in other contests of both local and national caliber.

"To encourage neophytes and new members to become soaring pilots to the extent of their desires, the Association owns a Schweizer 1-26 which can be rented

213

at the rate of $2 per hour and, recently, a Blanik which rents for $5 an hour. Both of these ships may be flown cross country for pleasure, badges or in contests.

"With direct and indirect help from the membership, it has become feasible for two independent commercial exclusively glider FBO's to operate facilities on a fulltime basis within the metropolitan Phoenix area. This benefits the membership, the public at large and the sport of soaring. None of these accomplishments would have come about were it not for many many individual members, who, singly or in concert, plied their skills to contribute when and where they could."

In line with this policy, The First Annual Invitational Team Soaring Symposium and Wine Tasting Contest was held in Prescott. "The original concept of the Meet," wrote Bob Hohanshelt, "was to team an expert pilot with an inexperienced pilot in a low key contest atmosphere so that the pundit would be inclined to pass on as much knowledge as possible to the neophyte."

It was the end of the season and a major thank you went out to Arnie Jurn and his assistant, Roy Radford, for being Contest Manager/Competition Director for the entire season, which had spared pilots taking the previously non-optional day off from flying to act in that capacity and run one day's competition. All pilots were immensely grateful.

Air Currents continued to hit the streets, and in October contained the news that there were 3 new Arizona Records that year. In June Andy Gordon (YR) from Tucson established a new 200 Km. triangle in a Standard Cirrus with 51.8 mph., in July Jim Slocum, with Leslie Horvath for a passenger, had flown a Schweizer 2-32 to claim the Arizona Open and Junior Multiplace 100 Km triangle which still stands with a speed of 64.5 mph. Also in July, Las Horvath flew a Schempp-Hirth Janus from Estrella to El Mirage in California to claim the Arizona Multiplace Distance to a Goal Record of 330 miles which has not yet been toppled either. Las had taken along Wes Morris as a passenger, who subsequently claimed some records of his own.

The Awards Banquet on October 2 was special that year since it was the first time the Joseph C. Lincoln Writing Award was presented. The Award is a beautiful piece of Steuben glass engraved with a bird motif and was presented by William English of the National Soaring Museum to Jim George, the first recipient, and coincidentally, guest speaker for the evening.

Jim spoke about the ability of a person to achieve early ambitions, citing his own experiences as an example, and Liam English showed slides of the present building of the National Soaring Museum and plans for its new home. A permanent building and the extra space meant its completion would be an appropriate time for the ASA to present the proposed Joe Lincoln Memorial.

There was a winter review of club activities and it was decided the $2 per hour rate for the 1-26 was on the low side. It was accordingly increased by 100% which was rather a jump but still very reasonable. The Blanik finally began to pay its way and it was democratically decided to keep the ship at Turf *and* Estrella. "This," reported Paul Dickerson optimistically, "is easier than it sounds - we will simply move the Blanik monthly between the two."

They were still vaguely aware of their responsibilities as far as enticing new members into the fold were concerned. Accordingly, "The ASA, in co-operation with Estrella and Turf, is planning a new form of introductory activities designed to provide a taste of soaring to a relatively large number of potential soaring enthusiasts, i.e. Boy Scouts, Key Clubs, adult flying clubs, professional organizations etc." For the sum of $12.50, each member of such a group would receive a copy of Air Currents, a back issue of Soaring, a 25 minute demonstration ride in the Blanik, one month's membership of ASA with an invitation to attend a monthly meeting, and an evening introduction to soaring built around the SSA film, "The Joy of Soaring".

In 1977 a new President was appointed, Giff Smith, and Bob von Hellens nobly continued for a second year in office as Editor. The earlier plans to bring in new members seemed to be working since they welcomed no less than 8 new members in February, Ed Belt and Wes Morris among them. They subsequently reported a total of 99 members.

With spring approaching, there was suddenly a real buzz of activity. Hank Halverson promised to start work on a new high altitude window, Pardon My Squelch was promised again for April and a most satisfactory increase in time in the Blanik was reported. Turf was reported to be relocating to "brand spanking new Pleasant Valley Airport. The airport is located on the northwest corner of Carefree Highway and Lake Pleasant Road intersection," reported Jean Engelke, "only 20 minutes from Turf Airport, which is now closed." She went on to report there was "plenty of elbow room for trailer parking, campers, tenting and so on. We will soon have additional tiedowns available. Soaring has already been excellent - on our first day we were topping 12,000 feet... Come on out and see the field," she invited. "It's not every day the Valley gets a new airport!"

They weren't the only ones anticipating an exciting new season. There was a sudden surge in interest in 1-26's in 1977. It was reported that all 55 slots for the 1-26 Nationals were filled by early March, 6 of the 55 being Arizona pilots. Hank was working "very hard in trying to cut through the morass of bureaucracy, officiousness, conflicting quasi-proprietary interests and pragmatics in order to co-ordinate with and receive the blessings of the FAA, GADO, military and commercial airline interests for a high altitude window in Arizona." It was a massive undertaking and while Hank was beavering away in Arizona, the Albuquerque ARTCC suddenly approved three in the Bisbee, Huachuca areas. Admittedly they weren't in the Phoenix area, but they were in Arizona. Effective date was August 11, 1977.

Last year's handicap system had been refined and revitalized and was explained at great length by Bob Hohanshelt in an article entitled, "Scoring Doesn't Always Mean An Erotic Experience."

"Now that I have your attention," wrote Bob, "please forget about erotic experiences because what I'm going to discuss is how we will score this year's ASA Contest Series."

For the first time it was noted in Air Currents that increased insurance premiums were beginning to make themselves felt. The deductible for off field landings in Club ships was increased from $500 to $1000, partly to reduce the premium and partly as an incentive not to land out.

After last season's practice run, Wilcox was declared a most suitable venue for a soaring weekend. Unfortunately, a massive dust storm descended upon the airfield just as the pilots and crews did, not an auspicious beginning. Jerry Robertson was in charge and was "ably assisted by (amongst others) John Lincoln and Judy Ruprecht", the lady who would eventually become Mrs John Lincoln, her first mention.

Region 9 at Estrella was a success once more, and Nancy Hume wrote it up in her own inimitable way for Pardon My Squelch. Bob von Hellens attended and wrote up the 1977 1-26 Nationals, where the weather started badly and got worse.

All this contest activity obviously inspired them. In August 1977 it was reported the ASA had put in a bid to the SSA to sponsor either the Standard Class or the 15-Meter Class Nationals at Marana Air Park in 1978. Next month Bob made readers plow through a whole paragraph before they discovered what they wanted to know. "The Editor has learned that the Open Nationals will be at Chester, South Carolina, the 15-Meter Nationals will be in Ephrata, Washington, and ASA, in conjunction with the Tucson Club, will host the Standard Class Nationals in Marana, Arizona."

They held a practice run to try out the place with a contest weekend of their own in July. The facilities were beyond their wildest dreams, wrote Paul Dickerson, "with motel units, bunk houses, food service, Olympic size swimming pool complete with retrieve telephone and shade trees, a barbecue grill (deluxe!), plenty of water, weather service, a concrete ramp big enough for all three nationals to be held at the same time (literally), rest rooms at the ramp, an open-air shaded area large enough to park 16 cars and most unlikely of all, a welcome mat for ASA." The only thing that let them down that weekend was the weather but that was unusual.

Bob von Hellens had done a grand job as Editor and ended the year looking back over the previous 24 issues. He thanked all contributors for the year and was happy to make a list. No less than 37 people had provided material for 1977 alone! The Club spirit was as strong as ever. In January of 1978, Ed Belt was appointed President and Bob entered his third - and final - year as Editor. Membership had increased healthily in 1977.

Also in January, a letter from the National Soaring Museum in Elmira was published soliciting contributions from Club members. The Museum was going into the new year having raised $300,000 and in need of a further $200,000. At the bottom of this letter, its author, William D. English, Jr., Director of the Museum, had handwritten, "I still think your newsletter is the best around!" Quite an accolade and assuredly a well deserved one.

That year the upcoming 1978 Standard Class Nationals, to be hosted by ASA and TuSC at Marana near Tucson, became the ongoing preoccupation. It was revealed that, "After ASA decided to bid for the 1978 Nationals, Fred Arndt took the time and energy to go to Texas and fight for ASA's bid. Fred really carried the ball and got the bid despite stiff competition. The Tucson Soaring Club will add their expertise to help ASA make this Nationals a success."

Despite having taken on so major a commitment, the weekend contest series was well supported and roving all over the place. That year contests were flown at Estrella, Ryan, Wilcox, Marana, Wickenburg, Aguila, Winslow and Prescott.

In March, two Tucson pilots availed themselves of the new window at Bisbee. Charles Tomlinson went to 26,400 and claimed a couple of records which still stand today. Also in March the Club's 1-26 returned to Turf for the season and was unfortunately damaged in an outlanding in April. Clarke Dunbaden, aged 16, wrote up what must have been quite a frightening experience.

"On a cross country flight April 1 from Pleasant Valley Airport to northern Arizona and flying on the front of a thunderstorm to an altitude of 7,000 feet AGL over very mean territory 10 miles north of Carefree, a very strange thing happened to me. The lift from the thunderstorm diminished leaving me in terrible sink of approximately 1,000 fpm. There was nothing but sink where ever I flew. Soon, I was down to about 4,000 feet AGL and not able to make it to my alternate airport (Carefree). I headed north toward somewhat flat ground.

"Over New River still in sink and down to 2,000 feet AGL, I started looking for a place to land. There was no place that even looked half decent so I headed for a last resort - an 800 foot ridge about half mile south of New River. By the time I got there I was about 50 feet too low to get over the top and the downwash of the wind blowing over the ridge was pretty bad - I knew it would be.

"I then turned around, now going down the ridge - it just had to be one of those ridges with saguaros and rocks everywhere. I was doing about 60 mph IAS which was about 80 mph groundspeed because of a 20 mph tailwind. I then spotted a small clear area at the base of the ridge on pretty level ground. Knowing I couldn't land going this fast, I tried to make a turn into the wind. I tried to make the turn at about 15 feet above the ground and going at 60 mph, which just wasn't enough altitude and speed. My left wing tip hit the ground then came back up. This swung me around into a palo verde tree which reduced the impact with the ground pretty well. The tail of the glider was stuck straight up in the air and the nose was the only thing touching the ground. I was not hurt at all, but you would think the town of New River found gold the way the whole town ran up to see what had happened. One guy said it was the biggest thing since the shootout in the bar over a six pack.

"The DPS jet ranger helicopter came and dropped a paramedic and his assistant. They came over to see if I was alright and asked if I wanted anything. I said, "How about some water?" One of them said, "Oh, sorry, I don't have any." I finally got a drink of ice cold water about four hours later. The KOOL News Helicopter also came and took a bunch of pictures.

"I really feel bad about wrecking the 1-26, especially right before the Contest series. I'll try to get it repaired as soon as possible."

In May, a far greater tragedy struck. Jim George was in a fatal accident on Sunday May 14, 1978 in his ASW-12. According to his close friend, Carl Herold, Jim had been suffering some tiredness of late and didn't seem to be coping with the heat very well. A physical examination indicated some heart problems but nothing that warranted giving up soaring. Practicing at Hemet in preparation for the imminent Region 12 Contest at El Mirage, Jim felt tired in the 107° heat and rested a while. Feeling better, he took off and enjoyed an hour and a half flight in the ship he had owned for four years. Returning to the field, Jim flew a normal pattern and called his crew to be ready for him with the tail dolly. As he turned final at an altitude of 400 or 500 feet, the sailplane spiralled to the ground. An autopsy revealed partially blocked arteries. Jim George had written and contributed many original articles to Air Currents and Soaring magazine, and was a great contest pilot. It truly was a major loss.

It certainly seemed to be ASA's year for tragedy. They say things go in threes and these two events were promptly followed by a midair collision over the Estrellas on the first day of the Region 9 Contest (see Ch.3). Miraculously neither pilot was killed and Russell Buchanan, no longer in his yellow Nugget, and Roy Desilets, no longer in a 1-35, parachuted to safety. (Roy Desilets was subsequently declared runner up for the Lead C Award for being involved in a midair while filling the role of Safety Officer!)

A newcomer to competition flying, Chris Woods, earned himself a mention that first day by coming second in 15 meter class. "Chris flew a 10 year old Libelle H-301 and flew it consistently well to assure himself of fourth place overall, an exceptional achievement first time out," wrote Paul Cordwell.

Woody Payne spent that first night out in the desert sleeping in his cockpit. A stuck trailer had prevented his crew from reaching him that night but they got through by first light next morning and retrieved him in time to fly the next task as scheduled.

On Day 2, history was made when Gwyn Gordon won the Standard Class task. She was the first woman to win a Region 9 day's task and flew well enough to place fourth overall for the week. On Day 3 only three 15 meter pilots returned to the field. Woody Woods came in third, a fortunate man who was looking for a place to land and found a thermal instead. John Ryan took first place overall in 15 meter unrestricted class, with George Gordon second and another youngster, John Lincoln, third.

They had just about recovered from the Regionals when it was time to host the long-planned 9th U.S. Standard Nationals which began on July 4 at Marana. They began as they meant to go on and said uncompromisingly, "Those not attending the mandatory pilots' meeting the night before would be punished by having to listen to a tape recording of the briefing."

Las Horvath took first place every single day so the final result was a foregone conclusion. On Day Two, five out of seven landouts were Arizona pilots. Carson Gilmer from Texas found a thermal that gave him 1000 feet per circle lift and third place for the day. By Day three, when Las Horvath's pattern began to emerge, some pilots tried to follow him but gave up after seeing Las' plane and its shadow almost converge over unlandable terrain on several occasions.

Day Four saw 36 landouts. Gwyn Gordon sadly lost her 4th place overall when she inadvertently opened her camera before winding the film and exposed pictures of her second turnpoint. She survived the week with no landouts and only 8 other pilots (out of 47) could claim that. Chris Woods won Day 7 and Woody Woods won Day 8 in their classes, but Las Horvath was still first overall.

Fred Arndt and Dick Townsend organized things beautifully, with the aid of many helpers, including Tucson's Andy Gordon on Operations and Laz' boys imported to do the hookups. The event cost $16,037 to put on (including 6 tow planes) and the $356 surplus they made was distributed to sponsors. Nancy Hume wrote it up for Soaring magazine and Bob von Hellens for Air Currents. Later Rainco kindly donated the start board that was used at the 1978 Standard Nationals, together with other soaring equipment, and that startboard is still used for the ASA Contest Series today.

After all the excitement of a Regionals and a Nationals, it must have been nice to return to the comparative sanity of weekend contests. The August weekend was held at Winslow and was attended by Winslow's Mayor, Harry Bates, also a pilot. It was ASA's weekend for being famous: Dick Townsend and weatherman extraordinaire, Julian Martin, were interviewed for a half hour program about sailplanes for Flagstaff radio.

For almost every ASA event, Contest Headquarters had been Roy and Jessie Radford's motorhome. "When the Arizona soaring group first met the Radfords," wrote Nancy Hume in August 1978, "Jessie was struggling to rehabilitate herself from the effects of an earlier stroke. Roy bought a large motor home but Jessie was seldom seen outside, preferring to stay inside with her little dog. As the ASA Contest Season started to develop, the Radford motor home became contest headquarters. The pilot briefings, start and finish gates, all originated from this location. As time went by, Jessie started spending more time outside "where the action was". During the months that followed, Jessie was able to move in and out of her motor home unaided and spend a great deal of time outside with the gang, getting caught up in the soaring scene. She seemed to thoroughly enjoy listening to the "pilot talk" and once in a while when a wife/crew chief decided to square away something with her pilot/husband, that was like the frosting on the cake!"

In August that year, Jessie suffered a final stroke and passed away. "The soaring scene brought pleasure to Jessie," Nancy continued her obituary. "And she, in turn, brought pleasure to us. We will miss her." Husband Roy then decided to commemorate his wife and her pleasure from soaring in one of the nicest ways ever: he purchased a beautiful Indian Kachina doll in a fine glass case and named it the Jessie Radford Trophy to be presented to ASA's Woman of the Year every year.

That first year it went to Ruth Petry, who had done so much in so many capacities for ASA over so many years. The only criticism one could level at Ruth was that she did it all so quietly, with so little fanfare, she rarely was mentioned in the newsletter. Nevertheless, she was very much appreciated and the Jessie Radford Memorial Trophy Woman of the Year Award provided the perfect opportunity to show it.

There was only one tiny problem with the Awards Banquet that year. "Well, when we goof we don't fool around with a little one!" wrote Susan Belt, Social Chairman. "Sincerest apologies to all those who will have to decide between spending the evening of October 14 with 100 ASA members at the Annual Awards Banquet at the Pointe, or with 70,000 ASU fans at Sun Devil Stadium for the USC game. By the time the Social Committee became aware of the conflict, rescheduling was impossible."

The evening was not a total loss, however. They showed the film, "Dawn Flight". Wally Raisanen had won A Class, George Kulesza had won B Class and each was awarded a brand new Trophy conceived and made by the Club's favorite artist, Woody Payne. The Lead C Award was presented to John Lincoln "not only for his straight glide to Stanfield from the start gate but also for forcing Judy to abort her successful flight to return to the field for the car and trailer, the keys to which were still in John's pocket." The Estrella Award for the longest/most commendable flight of the year went to Chris Woods and the Turf Soaring School Trophy went to Paul Dickerson for continuing and outstanding service to ASA.

In October, Secretary/Treasurer Hank Halverson received a bill from the U.S. Immigration and Naturalization Service in Minnesota. Hank replied thus:

"Gentlemen: We have recently received a billing in the amount of $25 for overtime wages on Wednesday evening, September 27, 1978. Apparently your customs agent cleared an aircraft of the registration N7JP.

"Please be advised that the Arizona Soaring Association does own a Blanik model L-13 with this registration number. However, after reviewing our log books, it appears that this glider was not used that evening and we would appreciate your reviewing the customs reports that we might be advised of which member might have flown this ship from Estrella Sailport to somewhere in Canada and return.

"Apparently the thermals were rather strong, since I note that the glider must have landed some time during the evening or the extra charge would not have been required. On the off chance that someone may have counterfeited our registration number, I would appreciate confirmation that this bill is due.

"I am aware of a longer flight charged to a glider for transatlantic service into Gander, Newfoundland, so in the event one of our members was flying the ship, I won't need official confirmation, since the record is already held by someone else."

Hank further had the effrontery to sign this masterpiece, "I remain, yours sincerely..." which he undoubtedly was not.

In December Bob von Hellens graciously, and possibly after 3 years a little sadly, retired from his position as Editor. He thanked his many contributors and said modestly the information and pleasure had been solely due to the authors of the materials published.

In January 1979, when the Club was still less than 25 years old, Bob von Hellens reported that the United States Pilot Entry Priority List (the national seeding list for sailplane contest pilots) had just been published. "This list identifies and categorizes pilots who have achieved scores during the last three years in Regional or National contests above certain minimum percentages of the respective winner's score. Of the ASA members named, eight are Category 1 pilots; four are Category 2 pilots; two are Category 3 pilots and twelve are Category 4 pilots for a total of 26 national rated pilots. In addition, five non ASA pilots who regularly fly in the ASA Contest Series are in Category 4."

Bob continued, "What does this mean? Simply, it means that the caliber of competition in the ASA Contest Series is very high, probably at least equivalent to that of any Regional Contests outside Region 9. It also means that for those of you who want to hone your skills, whether for badges, long distance flights, competition or just further enjoyment of the sport, the ASA Contest Series is an excellent learning experience."

Having extricated himself from one of ASA's busiest jobs, he plunged straight into another and, moving on to greater things, became Contest Director. His friend, Bob Hohanshelt, became President, and planned to foster the relationship between ASA and TuSC. Judy Lincoln took on the role of Air Currents Editor and the position of Safety Officer and that of Vice President. She was going to have a busy year.

It turned out to be busier than even she had anticipated since "the FAA (apparently in response to the San Diego disaster) proposed a ceiling of 12,500 feet for all aircraft flying under visual flight rules (VFR). It has just been learned that this proposed rule will include an exception for gliders, which exemption will allow gliders flight under VFR conditions to 18,000 feet, provided the local ATC is advised of the presence of a glider. It is believed that this exemption is due to a great extent to the petition drafted by Judy Lincoln and which so many of you signed.

"The present deadline for comments with regard to this proposed rule is March 4, 1979. All of you are urged to submit your comments and thereby let the FAA know, again, of the unique flight regime and flight requirements of gliders. To keep your comments well co-ordinated and have them addressed to the appropriate agency, please contact Judy Lincoln who will act as co-ordinator."

In April, Estrella was celebrating ten years of operation. "I can hardly believe it was 10 years ago," wrote Las Horvath in Air Currents. "On January 15, 1969 we drove into Phoenix. Betty, the kids and I in the car, trying to see 10 feet in front of us as we drove on I-10 East to Tempe. It was raining Gila monsters and rattlesnakes - I'll never forget it!" Estrella Sailport had subsequently opened on April 1 and Las was commemorating that day with an Open House complete with 1969 prices.

While others were celebrating anniversaries and thinking about flying, Judy Lincoln was becoming more and more concerned about the antics of the FAA. She gave lots of updates on airspace problems, and in February 1979 reminded members to write their congressmen, "pointing out both the deficiencies of the proposals, and their inflationary impact on the taxpayer." That month she also added, "According to an EAA bulletin, another NPRM scheduled to come out in March will require encoding altimeters and transponders in all 166 TRSA's, making them TCA's. By 1982, transponders will have to be replaced by new radar equipment to "answer" collision radar in airliners. Also, en-route radar services will be established below 10,000 MSL in certain traffic areas - these would operate like TRSA's. Controlled airspace marches on..."

So did Judy. Never had the membership been so well informed about air space and FAA threats thereto! Phoenix was earmarked to become a TCA which threatened Estrella, Turf Soaring School at Pleasant Valley Airport, and Carefree Airport, which would, by the following year, be owned by ASA member Woody Woods. The FAA also apparently had Tucson International Airport under its beady eye, which would ultimately affect TuSC.

In May, in a piece entitled, "More Is Less" meaning "More news about less airspace", Judy exhorted members to write letters, make phone calls and generally make a lot of noise protesting to the FAA. She had, she said, "been in touch with a Mr Clay Boring (I kid you not), Chief of Tucson Radar Approach Control." By opening paragraphs with statements such as, "And now the plot thickens!", and drawing similarities between Gulliver (the FAA) and Lilliput (us), and reporting the FAA was doing the polka on general aviation, Judy Lincoln is probably the only person in the whole country that can make dry old FAA rules and plans sound humorous and interesting. Her hard work paid off and she had the satisfaction of reporting to the ASA Board that the FAA may have been somewhat surprised at the 50,000 responses it received from the EAA, AOPA and SSA. The Phoenix TCA plan had been revised to allow access to wave soaring conditions off the Estrella Mountains.

At the May Board Meeting, Wally Raisanen made a suggestion that mercifully gave us all something more cheerful to think about. "Why don't we," said Wally, "put in a bid to sponsor the 1981 SSA National Convention." We did, we won and Wally was put in charge.

For National Soaring Week that year, June 3 through 10, Judy displayed her Libelle, HA, in the main office of the First National Bank for the week, together with photographs purloined from a German soaring calendar and plenty of brochures. The most successful day was Friday when the sailplane radio and audio variometer were left on and adjusted to echo airplane jargon in the bank lobby. The most common comment all week, reported Judy, was, "I've always wanted to try that!" One optimist enquired whether she was going to raffle it off afterwards. "I managed to stammer something about the aircraft being privately owned," reported Judy, "but wondered a) how many raffle tickets could have been sold and b) at what price? Hmmmm....."

The year continued in what by then had become a well established routine. Region 9 came and went: new member Orcen Irick made himself absolutely indispensable, Roy Radford's motorhome was headquarters once more, with Contest Manager Hank Halverson as his roomie. Lee and Boots Imlay did their first window and ASA's own personal weatherman, Julian Martin, received the Longest Commute award by traveling up from Tucson every day with forecasts and data that proved 100% accurate. Char and John Detwiler dogged everyone's footsteps picking up 1,650 beverage cans as they were discarded, hoarding a cache of 75 pounds of aluminum, the proceeds of which were donated to Muscular Dystrophy.

In June Turf Soaring School was rumored to be putting in a paved strip at Pleasant Valley Airport and Don Barnard, ASA's founder, then aged 68 years old, spoke at the July monthly meeting, recollecting pioneer days and showing a film of early Club activities. Paul Dickerson, Bob Hohanshelt and Wally Raisanen started the annual Father's Day "Soar Your Arse Off Regatta". (See Ch.7)

In July, it was reported that the Tucson Club was also having problems with the FAA. TuSC members also visited Mr Boring, a meeting requested because of several near misses between gliders and other aircraft in the vicinity of Ryan Field. The result of the meeting was that TuSC had to telephone ATIS and advise them every time they began flying for the day, and again when it finished. They also agreed on Kinney Road as the dividing line between TuSC on the southwest side and "them" on the northeast side.

Another fun note was added at the end: "Starting mid-July, the jets from D.M. will begin training flights in the vicinity of Marana. They will operate during daylight, five days a week, below 8500 feet altitude, within a 20 mile radius of the field."

ASA's indefatigable Editor, Judy Lincoln, followed up the following month with, "For A Real Good Time, Dial (202) 426 3656." She was calling Washington monthly, and having discovered a Mr Potts in William Broadwater's office last month, and a Mr Borden there this month, she was seriously pondering the reality and existence of Mr Broadwater.

It was appropriate to recall Derek van Dyke's Editorial from November 1959. He had said then, "Best beloved, it is no longer a matter of shrinking airspace; it has done shrunk." Now it had done shrunk some more.

The death of Jean Doty was announced in September. Jean had been newsletter editor for several years and had compiled for SSA a comprehensive index to Soaring magazine encompassing 305 issues from 1937 to 1971, an effort that took six years to complete. It had been a formidable but valuable task. Jean Doty's other claim to fame was that she was the first woman in ASA to earn a Silver C.

Speaking of formidable tasks, Bob von Hellens then took on re-writing the Club's bylaws and they were published in their entirety in the November issue. The work took several months to complete.

On a lighter note, ASA was still guiltily and sporadically spreading the word and had been invited to attend two breakfast programs in October and November, complete with sailplane on display. Both events were handled by Judy Lincoln, who, on her own admission, "was never one to turn down a free breakfast. (No cooking, no dishes)."

In November, it was reported three ASA members had taken State records in August - Feminine Absolute Altitude & Altitude Gain by Char Detwiler, Senior Speed around a 100 km triangle by Jim Fox in a Pik 20B at 73.5 mph which still stands, and Feminine Speed around a 100 km triangle by Judy Ruprecht at 43.8 mph in a H-301 Libelle. Judy Ruprecht and Judy Lincoln were one and the same and her record stood until 1987 when Elaine Cutri toppled it by flying the 100 Km triangle at 63 mph, also in an H301 Libelle.

Judging from Judy Lincoln's Editorial in December, entrants in the ASA Weekend Contest Series were at an all time low. There had been one weekend that season, she said, when ground personnel exceeded contestants! It was a time to look inward and reflect on the past, prepare for the future. Bob von Hellens, having completed the Club Bylaws and presumably finding himself with nothing to do, turned his attention to "ASA Long Term Goals and Structure of ASA Contest Activities". The piece was designed to permit the Old Masters the stimulating competition they craved while encouraging novices and neophytes to join in the fun.

In the same issue, John Baird put forward proposals in which pilots did all the work so that every person who could come up with a glider could fly the contest. "This sounds like a good objective," wrote John, "since on some days this season, the number of contestants was less than that which would make a competitive atmosphere for those flying, let alone a departure and arrival spectacle for those on the ground." The piece was reviewed, reported Mrs Lincoln naughtily, "by John (Sinkin') Lincoln also known as IF... and when..."

By the 1980's, the Club seemed to have settled into a pleasant routine comprising the Contest Series, Region 9, various Regionals and Nationals elsewhere, the Awards Banquet and the Annual Winter Party held at the Hume's home. There wasn't too much happening of major historical importance.

In 1980, Judy Lincoln took on the role of President, continued as newsletter editor and continued the fight with the FAA on all fronts. Wayne Roberts relieved her as Safety Officer. Chuck Doty became Treasurer and was amazed to receive, along with the Treasurer's bundles, a tired looking filing cabinet - the very same one he had purchased 15 years previously.

Judy's first order of business was a new game plan for the Club aircraft. She was determined they would be operated to break even. The Blanik was still at Estrella and the 1-26 suffered hail damage and was down for repairs at Turf. It apparently took some time. Not until April was it reported the ship would be ready to fly "as soon as we receive the blasted hinge pins from Schweizer." In January, Estrella started a new ground school and Turf reported Roy Coulliette had left for New Jersey to collect another 2-33 trainer, bringing their existing fleet up to four 2-33's, a 2-32, a Blanik, a 1-35 and two 1-26's.

1980 was the Year of the Flood and both FBO's became temporarily inaccessible. In January they sent out a dove but it was not announced until February that the waters had receded from the land and Estrella and Turf could finally be reached without too much detour. The Phoenix TCA question reared its ugly head once more, having been on the back burner for some months.

Region 9 also came under Judy's scrutiny and by March there were only a few slots left available. The Imlays were to do the window (it was now a tradition) and Bill Kolmeyer's name came up again and again. He was always just where he was needed.

It was also time to get down to some serious planning for the 1981 SSA National Convention. The SSA had sent Wally Raisanen a check for $1,000 to open his Convention Fund but it obviously wasn't enough. A mass Garage Sale/Auction/

Beer Bust was arranged. Straight donations of $25 were also solicited but Wally was really after "your old compass, compensator, instruments, battery, water bags, etc." Estrella donated a glider ride certificate, Rainco a whole passel of good instruments "and stuff," and various pilots gave all kinds of "good junque". "Almost anything cheerfully accepted," wrote Wally. "No donation too small (or too big)." It was to be the auction of the century - and it was! They made $1,000.

In April the monthly Club meeting site was moved to the Sheraton Inn at Skyharbor Airport and would continue there until February, 1988. And that May, the soaring Mom's missed out on Mother's Day, as usual. John Lincoln and Bob Mitchell were teased by Mother Nature out to the Diamond Mine, marked by a super lennie. "When John finally did call his Mom that evening," reported Judy, "she had already gone to sleep. Somewhere along the line he'd lost the card he planned to give to me... but, by Gawd, he had his Diamond altitude! One must have one's priorities straight."

Betty Horvath was probably thinking the same thing. Las Horvath had abandoned her and the Mother's Day party she was planning and flown off in search of a National Distance Record in a multiplace. 563 miles later he found it at Pueblo, Co. (See Ch.6). Billy Baird won the party's Guess-where-Las-Is pool, all 97 cents of it.

That season things were buzzing. ASA member Jerry Robertson won the Marfa Nationals 15 meter class. TuSC was asked to move from Ryan, the search was on for pastures new. And Judy discovered that after all her updates, directives, beseeching and pleadings to ASA members to write and protest, the FAA had received just *forty* letters. Judy was incensed! She ranted and raved at the membership - not without justification. "It is in extremely poor taste for me," she wrote, "either as Editor of this chronicle or as President of this Association, to rant and rave at the membership. Lacking taste, then, rant and rave I shall!

"For more than a year, Air Currents has carried TCA updates nearly every month. Last month, a special mailing went out to the membership, calling for response to the FAA's formal docket. Perhaps all this attention has made you jaded or complacent... Oh, here's the token TCA map for the umpteenth time... Perhaps the articles have been too long, what with background information and options for response; perhaps you've been discouraged by the lists of addresses..." It is to be hoped the membership felt suitably chastened and increased their letter writing habits accordingly.

With perfect timing, TuSC's plight highlighted every point Judy made. "The Tucson Airport Authority has requested the Tucson Soaring Club to discontinue operations at Ryan Field by December 1, 1980," it was reported in TuSC's newsletter, Thermal. "One reason for this request is that the Instrument Landing System (ILS) now being installed for runway 06 will be ready for operation at that time, and it will require a left hand traffic pattern. This FAA requirement will result in traffic over the north side of the field, presently designated for gliders only.

"TAA has also issued a NOTAM closing the first 1000 feet of the west end of our south runway. Construction of the ILS antenna and housing has started near the end of the runway. This event will affect operations for the remainder of our time at Ryan..."

TuSC members John Donatelli, Loring Green and Roger Wolf were actively seeking a viable alternative.

This was not the only cause of Tucson's troubles. On July 16, 1980 everybody's favorite weatherman, Julian Martin, died instantly in a tow accident at Ryan Field. "He was a familiar figure to one and all, with his clip-board cradling every scrap of weather information he could come by. Julian Martin presented rather a low profile in his khaki pants, soaring T-shirt, and crumpled hat; yet his was the profile every Regional pilot, every Marana competitor, and members of both ASA and TuSC came to associate with "The Weather Man." He was always there at the pilots' meeting and giving weather updates on the line; Julian and his reams of paper, lapse rates, temperature trends, winds aloft, forecasts for the valleys, forecasts for the hills. He was truly more important than the service he provided, for Julian was not just "The Weather Man", he was an institution." He was one of us. He had always been there, and now he wasn't any more.

That year the "new" membership roster came out in September, ("Better late than never" said the editor philosophically), Club meeting nights were changed from Mondays to Tuesdays and the October Awards Banquet was anticipated once more. Most important of all, plans for the 1981 SSA National Convention were going well. Wally had lined up some excellent speakers, including Gren Seibels, George Worthington, Bill Ivans, Dick Schreder, Eric Greenwell, Ed Byars, and, from our own ranks, Judy Lincoln, Don Santee and Fred Arndt. Jeri Raisanen and Maggie Alton had arranged some terrific western flavored side trips including Indian arts, Mexican tastes, Wild West party and Dinner at the Ron Nix Movie Set Ranch, Sedona Bus tour, Grand Canyon, and Nogales, Mexico flight tours, and, as a grand finale, the Estrella Bus Trip and lunch for Sunday flight operations!

All was going well, there was a detailed Schedule taking up almost two pages, the event was bound to be a success and January 13 through 17 was felt to be just around the corner.

In November Chuck Doty passed away, just a year after his wife Jean, and would be much missed. He always meant to go out and fall in love with soaring again but apparently he never quite got around to it. "It's ironic that Chuck had given so freely of his time and skills," wrote the author of the In Memoriam column in Air Currents, "making it possible for everyone else to fly, but it was typical of him too, to feel the need to get things done even if it meant his own flying had to wait... The soaring Chuck would have done when he had the time to fall in love again will now be done by us."

And fly they did, with a vengeance. In October more State records were announced, earned by Andy Gordon, Wayne Roberts, John Detwiler, Dave Jones, Las Horvath and Jim Nance.

In December, Judy was soliciting volunteers for Treasurer and Editor. Her farewell as Editor was a big thick January 1981 issue Special SSA Convention edition. It was a program and newsletter combined and distributed to visitors at the Convention.

In February, the Convention was voted a great success, everyone was duly thanked for their massive efforts, and then the Club seemed to suffer from anticlimax. Harry Alton became President, Wayne Roberts became Newsletter Editor and a letter from Pat Martin, Julian's widow, appeared, referring to the fact that her late husband's fatal accident had been caused by taking off with disconnected ailerons - a pilot error - and strongly suggesting that every person associated with soaring should take responsibility to encourage every pilot to do positive checks.

It was a sober start to the new year and the somber mood was not helped when the Club Blanik was written off in a soaring accident in March. "Juliet, our Club Blanik, went West last Sunday," wrote (I think) Wayne Roberts in the March Air Currents. "I saw her die. Her pilot made a low pattern, then failed to deploy spoilers to accomplish the landing. After floating past midfield, from an altitude estimated at no more than 50 feet, the pilot sealed her fate by attempting a 180° turn to a downwind landing. As the turn began, there was over 2,500 feet of clearway remaining ahead of the aircraft! When about 160° of turn had been completed, the nose dropped and the left wing hit the ground. The nose, aft fuselage and right wing followed in rapid sequence. To the last, Juliet protected her passenger and pilot by absorbing energy through crash damage. The passenger in the front seat was apparently unhurt. I have no report on the results of the pilot's back X-rays. Sic Transit, Juliet."

Under the heading of Safety, an unnamed contributor wrote, "I have just received my annual safety bill from Wyatt International. I don't think I can afford many more years of the present trend, and I collected more than I paid in last year... I had no airplane to fly most of last summer, and my ship log carries some pretty embarrassing items for any prospective buyer to read. And now we hit them again for the price of a Blanik!

"Friends, what we are doing is just not working. Sailplanes are not automobiles. Perhaps we would feel a bit more protective of them if we considered problems of a few years ago in soaring, to wit: To even sample the joys of soaring, a person spent hours and hours for months and months building the darn thing in the first place, and more hours to maintain it. If you crashed it and were lucky enough to escape, then you considered at length if you really wanted to do it all over again! It seems we get neither sadder nor wiser with our modern methods."

Despite the almost tragic air of desperation, and even a real dearth of contributors to Air Currents, which sort of added insult to injury, Region 9 was scheduled and looked forward to, the ASA series began and Skip Jackson was doing weather. In April 1981 an excellent Editorial appeared written by Wayne Roberts about the choices to be made regarding Club equipment. He pointed out that, compared to many other Clubs, ASA was in an enviable position and then continued, "You can pay for it or work for it, but flying is expensive either way. We have chosen to pay for it, but recent events point out that we also follow the normal trend, out of sight, out of mind, and we are not personally involved in any aspect of the Club operation to any great degree. This convenience perhaps has led to lax enforcement of procedures."

Losing the Blanik had undoubtedly cast a pall over the Club for a while and the concern was expressed that we might not be able to get *any* insurance in the future. A survey was conducted to discover the Club's wishes regarding replacement. Twenty five members responded, about a hundred did not, which loaned considerable color to suggestions of apathy. It was even suggested that the 1-26 and a replacement Blanik (or the insurance money from the old one) be donated/granted to non-owners so they could form their own independent Club and not be part of ASA at all. Don Barnard would have been horrified!

It was gloomily reported that a tornado had destroyed 4 ships and damaged 9 others at Chester, SC.; at Elmira there had been a collision between an ASW 19 and a pedestrian, and Wyatt & Taylor were considering another rate increase.

"Given our current losses," read Air Currents, "a rate increase is probably the kindest thing we can hope for."

However, in May a new note of optimism crept in. Contest flying cheered them up and a joint meet with TuSC - still at Ryan - cheered them even further. By the time they'd flown the Region 9 Contest in May morale was back to normal. Bob Mitchell won the Open Class in a Jantar, Wally Raisanen won Standard Class in a Cirrus and Mike Adams won 15 meter class in his ASW-20. According to Bill Ordway, the weather was not especially co-operative to begin with, with Day One resembling the Los Angeles basin with high fog and Day Two with a wind blowing like gangbusters out of the west which made just getting started tough.

On Day Two, John Lincoln was just climbing out of trouble over Sun City when his radio crackled, "Call the hospital, IF!" He and Judy were expecting a second crew member any minute so John finished his climb (first things first) and streaked over to Deer Valley to call the hospital. This was IF but not when - false alarm! Audra Lincoln did not put in an appearance until next day.

In July, ASA-ers were invited to fly at a new field - Carefree Airport had been purchased by ASA member Woody Woods and he invited fellow members to fly there as his guests by prior arrangement, with a Cessna 185 for towing. Estrella was offering flights at a discount, and Wayne Roberts made a Vulgar Downwind Dash to Salt Flats, Texas, taking 432 minutes to fly 436 miles. "Wally Raisanen got by for only a pair of diamond earrings," wrote Wayne. "I had to buy new tires and a new exhaust system for Spike."

1981 was a year in which ASA-ers again graduated beyond Regional contests and flexed their wings in more ways than one. A contingent of ASA-ers flew the sixth U.S. 15 meter Nationals in July at Minden, Nevada. Holighaus, Gimmey and Leffler took the top three places but ASA's Chris Woods took 5th place in an ASW 20, and other ASA-ers were Al Hume in 14th place, Wayne Roberts in his self-confessed "dated" Pik was 21st. John Baird in a Mini Nimbus, Ed Belt, Paul Dickerson in a Pik and Bob von Hellens in an LS-3 also competed. Every pilot in the top ten places had landed out at least once which prompted Wayne Roberts to write, "Bad luck will equalize and talent will tell."

Wally Raisanen, Pete Williams and Andy Gordon flew the 12th Standard Nationals at Hobbs that year too. The event began with 61 pilots and completed with 55. Wally finished 39th, Pete 43rd and Andy Gordon 46th. It was a Nationals and there were some big names in the top ten, four of whom landed out on Day 7 which offered some solace to lesser mortals. "Wally had a heartbreaker landing just short of the field that day," wrote our intrepid reporter, Pete Williams, "and Andy Gordon's canopy blew open shortly after take off. He grabbed the handle, held on and executed a smooth 180° turn at 200 feet, landing downwind with no speed brakes and a full load of H_2O. Excellent flying, Andy!"

In addition, we were represented at the 1-26 Nationals at Colorado Springs by Skip Jackson who wrote up the experience and sub-titled it, "I Came Here To Be Rained On." Skip finished a happy 16th.

At year end, President Harry Alton had the pleasant task of announcing the Club had purchased a replacement two seat Blanik. "It may already be available for you to fly," he wrote. "It is our hope you will use it and enjoy it often. It is a 1977 model, well equipped with radio, dual oxygen and full dual instrumentation. It has less than 500 hours total time." (ASA still flies and enjoys this Blanik in 1988!)

In 1982, ASA got busy! There was almost a bustle in the air. Air Currents resurfaced under the auspices of Pete Williams. He gave it a fine new format and a different color for each month of the year. Pete was soliciting Letters to the Editor and rounding up guest editors, contributors, and even galvanized Nancy Hume into action. She rashly promised a Pardon My Squelch column for late summer or early fall.

In January, Clay Hartman presented a slide/talk show of ASA soaring activities in the Valley vintage 1955. This inspired the Board to approve the production of a 5-6 minute slide show to promote soaring and seek ASA/SSA memberships. "This show will be available for use by the membership to be shown at malls, meetings and other gatherings where there is a need to let the general public know more about soaring activities in Arizona." Pete Williams put out a call for 35 mm slides and worked hard on the project which was completed in July.

Bob Mitchell, the 1982 President, in a somewhat tardy beginning-of-the-year address, ventured onto hallowed ground and took members to task about the direction the Club was taking.

"Since joining ASA three years ago," he wrote, "I have found it to be very heavily oriented toward individuals who own sailplanes... On the whole, orientation toward ownership is a very good thing but unfortunately I have on occasion observed an attitude bordering on contempt for those who have not as yet been able to go charging about the sky in the latest thing from Germany.

"I find this disturbing because such an attitude is indicative of severe myopia. I have found a manifestation of this attitude in the opposition to ASA owning sailplanes for general membership use. I do not imply that all opposed stand guilty - many good points regarding liability and pilot qualifications have been raised and are being investigated and implemented." Bob went on to weigh the advantages and disadvantages of the situation and ended on an admonitory note. "I hope that this interplay will be encouraged and perhaps we will begin to see ourselves as one organization." These animadversions seemed to have hit home.

In April, Wally Raisanen went to the SSA Convention in Houston and contributed "a highly biased and personal account of what happened". He in fact made some worthwhile observations. "Somewhat sparse attendance, (probably a function of sparse advertising, since they only got half an inch of Carl Herold's editorial in the issue preceding the convention, and no display ads!) of both attendees and exhibitors marred an otherwise interesting show. Attendees appreciated the star studded program and fine facilities. The exhibits showed little new... this being the fourth show I have attended, I started to recognize some of the regulars. The German designers show up only in even numbered years. The hot sticks of the racing scene only show up if they're paid to come, and/or speak. The SSA functionaries all show, and work really hard at SSA business. The major equipment purveyors are faithful but their ranks are thinning so the exhibits are slowly getting smaller and smaller. I think this event is suffering from over exposure and would be better if it were only held every two years, instead of annually."

It was summertime and the 1982 season was upon us with a vengeance. Marana was rumored as a possible site for the 1983 Open and/or 15 meter Nationals, the 1983 Internationals were moved from Argentina to Hobbs, New Mexico because the Argentineans suddenly discovered themselves to be at war with Britain, the 5 to 6 minute talking slide show was ready, the Club 1-26, which had been out of commission for several months, was back in the air, the ASA contest series was progressing as God intended and Region 9 took place. All was right with the world.

Region 9 was presumably as enjoyable as ever that year, although entry was down with just 8 in Standard class and fifteen in 15 meter class, and nobody wrote up the event for Air Currents. Wally Raisanen took third place in Standard Class, Tucson's Andy Gordon was 5th and Bob Hohanshelt was 7th. In 15 meter class, Al Hume took 3rd, Bob von Hellens was 6th, with John Baird 8th.

In July President Bob Mitchell was "out of town seeking greener ($) pastures" and Vice President Jean Paul Frignac was attempting to pour oil on troubled waters. ASA's wealthier members were still extremely concerned about the liability of owning two Club ships and understandably did not wish to be sued by the relatives of anyone who came to grief in either one of them. Jean Paul investigated the matter and declared "the incorporated status of ASA is intended to protect its members and its officers against liability claims arising from the actions of other club members.

"The officers possibly could be held liable if they had condoned some poor maintenance or operational practice which, in turn, could be shown to have contributed to causing an accident. Present insurance covers the Club as well as qualified pilots operating the club ships for a maximum liability (single limit bodily injury and property damage liability) of some $1M." Having reassured everyone very nicely, Jean Paul ended on a doubtful note. "$1.5M might be preferable."

He also covered maintenance practices, pilot eligibility and the fact that a liability disclaimer was being prepared for non-club members flying as Blanik passengers. Separate accounting books were also to be introduced for each ship, and a "1-26 Club" and a "Blanik Club" were to be set up immediately.

In August the big news was that Marana had finally been confirmed as the site for the 1983 Open Class Nationals and another big event, for two members anyway, was the Heber City Safari. "Steve Fahrner piloted his Standard Astir over 650 miles in 3 flights toward Heber City to win the most air miles award. Compiled with Peter Williams' 562 total air miles, the Arizona contingent amassed over 1200 air miles. Steve's Route: Ryan to Turf; Turf to Boulder City, Nev.; Boulder City to Nephi, Utah, 56 miles short of Heber City. There were between 40 and 50 participants flying out of the lush green Heber Valley ringed with 12,000 foot snowcapped peaks."

During the event, on Wednesday July 14, a 2-32 was flown from Heber City to Salt Lake City carrying U.S. mail commemorative postcards to celebrate the 50th Anniversary of soaring.

That month, Bob Hurni gave himself a nasty fright by having his altimeter set at the wrong altitude. He got into trouble with his final glide and managed a landing that only just avoided being a controlled crash. "Before unbuckling from the ship at the end of the rollout," confessed Bob, "I checked the altimeter. It indicated 2300 MSL. The local field elevation is 1275 MSL!" Having survived that flight in a 2-33, Bob returned to his first love, the 1-26, and flew the 1-26 Western Regionals at Rabbit Dry Lake in California. The weather was unpredictable to say the least, with the winds and blowing dust exclusive to desert dry lakes, and a great time was had by all.

Wally Raisanen was also in California, flying the Standard Class Nationals at El Mirage, although no ASA names featured in the top ten of the results list that year. In October, Bob von Hellens drove 2,433 miles to fly the Canadian Nationals and was greeted as a celebrity for being the only foreigner there. Bob finished 7th overall and ended up saying, "I have never before flown so low, so slowly, for so long but I will go back any time I can... It was the most enjoyable contest I've ever attended."

He returned home to discover the results of the ASA series had been published and he had won A Class! Paul Dickerson took second place, followed by John Baird in 3rd and Al Hume 4th. Class B was won by Wes Morris, Bob Hurni was 2nd and Skip Jackson took third.

At the end of that season, they all went wildly social. There was a summer party at the Lincoln's domicile, a hayride was arranged at Pointe Tapatio Stables and the date for the Awards Banquet was discovered to be so near Halloween, everyone was instructed to masquerade as their favorite aviation person, place or thing. This was later declared optional by the Board but many people entered into the spirit of thing, notably Mark Arndt as Superman, Mary Ann Ardnt as the Wicked Witch, Al Hume appeared as the Patron Saint of Soaring and his wife, Nancy, was the Princess of Lift. "In the final analysis it was a neat, trim and very orange wind sock that fluttered away with the prize - our very own Judy Lincoln."

The ASA Weekend Contest Series as presented in the January/February 1983 newsletter, seemed as if it might be a somewhat desultory affair. Pilots were asked to work 2 days, the window person was expected to do the weather and, except for the Tucson weekend - at a site to be announced - all meets would be at Estrella. Nobody minded too much, just so long as they got to fly. Even the newsletter was reduced to once-every-two-months instead of monthly. Were ASA members suffering from burnout?

Estrella purchased a new motor glider and Jim Dean and Mike Garcia flew the self-launching Grob 109 through some pretty dire weather from Cincinnati to the sailport. Jim refused to give a full PIREP (Pilot's Report), however, because, "Too many people read that kind of thing, form a prejudiced impression about the airplane and go round talking like someone who helped design it and they haven't even seen the thing." Jim insisted, "You owe it to yourself to do more than just read about this new generation of sailplane. Give Estrella a call and actually fly it."

With effect from February 1, 1983, TuSC was firmly and finally removed from Ryan Field and soaring operations there were terminated. The Tucson Airport Authority acknowledged materials from SSA's Airport Utilization Committee with a terse comment, "We hope you will understand our position and that you do not force Tucson Airport Authority to adopt an adversary position." TuSC temporarily relocated to La Cholla Airport and Taylor Field, hosted a local level contest weekend at Marana (Pinal) and kept its collective fingers crossed that tentative plans for a permanent airfield nearby would materialize.

Having lost Ryan for ever, soaring pilots were then told Scottsdale Municipal Airport prohibited glider landings too. "The attitude was," reported Judy, "Well, it might be the controllers' airspace, but it's *our* asphalt!"

Airspace was further eroded that month around Coolidge and Florence because the Grunts were lobbin' joes. President Wayne Roberts, a military man, translated this to mean army guys were lobbing projectiles, shortened to projoes shortened to joes. "Superior is not a good turnpoint," wrote Wayne, "while the Army National Guard is conducting live firing exercises." The exercises would take place in April, May, July and August, which coincided nicely with the soaring season.

As if all this was not enough, a revised FAR now required a log book entry for both rigging and de-rigging gliders!

By March TuSC's crossed fingers had worked and they officially had "a new base of operations located about 5 miles south of Pinal Airpark (Marana) at an old military landing square." This was great news indeed and credit for finding it and obtaining access goes to Irv Rubenstein. The auxiliary field was called El Tiro, which Andy Gordon claimed meant "mineshaft" in Spanish and concedes that Ryan gave the Tucson Club just that when they were forced to move.

TuSC's new site would never be mentioned in the future without someone noting it was Arizona's third largest airfield in terms of runway length, the first being Skyharbor and the second being Tucson International. The gliderport comprised 182 acres of Bureau of Land Management land, 11 miles west of Marana. There were 5 miles of runways, 1300 feet of which were paved. It was a gem indeed.

The first ASA Weekend Series event in April did not get off to an auspicious beginning when all of B Class launched and promptly landed again. However, by May, the 1983 Open Nationals at Marana had attracted 29 entries and some gratifyingly familiar names were among the 45 registered to fly Region 9.

"A genuine water shortage for use as ballast is expected at Estrella," wrote the indefatigable Mrs Lincoln. "Contestants are encouraged to bring their own ballast water to the field daily, if possible." Other arrangements were also mooted and Judy ended with a great suggestion. "On an average day, over 2,000 gallons of water (16,400 lbs.) could be dumped on final glide into Estrella. Perhaps we could work out a sprinkling fee arrangement with the local farmers and recoup some costs!"

The water shortage didn't slow them down a whole lot. "Some called it a mini-Nationals as 44 pilots assembled... The weather was hot at well over 100° for 3 out of 5 days. Hot blustery thermal-bending winds buffeted the contestants for 3 days. The last 2 were relatively calm but the thermals were not strong and a long way apart. No mishaps. No damage. All in all a well run, safe contest." Woody Woods took 2nd place in Open Class and Chris Woods took 6th. In Standard Class, Wally Raisanen took 1st, Bob Hohanshelt came 5th and Andy Gordon took 9th. In 15 meter, no ASA-er appeared in the top five but John Baird came 6th, Pete Williams was 8th and Paul Dickerson came 10th, so we were well represented in the top 10 if not the top 5. There was stiff competition in all classes.

The same could be said of the 1983 Open Nationals at Marana but ASA still was well represented with one of the Woods in 5th place (the list doesn't show whether it was father or son!), and Las Horvath, flying a 15 meter ship, was 13th out of 33 contestants.

As the Contest Series ended that year, at the Club's September meeting members voted to appoint a Committee to study the contest rules and suggest possible changes. The event had become so well supported and popular, it was becoming unwieldy and too much for one Contest Director to manage unaided. Paul Dickerson agreed to chair the Committee and John Lincoln was to work with him.

In retrospect, 1983 seems to have been a somewhat flat affair. Oh, everyone enjoyed the flying and the friendships, the competition and the camaraderie, but no one had contributed anything to the newsletter, other than various Board members in an official capacity, and apart from the Open Nationals, no one seemed to have done anything major about anything. As such, it turned out to be something of a catalyst and made us look inward instead of upward.

231

At the beginning of 1984, ASA seems to have had a collective attack of bad conscience. Bob Hohanshelt took on the job of President once more and Judy Lincoln took on the role of Secretary and even managed to make dull boring Minutes of Meetings lighthearted and interesting to read. After 2 years as publisher, Pete Williams said he would continue - with assistance - so Jane Jackson helped by soliciting articles.

At the February meeting of the new Board, Paul Dickerson moved that ASA develop a membership plan to encourage new members, likely prospects be targeted, and existing members be encouraged "to bring their non-soaring friends into the sport, on the theory that friends of a feather should fly together. (Pun intended)!" finished Judy defiantly.

The Board meeting ended with a general discussion of promoting ASA and soaring. Paul Dickerson closed with a suggestion we identify, "What has changed? Where is the next generation of soaring pilots?" Thereafter, "Mrs Lincoln noted that Dorothy Hohanshelt had just put the Lincoln contingent of future soaring pilots to bed and there being no other business the meeting was adjourned at 9:40 pm."

This new mood of dynamism was further augmented by the advent of several new members. The February meeting was enlivened by "humorous antidotes" from crews about their experiences while chasing wayward pilots, and pilots were promised the opportunity to tell their side of things later on. Air Currents became more "newsy" again, and contained such reports as El Tiro's new hangar was complete and now housed the Club tow planes, just in time since their Ryan hangar was condemned some 3 months ago when one of the main roof beams gave way. Their new asphalt runway was also completed and the first take off took place February 18, 1984. "Now," continued Andy Gordon, "if we had the Club house completed, a power line and water pipe, we'd be all set... come down for a visit."

ASA was not the only soaring group concerned about the need to recruit new members. SSA began a new recruitment program offering to pay recruiters a dollar for each new recruit gathered into the fold. It is doubtful if ASA's coffers swelled very much as a result of this largesse but it drew attention to the problem.

As discussed at the end of 1983, new contest rules were introduced for the Series in 1984. "Briefly, there will be two classes racing this year: Class A and Sports Class. Sports Class will be open to all pilots regardless of experience or equipment. Class A will be as before. Sports Class will be handled along the lines of Herold '81 handicapping with slight changes." There would be a 5,000 foot start gate, everybody had to work one day (instead of two as last year) and scoring was on best of 9 days, which allowed for days lost working the contest, due to weather or simply not flying at optimum personal levels!

On Labor Day weekend, the very first 3 day event was held at El Tiro. Unfortunately, it was not an auspicious beginning since the weather was most uncooperative. "If anyone was at Ryan after 3.00 pm," reported Bob Hurni, "he got very wet indeed." Day Two was soon summed up: "No thermals, no contest," but by Day 3 the weather had remembered what was expected of it in Arizona and was conforming obligingly.

Bob Hurni was getting in a lot of soaring and a lot of writing that year. He and Gary Beaver, Rohn Brown and Russ McAnerny flew the 1-26 Nationals and Bob wrote up the event, divulging at the same time that Gary Beaver had driven safely the many miles to Hobbs, New Mexico, only to wipe the tail off his trailered 1-26 as he drove under the hotel awning.

In September, Soarathon '84 was held in aid of the Cancer Society. It had been arranged for June but "rains of almost biblical proportions" meant it was postponed. Members raised money by having friends and colleagues pledge so many cents per mile distance or foot of altitude. Ken Hartzler won a Grob aerobatic flight at Estrella and three 3,000 foot tows at Turf for the highest dollar amount in pledges. The event raised a total of $1,545.69 and ASA-ers were well pleased with themselves.

At season's end they reviewed the ASA Weekend Contest Series and could do so with some satisfaction. "25 pilots flew more than 14,600 miles. Their ships ranged from state of the art Ventus' and ASW-20's to 1-26's. We finally got out of the valley and into the Prescott highlands. Some of us got to see the Grand Canyon and San Francisco Peaks in addition to the familiar Phoenix-Tucson countryside. We spent two weekends at El Tiro and enjoyed the fruits of their labor on the new club house and deck... All in all the season turned out very nicely, nobody was injured, only one ship damaged (not severely) in all the miles flown. The contest went down to the wire, three possible winners on the last day. That makes for a good season with the contest in doubt to the last."

When the figuring was finally done, Class A had been won by Bob von Hellens (1X) with Wally Raisanen (2E) second and Paul Dickerson (19) third. In Sport Class, Bob Hurni excelled himself and came first, Kevin Harrenstein was second and Gary Beaver third.

Although the season had gone well, there was a new threat building on the horizon. "At the October 29 CIVV meeting in Europe, a formal proposal is expected to define a new competitive class," reported Judy Lincoln. "The current CIVV recognized classes of Standard, 15 Meter and Open Class may be altered somewhat if foreign manufacturers and European representatives have their way. For sometime, the rumor mill has been grinding away with word of a 17 meter class... more recently, a new 18 meter class has been the subject of much speculation."

This may be all very well for the Europeans, but the Americans weren't having any of that! Wally Raisanen responded with a letter to Bill Ivans that uncompromisingly summed up the situation and put his finger right on the mark.

"...I believe the present activity in promotion of a new class, 17 meter, 18 meter or whatever, is motivated purely by the manufacturers to create a new market. There is no corresponding benefit to the pilots that I am aware of. Canceling any of the existing classes to make room for a new class of no discernible advantage in performance, cost or safety, makes no sense at all.

"I believe that if the Europeans succeed in creating a new class, it will dilute the already thin supply of pilots in the Open Class, and that if the 15 meter racing class is abolished, a new racing organization for the disenfranchised 15 meter competitors will be organized in the U.S., to the great disadvantage of the SSA and CIVV.

"I strongly urge you to oppose creation of a new class, in the interest of protecting the investment thousands of SSA members have made in existing sailplane designs. I also strongly urge you to oppose cancellation of any existing class, for the same reason." Strong stuff. The specter of a 17 or 18 meter class remains today.

Sure as fate, the Awards Banquet rolled round again. Gary Beaver won the Lead C Award for losing his tail in a motel and Wally Raisanen walked away with two trophies - the Soar Your Ass Off contest of his own creation and the Estrella

Trophy which carried with it a prize of $500. "Wally donated the $500 prize to ASA's Board of Directors with the stipulation that it be used to further cross country soaring."

Now all they had to do was make it through the dark dull days of winter until the next season! However, winters in Arizona aren't always dull or dark, and by January they were off to a flying start with the Region 9 Annual Contest bid and paid for, (the sanction deposit anyway), and a Contest Director all arranged - Bill Ordway.

Even if they couldn't fly as much as their little hearts desired, no one could stop them talking, thinking and writing about it. And then, on the very last page of the February Air Currents, Good Grief! What's this??? Pardon My Squelch!

Irreverent as ever, in among the usual gossip and news was the revelation that Al Hume had inadvertently "fallen asleep at the last Board Meeting and was thereby elected President". This meant his good lady wife was automatically Social Chairman for the year and Mrs Hume had burst into print with a long list of the people to whom she would be delegating all social responsibilities for 1985.

Bob Hurni's recent writings had not gone unnoticed in high places and he received the consummate honor of being made Editor of the 1-26 Association Newsletter. The Board was in sore need of a Safety Chairman and also had gaps in its list of officers under Weather, Technical and Equipment. The Pete Williams/Jane Jackson team was continuing yet again with the newsletter.

To celebrate the upcoming season, Rohn Brown designed a rather nice ASA logo for Club tee shirts which sold well, and Turf Soaring School put in a new runway. Roy Coulliette made the mistake of scheduling this on April 1 - All Fools Day - so no one would believe it was actually going to happen, but it did, and Roy generously invited members out for a free tow to celebrate.

Kevin Harrenstein became Contest Director for the Contest Series, cross country flying was being encouraged with Wally Raisanen's generously donated grant and it was reported there were 3 new members, not the least of which was Andy Durbin and wife (even if I say so myself!)

Just in time to coincide with the beginning of the season and the upcoming Region 9 Contest, Paul Dickerson sounded a warning and published some interesting figures. "Most racing pilots will agree that regional and national contests can be tiring," wrote Paul. "Tiring, however, is a relative term, difficult to quantify. One way to breathe some life into the word is to compare the maximum cumulative flight duty for an Army pilot to the flight hours of a soaring contest." Paul then printed a table showing permitted Army pilot hours, factoring in such considerations as traffic, close to terrain, night flying etc., against the cumulative hours flown in consecutive days of contest flying.

"It clearly shows," continued Paul, "that even a regional contest would exceed the flight hours limit for Army pilots. A National contest exceeds the Army limit by a factor of 2 or 3, depending on the length of the days (not just the task). Consider also that the Army limit is for people who are in physical condition that most of us only dream of. Now mix in a little heat, a little dehydration, a little bit of rust behind the stick (five hours since last September?) with the fatigue. The elements of an unpleasantness are at hand."

In May, the Editor published an item entitled Durbin's Diamond, accompanied by a contribution from his crew entitled, "How It Looked From The Ground." (See Ch.9) While Golf Yankee was delighted to have completed all his Diamonds, the reporting thereof was to have far reaching effects. Jane Jackson read the reports with relish, and when a further piece of mine appeared the following month in Soaring magazine, How Soaring Really Started, she put two and two together, and figured we had a writer in our midst. Jane had a relief Editor in sight for 1986, and Trish Durbin was a marked woman!

Pete Williams wrote up Region 9. The enthusiasm was back, the pleasure had never gone away, but where were all the contestants? Just 24 pilots and one guest participated that year, fifteen 15-meter ships, six Standard Class and four in Sports. Attendance might be low but enjoyment was high and the 24 flew a total of 26,573 miles between them.

Pete presented several cameos: Jim Kett will never forget his spectacular "save" over the rocky strip north of Lake Pleasant on the way to Prescott. Marion Cruce won Day 6 in his 1-26 against 3 glass ships. Joe Carter won his first contest day. Jim Johnson swamped Standard Class with his LS-4. Dick Mockler edged Raisanen and Dickerson in 15 meter. Art Pasquali went the extra miles to Kearny via Superior for a photo he did not need. Paul Dickerson was the fastest man until he passed Turf without a photo on Day 5. John Baird landed after 7:00 pm to capture the true grit prize. Skip Jackson did just about everything except get his computer to print the daily results. Bill Ordway herded the brood in his usual professional manner."

The continuing water shortage at Estrella meant Bill Story of Maricopa earned the undying gratitude of all pilots for permitting unlimited use of his water supply. A religious group brought its water truck to Estrella too, thereby earning a grateful letter of thanks and a donation to funds at the end of the event.

Meanwhile, Turf quietly continued its program of improvements. In addition to a paved runway, it could now boast an air conditioned pilots' lounge.

Paul Dickerson had located a tow pilot, with plane, who would tow for "away" contests at a reasonable fee, and TuSC had also indicated being prepared to "lend" pilot and plane when necessary. This meant the Club again had the capability of conducting contests at sites other than an FBO. The first "away" event of the ASA Contest Series was a wet and wild weekend at Wilcox with "wet, soft thermals" which caused multiple landouts. "Sunday was the same except the rains started sooner" so everyone boxed up and went home in disgust.

About that time, Tucson's Steve Fahrner also joined ASA, which was to presage great things. Steve enjoyed flying out of different sites and was destined to become the Series Contest Director for the next few years and would arrange a positively nomadic existence for the Series.

At the end of the year, the Annual Awards Banquet was rendered extra special with the showing of ASA member Chris Woods' latest film, "The Quiet Challenge". Awards went to Class A winners Bob von Hellens, Paul Dickerson and John Baird, Class B winners Orcen Irick, Rohn Brown and TuSC members Roc & Elaine Cutri who flew as a team. Skip Jackson was Man of the Year; last year's Woman of the Year, Jane Jackson, presented the beautiful kachina doll award to her successor, Connie Brown; the Turf Award went to Judy Lincoln, and Wally Raisanen, having dusted and returned the Estrella Award for the Banquet, then had to turn around and take it home again.

The Banquet must have inspired everyone afresh since immediately afterwards a positive rash of Records was announced: Moe Morris, Elaine Cutri, Steve Fahrner and Andy Gordon were listed as new record holders for the year, every last one of them from Tucson Club. ASA had better watch out!

1986 was a pleasant ticking-over sort of a year, with Rohn Brown as President. On February 4th through 9th 1986, the very first U.S. Sailplane Aerobatic National Championships took place at Estrella. Las Horvath won the Open Class, with his pupil, Nancy Blank, in second place. Kevin Knutsen took the Intermediate and the Sportsman Class went to a non-ASA-er, Frank Demiceli. The weather was positively cruel but Las was impressed by the standard of judging, which was remarkably consistent.

Roy Coulliette started a Just For Fun contest series at Turf, one or two per month fitted neatly around the ASA Contest Series, with a barbecue to follow and a moonlit hayride through the sage-scented desert for dessert.

The Club Blanik and 1-26 were still a cause for concern. They simply weren't breaking even, let alone paying their way! The 1-26 had been based at Turf's Pleasant Valley Airport for some years, but was looking somewhat tired around the edges. Kevin Knutsen, tow pilot, glider pilot, glider instructor and A&P Mechanic, took on complete refurbishing of 454 and did an absolutely superb job on her. The basic design of the new paint job was based on the Arizona flag, with a copper star as a symbol of the copper State. "The fun part," reported Kevin, "was getting the lines of yellow and red round the fuselage to appear straight." The mechanical mysteries under all this exterior beauty were also given a bit of a birthday, and, to all intents and purposes, ASA had a "new" ship.

A questionnaire was circulated to discover what members wanted to do about the Blanik. Some suggested they'd be more interested in flying the ship if it were better instrumented, a few said they'd use it more if it were based at Turf, not Estrella, and there were several definite yeses to the idea of replacing the Blanik with a Grob. As a result of this questionnaire, the Blanik was moved to Turf. Private owners still seemed to prefer Estrella but more non-owners were congregated in the north of Phoenix, which made Turf more geographically convenient. This move has certainly resulted in greater use and, consequently, greater financial independence although it's always a fine line between the red and the black, especially when insurance premiums are due!

In June, it was gratifying to discover Region 9 entries were healthily up once more - 38 ships, 39 pilots. It would have been 40 but Mike Adams' trailer was involved in an accident en route to the contest which slightly damaged the LS-4 inside. There was a good mix of ships - 5 Ventus' (Venti?), 4 ASW-20s, an LS-3, LS-3a, a Mini-Nimbus, Speed Astir, Mosquito and a DG 202. In Standard Class, there were 3 brand spanking-new Discus' (Disci?), 3 LS-4's, two Pegasus (Pegasi?), two DG-300's, an ASW-19B, and, getting toward the Vintage Department, a Cirrus and a Jantar.

The first day was almost stopped dead in its tracks by a power outage, which left contestants on the grid a little longer than they would have chosen in 100°+ temperatures. No power meant no pump to refuel the tow planes! Las Horvath ingeniously resolved the problem with his now-famous Lawn Mower Solution. He resourcefully decanted gas from an old lawn mower into a generator which was in turn used to power the electric pump to fuel the tow planes s-l-o-w-l-y.

That was also the year the Bradshaws north of Phoenix were IFR on the Tuesday and many pilots had navigational difficulties, which is a polite way of saying they got lost. Veterans agreed it was the worst visibility ever seen (or rather, not seen!) in the area and there were mass landouts. Several pilots did not find their respective ways back to Estrella until 2:30 am or so, and at the pilots' meeting next morning, the crews received a round of applause.

Days 1 and 5 were even more remarkable - every pilot completed and the gate was closed before 5:30 pm. "This," said the crews, "is how it should be." Paul Dickerson undoubtedly felt the same, since he won 15 meter class. We did not know it then but the 1986 Region 9 was our last one hosted by Las Horvath at Estrella.

The Women's Soaring Seminar was hosted by TuSC at El Tiro in June, 1986, their first major event which earned them well deserved recognition. Elaine Cutri, assisted by husband Roc and a great TuSC team, worked hard to make the event a success. 32 women and 3 men participated, 210 aerotows and 20 winch launches got them up, up and away with many lady pilots flying above 10,000 MSL for the first time.

In August winds of biblical proportions resembling a tornado tore through Pleasant Valley Airport during the Saturday night of an ASA Contest weekend, when several members' ships and trailers were tied down north of the runway. Miraculously, damage on the tiedowns was slight considering the havoc caused elsewhere on the field.

"Roy Coulliette's home, to the south east, lost an awning built two weeks previously. Incredibly, the winds passed around the hangar-next-door, which left Roy's beloved N3N unscathed, but concentrated their ferocious energy on the hangar beyond that one. Steel support posts were ripped out of the ground and the whole structure was blown some 200 feet to the south, dragging with it and destroying a Grob fuselage and a Blanik wing. Steel roof beams fell and crushed all that had not been blown away, including the little blue Citabria, which sustained a smashed canopy and a broken wing.

Several ASA trailers were moved around and modified slightly, but incredibly, only one sailplane sustained minor damage when a whipping cable reared through the main wheel mudguard.

A second massive storm followed a week later and did most damage over the road at the parachute school. 80 to 90 mph winds moved a 6000 lb Beech aircraft 300 yards and a second Beech was saved only when the owner jumped in and "flew" it on the spot.

Steve Fahrner flew Region 12 at Bishop in his trusty Speed Astir and won one of the days against fierce competition. He was thrilled to come second over all. Paul Dickerson and Wally Raisanen also flew Bishop that year, Wally finding himself in 18 knot lift being sucked up into a thunderstorm at one point. Wally also flew the 15 meter Nationals at Uvalde that year, and ASA was proud to have a pilot - Las Horvath - who qualified for an invitation to fly the first Hitachi Masters of Soaring Championship in Minden.

The monsoon was certainly a vicious one that year. The now-traditional Labor Day weekend at El Tiro was a great though soggy success. "A record 22 pilots attended and the 1-26 Western Regional Contest was run in conjunction with the event. Saturday started off with leaden skies and became worse. Day One was enlivened by a brand new contest pilot who did his own start. "For a start!" he called over the airwaves. "Three! Two! One! Good Start!" Roc Cutri, manning the gate, said plaintively, "I'm supposed to say that!"

The day died early and everyone was ready for beer and barbecue by 4:00 pm. We also enjoyed an unexpected cabaret. Three superbly renovated Stearmans, WW2 vintage trainers, treated us to our own private air display, after which they landed and joined us for Seven Up. Flown by a father and son team, and a third pilot who is regarded as an adopted son for flying purposes, you'd be hard pressed to find three nicer guys or a more delightful sight.

The Sunday started with sufficient docility to lull us into having a pilots' meeting and calling a task. It even let us launch and waited till pilots were out on course. Then the weather sneaked up on us again and let rip! We had four storms roar through El Tiro that day. We had horizontal rain, the runways were obliterated for minutes at a time, the lightning speared the ground close by and hissed like a whiplash. Not to be outdone, the thunder crashed immediately on its heels, deafening the ear, vibrating the building.

Many pilots made the first turnpoint and returned to the field. Andy Durbin was cornered by 3 thunderstorms and deemed it expedient to make a field landing 2 miles north of Taylor. A couple of guys in a truck gave him a lift to the nearest phone but no-one at El Tiro heard it ringing because of the storms. So GY got a lift back to the field, collected his trailer and crew and went back to retrieve himself. All crews had to wait until the washes receded before they could leave, however. They were full and impassable due to the runoff from the mountains. Meanwhile, a trainer ship landed safely at Taylor, the pilot dismounted and the winds flipped the trainer over on its back, damaging it beyond repair.

Fortunately it was a 3 day contest and the third day dawned bright and clear, with a sparkling blue sky and puffy white clouds to gladden the heart. The sun was almost whistling nonchalantly in its innocence. Everyone flew a successful task, dried out and forgave the elements. It takes more than the sky falling to stop ASA pilots flying. Come rain or shine, hell or high water, (and believe me, we had all four!) ASA contests take place.

That was the final contest of the season and Wally Raisanen, Steve Fahrner and Bob von Hellens were declared 1st, 2nd and 3rd in 15 meter class with Jeff Turner, Andy Durbin and the Cutri team in the corresponding places in Sports.

At year's end, the flourishing though tiny Prescott Club merited a mention since it offered safe winch launches not available at Phoenix' FBO's; our only female contestant, Elaine Cutri, had earned herself a record, the women's out and return distance, and it was announced the next Hitachi Masters of Soaring was going to be held at Estrella. 1987 was going to be a great year!

And it was. It started with a dramatic save at Turf, reported in Air Currents and taken up by almost every other editor who read it, including Bob Gaines in Soaring magazine. Australian Tracy Tabart, an experienced pilot, and his guest/passenger, owe their lives to Tracy's quick thinking and his familiarity with the inner workings of the Grob 103 Acro. "Avoiding The Parachute Option" (See Ch.5) was Tracy's story of how he resolved the problem without evacuating either the plane or his bowels.

In March there was a new man in town and the Civil Air Patrol benefitted enormously. Thanks to the sterling efforts of Mike Hull, teenagers in Arizona who were members of CAP were enjoying the opportunity to restore a glider and would later learn to fly in it. Mike was a member of CAP when he was a lad and had always longed to fly gliders. He finally achieved this ambition through a barter club. As he put in time to add a glider rating to his power license in September 1986,

Mike met Turf's CFIG, John Hanauer, part-owner of a somewhat decrepit 2-22. After a little wheeling and dealing, the 2-22 was transported to Mike's home and the teenagers started work.

Mike got in touch with ASA because the kids needed a trailer for their ship and Mike needed suggestions. It did us a good turn too: we needed someone to provide lunches at Hitachi and Mike's CAP group, smart in their probably rather warm uniforms, filled that need and made $338 profit toward their beloved ship. In August the happy band was featured in the local newspaper and Mike's modest secret was out. It transpired he was not only donating time and expertise to the project, but also his half share in the glider.

History was yet again repeating itself. Mike was following in Ruth Petry's footsteps since Ruth helped 5 junior ASA members acquire a Schweizer 1-19 in 1960 and part of the fun then had been getting the ship in flying shape. It is also to be hoped Mike's project is breeding future pilot members for ASA.

In April Woody Woods generously held an open day for ASA at Carefree Airport. Qualified pilots enjoyed launches from Arizona's smoothest runway and an impromptu contest, although we'll never be sure who won because Hank Halverson was too busy talking and forgot his duties at the finish gate.

And in May, Estrella and ASA hosted what was probably its most glittering, most prestigious and most rewarding event ever - the 1987 Hitachi Masters of Soaring. Nineteen of soaring's best known pilots descended on the desert for a battle of champions. Chris Woods filmed the proceedings and produced Running On Empty, which was later taken up by National Geographic for their prestigious Explorer series. And ASA members worked and contributed and enjoyed as they had never done before! Judy Lincoln worked more hours than you would have thought humanly possible to make the event a success and I had the pleasure of crewing for George Lee, Britain's three times world champion, while covering the event for Soaring magazine at the same time!

At the Hitachi Masters of Soaring Awards Banquet, Mr Tomoo Yoshikawa, Vice President and Corporate Secretary of Hitachi America, Limited, said in his speech of thanks, "There is a beautiful Japanese proverb that says, As you drink of the cool water, do not forget the hands that dug the well." He undoubtedly had in mind many members of the Arizona Soaring Association who had contributed many hands for the digging. Our star turn, of course, ASA Member Extraordinaire, was Las Horvath: as recent owner of Estrella, our host, and a contestant. ASA produces good workers *and* good pilots!

Yes, we did say "recent owner". At Hitachi news filtered through that Las Horvath had sold Estrella. It seemed unbelievable but Las himself confirmed the news. He was happy about the decision, since it would relieve him of the business side of things which he did not particularly enjoy, and permit him more time for instructing and contests, which he did. He was also very happy about the purchaser, Bruce Stephens, and was confident the two would work together well. Bruce has subsequently become a member of ASA and he and his wife Karen are two of us now.

Following shortly on the heels of Hitachi was Region 9. Because of involvement with the Masters, and the anticipated change in ownership, Estrella did not bid for Region 9 in 1987. This broke the tradition of 13 years (Arizona's first Region 9 had taken place there in 1974) and the event was held at El Tiro, hosted by TuSC.

Region 9 at El Tiro was memorable. ASA-ers were possibly a little relieved not to be hosting it that year. Everyone wanted to fly, no one wanted to be Contest Director. For the first time, an "outside man" was brought in, and Bruce Bowmar nobly left wife and brand new baby in California and ran the meet. As hosts, TuSC had had little experience of contests and their members were stretched to the limit. However, what they lacked in experience they made up for with enthusiasm and learned quickly.

It was also big, with 39 pilots from six states who provided what was probably the highest seeded competition for some years. The Wednesday will always be remembered by all those present, being the boomingest day ever! In 15 meter class Ken Sorensen (KM) flew his Ventus 100.32 mph that day, undoubtedly a State record, and in Sports Class, Andy Durbin (GY) flew an unballasted Jantar at 70.55 mph, which wasn't too shabby either. It was Golf Yankee's first Regional day win and overall the winners were in 15 meter class Wally Raisanen 1st, Ken Sorensen 2nd and Art Pasquali 3rd; Out-of-Staters took all top three places in Standard Class but ASA held its own in Sports with John Lincoln 2nd and Pete Williams 3rd although Out-of-Stater Ned Wilson took 1st.

One reason for El Tiro's popularity as a contest site is the attitude of traffic controllers at Tucson International Airport. Paul Dickerson sums it up: "The ARSA people know glider pilots are a little bit retarded or they wouldn't be flying without engines, so they're very patient with us." Unlike Phoenix ARSA, who invariably instruct gliders on squawk numbers and altitude to maintain, Tucson seemed to understand and was diverting commercial traffic around sailplanes. They could see these tiny ghosts on their radar screens provided they kept moving, but if a ship stopped to thermal, it disappeared.

Those were significant events for ASA in 1987. The Hitachi event, the sale of Estrella, the break with tradition for Region 9. And then, on June 1st, 1987, our founder, Don Barnard, aged 76, passed away. It was as if he had waited to see the little Club he'd founded so many years previously establish itself in its own routines, learn from its mistakes, suffer a few setbacks, pick itself up and carry on, and finally to reach a pinnacle of recognition by hosting Hitachi. Like a fond father figure, Don realized we were up and running on our own. It was time to free his fettered wings and we must not be sad.

Unfortunately, in the middle of this euphoric mood of achievement, this feeling of, "We've arrived and we're here to stay", FAA NPRMs, TCAs and ARSAs, and all those other ominous alphabet soup problems, once more reared their ugly heads. Only this time, they were uglier than ever! Phrases such as "Soaring Survival" and "Endangered Species" were being bandied about and it wasn't in relation to dodos or condors any more, it was in relation to us.

Along with myriad other airports throughout the country, Phoenix Skyharbor was destined to become a Super TCA. (What was super about it?) The inverted wedding cake plan consisting of three circles, commandeering 10, 20 and 30 mile radii of our airspace, could effect Estrella, Turf, El Tiro and Carefree. There was a slim possibility of a special case for gliders if we shouted loudly enough, and members were begged, beseeched and bullied into writing letters of protest.

Life continued. Las Horvath, Nancy Blank and the rest of the US team departed these shores to compete in the World Aerobatic Championships in August. Nancy placed 3rd and Las was ill but still took 13th. John Serafin also attended and crewed for his Polish friends at the subsequent Polish Nationals as he had done at Marfa 17 years previously in 1970. Sweet Marcel Godinat passed away at Minden and his badges and trophies were destined for permanent display at the SSA Museum in Elmira, New York. Woody Woods came 7th at the Open Nationals at Hobbs in *that* ship (an AS-H 25) with George Moffat as navigator, a formidable team.

Chris Woods was hard at work on "Running On Empty" and asked me to co-write the script with him. I didn't need too much persuading and spent a pleasant week in Santa Monica reliving Hitachi and reloving every minute of it.

In July, Wally Raisanen (2E) attended the 1987 15 Meter Nationals at Barstow, and, along with 16 other pilots, lost his sailplane, a Ventus, in the now famous fire. Despite subsequently replacing the ship with a brand spanking new LS-6b with very reasonable settlements, Wally and his Ventus had been through a lot together. It was like losing a friend.

"At 11:30 pm, July 10, I was awakened by a phone call from Mike Adams. He had just been called by the airport, and said the hangar was on fire, and all the ships in it were lost. Arriving on the scene 20 minutes later, I found 5 fire trucks spraying water on the collapsed building, still burning fiercely. Trudging through choking smoke and flying embers, driven by a 20 knot wind, I found the remains of 2E with a burning roof truss astride it. Nothing was left but sheets of carbon fiber fabric, the steel push rods and undercarriage, and the remains of the oxygen system. All the resin and aluminum had burned up in the intense heat." Wally's only crumb of comfort came next day when his son/crew, Eric, found 2E's metal identification plate among the ashes.

Labor Day that September found us back at El Tiro once more for the final 3 day jousting to discover the ASA Weekend Contest Series Champion. Scores were the closest ever, anything could happen - and it did!

The first thing you noticed as you arrived for the contest was Steve Fahrner's survival hat. (The one with the flaps). (A 15 meter hat?) Steve had been saving his hat to make soup in the event of an outlanding. Incredibly, on Saturday, his hat was *clean*. Had Steve indeed landed out and boiled his hat to make soup? Steve is now a broken man and reports disgustedly that he inadvertently left his hat at a friend's house. When he went back next day to retrieve it, his friend's wife had *washed* it!

The first day of the Contest was enlivened by a considerable number of landouts and subsequent retrieves, with no less than three pilots choosing fairways instead of runways on which to land. Steve Fahrner was effusively welcomed by the management of Tubac Golf Course who said he was the second plane to land there, the first being President Ford when he was introduced to the Mexican President. They didn't have a Mexican President for Steve so they substituted a Mexican beer, which was probably far more to his taste. (Thank goodness the boy was wearing a clean hat).

Landing out was not his exclusive prerogative that weekend. In fact, only one Class A pilot made it home on the Sunday, which leant considerable substance to the theory that it was a bum call. Elaine Cutri (RGA), our only female contestant, landed at Continental, a lonely place for a lady, and had to walk out through fruit orchards harboring illegal aliens who began hastily packing up their belongings at the sound of her approach.

The results? Paul Dickerson (19) took first in 15 meter, followed by Wally Raisanen (2E), despite having no ship for the final days, and Bob von Hellens third.

In Sports Class, Andy Durbin (GY) took first, John Lincoln (ELF) took second and the Cutri team (RGA) took third.

In October, TuSC celebrated its twentieth anniversary the old fashioned way, with spot landings and bomb dropping competitions. Also in October, the Annual Awards Banquet was being specially groomed and planned by Nancy Hume and Bill Ordway. Last year's event, by common consent, had not been an unmitigated success, and, always ready to learn from our mistakes, this year's event was to be extra special. It certainly was for me. I was proud to receive an award in recognition of my literary efforts for ASA and SSA, only the second time such an award had been presented. The first one went to Nancy Hume in what she refers to as "1971 B.C." It was an extra thrill that my framed award also referred to me as Club historian.

The Banquet was scheduled to include the Arizona Premiere of "Running On Empty". Unfortunately, due to circumstances beyond Chris' control (as they say), the film was delayed and didn't quite make it in time. The Banquet organizers, however, did not miss a beat and in its place we enjoyed a look back into our past. A brief synopsis of the Club's history was shared, and a slide show, "We Were Younger Then" took its place. This could easily have been re-titled, "We Were Slimmer Then" but the reminder didn't stop us enjoying an excellent dinner.

Afterwards, there was still the pleasure of seeing Running On Empty to look forward to. There was a small SSA Premiere at the Beverley Hilton Hotel in Los Angeles and ASA was well represented by Chris and Lesley Woods, Woody Woods, the Lincolns and the Durbins. It was a delightful evening, and for me, an adventure of discovery to see the film in all its glory, complete with Cliff Robertson narrating Chris' and my script and to discover the difference the addition of music and a polished sound track can make!

ASA-ers had to wait a little longer for their view of Chris' masterpiece. It was shown instead at the Christmas Winter Party, held at the Hume's home for the seventeenth consecutive time. It was a fitting end to a triumphant year. "The challenge draws him, frustrates him, eludes him - then, one day, rewards him. Just enough to let him know he can win sometimes. Just enough to keep him coming back for more."

1988 found us coming back for more on many fronts. Pilots are again enjoying this season's ASA Contest Series. Several intend flying nationals and regionals elsewhere, and a few of us attended the Hitachi Masters of Soaring Championship at Winter Haven, Florida. George Lee asked me to crew for him again so I guess I must have done OK last year!

Region 9 for 1988 was again scheduled at a different venue, Turf Soaring School's Pleasant Valley Airport. Turf is Arizona's oldest soaring operation, despite several moves over the years. Although the formidable terrain to the north, about which Joe Lincoln sounded a warning so many years ago, probably caused the reduced field of just 25 pilots, most contestants found it enjoyable and challenging. Steve Fahrner, EU, justified his recent purchase of Las Horvath's Ventus and beat Wally Raisanen (2E) into second place, with Kevin Harrenstein (F) third. In Standard Class the top three places went to out of staters but Sports Class was won by Glen Stiles (YU), with TuSC's Kumm/Parker (YR) team second and Bob Hurni (382) an honorable third in a 1-26.

And if that is our past, what of our future? In common with the rest of the soaring fraternity, ASA is threatened as never before by FAA regulations, NPRMs,

TCAs and ARSAs. New proposals could seriously curtail Arizona airspace in addition to calling for transponders. It is indeed American soaring's darkest hour. However, recent meetings with the FAA show an apparent willingness on their part to listen, and ASA-ers are cautiously optimistic that counter proposals supported by the majority *may* produce an acceptable compromise and could result in Phoenix having one of the smallest TCA's in the country.

The feeling remains that we have been threatened before and survived. We will continue to fight on every front possible and we have the capable Judy Lincoln, currently one of two SSA Vice-Presidents, leading the fray. Backed up by many professional, capable members, notably Paul Dickerson, Bill Ordway and this year's Club President, Jeff Turner, and the SSA too, Judy presented soaring's case, with Larry Sanderson, in an outstanding article in Soaring magazine dated March 1988.

Interestingly, that same issue of Soaring carried articles written by no less than three ASA members, Judy, myself, and a new discovery, Bob Welliever. Bob's charming article entitled "The Dowager Queen" (see Ch.5) first appeared in the January 1988 Air Currents where it was spotted by the National Soaring Museum who declared it "absolutely outstanding" and submitted it to the Harris Hill Soaring Corporation as a nomination for the 1988 Joseph C. Lincoln Award. We won't know the Editorial Board's decision until after this book is put to bed, but history repeats itself once more.

After those who pioneer and lead the way, there will always be those who will follow, carry the torch and eventually lead those who in turn come behind them. With the structure we now have, which encourages contest flying above all, it seems very likely that ASA in the future will produce more champions at regional, national and world level. And even if we don't, we will continue to enjoy our Association, our friends and our flying. From the acorns that Don Barnard planted just 33 years ago, we are now enjoying the shade of the oak trees.

CHAPTER 12 - THE PEOPLE

DON BARNARD almost certainly written by Joe Lincoln, December 1957.

This century was only eleven years old when Don Barnard decided to start his life story, and Portland, Oregon, was the locale for the opening scene. His interest in flying started at an early age when he saw a flying circus of World War I planes in 1918. Throughout the twenties he was always hanging around airports and in 1928, with all the magazines showing plans on how to build gliders, he sent for plans for the Zogling primary and finished the glider in little over a year of hard work. First tows were off a hill using shock cord launchings, which gave flights of up to 30 seconds. After months of this type of launch he figured out it would be possible to auto tow, so he took the glider to an airport and proved this method. Many flights were made with his first ship and distances up to about 500 feet were achieved.

In 1931 Don went to Seattle, hoping to work for Boeing. While there he flew with the Seattle Glider Club, at that time under the direction of Otto Viewig. The Club had about 7 members and a two-place primary glider which Otto had designed and built. Don made many flights with Otto in the glider and on one occasion they trailered the ship into eastern Washington to try to soar off some large hills there, but the primary was a very poor excuse for a sailplane and although no flights over 3 minutes were made, a lot of fun and experience was gained. A year later Don returned to Portland and found his glider had been stolen so he set to work to design and build a ship, a single place with a pod and boom and a wing span of 47 feet. When the ship was all finished but the boom, Don threw a primary type tailend on it and off into the blue he went. Many, many flights were made with this ship, some good ones too, with times up to five minutes. As there were no instruments, soaring was out, although many attempts were made.

In 1935, Don went on the road in show business (he gave the glider away) and through the following years no gliding was done but flying was kept up with power planes. Santa Cruz, California, in 1940, saw Don entertaining at the big hotel there and he discovered an Eaglerock primary glider in a section of the building.

He finished some work which had to be done on it and again he took to the air in a motorless craft. A lot of tows were made there at the local airport but when Don moved on to Monterey he left the glider in Santa Cruz. In January of 1942 Don moved to King City, Ca., where he spent the next three years at a primary training school for the Army Air Corps. Marysville, California, was the next stop for Don and there he started a flying school along with his entertaining at nights.

His first real sailplane was acquired when he bought a Baby Albatross from the Bowlus factory. Soon he owned his first two-place ship, an LK, and after acquiring his Commercial Glider Licence, added glider instruction to his power plane flying school. When in the spring of 1947 he managed to buy a Super Albatross, one of only two such ships ever built, he knew he had a ship good enough for the Nationals. So that summer he trailered to Texas and was one of the participants in the mightiest flying endurance contest ever held. Enough to say that Don did finish the two weeks of open days flying and dragged his trailer home, sadder but wiser. Don's school was doing fine so the Super was traded off on a deal with Herman Stiglmeier for two Pratt Reads.

During these years Don was trying to burn the candle at both ends by operating a bar, doing his own entertaining, a radio show, and a flying school. Something had to give so Don sold out everything and moved to Carmel, California. The fog there turned out to be too much for him, however, so after looking at the map he decided Phoenix was the place and up and away he went.

Don wasn't long in Phoenix before rumors of a glider brought him in touch with Jerry Hopf with a TG-3 and Roy Graves with a Cinema. Soon Don and Roy were on their way to El Mirage to pick up an LK for Don, and from there on it wasn't long until the Arizona Soaring Association was born. From here on we all know the story, with Don the main power behind putting gliding on the map again here in Arizona. He was ASA's first President, and without his efforts, vision, admonitions, instruction and never-ending promotions, soaring in Arizona would still be unorganized.

Don's log book on gliding shows to date 1349 tows, 558 hours and 353 hours as an instructor. Although at the moment Don owns no sailplane he has a ship of his own on the drawing board with plans for construction in the near future. He is always in there selling gliders and soaring to anyone who will listen, even to his best friends who are as enthusiastic as he. "Is there anything more beautiful than a sailplane soaring up there in the blue sky?"

THE GEORGE LAUMAN STORY by Don Barnard, June 1957.

George Lauman was the Arizona Regional Governor for the SSA in 1956 and Club Secretary. He was born just 30 miles from Elmira which was thought to account for his love of soaring. He attended the Second National Gliding & Soaring Contest when he was 16 and most of the contests held at Elmira before World War 2. George helped launch vast numbers of utility gliders by shock cord and crewed for many of the pilots including Art Schultz, John Nowak, Dallas Wise and Udo Fisher.

Lauman attended Cornell University and helped organize the Cornell Flying Club and later the Ithaca Gliding Club during the late 1930's. The latter provided George with his first glider flying, and consisted of auto tows on the local municipal airport behind a Chevy two door sedan. Instruction was mostly by trial and error on the part of the glider pilot, all solo. The airport manager was also a member of their club which helped tremendously, having his sanction and co-operation in flying on the field. The Club consisted of ten members, some university students, and they had purchased for $300 a Franklin Utility PS-2 from Udo Fisher.

George decided to make aviation his career and studied at Elmira Aviation Ground School under the direction of Floyd Sweet, the 1957 president of SSA. In November 1939 George enlisted in the US Army Air Corps and became involved in radio and communications. He subsequently left the Service but returned to active duty in 1948 and was shipped to Japan, his family following later.

George met many of the foremost glider pilots and enthusiasts of Japan and met many times with them to just talk about gliding and soaring as all soaring enthusiasts do. Only one of them, Shiro Kawase, had a good command of English and he had to do all the translating. Many enjoyable hours were spent with these new friends, and it also included an overnight trip to Kiragamina Heights, one of Japan's foremost primary glider and slope soaring sites, a really beautiful spot.

While stationed at Johnson Air Base just outside Tokyo, George attempted to obtain permission for the Japanese to build him a Grunau Baby II intermediate sailplane, which they promised to do for about $250. Since the surrender the Japanese had not been permitted to build or fly any aircraft. The permission had to be requested through lengthy channels including headquarters of the Far East Air Forces in Tokyo, and finally General MacArthur's HQ. Permission was approved all the way through FEAF but disapproved by General MacArthur.

After leaving the service in 1953, George settled in Phoenix and selected the investment securities business as a likely profession to keep his family in boots and beans. He was one of the group that helped set up the ASA, being elected Vice President the first year and Secretary the second. From his past connections with Floyd Sweet and his 30 years enthusiasm for gliding and soaring, George was appointed the Arizona Regional Governor for the SSA in 1956 and reappointed this year (1957).

I LIKE IT by Derek Van Dyke, December 1956.

For thirteen years, flying has been a way of life for me. Little puddle jumpers with their short takeoff and landing and their shake, rattle and roll flight characteristics on up through 4 engine Douglas transports, had been my magic carpets which carried me to many corners of the world. Even now, each takeoff is thrilling because of its miracle transformation from dead weight to surging lightness. But far back in my memory was a picture of a small boy standing by the rail of an ocean liner watching the sea gulls course down the ship's wake. What fun it would be to fly as the birds did.

It wasn't until last September (1955) out at Cactus Airport, 35 years after the dream on the deck of the ocean liner, that I felt that first real thrill of true flight. For some of us it is given to understand art in its many forms, some gain happiness from music, others revel in the accomplishment of competitive athletics, and there are those of us who love the sky. Not because we know too much about the home of the clouds but because somehow being, even for a short while, part of the sky's vastness restores our souls. Power flight does that for you - but how infinitely more satisfying it is to soar quietly through the air in a sailplane.

As the rushing air ruffles the feathers of a hawk, so does it flutter the fabric of the soaring glider. The drumming moan of the wind against the wings of the sailplane is a fugue for flyers in the truest sense. One cannot sit in the cockpit of a sailplane as it surges to the lift of a strong updraft and remain unresponsive. The quickening of the entire aircraft to the tremendous power inherent in the rising air is felt completely only by the soaring pilot.

Gliding and soaring have something for everyone who wishes to expose his flying skills to a really critical and impartial judge. The careless flyer won't have too much fun, for it is by increasing his skill and delicacy of touch that the true sailplane pilot derives his greatest satisfaction. The pleasure of soaring is directly proportional to the skill you develop in flying finesse. The heavy-handed and lead-footed have no place in a sailplane. But approach the sport for the sake of sport and with a desire to improve in the art of flying and your future as a soaring pilot is bound to be happy and long. No finer way of flight can be found.

DEREK VAN DYKE by Himself! July 1957.

It is uniquely fitting that I am writing this on the evening of Charles Lindbergh's thirtieth anniversary of his flight to Paris. I'll always feel that his example has been my lodestone. Shortly after his flight, I embarrassed my father no end by writing to the Ryan Company and being offered a demonstration flight by a truly aggressive salesman pilot who flew up from Chicago. Dad had to dissuade him by pointing out that even if it were possible for a seven year old boy to have the necessary funds, the law was quite explicit even then about seven year olds flying aircraft. I had to wait.

My first formal instruction came when I enrolled in the airline pilot and engineering course offered by the old Boeing School of Aeronautics in Oakland back in 1939. Just before I was to receive my degree, the Japs unloaded on Pearl Harbor and the school was commandeered by the Army to train mechanics. I was turned down by the Army, Navy and Marines as a prospective flyboy, and so I solved the problem by signing up in the British RAF. The British had been fighting for several years and weren't quite so fussy and were happy to have me in spite of a couple of extra inches. I am sure that they subscribed to the theory of Sherman's that, "War is hell" and if I was going to be a bit cramped sitting in a flying machine, well, I could just reflect on this piece of philosophy and be comforted.

However, before I could complete my course of training, our Air Force started screaming for flight instructors for their accelerated program and the British released me on the theory that I could train more men and we could win the war more quickly if we had more pilots flying more planes and dumping more bombs on Hitler's Reich. Sound thinkers they. Two years in Phoenix at Thunderbird II and then on to active duty in the ATC at Long Beach with the Sixth Ferry Group and in India flying the Hump for 15 months.

After the war, I joined the ranks of returned flyboys who were going to revolutionize the aircraft industry. I bought a major interest in a flight operation at Sky Harbor, helped re-organize it, beat my head against various stone walls for 3 years and sold out. Since then I have been content to charter aircraft and fly around the country on business. I've enjoyed each moment to the utmost. I wouldn't change any of it. I've flown all types and sizes in just about every corner of the world but, as I've been heard to say before, I enjoy soaring best. The flying which preceded a certain flight at a dusty little strip called Cactus Airport over a year ago, where I was introduced to the freedom of real flight, seems incidental.

Editor's Note: Derek van Dyke retired to live at SkyRanch, the aviation community at Carefree Airport, owned by ASA member Woody Woods. Derek was very supportive during the sometimes difficult transition period at Carefree, and passed away in 1987.

MARCEL GODINAT probably by Joe Lincoln, November 1957.

Marcel was born in Landerson, Switzerland and raised in Porrentruy, just 4 miles from the French border where he saw fighters in action during WWI. A grandstand seat without being involved but it whetted his appetite to learn about flying. The first plane he ever saw on the ground was a German fighter that made an emergency landing near Porrentruy and the pilot was interned. His longing to fly had to be suppressed while he began to earn his living in Zurich but was triggered again when he saw his first glider, a Farner, piloted by Willi Farner, at the Dubendorf airport performing acrobatics.

Then in 1931, Guenther Groenhoff, one of the foremost German soaring pilots, came to Switzerland in his high performance Fafnir and took part in an Alpine glider expedition to Jungfraujoch, at an altitude of 10,200 feet. Takeoffs were by shock cord from the glacier. Marcel did not see this but he read about it in the paper which inspired him to buy Groenhoff's book, "I Fly Without Motor and With Motor". By 1934 Marcel had joined the Soaring Club of Zurich where he started flying Zoglings and Falkes, primary and utility gliders of German construction. Launches were from the top of a slope by shock cord and winch.

That year, 1934, was a big one for Marcel. He earned his A, B and C pins and tow licenses. The C pin was accomplished with a flight of 1 hour 23 minutes on a mountain slope near Porrentruy in a Spyr III. Marcel had gone there for an air show and was the only glider pilot there. The following weekend he broke the Swiss duration record with a flight of 8 hours 45 minutes, 5 hours of it at night in a storm where the wind built up to 70 mph. He landed because the clouds came in and he couldn't see the mountains any longer.

With two brothers, Marcel built the fuselage of a Spyr III in 1000 hours, the wings were contracted out to a woodworker. The Spyr III has a 30 to 1 glide angle and sink of less than 2 feet per second.

Another Swiss record was made early in 1935 when he accomplished his Silver Distance with 33.6 miles. On a later flight he gained an altitude of 3,900 feet to earn the second Silver C issued in his country. In 1936 he made another distance record, this time 86.8 miles. The Olympics were held in Berlin that year and for the first time, soaring was included. With 4 other pilots, Marcel made up the Swiss team with 4 ships. The competition was in acrobatics and soaring. The following year he also flew in the International Contest at the Wasserkuppe, Rhon, Germany. In 1938 he set the first goal and return flight record for Switzerland of (twice) 40.3 miles. That year he was also National Soaring Champion.

During the war flying in Switzerland was restricted to a 32 mile radius but that didn't seem to stop Marcel. He continued to earn badges and establish new records, notably the altitude record in 1943 with 14,100 ASL in a Spyr IV. Marcel left Switzerland in 1951 and came to America, finally ending up in Prescott, Arizona where he flew Bob Sparling's LK. Later he moved to Phoenix and co-owned a Pratt Read with Joe Lincoln, Bob Moore and Chuck Schmid.

Editor's Note: Marcel Godinat ended his days peacefully at a nursing home near Minden, Nevada, in July 1987, surrounded by some of his soaring memorabilia and visited by many soaring friends. Badges and trophies won by Marcel are to be on permanent display at the SSA Museum in Elmira, New York.

THE JOHN RYAN STORY by John Ryan and Trish Durbin, May 1988.

John Ryan has a million soaring memories. His favorite took place during the Nationals at Reno, Nevada, in 1966. "Phil Paul, tow pilot, dropped me at about 1800 feet in smooth 1800 fpm lift," recalls John. "The Peavine Wave! I went straight to 27,000 feet, and flew the task triangle down to Mount Rose, off to Smith Valley, back to the secondary wave and home at redline - where they were still doing the launches! My Crew Chief, Ed Butts, asked if I wanted to go again. My reply - Why?" Why indeed. John won that day and took 4th place overall.

There have been many highlights before and since. Born in 1925 in New York City and raised in Butte, Montana, Military Naval Air Service and a medical discharge due to injury came first, followed by learning to fly at Dartmouth in 1944. John's licence includes Commercial airplane single and multi-engine land, single engine sea, instrument and glider. His first airplane came in 1946, a Waco ATO taper wing.

His soaring began in 1958 at Turf Paradise in the Pratt Read under the tutelage of Marcel Godinat, Kenny Bowden and Don Barnard. He was so captivated by it, he ordered a Schweizer 1-23G before he'd even entered a thermal. (He started learning in November so there weren't many thermals around).

His first two cross country flights earned him two badges and in 1960 he made the wave flight at Bishop to 35,100 feet with a height gain of 24,000 feet that earned him a Two Lennie pin. That year he completed his Diamonds and holds Badge Number 16, International Badge number 140.

John's over achieving continued. In 1962 he won the Barringer Trophy for the longest flight of the year, from Kingman, AZ to Santa Fe, NM. The same year he won the US Championships at El Mirage and was chosen to represent the US in the 1963 Internationals in Argentina. He hogged the top spots in subsequent Nationals and Regionals and took 3rd place in the Smirnoff in 1972 and 2nd place in 1973.

On the ground, there is a similarly illustrious list of achievements. He crewed for Dick Schreder in Germany in the 1960 Internationals, was elected President of ASA the same year, and was an SSA Director in 1961, 1962 and 1963. In March 1964 he was elected SSA Vice President and was SSA President for 1965 and 1966. He was Assistant Competition Director for the 1970 Internationals at Marfa, Texas.

By 1978, for John contests had ceased to be fun. "My pleasures started interfering with my pleasures," he said. "It became too blood thirsty, there were too many accidents, too many friends hit the rocks."

Despite that, John still enjoys his myriad memories. Another favorite was a contest flight from El Mirage to Tehachapi to Red Mountain and return to El Mirage. "I deviated about 25 miles north of Tehachapi into the mountains and caught a boomer. I went to the turnpoint and saw my friends polishing rocks. I went back to the same thermal and went non-stop to Red Mountain and home. Elation is when you fly home at redline, pull up and look down, and there's not another glider on the field. Then, the elation builds as time goes by. That day it was an hour and a half before another ship showed up!"

RUTH PETRY some of it by Joe Lincoln, July 1967.

Ruth came to Arizona in 1957 after living in New York, Washington and Cleveland. She is a Technical Editor at Sperry. As a result of their father's interest in gliding, Ruth and her brother Peter were exposed to the sport at an early age, at Elmira and at the Corn Hill site on Cape Cod. After the war she flew with the Metropolitan Soaring Association in Wurtsboro, NY., and the Mid-Atlantic Soaring Association of Washington, DC. Ruth earned her Silver C Badge in 1950 and was Women's Champion at the Nationals in 1949 and 1950. She has been a member of ASA since 1957 and has been on the Board of Directors since 1959. Since coming to Arizona she has crewed at two nationals, but most of her flying has been at the towplane end of the rope.

In his July 1967 Arizona Highways article, Joe Lincoln wrote, "Ruth Petry is the chief tow pilot of the Arizona Soaring Association. She has been in soaring since the summer of 1941, when Professor R.E. Franklin gave her no less than fifty automobile tows between 2:30 in the afternoon and sunset, during one of the days of the National Soaring Contest at Elmira, New York." (Only to be grounded shortly thereafter by Pearl Harbor). "In 1949 she competed in the National Contest at Elmira, and then in 1950 she took the Wurtsboro, New York, Club's Laister-Kaufmann sailplane out to Grand Prairie, Texas, where she won the National Feminine Championship. That year she became a Silver C pilot.

During her early years out here, she did a good deal of crewing for various pilots. She crewed for me on my Diamond Distance flight from Prescott to Albuquerque and towed John Ryan aloft on his flight at Bishop, which carried to an altitude of 35,000 feet. In 1958 her sailplane was brought out from New York and in 1959 she began her steady work as tow pilot for ASA."

THE LAS HORVATH STORY by Trish Durbin

As a teenager in Hungary, Las was introduced to soaring, the sport in which he would later become a Regional Champion, U.S. National Standard Class Champion, U.S. Sailplane Aerobatic Champion, represent the United States overseas, write a book on basic aerobatic techniques, twice be invited to fly the Hitachi International Masters of Soaring Contest, hold a multitude of records and earn his living.

It was in 1956 that the Hungarian Revolution collapsed and Hungarians began leaving their homeland by the thousand. The Communists had been back in control for just three weeks and Las, aged 20, was called up for the Army. "I decided I was not going to do that!" said Las gently but very, very firmly.

On the day he was due to enlist, Las, with brother Stephan and Frank, a friend, boarded a train for Austria. Las was technically a deserter and deserters were shot on sight. Word filtered through the train that the Secret Police were evicting anyone without papers so Las, Stephan and Frank de-trained, without their bicycle. After a long, cold walk, during which they were captured by guards but bribed their way free, midnight found the trio at the Border. They were in Austria.

Later Las, Stephan and Frank were assisted to America by a religious charity group. Speaking only Hungarian, Las' experience as an electrical engineer was useless. He took jobs in a sanatorium and a factory while learning English, and eventually resumed his electrical career with Sperry Rand Univac, working on the second computer ever made.

The Hungarian refugee Made Good and did well with the Company. He bought his family a home and in 1963 he could even afford to go back to his beloved sport of flying engineless sailplanes.

Soon our intrepid hero decided what he really wanted to do with his life was "build an airport". He arrived in Phoenix, Arizona on January 15, 1969. With his brother Stephan, he leased a patch of sand in the desert, eight miles down a dirt road near Maricopa. The operation, christened Estrella Sailport after the nearby Estrella mountains, boasted two sailplanes, a towplane, a tied down parachute for shade, an old green Chevy truck with a drinks cooler on the back, and a cash box. All they needed now was a customer.

The rest, as they say, is history. Having your own airfield and fleet of sailplanes certainly encourages regular practice. Las flew frequently and began entering contests. His career as a champion spans several years. In 1975 he took the Standard Class 100 Km Speed Record and won the Region 9 Soaring Contest. He went on to become U.S. National Standard Class Champion in 1978, taking numerous second and third places along the way. In 1980 he took the U.S. National Two Place Distance Record by flying 560.43 miles, taking 8 hrs and 10 minutes to do it.

He represented the U.S. in aerobatic contests abroad in 1983 and 1985, and in 1986 he won the Open Class of the first U.S. National Sailplane Aerobatic Championship which he also hosted at Estrella. A special thrill was that his pupil, Nancy Blank, took second place and he had taught her everything she knew. History repeated itself at the same event in 1987, held in Stillwater, OK., when Las and Nancy again took first and second places respectively.

To go from being a Hungarian refugee with nothing to being a successful business man and soaring champion demonstrates what a remarkable man Horvath is. Las sold Estrella in 1987 but continues there, doing what he loves most.

CHAPTER 13 - PARDON MY SQUELCH

Nancy Hume was an Air Currents Newsletter Editor who became a legend in her own time. Her first Editorial, in May 1968, appropriately entitled, "From The Editor's Kitchen Table", solicited contributions and Letters to the Editor, but ended with a P.S. "I'm a lousy speller, so no letters about that please!"

Nancy was simply standing in for Jean Doty for a few months while Jean worked on the index for Soaring Magazine and took a vacation. Confident that there was at last someone who could more than ably fill her shoes, Jean subsequently retired in September 1969, and Nancy took over the job which she would fill - usually hilariously - until December 1972 - just over three years. Two years after retirement, her monthly column "Pardon My Squelch" began and ASA would never be the same again.

As an experienced reporter employed by The Phoenix Gazette, Nancy was a natural choice for the job. She had a talent for writing and for scatty humor although she never re-wrote, cut or polished anything (which accounts for a lot). One of her strengths seemed to lie in scouting soaring associated gossip and tidbits.

She harassed pilots into writing reports of interesting flights, there were updates on the progress of on-going ship repairs, there were declarations that the Humes hated missing this or that trip and instructions to "save us some thermals". Like all good writers, she could not resist reporting on her friends, preferably in their most embarrassing moments.

Sometimes things became a little confused as Nancy always typed directly onto duplicating "skins" which did not permit rearrangement or alterations. Often she would say, "We don't have room for so-and-so" and then discover that she did. The explanation was that "the Home Office really isn't as satisfactory as the Office. So I hope you understand that it is confusion, not stupidity, makes my contributions to Air Currents a bit jumbled from time to time. In an Office, one doesn't have to remember to tell the diaper man to leave two sacks instead of one, the milkman to leave an extra quart of cottage cheese but only one dozen eggs, and most important of all, to keep two little boys from literally murdering each other. And so," Nancy would end with a flourish, having explained things to her own satisfaction, "with pleasure I now present to you - the missing piece!"

In November 1969 she was getting into the swing of things, still soliciting material and, in desperation, even offering to take things down over the telephone "via very stale shorthand and save you 6 cents." Somewhat disconcertingly, she added, "Judging from my notes, this promises to be a full issue. (I'm never very sure, you know!)"

Having an editor for a wife and being employed as Official Proof Reader seemed to go to Al Hume's head and inspired him to write an article of his own. In December 1969 the first of a very boring series of articles on variometers appeared. It was rumored that although they were published, no one had actually read them.

Also in December 1969, Nancy exposed what would seem to be one of Al's darkest secrets: "Hume Picks Up New Girlfriend - by his wife. I haven't met her but I don't like her. By his description she is fast and smooth. By mine, she has a long pointed nose and is so pale, she is actually white. Her name is Diamant 15. She must have something - he drove all the way to Houston to pick her up. She is bringing with her a better dowry than I did - even her own covered house. However, I have been informed that she will occupy the carport and my car will remain in its present location outside! I know she will lead him astray by many miles next spring and I also know that I will be dumb enough to follow them and bring them back!" It was a love/hate relationship that continued for several months, principally because Al moved his new girlfriend into the living room!

Two months later Nancy apologized for not providing "a January Air Currents to scan, absorb or rip into a million pieces (frustration pacifier)" but had been down with 'flu. As recompense she was offering the loan of newsletters from all the California soaring clubs, Yuma and Tucson. She also had the New Zealand soaring magazine and as a final blandishment said, "If you come by, and I hope you will, for the small fee of 25 cents a head, you can enter our living room and view Her Majesty, Diamant. (STILL!)"

The new Diamant was Al's reward, it seems. In 1969 he had won the Schweizer 1-26 Sweepstakes with a flight to Albuquerque of 327 miles. Nancy was inordinately proud of him and wrote it up for Air Currents. "I don't want to sound proud but it will be difficult not to because I am," she started off. And after reporting the triumph, ended up with,"I knew I couldn't do it. But I don't know how to do it differently. So chalk it up to an emotional female and wife and read on."

Meanwhile work on the Diamant continued apace. "An unready ship and popping cu's can be pretty hard on a guy, you know. We are still soaring in the living room where the lift leaves much to be desired." Eventually, in April 1970, Nancy wrote, "A word of warning to all you pilots - make room in the sky - the Diamant will be there! (And am I ever glad to see her get out of the house.)"

The new Editor liked trivia, and so did her readers. During her reign she was to report there were 227 soaring clubs and 100 schools in the U.S.. She told us all there were 71 Soaring Club newsletters in the country and their titles included Birds I Views, Cloud Nine, Cross-Winds, The Cu-Bird, Cu Cues, The Dope, The Eagle Call, Gliding Gators (from Florida, of course), Lift's Up, The Ridge Runner, Shear Lines, Soar Spots, Spirals and The Wisconsin Thermal Sniffer. Most popular title? Towline.

Having run a poem on the title page ever since she became Editor, Nancy was now scraping the bottom of the barrel. Her final offering, penned by a member who understandably insisted on remaining anonymous, read, "Roses are red, Violets are blue, I like to soar. How about you?" Ending with a definite whimper and not a bang, Nancy wisely said that was the end of the poetry unless she received more poetic contributions pronto, and thanked this month's contributor for, "at the very most, supplying a few lines to a blank page."

The following month she was thanking everyone for sending in so much poetry and in May she printed that well known piece, "Aviation is not inherently dangerous, but to an even greater degree than the sea, it is terribly unforgiving of any carelessness, incapacity or neglect." She also attributed the lines to the correct author, D. Dixon Speas, which is rare and something worthy of note. It had been contributed by Darlene Coulliette who revealed that husband Roy carried it in his billfold.

In April 1970, in an unusually reflective mood, Nancy told her readers, "If, from time to time, black dots appear in this newsletter, there is a very good reason - the "o's" are being cut out of the stencil. Did you ever stop to think how many o's appear in a newsletter? Lots. Count them!" If there was space left at the end, we were treated to "Kitchen Table Left Overs".

Comfortingly, there was room in between for more important revelations. Despite having his sailplane airborne once more, Al struck again with another article on variometers. He ended with a modest question: Shall I continue????? Nancy was still rejoicing at the Diamant's departure and having the opportunity to do "three cartwheels in my living room without hitting anything."

In November 1970 Nancy actually took a flight at Estrella. To the President of the Cowardly Lion Club this was a big deal.

"They all work fast at that sailport. I was still telling Las why I really couldn't go this particular day, when I realized we were airborne. Somehow, what ever reason I gave seemed the deadest excuse of a lifetime at that moment. The tow went well until I was informed that I had a small task to perform (since I was sitting in the front seat). (I remember objecting to the front seat in the beginning but...) and the task was to pull the release knob upon a command from the back seat pilot. At least twice, I was informed, "Keep your eye on the rope when you pull the release. It's very important that you see it fall away." Las, I must tell you now that... (I was pretty sure he was watching too.)

My only other stomach-in-the-mouth situation occurred during banks. Banking in a glider (even a 2-32) and banking in a jetliner are simply not the same thing at all. Al once said, "With Nancy in the plane, who needs a turn and bank..." Shoulders hunch, back stiffens, hands clutch the shoulder harness and eyes look the opposite way. All of these signs immediately told Las that I was somewhat nervous.

"Relax," said he.

"But," said I, "look how high that wing is!"

"Yes," said he, "and look how low the other wing is!"

And so it went. Even, at one point, with hands comparable to half-set Jello, took the stick and flew that glider. Las said I did it by myself. I believed him then and I believe him now.

"It was time to land. That is an interesting sensation - particularly when you are in the front seat, particularly when you are a Cowardly Lion in good standing.

The greatest compliment that can be paid to Las is for ME to say, "I had a good time, and I want to go again - sometime!""

Having discovered (and conquered) the joys of flight, Nancy took a new interest in flying arrangements and took charge of Line Chief Assignments. In January 1970, she published a list of Line Chiefs from February through April, but in the inimitable Hume manner, seems to have got things slightly muddled and Bernie Skalniak ended up in the wrong slot. Unperturbed, Nancy added, "Note to Bernie Skalniak: You were put where you are because I forgot you. So I put you where I was when I thought of you. (Wonder if Victor Borge would buy that bit of grammatical genius?) However, if you would like to be where you belong, I'm sure you can trade (or would you rather just forget the whole thing?)"

After sixteen months in office, in January 1971, Nancy took a month off and Al Hume took over as Newsletter Editor. Instead of "From The Editor's Kitchen Table", we had "From The Editor's Husband's Workbench". "Last November," wrote Al, "in the midst of Nancy's monthly mad rush to get out the newsletter, (accompanied by the usual vows that this was the last time she'd ever go through *this* again), I rashly offered to take on the Editor's job for one month. Ever since, she's been hovering around like a mother hen, fearful that I may not produce a suitable work of art. I finally agreed to follow her format, with suitable changes in titles to reflect the vibrant personality of your temporary editor. Besides, I've been trying to no avail for months to get my next variometer article published. At this point I'm willing to agree to anything just to get into print.

"Seriously," continued Al, "some of you should try the job if you think it's an easy task. Nancy, by some gift from heaven I suppose, composes directly onto the stencil. Not I. It's all done in longhand first, and laboriously at that. Next month I'll appreciate that newsletter just a little more than in the past."

His comments were only partly in jest. The power of editorship quite went to his head and he did indeed publish his third piece on variometers. He ended this gargantuan effort by saying his editor/wife "has been bugging the devil out of me all week - looking over my shoulder, making suggestions, bringing me items to put in. You should hear the spluttering when I reply that I'll check it over and see if it's suitable! You can't be the Chief Honcho if you don't act like one."

Nancy had the last word the following month, however. "I think I'm expected to make some reference to last month's Air Currents or its Editor or something," she wrote. "Actually, I felt it was "reasonably" well done! Certain parts of the editorial, *I* felt, were largely exaggerated and therefore not in keeping with the "straight reporting" policy of this publication. However, be that as it may, comments from subscribers indicated popular acceptance of the guest editor. So hate to disappoint you but the guest editor gave absolutely no indication of wishing to continue his assumed role this month, and frankly I doubt that he will until he has another variometer story ready for publication." She did unbend with a PS at the end. "Seriously and not in jest, I say thank you, love. You were a big help!"

In the ensuing April issue, Nancy made *the* classic booboo of a lengthy career and announced the upcoming publication of Joe Lincoln's new book, "Unquiet Wings". (Maybe it was due to the exigencies of house moving). "Those of you who have read "Soaring For Diamonds"," continued Nancy authoritatively, "will know why "Unquiet Wings" will be a must for your library."

That April, Nancy had a new preoccupation - they were moving house. It was an on-going soap opera that summer. In May it had not happened "because nothing is certain except death and taxes" and in June Bill Ordway was a guest editor while Nancy took leave. They were hoping for two more guest editors for July and August but Nancy was back in the Editor's seat in July saying the move would definitely happen but not til September.

Nancy did not report Mission Accomplished until the November newsletter, however. Although the move had been traumatic, all was well. "Brad found Pooh Bear. Steve found his P.E. shirt. Al found his sailplane and I found my sanity. We are a complete family unit again!"

Joe Lincoln's book was published in October and the Humes and Ordways were fighting over the privilege of who would give the autograph party. "If the Humes can clear a path to the bar, find the other sofa and hang the bathroom door, they will give the party," wrote Nancy. "In the meantime, the Ordways are hoping none of this will get done so they can give the party."

Crewing was inevitably a major part of Mrs Hume's life. She relished the company, the camaraderie and the friendships. She shamelessly got a bridge game going when ever she could and, in one issue, publicly instructed Nancy Ordway to bring her "rigged Scrabble game". "Crewing?" she asked nonchalantly. "Oh, we'll all work it in somehow."

Her other preoccupation in life was getting Al to do his Honey Do's, and recommended other wives with a similar problem to "allow" their pilots to buy a new sailplane, since said pilot would (in theory) be keen to get all the "job jar chores" out of the way before delivery. In March 1972 she further revealed that during UnSoaring Season the Hume family did "what I want to do. It's a season of relaxation, reading, bridge, plays and good conversation with each other. Then, one morning, all of a sudden, it's Soaring Season! "Up and at 'em is the order of the day! Pack lunches, fill canteens, think soaring! Can't talk! But, no matter really. This has been a successful arrangement for us. And - I'll let you into a little secret - I'm glad it's Soaring Season again. It gives me a chance to plan, without rush, what I would like to do next UnSoaring Season."

At the end of 1971, a special framed award was created to acknowledge Nancy's literary efforts for ASA and the great job she had done - and was doing - on the newsletter.

In April 1972 she was delighted with a new cover designed especially for her (and ASA) by Woody Payne, "an esteemed artist with an impressive list of credits." The remainder of that issue progressed happily until we reached the back page and found another little note from the Editor. "As you can see," she apologized, ""Turf Notes" has ended up on the back page. Normally it would be in the middle of the newsletter with all the rest of the soaring news. However, these are not normal circumstances. I left "Turf Notes" in my bedroom. Al Hume is asleep in my bedroom. If I go get them I will awaken him. When he is awoken unnecessarily, he can become ugly and emotional. I had only two choices - emotional ugliness or put "Turf Notes" on the back page."

One wonders if Al ever felt he was living life in a goldfish bowl, with even his most private moments of emotional ugliness revealed with innocent candor to the entire membership.

In May 1972 there was a delightful story in Air Currents entitled "Battle By the River" by Little Walking Bear (alias Gordon Dutt). Little Walking Bear told the story of how he and Eager Beaver plan all through the snows and dream of coming suns when the Great Soaring Gods twist the skies and the 1-26 soaring birds can climb toward the home of lightning, rain and clouds. Little Walking Bear enjoyed his flight, climbing three hills high, then four hills high and back to three hills high, and ended the piece asking why ASA no challenge TuSc tribe.

Nancy had the last word, as usual. "Squaw Editor say Indian who smart off do battle with blunt tomahawk! ASA tribe on warpath - no more kemosabe stuff til star of Big Dipper appear and tribes join for stomach fill." If the local Indians had seen all this they would have undoubtedly sued for defamation of character!

By this time, Nancy must have begun to feel a little "written out" if not burned out. Running a home, a family and crewing were time consuming enough without adding a full scale newsletter. She wasn't just composing it and typing it either, she was duplicating, stapling, licking stamps and mailing it too. A couple of issues were subsequently edited by Ruth Petry and Dan Halacy and by August, Nancy had recruited some help with a consequent change in deadline. "Wish I had a dime for every person who is now thinking "I don't remember the old deadline!"" challenged Nancy.

In December, 1972 she announced that she had been doing Air Currents for three and a half years and profusely thanked everyone who had contributed. It was an omen, and in January she wrote her last Editorial From The Editor's Kitchen Table.

"In very unprofessional terminology, a "30" at the end of newspaper copy means "That's all, folks." And so it is with "Kitchen Table." Being Editor of Air Currents the past three and a half years has been, in all sincerity, a "very neat experience". The help, co-operation, encouragement, praise, and, most of all, friendships developed through this association, mean a great deal to me. But - it seems to me - the time has come when we all would benefit from the thoughts and style of a new editor and I must confess that a little bridge and some special crafts are really tempting my spare time.

"My deep and sincere thanks to all with whom I have worked during the past few years. I know I can count on you to lend your support to the new editor (as yet un-named). You know, it's going to be kind of fun to read the next issue of Air Currents with anticipation instead of knowledge.   - 30 - N."

For members of the Arizona Soaring Association, 1973 and 1974 were Nancy-less years. However, in February 1975, new Editor Ben Stanton offered a glimmer of hope on the back page. "Although her arm is still too sore from twisting to appear in this month's issue," wrote Ben, "Nancy Hume has "offered" to develop a monthly column for the newsletter."

Sure enough, the following month, March 1975, Pardon My Squelch was born, starting off with an injunction from Nancy saying, "If you want a juicy and interesting column, (1) Do juicy and interesting things and (2) then let me know about them". There was also an explanation of how Pardon My Squelch received its name.

It seems the Bairds, the Ordways, Arnie Jurn and Josh Voynick met at the Humes' home to view slides taken by Josh while crewing for those present. "After dinner and a little wine, and then a little more wine, I asked for suggestions for a title for my new Air Currents column. The group was enthusiastic and I was delighted with the way they really applied themselves to the task. The following names were tossed in the ring but never reached a vote: Canopy Capers; Nancy's Nonsense; Hot Air by Hume and Big Wind. Billie Baird's Bird Droppings received more than just casual consideration. However, Al Hume felt it sounded crude and therefore submitted Poop and Scoop. Arnie Jurn yelled out Turn Down The Squelch and Bill Ordway immediately countered with Pardon My Squelch. When the vote was taken, Bill Ordway's contribution won. When you see Bill, do congratulate him on his cleverness. It will make him feel good."

One of Nancy's first "juicy and interesting" revelations was that "Billie Baird has purchased a new scrub bucket with which to start the season." Unfortunately Nancy forgot to ask the color so the report was incomplete but she did add, "Billie really, truly did not believe that I would print this!"

The content of her column was far reaching and wide ranging. She mentioned that Joe Lincoln was now feeling pretty good after his recent bout in hospital, had certainly enjoyed the cards, letters and visits from friends, and was continuing work on his new book about the Marfa Internationals.

Finally, she was able to continue the saga of the Hume Daily Doings for a waiting world, her readers having been deprived since she quit as Newsletter Editor at the end of 1972. Little had changed. "Al Hume has been busy doing chores," she wrote of her beloved spouse. "The home in which he lives has a leak in the shower and a leak in the roof. However, his Cirrus trailer has a new paint job and brand new chrome-plated handles. Somehow, this year I just didn't seem to be able to stay on top of the "Honey Do's." In May 1975, Nancy's "squelch was turned way down this time" because of the death of her dear friend, Joe Lincoln, a loss she felt personally as well as for the soaring fraternity. She remained subdued for sometime but in July reported having enjoyed the contest at Minden, even though daily retrieves meant she had not even shuffled a deck of cards, let alone played a hand of bridge. She did have time to meet Paula Mannie of Rainco, however, and Paula had given her a quote that Nancy felt should be adopted as the official crew chant: "We, the unwilling, led by the unknowing, are doing the impossible for the ungrateful. We have done so much for so long with so little, we are now qualified to do anything with nothing."

No one was safe any more. She was mischievously quoting friends again, in black and white, and probably getting them into no end of trouble at home. She reported that Mrs Nancy Ordway had said, "Bill Ordway will do a fine job of flying this summer because he is so full of hot air!!!" Joyce George was her next victim, when Joyce said, inadvertently within earshot of Nancy, "This whole crewing business is like practicing bleeding!" It was trivia, and some of it was nonsense, but it was fun and it was nice to have her back.

Nancy squelched on through the remainder of the year and naively thought the advent of a new editor (Bob von Hellens) was going to let her off the hook in 1976. Bob soon disabused her mind of that and promptly requested Nancy continue her Pardon My Squelch column. She expressed some reservation about the lack of news. Bob, in desperation, suggested she be creative and make some up! Sooooo...

In February 1976 the irrepressible Mrs Hume played a huge joke on the membership, some of whom swallowed the whole thing hook, line and sinker. "Al Hume *and* John Baird have just sold their ships," wrote Nancy creatively. "John's Nimbus *and* his motor home have gone to help swing a house purchase deal." Al's Cirrus had been sold and the proceeds put toward a cabin in Alpine "so he could spend time with the family." John Baird was even quoted as saying, "What's the big deal? First things first!" which really was stretching the realms of credibility a little too far and should have alerted the most gullible of readers.

The following month found Mrs Squelch gleefully crowing over her triumph: several members had read with stunned acceptance but some knew Nancy too well to be conned. She gleefully apologized, brazenly confessing last month's column had all been "a pack of lies! The devil and the Air Currents Editor made me do it!" She also admitted to being a little sobered by the realization that what had alerted most people to the fraud was the report of Al selling his ship. She didn't care to think this was such an unreal and impossible thing for Al Hume to do!

Nothing got past Nancy. In addition to who was getting married, who'd moved, and who's dog had done what, she also included who was getting a new ship and who was flying in which contest this summer. She was one of the people destined for a contest in 1976. "Today is July 3rd. At least one half of the soaring population is at Prescott today - and tomorrow - and the next day - enjoying the cool weather, soaring, bridge, friendships. They will enjoy this tomorrow and then they will enjoy it again the next day.

"Bill Ordway is not at Prescott with the rest. He is enjoying heat, no soaring, a dead truck battery, no friendships and the trauma of readying himself for his trip to Kansas in exactly five days! Al Hume is not at Prescott with the rest either. He is enjoying heat, no soaring, a sprung water plug, no friendships and the trauma of readying himself for his trip to Kansas in exactly five days!

"Nancy Ordway and Nancy Hume are making a concerted effort not to think about Prescott and bridge and friendships. Their trauma has not yet started. It will start on July 10, opening day of the Nationals. I don't know what Nancy O. has planned in the way of revenge when the season ends, but Nancy H. has just completed her list and it's a real winner!" It was indeed, and during the event, had the ultimate deterrent added to it at the last moment.

So, in August 1976, after the usual information and gossip, Nancy continued her column, "...and then there was Kansas and the Standard Nationals. Al has written a story about the affair but he left out all the good stuff. He wrote about the weather, pilot performances, tasks and unusual flying experiences, if you can imagine. So I guess it is up to me to tell you about the really important things."

The important stuff, as far as Nancy was concerned, was leaving Phoenix on the Thursday evening and getting as far as Winslow hospital with Brad, who developed stomach 'flu, which his fond parents diagnosed as appendicitis. When they eventually arrived in Kansas, the rest of the contingent went down with 'flu too, the muffler broke on the crew car, and various other disasters befell them in true Hume style.

"The actual crewing was not that difficult, save for the day of the Big Front. The storm hit the airport like gangbusters dropping more rain in one hour than we get in Arizona in half a year. I have never seen such black clouds and hard rain. We all knew we were going to have to go out as no pilot could get back. It was raining cats, dogs, horses and cows! Pilots were falling out of the sky all over Kansas. By the time we arrived in Newton, I was weary from all the rain and it was still pouring!

"I selected a building with a large parking lot, as the place from which to call Hutch. As I approached the door, I noticed a sign that read, "Livestock Exchange". That didn't bother me as long as they had a phone. After I got inside, I discovered that it was apparently hog exchange day and that bothered me! I'll spare you the details but if I escape swine flu it will be a miracle! A quick call to Hutch informed me that my pilot was down near Newton in a recently cut wheat field and could be reached at a farmhouse. I called the farmhouse. Al, along with Bob Klemmendson of California and Chicho Estrada of Florida and Ecuador, were there. Al gave me directions to the field. I must say here that I can always pass a test telling right from left. No guarantees are given for North, South, East and West. Al is a North, South, East and West man. To save face, I will spare you more details and simply say that we did find the field and there sat 3D, 7A and E8 in a mire!

"There was only one way to get the planes out - carry them all piece by piece across the field, over a ditch and onto the dirt road where the trailers were parked. I must at this point tell you that I was wearing a $30 pair of white slacks and a new pair of white tennis shoes. My hairdo was long since gone from the rain.

"We started toward the plane, sinking down to our ankles and above sometimes in mud and slush and slip. The pilots and crews all joined forces to help each other with the planes. Klemmenson's 7A was the first to be removed and loaded. My job was to stay with 3D and keep the wings out of the mud. 7A was eventually loaded and they all came for 3D. I was told by my pilot to carry out the canopy, bringing up the rear (the story of my life!) At this point my pants, shoes, legs, feet, blouse - all - covered with mud. I am standing in mud well above my ankles. My thoughts ranged everywhere from !@#$%^&*()+! to, "Al Hume, you are going to take me to the Liberace show this year - and furthermore, you are going to be nice about it!!!

"While I stood in the muck, I thought about Becky Townsend, Beth Halacy and Camille Carter, all new crew chiefs! I thought about Helen and Graham Thomson who go to Hawaii every year. I thought about Nancy Ordway and Mary Robertson - wondered if they were standing in the muck somewhere. And then the humor of the whole situation hit me as I realized how funny Al, Steve and Brad looked covered with mud. I had not seen myself in a mirror but if the neck up looked as bad as the neck down, I had the prize for any clown costume. It was later verified that I won hands down! The day ended at the Yoder cafe, always the perfect end to a day."

Our intrepid reporter was temporarily mollified with Yoder Cafe's Peanut Butter Pie but there is little doubt that it was left to Liberace to completely heal her wounded soul and restore her equilibrium at a later date. "This was a successful Nationals for me," she finished. "I was reduced to hysteria followed by, "I'll never do this again!" only once - an improvement of two times in a 10 day period."

By September our intrepid reporter was looking forward to chilly nights, fireplaces and summer reflections, and putting the Pardon My Squelch column to bed for a long winter's nap.

The nap turned out to be longer than even Nancy had anticipated. In April there was a brief entry proclaiming, "Pardon My Squelch Lives!" but it was not until the June issue, long after everyone else had been up and running, that Nancy yawned and stretched and emerged, blinking in the bright sunlight of approbation once more. "Greetings, everyone!" she said. You could almost see her standing in the doorway in her nightgown, with a teddy bear trailing from one hand.

"First I want to thank all of you who have requested Squelch and complained because it has been absent. Your complaints have been truly appreciated." She had been coerced back into action by a desperate editor (still Bob von Hellens) who wanted news from Motor Home Village at Region 9. He'd promised her she did not have to write about tasks, scores, winners and all of that stuff, just the things going on "behind the hangar, in front of the A-frame and beside the J-Johns. When word drifted back to me that a couple of sidewinders had been spotted by the J-Johns, I made other arrangements and therefore, any J-John news will go unreported for ever! Mr von Hellens grimaced and cringed so intensely when I requested permission to sub-title the Squelch column "Squelch Squealings From Region 9", I had to assume it met with his approval."

Fortunately, all was "as usual" in Motor Home Village so there was plenty to report. "Day One: Billie Baird runs over a chair shortly after her motor home was clipped in the back by another car. Nancy Ordway hit in the head with a Cirrus wing by Bill Ordway. Nancy Hume hit in the head with a Cirrus wing by Al Hume. Patsy Brooks hits son-in-law's car while backing up her motorhome and leaves some noteworthy dents.

"Day Two: Josh Voynick and Nancy Ordway experience a trailer hitch break during a retrieve of Bill Ordway in Stanfield. Fortunately no damage and the break occurred as they were stopping. Thanks to a full moon, the hitch was welded back on that night by a Stanfield welder and the 81 team was back in business. Nancy Hume makes another retrieve worthy of another evening with Liberace. However, no commitment was made this time.

"Day Four produced a long task in less than perfect weather. Balked of another retrieve, Nancy filled her time eaves dropping on the radio and recorded the following.

"Ooee!!!"

"I'd feel safer in a balloon."

"Anyone for hail?"

"Was it supposed to lightning today?"

"Anyone who isn't flying this task is missing all the fun."

"Aborting task - returning to Estrella."

"YR is OK with a face full of dust."

"Boy, did you see that?"

"Do you have a radio channel where we could have a private talk?"

"You guys won't believe me, but my boss at Continental Airlines just flew past me!

"Boy, are you in a heap of trouble."

"Day 5: I was sitting at the start gate waiting for my pilot to make his start. As the words came across the speaker, "3D turning IP", all heads turned toward the IP. No sign of a plane there. I jokingly, truly jokingly, said, "Maybe he has the wrong IP!" Instantly, all heads jerked in the opposite direction - and here came 3D! As he was just about over the gate, Contest Director Peter Petry called and said, "You're beautiful 3 Delta, but you're going the wrong way!"

There were yet more Squealing Odds and Ends. Having spied upon and exposed her own husband, Nancy proceeded to do the same to her friends. "The first thing Sherry Dickerson bought for her motorhome was a set of wine glasses," she wrote. "The first thing Mary Ann Ardnt bought was an ironing board. Before Region 9 even started Fran Petry and Sherry Dickerson reportedly had car trouble on their way in to Maricopa for groceries. They hailed down a carload of Indians, whose only English was Headquarters Bar and Cafe, where they were driven to use the telephone.

"Would you believe Rusty Ordway became lost again," revealed our intrepid reporter, obviously shocked by the cavalier behavior of Rusty's owners. "Or perhaps left might be a better word. This time at Maricopa and this time Bill Ordway was

261

the culprit. Happily, Rusty was found again. One wonders if Rusty is really happy in her present home situation."

She finished with "A Closing and Disgusting Quote" from Al Hume. She called him 3 Delta or My Husband when he was in favor, and Al Hume when he wasn't.

Nancy Hume: I don't know what it is but I'm having trouble writing up this soaring stuff.

Al Hume: You're not supposed to write the soaring stuff. You're supposed to write the crap!

Shortly afterwards, she was dragged off to Region 12 at El Mirage and had to write the non-crap stuff as well for the July issue.

In August our heroine excitedly reported ASA's bid to the SSA to sponsor either the Standard or 15 meter Class Nationals at Marana Airpark near Tucson for 1978. During a trial weekend, the facilities there were discovered to be superb and some had likened Marana to Glider Pilot Heaven. Nancy had her doubts.

"Along with the beautiful Olympic size swimming pool, they also have very large green frogs and "Somethings" that bite knees deep and painfully. If I were going to design a glider pilots' heaven, I would omit these last two items. I was the recipient of the Something bite and honestly thought it might have been a) scorpion; b) black widow, and, during the most intense period of pain, c) two rattlesnakes. Upon learning of my distress, Bud Munzer, Nancy Ordway, Dorothy Hohanshelt and naturally Bob Hohanshelt, immediately started planning my "wake". I don't think wine and dancing in the streets is indicative of sorrow and respect - so I recovered (but not without a lot of verbal suffering).

"I've been telling Camille Carter for months now that she is in grave danger of losing the female friends she has in ASA (and for the moment they are many). Camille smiles all the time, acts happy all the time, doesn't complain, is a good sport and is pleasant and friendly to everyone at soaring events. At the Marana affair, she prepared a beautiful crock pot dinner for her family, prepared and delivered lunch to the lone "window person", and the last day provided assorted snacks for the poolside glider pilots and their crews. (No, we weren't there - we were having a gala time in a field taking apart 3D. No, of course I'm not jealous, resentful and hateful!)

"The Marana weekend was an exciting experience for Dorothy Hohanshelt. She experienced two "firsts" - she retrieved pilot/husband Bob before sunset and she caught his wing for the first time. I have never caught my pilot's wing and I doubt if Nancy Ordway has either. But probably Billie Baird, Sherry Dickerson and Fran Petry have. They are just the type!"

Having emerged for the summer, and covered the season's three most auspicious events, Pardon My Squelch returned once more to obscurity and hibernation. Although it seemed he could not wring another Squelch out of her, Editor Bob von Hellens did manage to persuade ASA's most popular author to co-write up Day Two of the Wilcox weekend with husband Al.

Nancy went first with the Important Stuff, and mentioned early on that Day Two at Wilcox was Mother's Day. After a sympathetic report about poor 14 year old Rusty Ordway, who had been unable to fulfill her owners' commands to jump up on the back seat of their vehicle because her tail had been inadvertently shut in the vehicle door, Nancy returned again to what was apparently bugging her most, crewing on Mother's Day. "In times past," she said, only a little wistfully, "Mother's Day was for Al and Father's Day was for me." The other wifely crews were apparently laboring under similar feelings of deprivation. A clarion call went out.

"Attention all females involved in soaring," Nancy wrote. "A new group has been organized and you are encouraged, urged and begged to join! The new group, hereinafter referred to as the ERA (Erp Regarding Aviation), quite by accident met, formed and elected officers after the pilot's meeting, on the airport porch. Any female who was fortunate enough to be in the vicinity became an automatic member. Officers include: President, Susan Belt; Secretary, Nancy Hume; Program Chairman, Sherry Dickerson; Trimmer (Bouncer), Roberta Desilets; and, Mother Figure, Nancy Ordway. Items of business established at this first meeting included plans for Mother's Day 1979, when the pilots shall clean their own planes, cook dinner and clean up. A complaint was voiced that Wife Mothers did not receive a bouquet of flowers from the pilots this year! The meeting had to be adjourned when the Bouncer was asked to leave to wash wings and the Program Chairman buckled under pressure from her pilot."

Al Hume's version of Day Two at Wilcox then followed. He had enjoyed a good flight and ended, "It was great to experience that fine May soaring weather - one of the best Mother's Days in some time."

In June, Nancy addressed the membership. "Dear ASA Members: I wish to start by saying thank you for your desire to see "Squelch" continue. I am truly not trying to play hard to get. Perhaps it is a case of the writer seeing the copy differently from the reader. I felt that it had run its course. You say no, and so it shall be. Actually, the two obscene phone call attempts set me to reassessing the situation. Perhaps this all points up the need for the "dumb stuff" in this busy, often complicated world we live in."

She started with an in-depth report of all the daily doggy doings she could muster, including mention of Snooky Baird's first witnessed love affair at Region 9 with Brandy Gray. It was all just an excuse to be able to mention the fact that the Humes had a brand new, white German Shepherd puppy which Nancy had lovingly named Heidi and which Al had promptly (and, according to Nancy, disgustingly) re-christened Heidi Ho Hume. Only then did she manage to elevate her mind to the usual soaring minutiae.

"Because I'm a poor sport," she wrote indignantly, her hackles high and her sense of fair play severely damaged, "I'm going to tell the dirty trick that Region 9 winner Wally Raisanen pulled on Al Hume the last day of the contest. Wally knew that Al was out to get him if he could (he didn't get him enough!) Out on course, perhaps sixty miles from the finish gate, Wally spotted Al ahead of him and higher in a thermal, working his little heart out. Wally then (while watching Al) called his ground crew and told them to switch to 5 (the finish gate channel). Al Hume almost fell out of the sky! But recovered and of course switched to 5 also. Wally waited a reasonable time and then asked his crew what the ground winds were at Estrella, all the time watching Al Hume ahead of him. The devil himself never snorted more fire than Al Hume at that moment, but he put his nose down and pushed a little harder. When he landed back at Estrella, Al's first words to me were, "How long has that damn Wally been back?" I responded, "He isn't back yet." With that the 3D pilot just crumpled in the cockpit, later to hear the whole ugly story from Wally."

Nancy ended that column with the news that Al had sold his trusty Cirrus and purchased an LS-3 all within 5 days. "This may disqualify my membership in the Soaring ERA," she admitted, "but I confess I cried when Gus Miller drove off with the Cirrus!"

In August 1978 it fell to Nancy Hume's unhappy lot to write not one but two obituaries, one of which was for Jessie Radford whose passing inspired husband Roy Radford to provide the Jessie Radford Memorial Trophy. The trophy was in the form of a beautiful Kachina Doll and was to be awarded to The Woman of the Year.

In a volume bulging with Marana Nationals News, Pardon My Squelch was conspicuous by its absence. Nancy had been busy writing up the event for Soaring magazine. Having amply spread herself over 12 pages of that august publication, Editor Doug Lamont gently and tactfully told her he simply did not have room for more. So she contented herself with inflicting the remainder on Air Currents readers in October who, needless to say, welcomed it with open arms.

For the last three months, Nancy's Pardon My Squelch column was "positively the last one of the season". Another "final" appeared in November, still having some leftovers from the Nationals, and they appeared under the inspiring heading, "Junque".

When Judy Lincoln took over Editorship of Air Currents in 1979, she had to manage without Pardon My Squelch. Nancy had taken refuge in hospital, ostensibly for the removal of staghorn kidney stones *and* kidney. (Trust Nancy to have the unusual kind). In reality, her sojourn was undoubtedly to avoid having to write yet another column by popular demand. The merciless membership did let her off for a while although by June she was recovering nicely and had formed HICUP (the Honored Ideal of Crews Under Protest).

In 1980, it was only fitting that the Jessie Radford Woman of the Year Award should go to Nancy Hume. She might be writing less these days, but she was living life to its fullest, as usual, with her irrepressibly mischievous sense of humor and fun. She responded to the Award in the October 1980 Air Currents in her own inimitable style.

"The first word that I learned to say was "shoe". The first sentence I uttered was "Tie Shoe". From then on, I never seemed to be at a loss for words or sentences - or so I am told. At the recent ASA Awards Banquet, that changed! Total surprise prevented me from being able to verbalize what I felt in my heart and it is important to me to do that.

"I am deeply appreciative to you, Roy, for selecting me to receive "Jessie's Award". To you ASA folks, I am equally appreciative for your response to my selection. The Jessie Radford Memorial Trophy is given in recognition of important female contribution to the ASA. Friends, your contributions to me in the form of friendship far exceed any that I may have made to the ASA."

Everyone thought that was the end of the story but it takes more than hard work, a tight schedule, various surgeries and excessive amounts of hospital volunteer time to slow down Nancy Hume. Everyone was still requesting Pardon My Squelch and she did vaguely promise a column now and then but nothing materialized immediately.

By August 1984, Nancy had taken refuge in hospital again, not only to avoid having to write Pardon My Squelch, but, on her own admission, for a respite from crewing! She wrote to thank the Club for the flowers they'd kindly sent and confessed she was running out of reasons for surgery to avoid crewing and added,

"Soaring folk are so special. Thank you for again confirming that and in such a lovely way."

By 1985 Nancy was fit and blooming once more. Good Lord, what's this? On the very last page of the February 1985 Air Currents, Pardon My Squelch reappeared! Irreverent as ever, in among the usual gossip and news was the revelation that "Al Hume fell asleep at the last ASA Board Meeting and was thereby elected President." (This was the official published version. Verbally, Nancy let it be known he hadn't fallen asleep, he had gone to the bathroom, but she hadn't felt she should publish this in the newsletter. Had she changed? She had never displayed such maidenly modesty in the past!) "In a monarchy," continued Nancy, apparently going off on something of a tangent, "when the heir to the throne is crowned King, his wife becomes Queen." And so it was that Nancy inherited the traditional role of Social Chairman, and burst into print with a long list of people to whom she would delegate all social responsibilities for the year.

In April 1985 Pardon My Squelch was back with a vengeance.

"I usually have 29 days and 23 hours to write this column before Jane Jackson's deadline to turn it over to the Air Currents Editor, Pete Williams. Usually I spend 29 days thinking about it, but this time I'm really under the gun - the time factor is 29 days and 22½ hours. If you are confused, very simply, I have 30 minutes to wrap this up before Jane arrives to pick it up.

"And to add to all of this mass mania, five minutes ago I received a telephone call from Bob von Hellens which went as follows:

"Hello, Nancy. This is von Hellens."

"Hi, Bob. How are you?"

"Good, I'm returning your call."

"My call was returning your call yesterday."

"I called yesterday returning your call of the day before."

"I called you the day before but you weren't in so I left a message for you to call me. Do you want to talk to me?"

"No."

"I don't want to talk to you either. Oh, I know what happened! Your original message to talk to me wasn't erased off my answering machine and I thought your message of yesterday to call you was a fresh one."

"I don't send fresh messages."

Having got that sorted out, Nancy continued with her usual round of thanks for hospitality, sympathies to the recently bereaved, and sundry congratulations. Congratulations to Bill Ordway on his recent retirement and more congratulations for Woody Woods on being featured on the cover of Phoenix Magazine dressed in his Red Baron suit. Woody also came in for some gentle teasing about the glamorous lady pictured next to him who, Nancy declared, "did not look to me like she washes wings or carries fuselages out of muddy fields somehow!"

In June/July of that year, Nancy fulfilled the main purpose of Pardon My Squelch and wrote up news of Motor Home Village, Region 9, Estrella. Dan Halacy was writing up the event for Soaring magazine, and Nancy was in no way attempting to stomp through his territory, but she could put things in Air Currents that would never be included in Soaring magazine.

"Motor Home Village was sober, relaxed and the site for much good conversation. For example, I discovered for the first time that not all pilots carry a potty bottle in their plane. Further research revealed that some carry none and some carry two. As should be pretty obvious by now, age of the pilot has great bearing on this decision."

She continued by embarrassing new member Jim Kett with the revelation that, "after a day or so, Jim felt comfortable enough to introduce us all to his special soaring friend, Hector. Hector is, I think, the most unattractive stuffed animal I have ever seen. Lime green body, long orange tail, yellow furry ears, weird eyes. Hector rode with Jim one time but the flight resulted in a land out, so Hector now stays on the ground and obviously has a very special place in Jim's heart. He cuddled him!

"On a day so overcast that the line was not launched until 4:00 pm, several of us watched the lifestyle of a group of wasps. During this observation period, Betty Irick made the best quote of the entire contest. 'I should have married a wasp. They fly and don't need a crew!'"

"So much for my Region 9 stuff," finished Nancy with a flourish. "I feel very sure that what I have revealed will not in any way interfere with Dan Halacy's story!"

And then, in October 1985, although no one knew it at the time, least of all the author, came her swan song, the final Pardon My Squelch (so far, anyway!) Written the day after the Awards Banquet, when the assembled gathering had enjoyed Chris Woods' The Quiet Challenge, she took pleasure in announcing Leslie and Chris were expecting their first wing runner in April.

Nancy likes babies, and she especially likes being the first to announce someone is getting one or has just got one. She also likes announcing who has a new sailplane but announcing new babies is best. Briefly interrupting herself to thank everyone for all their hard work making the Banquet such a success, Nancy suddenly discovered herself in possession of a very Pardon My Squelch nugget of information. You could almost see her toying with it and savoring it like a monkey with a peanut.

"Interesting little item here," she wrote innocently, setting her audience up very nicely. "Rohn Brown has a new Mini-Nimbus and a new son. Gary Beaver has a new ASW-19B and a new son. Al Hume has a new Ventus... and nothing more! I just hope through the miracles of modern science, there hasn't been a new development involving soaring, biology and physiology of which I am unaware!"

Nancy Hume's perceptions of life in general and soaring in particular are unusual to say the least, make great reading and are endearingly funny. She has written a Pardon My Squelch column, on and off, for over ten years and has done so for every subsequent Editor - except me! Should I take this personally?

I took on the pleasant though time consuming task in 1986. And people still ask me, "Can't you persuade Nancy Hume to write another Pardon My Squelch column?" Believe me, I've tried! Regretfully, the answer has always been No. Maybe one day Nancy will have the time and inspiration to turn up the Squelch once again. In the meantime, all we can do is - as usual - let Nancy have the last word.

"I don't like to glide! I tried it once and didn't like it. I tried it again and didn't like it again. However, this hasn't prevented me from having my own type of fun in the soaring game. I have found that there are no real strangers among people in this sport. Affluence, or lack of it, social position or occupation - none of these things carry weight with a soaring type. The achievers in soaring are admired by their peers but not unreachable. I have visited glider ports in Miami, Florida, Albuquerque, New Mexico and of course Arizona's Tucson, Yuma, Flagstaff and

Prescott groups and the story is always the same. There are really no strangers. I am a firm believer that everyone should have some degree of group relationship in their lives. Through my wanderings over the years, I hadn't found this. Then, in self-defense because of Al's intense interest in the sport, I started participating in soaring "on the ground". And it's been great. I wouldn't trade friendships developed through soaring for anything."

CHAPTER 14 - CLASSIC SOARING POETRY

THE SUBLIME AND BLISSFUL WORLD OF SILENT FLIGHT by Phil Thorndyke. Wind & Wings, January 1970.

If Satan followed gliders,
He'd surely have it made.
How many souls he could have had
Along the Baker grade.

"I'll sell! I'll sell!" would come the cry
From pilots in despair.
Surprising what a man would pay
For half a mile of air.

But maybe not surprising
To those who might be found
Where happiness is measured
In distance from the ground.

Five hours out, about on course,
Lift's getting far between;
A lot of miles still to go
Which now may not be seen.

You had it good there, for a while,
But now you're getting low.
The only place that's fit to land
Is that clear patch just below.

But then ahead - a wisp of cloud,
And so you drive it on.
Just past the point of no return
The cloud dies and is gone.

Always have a landing site,
This time you didn't think.
The rocks below, no place to land,
The gage shows zero sink.

Now come the curses muttered low,
Obscenities for prayer.
50 down and 40 up,
Ease back the stick a hair.

Five minutes; fifteen; twenty; damn!
You've gained a hundred feet;
Vario - airspeed - altitude;
Sweating in the heat.

Below, the hikers glance aloft,
And think that they might too
Enjoy such silent graceful flight;
The vario marks "Down 2".

Roll it in; roll it out;
Fly at lowest sink.
Til, with agonizing slowness,
The rocks begin to shrink.

Ah, the quiet grandeur,
Of soaring like a hawk.
Do they tremble from the tension
With their stomach like a rock?

At least you'll make that clear patch now,
You're luckier than some!
You should be sharp for landing
But the strain has left you numb.

Approach will have to be straight in;
Can't check the field that way.
Rely on what you saw before
So far it looks OK...

Spoilers open, watch your speed;
Keep the....
"----------!!" POWER LINES!

LAMENT by Mary Baldwin From Wind & Wings, February 1972.

When I get out to the gliderport
All set for a day of soaring sport,
There's one thing the troops are sure to say -
"You should have been here yesterday."

The thermals then were big and strong;
They started early and lasted long.
Three students in the 2-33's
Got duration for their Silver C's.

Four 1-26's went 300 miles
And you should have seen the pilots' smiles
While they were describing their soaring lark
And how they landed because it got dark.

The local fliers around the field
Climbed and circled and turned and wheeled.
"My vario's pegged," was the happy call;
"The needle's jammed against the wall."

Higher and higher the sailplanes flew
Til they were specks against the blue.
Each pilot, in turn, as he touched the ground,
Maintained, "I thought I'd never get it down."

You ask, "How does the weather look today?"
"Well, there's lots of cirrus, the sky is gray.
The air is stable, old pal, but say --
You should have been here yesterday!"

THE WEATHERMAN'S LAMENT from the Marfa Nationals Journal.

As I watch the dying embers
These are my last regrets.
When I'm right, no one remembers,
When I'm wrong, no one forgets!

"SAM" is Shirley Marshall, who worked at Black Forest Gliderport when it was owned by Mark Wild, who liked her poetry so much he published it in a volume entitled, "Views From The Arena."

AUTUMN by SAM, Birdseed, November 1970.

> Remember how the Aspen on the hills
> were splashed with yellow overnight
> When Autumn wandered by?
> Remember how she daubed the peaks with white
> Then cleaned her brush with random strokes
> Across the light blue sky?
> And as she strode through a dry brown field
> You saw where the drops of orange
> Were laced with pumpkin vine.
> And the crimson she spilled on the sumac
> Seeped along the banks and down the wash
> Drawing a careless line.
> Surely you remember?
> The festival of fall was everywhere,
> Golden oaks dropped golden leaves
> Into a lazy stream.
> Remember how you shared your love
> with me and Autumn long ago?
> It wasn't just a dream.
> Tell me you remember.

POEM by SAM, Birdseed August 1972.

> Cotton clouds cast shadows
> In a summertime ballet.
> They lilt across the fields
> In a most enticing way.
>
> They call to all the fledglings
> And the masters of the air
> To ride the rhythmic turn of winds
> And pirouette out there.
>
> The wind's song, rising high,
> Echoes nature's symphony
> And lifts the slender wings
> To unfold the melody.
>
> Make haste, you graceful birds,
> And go dancing while you may.
> Quiet comes with evening,
> and you'll miss a perfect day.

FINAL GLIDE by Sue Grosek

Blue melts to orange,
The sun hangs low,
Around you the sky goes stale.
You're thirty miles out,
Right on time,
And high enough to make the field.
Below, the earth is silent;
Long shadows, purple in hue,
Stretch across the desert, threatening you.
Again you whisper
Above the heads of those less fortunate,
White shapes held firm
In the velvet clutches of twilight.
Another friend goes down,
Another trailer is loaded,
Another crew wanders home for the night.
You're a flash of light in the distance,
A finishing window blur.
A chandelle, a smile, and
"Welcome home, Champion."

FIRST SOLO FLIGHT by Mark Masters, February 1971.

Alone free now
To turn as I please
Be it left, right, or not at all
The choice is mine
To do what I like
Going up, or down, or not even caring.

Co-ordinated turns and proper procedure
are no longer his decision
They are mine alone
Just as is the world below
Because I see it all!

With excited breath and
A quick glance to the left
My notion is confirmed
No longer wings of metal or glass
They are my arms now
No separation between,
We are one.

Through the canopy
The earth below is seen in all its miniature splendor
So far below is my world
And even the sky seems
Smaller, or I much bigger.

The machine has done its job and now I am
Free to share the view with God
The routine of those with feet wasted
On the earth is gone,
I never really knew it.

Dream and fact have merged and now
Are hesitant to separate
Time moves neither fast or slow here
But that is because of the special clock.
The clock runs fast when my
Thoughts become hurried, yet I have
spent years aloft in one flight.

Think about it when you fly
And should you see that actually you
Are the world's best - proclaim it.
But do not expect recognition from the others,
For each of them are champions to themselves.

SKY FEVER by J.M. (Ace) Field, based on John Masefield's "Sea Fever".
First appeared in Canada's Free Flight, circa 1968.

I must go back to the sky again,
To the world of air smooth and soft.
And all I ask is a sleek ship
And a thermal to keep her aloft,
And the cu's kick and the wind's song
And the green ball hopping.
Six thousand feet on a June day
And the white clouds popping.

I must go back to the sky again,
For the call of the mountain wave
Is a wild call and a clear call
That lures the bold and the brave.
And all I ask is a west wind
With the cap cloud standing
Twelve thousand feet o'er Saddleback
And a ship that heeds my commanding.

I must go back to the sky again,
To a soaring nomad's life.
To the hawk's way and the eagle's way
Far from daily strife.
And all I ask is a street of cu
Til the long trek is over,
And a gentle glide at the set of sun
To a soft field of clover.